Preparing for Victory

Thomas Holcomb and the
Making of the Modern Marine
Corps, 1936–1943

PUBLISHED WITH THE MARINE CORPS ASSOCIATION

Preparing for Victory

Thomas Holcomb and the Making of the Modern Marine Corps, 1936–1943

DAVID J. ULBRICH

Foreword by Lt. Col. Charles P. Neimeyer, USMC (Ret.)

Naval Institute Press
Annapolis, Maryland

This book has been brought to publication
with the generous assistance of Edward S. and Joyce I. Miller.

Naval Institute Press
291 Wood Road
Annapolis, MD 21402

Library of Congress Cataloging-in-Publication Data
Ulbrich, David J.
  Preparing for victory : Thomas Holcomb and the making of the modern Marine Corps, 1936–1943
/ David J. Ulbrich.
    p. cm.
  Includes bibliographical references and index.
  ISBN 978-1-59114-903-3 (hardcover : alk. paper) 1. Holcomb, Thomas, 1879–1965. 2. United
States. Marine Corps—History—20th century. 3. United States. Marine Corps—History—World
War, 1939–1945. 4. World War, 1939–1945—Campaigns—Pacific Area. 5. United States. Marine
Corps—Officers—Biography. 6. Generals—United States—Biography. I. Title.
  E840.5.H65U53 2011
  355.0092—dc22
  [B]
                              2010047478
Printed in the United States of America.

19 18 17 16 15 14 13 12 11   9 8 7 6 5 4 3 2 1
First printing

▼

In loving memory of my parents,

Jill G. Ulbrich (1936–1996) and Richard W. Ulbrich (1921–2008)

TABLE OF CONTENTS

▼

ILLUSTRATIONS

CHARTS

▼

ACKNOWLEDGMENTS

MY BOOK HAD ITS GENESIS in 1994 at Ball State University, where I started my master's thesis on Commandant Thomas Holcomb and Marine Corps defense battalions under Phyllis Zimmerman's direction. The next stage—research and writing at Temple University—resulted in my doctoral dissertation, titled "Managing Marine Mobilization: Thomas Holcomb and the U.S. Marine Corps, 1936–1943." I am grateful to my adviser, Gregory Urwin, for believing in my potential. Greg offered unfailing and unflinching support of my professional development, and he was unsparing in his high standards. I also benefited from receiving excellent advice from James Hilty and Nguyen Thi Dieu, both of Temple; and Donald Bittner of the U.S. Marine Corps Command and Staff College. Don deserves my special thanks for more than a decade of encouragement and friendship, including many discussions about military history over meals at the Globe and Laurel near Quantico and during several extended stays at his home.

Financial and institutional assistance came from several sources. The most vital aid came in forms of the General Lemuel C. Shepherd Jr. Memorial Dissertation Fellowship and a subsequent grant-in-aid, both awarded by the U.S. Marine Corps Heritage Foundation. Susan Hodges, vice president for administration at the foundation, always went out of her way to assist me. The fellowship allowed me to conduct extensive research at the Marine Corps University in Quantico.

The entire Marine Corps community was gracious and helpful, especially staffs in the Archives Branch and at the Marine Corps History Division, including A. Kerry Strong, J. Michael Miller, James Ginther, Alisa Whitley, Charles Melson, Charles Smith, Charles Neimeyer, Fred Allison, Daniel Crawford, Richard Aquilina, and Annette Amerman. Thomas Holcomb's late daughter-in-law, Suzanne Holcomb; and his granddaughters, Sarah Holcomb and Clover Holcomb Burgess, should also be acknowledged for their generous donation of his family papers to the Archives Branch in 2006. These documents and photographs enabled me to better understand Holcomb's personality. To their great credit, never once did any staff or family members unduly influence my interpretations in this book.

Apart from the Marine Corps' archival collections, the National Archives and Records Administration held many sources essential to my research. Among the most helpful archivists in Washington, D.C., and in College Park, Maryland, were Gibson Smith, Barry Zerby, Patrick Osbourne, Trevor Plante, Timothy Nenninger, and Nathaniel Patch. "Sandy" Smith merits special appreciation for his donation of two dozen boxes of Holcomb-related materials to the Marine Corps University Archives Branch. The sources collected by Sandy in the 1970s played crucial roles in my exploration of Holcomb's commandancy.

The staff at the Naval Institute Press deserves my recognition and appreciation for expert advice and a handsome finished product. Rick Russell, Thomas Cutler, Adam Kane, Annie Rehill, Judy Myers, Wendy Bolton, Emily Bakely, Susan Corrado, Chris Onrubia, Brian Walker, George Keating, and Judy Heise were helpful and supportive throughout the entire process, from our initial tentative conversations about my proposal to the final stages of production. Edward S. Miller, author of the seminal book *War Plan Orange*, also played instrumental roles in bringing my book to publication.

Neither the book nor the many years of graduate study could have been completed without friends and colleagues, including the late Edwin Simmons, the late Benis Frank, the late Russell Weigley, Linda Jones Hall, Amy Hollaway, Kenneth Swope, Mark Fissel, Dennis Showalter, Bobby Wintermute, Michael Matheny, Stewart Lockhart, Abel Alves, Colin Colbourn, Elizabeth Greenhalgh, Mark Danley, Jerry Sweeney, Beth Bailey, Robin Higham, David Rismiller, Kevin Smith, Richard Immerman, Bruce Geelhoed, Norman Goda, James Ehrman, Dorothy Lassen, Peter Lassen, Larry Roberts, Jennifer Harper, Chris Brown, and John and Sherri Burkardt. They rendered an enormously wide range of assistance, from sympathetic ears and chapter critiques to professional opportunities and timely kicks in the pants. Three individuals stand out for extraordinary kindnesses. Ken and Amy spent many hours reading endless drafts and feeding me countless meals in Muncie, Indiana. Linda has been my friend, confidante, editor, colleague, and substitute mother since 1992, when I was an undergraduate and she an instructor in the History Department at the University of Dayton.

Last and most important, I wish to acknowledge inspirational support from my family. My brother and sister-in-law, Tom and Pat Ulbrich, always took time to talk with me and gave me great places to spend my infrequent vacations. My late father, Colonel Richard W. Ulbrich, U.S. Air Force (Retired), generously provided financial assistance, counsel, and a sounding board for ideas about military history. He read and critiqued my entire dissertation during the final years of his life. My late mother, Jill G. Ulbrich, inculcated in me an early love of reading about history. She was my role model for what a Christian teacher should be like. My only regret is that my parents did not live to see this book in print.

▼

FOREWORD

A THOROUGH STUDY of World War II era Commandant of the Marine Corps, Major General Thomas Holcomb, has long been overdue. Fortunately, David Ulbrich's *Preparing for Victory: Thomas Holcomb and the Making of the Modern Marine Corps, 1936–1943* now nicely fills this missing piece of Corps institutional history. Few historians are aware that it was Thomas Holcomb who took a diminutive Depression-era Marine Corps of just 18,000 officers and men and, by 1943, expanded it to over 385,000 men. The Corps would grow even larger after Holcomb's tenure as Commandant was over. Moreover, building on the work of his predecessors, Thomas Holcomb laid the groundwork for creating the most effective amphibious-based combat force the world has ever seen. In that he was able to accomplish this task in just a few years was nothing short of phenomenal.

David Ulbrich is a historian of the highest order. His work throughout the entire book is scholarly and compelling. He was able to complete much of the groundwork for his pathbreaking study of this very influential military leader due to his competitive selection as the General Lemuel C. Shepherd Jr. Dissertation Fellow (2003–2004) sponsored by the Marine Corps Heritage Foundation. Further, in the course of his research, Dr. Ulbrich utilized the vast resources of the Marine Corps History Division and Special Archives collections located at the Gray Research Center, Quantico, Virginia.

Ulbrich's research makes it clear that Thomas Holcomb's impact on the Marine Corps was tremendous. Using experience acquired during tours at Headquarters Marine Corps and then honing his leadership skills on the battlefields of France during World War I, Holcomb was well prepared to become Commandant of the Marine Corps in 1936. Throughout his Commandancy, Holcomb saw the likelihood of war with Japan growing year by year. His role in getting the Marine Corps ready for its first offensive ground operation against the Japanese on Guadalcanal in August 1942 was absolutely crucial toward the Marine Corps being given greater national resource allocation as the war progressed. He instinctively recognized, especially during those dark days, that nothing impressed the Joint Chiefs of Staff more than success on the battlefield. Indeed, unlike the First World War where Holcomb's combat skills were in high demand, during World War II Holcomb's greatest contribution were his bureaucratic skills within the halls of the Navy Department. Holcomb was a strategic leader. Instead of worrying about immediate activities on the battlefield, he focused instead on resource allocation, personnel, logistics, and command structure, and balanced them off against the larger priorities of the war in the Pacific. However, if Holcomb had one Achilles heel, it was that he was not especially progressive when it came to issues of race and gender. These faults notwithstanding, after the conclusion of his career as a Marine in 1944 and following his brief service as the American minister to apartheid South Africa, Holcomb seemed to realize that his views, especially regarding race, may have been wrong. And while it is hard to definitively tell if he had truly changed as a result of his experience in South Africa, it was clear that his up close and personal experience with apartheid certainly had an impact upon him.

We are thankful to Dr. David Ulbrich for producing such a fine history of this very important Marine Corps leader. And despite Thomas Holcomb's obvious flaws, he can now be considered as one of the giants in Marine Corps history and ranks alongside that of his mentors, John A. Lejeune and John H. Russell. Holcomb was a man for all seasons—equally comfortable on a battlefield or in an executive boardroom. I anticipate this book will soon become required reading for all students of World War II Marine Corps history.

Lt. Col. Charles P. Neimeyer, USMC (Ret.)
Director and Chief of Marine Corps History

Preparing for Victory

Thomas Holcomb and the
Making of the Modern Marine
Corps, 1936–1943

▼

INTRODUCTION

The United States Marine Corps fell on hard times in the two decades that followed the First World War. The Corps hit its nadir during the Great Depression, dwindling from 75,101 Marines in 1918 to only 17,234 in 1936. This was not a propitious time for the country to weaken the Marine Corps or its other armed services, as international tensions escalated around the world during the 1930s. Nazi Germany and Fascist Italy expanded their military power, while the militarist regime in Japan undertook an imperialist program by invading Manchuria and menacing China. The United States possessed neither the will to fight nor a sufficiently strong military to counter these threats looming in Europe and East Asia. At this low point in December 1936, Thomas Holcomb became the seventeenth commandant of the Marine Corps.

This book examines how and why Holcomb solved so many problems that the Corps faced in the lean prewar period and the frenzied war years that followed. I argue that he exhibited a rare combination of abilities: he was a progressive manager, meticulous planner, visionary leader, and shrewd publicist. During those seven years until his retirement in December 1943, Holcomb molded the Corps into the modern amphibious force that helped win the Pacific War.

Thomas Holcomb measures up well in achievements and abilities when compared with such great American military managers as Dwight D. Eisenhower, Chester W. Nimitz, and George C. Marshall. Like these unassuming yet highly effective flag officers, Holcomb shied away from the limelight and thus never garnered the attention that such Marines as "Red Mike" Edson, "Chesty" Puller, or "Howlin' Mad" Smith sought or received. Indeed, much credit for the Corps' success in the Second World War has gone to Alexander A. Vandegrift, commanding general of the 1st Marine Division on Guadalcanal and later Holcomb's successor as commandant. Taking nothing away from Vandegrift's efforts and accomplishments, Holcomb rightly deserves a more prominent place in Marine Corps history. It is likely that he has been ignored or given short shrift due to the propensity of most service histories to be operational in their content. Marines fighting in battles attract historians writing about the Corps. Meanwhile, despite his significant accomplishments and major contributions, Holcomb's commandancy gets quietly sandwiched between those of Lejeune and Vandegrift.[1]

The dearth of coverage notwithstanding, one scholarly work does focus on Holcomb's career. John W. Gordon's article "General Thomas Holcomb and 'The Golden Age of Amphibious Warfare'" appeared in *Delaware History* (1985) and was later revised and reprinted as a chapter in Allan R. Millett and Jack Shulimson's anthology *Commandants of the Marine Corps* (2004). Gordon likens Holcomb to George C. Marshall "in terms of personality, style, and even intellectual equipment."[2] This is high praise. In fact, Gordon characterizes Holcomb as "a sort of 'mini-Marshall,' juggling far tinier resources but coping with the vaster geographic sweep of the war in the Pacific."[3]

Gordon does not, however, press comparisons with Holcomb and Army chiefs of staff far enough. For instance, Holcomb encountered severe budgetary restrictions during the early years of his commandancy, from 1936 through 1939. It was Marshall's predecessor as chief of staff from 1935 to 1939, the very capable General Malin Craig, who endured fiscal constraints comparable to Holcomb's and who set the Army on paths toward modernization and mobilization that Marshall, in turn, brought to fruition from 1939 through 1945. For his part, Holcomb did not head an independent branch of the armed services such as the Army, with its own resource base and manpower reserve. Instead, Holcomb and the Corps were inevitably beholden to the Navy for equipment, weapons, and other resources. Rather than portraying Holcomb as Marshall-in-miniature as Gordon has done, I believe it is more accurate to characterize him as an amalgamation of both Malin Craig and George Marshall.

Two additional works merit attention because they offer useful, albeit episodic, insights into Holcomb's personality, leadership, and historical context. First, in *In Many a Strife: General Gerald C. Thomas and the U.S. Marine Corps, 1917-1956*, Allan R. Millett examines one of Holcomb's subordinates. Because Gerald Thomas became acquainted with Holcomb in the First World War and crossed paths with him for decades thereafter, this biography frequently mentions Holcomb. Millett relates how he lobbied for a larger Marine Corps and competed for limited material resources with the other military services. Once the Second World War started, the commandant's tasks were no easier, because of nearly impossible mobilization schedules in the United States and counterproductive command problems in the Pacific theater of operations.[4]

The other book containing material on Holcomb is *Once a Marine*, by Alexander A. Vandegrift with Robert B. Asprey. One of Holcomb's contemporaries, Vandegrift served as his military secretary and then as assistant to the commandant at Headquarters, Marine Corps (HQMC) from 1937 to 1940. Vandegrift then commanded the 1st Marine Division on Guadalcanal in 1942. These assignments afforded him ample opportunities to assess Holcomb's abilities and to glean lessons for his own commandancy, which immediately followed Holcomb's in 1944 and lasted until 1947. Most compelling are Vandegrift's observations about Holcomb's management skills and personal character. Because Vandegrift so often unabashedly praises his mentor and friend, however, his book must be filtered for bias.[5]

Despite their many strengths, the works by Gordon, Millett, and Vandegrift do not portray Holcomb to the fullest extent as the visionary leader or progressive manager that he actually was. Nor do they examine such topics as his considerable influence on the Corps' public relations and recruitment activities. Finally, these works do not deal in sufficient detail with social or cultural factors affecting his commandancy.

My book conclusively redresses the deficiencies in the existing literature by demonstrating that before and during his commandancy, Holcomb helped shape the evolution of amphibious warfare and supported innovations that allowed the Corps to fulfill its new amphibious missions. His expert guidance of the service from December 1936 through December 1943 cannot and should not be ignored or understated. Thus he helped transform the Corps into the modern force-in-readiness in the Pacific War and long into the twentieth and twenty-first centuries.

PERSPECTIVES FROM OTHER DISCIPLINES

Assessing Thomas Holcomb's skills as a manager, leader, strategist, and publicist required me to borrow modes of analysis from other fields in history and from other disciplines. These new lenses allowed me to examine Holcomb's policy making and implementation processes, his employment of progressive management principles, the effects of the reforms he initiated in the Corps, his grasp of naval strategy and amphibious operations, his efforts to cultivate good relationships inside and outside the Corps, his knack for matching the right subordinates to the duties they could best fulfill, and the degree to which American society and culture influenced Holcomb and his Corps. To craft new interpretations of Marine Corps history and Holcomb's commandancy, I employ methodologies drawn from leadership studies, organizational theory, and social and cultural history. My conclusions often fall outside those of mainstream studies of Marine leaders and battlefield exploits.[6]

Leadership studies blend social science and business management to determine the qualities needed for administrators to achieve their goals and whether individuals can influence their organizations in any significant way. Effective leadership, according to political scientist Fred I. Greenstein, consists of more than "political prowess" or "intellectual ability," both of which Holcomb possessed. Greenstein argues that neither trait is absolutely essential for successful leadership, though they can strengthen any leader. He enumerates several less tangible qualities common to effective leadership: "organizational capacity" as the leader's "ability to rally his colleagues and structure their activities effectively"; "cognitive style" as the capacity to process "the Niagara of advice and information that comes his way"; and "emotional intelligence," as the "ability to manage his emotions and turn them to constructive purposes, rather than being dominated by them and allowing them to diminish his leadership."[7]

Greenstein concentrates on American presidents and does not examine senior military officers. Nevertheless, I utilize his criteria for ascertaining effective leadership and apply them to Holcomb to show he exhibited organizational capacity, cognitive style, and emotional intelligence. Holcomb could synthesize vast amounts of complex information and make knowledgeable decisions accordingly. His calm temperament helped him maintain self-control during emergencies and keep focused on the tasks at hand. Once he decided on an action, he delegated the authority to a particular subordinate or groups to execute that action.

In addition to Holcomb proving himself as an effective leader, he also developed considerable managerial skills during his long career. His management of the Corps can be best understood by viewing those skills through the lens of organizational theory. In the late nineteenth and early twentieth centuries, the "classical school" of organizational theory, including Max Weber and Chester Bernard, argued that the quest to create a successful organization centered on the "rationality" and "efficiency" of its administration.[8] These ideas helped constitute what became known as "progressive" management as Americans struggled to come to grips with industrialization.

The rapid expansion of railroads, energy production, and manufacturing posed uniquely huge and complex challenges for managers. Consequently, the classical organizational theorists set out to create institutional structures and functions to control those ponderous business enterprises and ultimately make them profitable. A good progressive manager in the early twentieth century employed the following techniques: delegate authority to subordinates and coordinate their efforts; balance vertical levels and the horizontal divisions with an organizational structure; cooperate with outside entities to determine and achieve common goals; and protect the organization from threats and unanticipated variables.[9]

No evidence exists that Holcomb studied organizational theories in a formal setting, but his activities as commandant fit the progressive-management mold outlined by classical organizational theorists. His decisions at HQMC in Washington, D.C., can be tracked up and down the chain of command. Consequently, a meaningful analysis, not only at the macro level (Holcomb's roles at HQMC) but also at the micro level (specific examples out in the Corps), becomes possible. Holcomb embraced most changes as opportunities for improvement. He used progressive techniques to reform the Marine Corps' administrative and command structures, chose the right subordinates for the duties that best suited them, and safeguarded his service's place in American strategic plans and military operations.

Increasing the Corps' efficiency was no easy task, considering the obstacles Holcomb faced during these periods of depression and war, each of which required him to employ different skills in divergent military, political, and economic contexts. The prewar period required him to be parsimonious in matching the Corps' severely limited resources to its many missions, and the wartime period required him to be conscientious in balancing the Corps' unprecedented growth with the maintenance of a specialized force.

Holcomb may have followed what could be considered progressive principles, but he also believed that effective management could not solve some problems. Sometimes, delegating authority or streamlining bureaucracy was not enough. Looking back on nearly seven years as commandant in August 1943, he encapsulated his philosophies of management and leadership in a letter to a close friend. Writing in the third person, Holcomb observed, "The Commandant perhaps undervalues the virtue of a perfect paper organization. He is, however, convinced that even if it has an ideal chart, any large organization, to be successful, must be headed by a personality; one possessed of those qualities of leadership which command respect and loyalty; which inspires in all hands the determination, and which is more important, the compelling desire, to work together for a common end."[10] Holcomb pointed to something less tangible than rational administrative structures and efficient managerial methods. Instead, he highlighted traits akin to Greenstein's notions of organizational capacity, cognitive style, and emotional intelligence.

Making use of leadership studies and organizational theory is useful in understanding Holcomb's leadership abilities and managerial skills, but no examination of his commandancy can be complete without placing him against the backdrop of American society and culture. Determining these external factors necessitates using interpretative methods of social and cultural history, as most military histories, let alone histories of the Marine Corps, do not. For millennia, traditional military historians have studied grand strategies, individual commanders, and significant battles. But beginning in the 1940s, historians probed the effects on warfare of politics, technology, ideology, and diplomacy.[11] In the 1960s, the historical profession as a whole increasingly opened up new avenues of inquiry by delineating social and cultural influences on the past. By the 1970s and 1980s, some military historians applied these "new" approaches to studying warfare and military institutions.[12] Peter Karsten contended, for instance, that the American military could be studied "as process, as institution, and as system interactive with society." He acknowledged "what most Americans forget: that our military has always been, far more so than is the case of most other states, the creature of our culture, not its mentor."[13]

Therefore, Karsten rejects Samuel P. Huntington's argument in *The Soldier and the State* that the American military has existed in isolation from civilian society. Karsten instead accepts positions held by sociologist Morris Janowitz in *The Professional Soldier* and military historian Walter Millis in *Arms and Men*, both of whom contend that the American military and society developed in mutually interdependent systems.[14]

Placing the Marine Corps and its commandant within American social and cultural contexts exposes some intriguing wrinkles in the debate over their interrelationships. For example, Holcomb's policies on race, gender, and sexuality make this relationship more complex because he saw only physically fit, heterosexual, Caucasian men as acceptable candidates to become Marines. He may have followed "progressive" management principles of the early twentieth century, but he was no progressive when it came to social issues. Holcomb resisted inclusion of women, African Americans, and certain other minorities into the Corps.[15] This exception in the record of an otherwise forward-looking commandant reveals much about Holcomb and his service in their larger political and social contexts.

To accomplish the twin tasks of appraising Holcomb's often overlooked commandancy and enriching Marine Corps history with new modes of analysis, this book draws on a large number of primary sources from the Marine Corps University Archives Branch in Quantico, Virginia, and the National Archives and Records Administration facilities in College Park, Maryland, and Washington, D.C. Most of the archival documents cited on the following pages were declassified, discovered, or donated during my research for this book. Perspectives from many oral history interviews also helped me craft a more complete and nuanced interpretation of Holcomb's commandancy.[16]

STRUCTURE

This book is divided into three principal sections. The first covers Thomas Holcomb's thirty-six-year career before he assumed the commandancy. He learned invaluable lessons about management and leadership during tours of duty in China, in France during the First World War, and at HQMC. He likewise helped to develop the service's amphibious capabilities and situate the Corps in naval strategy, both of which would be crucial to his service and to America's success in the Second World War. Holcomb's combat experiences, educational achievements, and administrative duties prepared him to become commandant.

The second section, which comprises Chapters 2 and 3, explores the prewar years of Holcomb's commandancy. When he assumed this position on December 1, 1936, he inherited myriad internal and external problems. He competed with other armed services for limited manpower and material resources, while cultivating good relationships with Congress and the Roosevelt administration and portraying the Corps to the American public as a viable and elite fighting force with a legitimate place in national defense.

Holcomb kept the Corps from becoming a marginalized part of the otherwise expanding U.S. military establishment. Not only did he navigate the Navy Department's bureaucracy, he also tamed the Corps' bureaucracy. Holcomb reformed the Marine Corps mobilization, recruitment, personnel, innovation, education, procurement, strategy, and plans and policies. Meanwhile, he supervised the service's preparations for amphibious warfare and achieved his greatest success by ensuring on paper, if not yet in reality, that the Corps could fulfill its dual mission of amphibious assault and base defense. The challenges multiplied as the United States appeared to be drawn inexorably closer to conflict in late 1941.

The third section (Chapters 4, 5, and 6) critically analyzes Commandant Holcomb's activities during the first twenty-four months of the Second World War. Once hostilities with Japan erupted on December 7, 1941, Holcomb suddenly faced a completely different set of challenges. He poured himself into holding Marine mobilization in step with the demands of the nation's strategic plans and military operations. Only in 1943 did the Corps' strength begin to match the country's strategic priorities. The campaign for Guadalcanal served as a case study of Holcomb's coordination of the Corps' war effort at HQMC and in the Pacific theater of operations.

In an effective leadership style, he dealt with delicate but important matters of personnel assignments, command structure, resource allocation, and interservice rivalries. As stated earlier, he also consistently upheld the Corps' positive image in the eyes of the American people and their Congress, displaying talents that exemplified the best progressive notions of efficiency and rationality—except, as noted, in areas pertaining to race and gender. While the American military's prohibition against homosexuals remained intact throughout the Second World War, Holcomb obeyed orders to accept African Americans and women into the Corps. He adapted grudgingly to societal changes that would eventually alter the nature of his service and the nation it served. His wartime social views notwithstanding, when Commandant Thomas Holcomb retired in December 1943, he left the Marine Corps at an unprecedented strength of 385,000 men and women.

As an epilogue, this book's final chapter covers Holcomb's activities following his retirement, when he continued to serve his nation as U.S. minister to the Union of South Africa from 1944 to 1948. In this post, Holcomb worked to maintain good relations with the South African government—while witnessing the effects of unimpeded racism in that nation's oppression of its black population. In his reports to the U.S. State Department, Holcomb leveled damning criticisms against the white South African government's brutal policies. His reports indicated a transformation in his previous racial views. After his second retirement from public life in 1948, Holcomb spent his waning years as a gentleman farmer, and he cared for his beloved wife, Beatrice, who suffered from chronic illnesses.

CHAPTER 1

HOLCOMB'S FIRST THIRTY-SIX YEARS IN THE MARINE CORPS

1900–1936

Thomas Holcomb spent thirty-six years rising through the ranks of the United States Marine Corps. He always seemed to be in the right position at the right time to maximize the benefits of fighting in the First World War, studying in the American military's advanced education system, and serving in key line and staff positions. These duties helped Holcomb hone his managerial skills, expand his circle of contacts, and carve a place for the Corps in the nation's war plans. The experiences also readied him to become major general commandant in December 1936.

Holcomb's career path paralleled many changes in the United States and its military during the early decades of the twentieth century. Victory in the Spanish-American War in 1898 gave the nation new strategic priorities in the Pacific Ocean, and this new international position provided the Corps with a relevant raison d'être: amphibious operations. Holcomb helped lay the foundation for the Marines to fulfill this new mission.

FORMATIVE YEARS

Elizabeth Barney and Thomas Holcomb Sr. celebrated the birth of their son Thomas Holcomb Jr. on August 5, 1879. The elder Holcomb, an attorney and Delaware state legislator, provided a middle-class standard of living for his family in New Castle, Delaware. His family traced its lineage back nine generations to a namesake, Thomas Holcomb of Devonshire, England, who landed in Nantucket, Massachusetts, in 1630. Elizabeth Barney's ancestry was also impressive: she was descended from Joshua Barney, an American naval officer who served with distinction in the Revolutionary War and War of 1812.[1]

Growing up in Delaware, young Thomas attended a private school until 1893, when his father took a job with the U.S. Treasury Department and moved his wife and four children to Washington, D.C. The teenaged Thomas entered the capital's public school system, where he was first exposed to military-style drill and discipline that resonated with the young man hailing from a family of proud military heritage. After graduating from Western High School in 1897, Thomas hoped to enter the United States Naval Academy in Annapolis, Maryland. But, because his family fell on hard times in the economic depression of the mid-1890s, he set aside this goal to help support his family. Thomas worked as a clerk for Bethlehem Steel near Baltimore so his younger brother, Franklin Porteous, could attend the Naval Academy. A few years later, Franklin proved to be an outstanding midshipman.[2]

Thomas Holcomb Jr. never did receive a baccalaureate degree, something that set him apart from most other Marine Corps commandants in the twentieth century. His predecessor, John H. Russell, graduated from the Naval Academy, and his successor, Alexander A. Vandegrift, from the University of Virginia. It was not that Holcomb made a poor student, nor that he was uninterested in intellectual development. Quite the contrary, he voraciously read books and poetry.[3]

Once the younger Holcomb reached adulthood, he dropped the "junior" from his name and simply went by Thomas, or "Tommy" to close friends. In the wake of the Spanish-American War, he applied for a commission in the Marine Corps in 1898. This would have allowed Holcomb to achieve his ultimate goal of becoming an officer while still supplementing his family's income. His first attempt to join the Corps ended in rejection, because he was deemed to be too thin and too short.[4] As the story went, the Marine recruiter took one look at him and said, "Youngster, better go home and forget about the Marines. You'd never stand the gaff."[5] In the 1890s, that was slang for enduring harsh treatment or criticism.[6]

A disappointed but not disheartened Holcomb returned to the steel mill. The job doubtlessly helped him develop an eye for detail and an understanding of organizational structure, both of which would serve him well throughout his military career. Working as a clerk also likely exposed Holcomb to progressive management principles and techniques that played such prominent roles in American business at the turn of the century and that subsequently seemed to influence him so greatly.

In his spare time, he took dancing lessons, enjoyed social events in Baltimore, and attended an Episcopalian church nearly every Sunday. After two years, he gave the Corps' enlistment process a second try in 1900. With help from his father's political connections in Washington, twenty-year-old Thomas Holcomb secured a place in a pool of fifteen applicants who would take the intensive examination required to become a Marine officer. Never a slacker, Holcomb diligently prepared. In February, as the testing dates drew nearer, he moved into his church's rectory, studied many hours each day, and received tutoring from his parish priest. Rumors also surfaced that Holcomb had himself stretched, in a long and painful process to add inches to meet the Corps' requirements. In interviews in recent decades, however, no Holcomb family member has provided concrete evidence that either affirms or refutes this rumor.[7]

Thomas Holcomb as a young Marine officer, early 1900s.

(Holcomb File, Reference Branch, Marine Corps History Division)

Holcomb started his testing at the Marine Barracks on March 3, 1900. In addition to a physical fitness component, the examinations evaluated would-be officers in grammar, constitutional law, history, geography, arithmetic, algebra, geometry, trigonometry, surveying, reading, writing, and spelling. Holcomb noted in his diary that each subject took all morning or afternoon, and that the arithmetic examination lasted four hours and fifteen minutes. He finished the last test in the morning twelve days later, and then proceeded to his boyhood home of New Castle, Delaware, to wait for news of his performance.[8] Holcomb's diary entry for March 20 reads, "Rec'd telephone message about 1 pm . . . that I had passed exams."[9]

He earned the fourth highest grade and was one of only five applicants who passed all examination fields. On April 13, Holcomb received a commission as a second lieutenant in the United States Marine Corps. Never an imposing figure physically, the new second lieutenant stood five feet seven and a half inches tall, weighing 135 pounds. Navy physicians conducting his medical examination noted that the brown-haired, blue-eyed Holcomb had especially strong hearing and eyesight. This latter trait would be particularly useful to Holcomb as he developed into a superior rifle marksman.[10]

After completing the Marine Corps' School of Application in Philadelphia, Holcomb took up his duties with the North Atlantic Fleet in Newport, Rhode Island. He participated in naval exercises and got his initial exposure to seaborne operations. The new officer also received the first of many promotions to first lieutenant. Beginning in 1903, Holcomb served several tours of duty overseas in East Asia. He served with the Legation Guard in Beijing, China, from 1905 to 1906. He advanced to captain in May before again departing in 1908 for East Asia, where he stayed for two tours, until 1914. Receiving a three-year extension in China from 1911 to 1914 bears witness to the high regard that Holcomb attained in the eyes of superiors.

Service in China ranked as the most sought-after assignment in the Corps. American dollars went much further there, and enlisted Marines could even afford to hire personal servants. Freed from having to make beds and polish buttons, the Marines devoted much of their time to drilling and parading. Officers like Holcomb also enjoyed hunting, traveling, and participating in sporting events and rifle matches.[11]

But Holcomb was hardly idle. He took advantage of many opportunities to better himself as an officer. While serving as attaché to the American Minister in Beijing, he studied Chinese language, culture, and politics. Holcomb acquired language proficiency, earning the grade of 95 percent on one Chinese examination in 1914. His evaluator of his translation work said that Holcomb "has an accurate and fluent enunciation, and his knowledge of present day Chinese idioms, as exhibited in the reading aloud and translating of both the 'Wen Li Lessons' and the newspaper, guarantees his efficiency in translating work of more than usual difficulty."[12] Tributes like these became hallmarks of Holcomb's career. These tours likewise made him a "China Hand," as those guarding international settlements came to be known.

Holcomb's other assignments included stints as acting quartermaster and acting assistant paymaster for Marines stationed in Olongapo, the Philippines, in 1905, and as post quartermaster at the Marine Corps Barracks in Washington in 1907. While in the nation's capital, he also landed a plum appointment as a White House military aide to President Theodore Roosevelt.

These duties gave the young Marine a more thorough understanding of staff functions and military bureaucracy. When not on duty, Holcomb and other bachelor officers gave parties for young women from prominent Washington families. These social gatherings played important roles in officers' lives, in terms of both

Holcomb (left) was on the winning American rifle team in Peking, 1910.

(Marine Corps University Archives, Holcomb Papers, Box 26)

leisure and networking. Holcomb always enjoyed the events, and he would continue to entertain guests throughout his military career and into his retirement. It was at one of these parties during his next tour in Washington, from 1914 to 1917, that he would first meet his future wife, Beatrice Clover.[13]

Very early in his career, Holcomb achieved his greatest distinction as a marksman and commanding officer on the Marine Corps Rifle Team. He had done no competitive shooting before receiving his commission, but he immediately demonstrated natural skills. At the behest of some observant Marines in Newport, the young second lieutenant qualified as sharpshooter, which was then the highest marksmanship classification. Holcomb subsequently secured a spot on the Marine Corps Rifle Team. He served as either a team member or commander in 1901, 1902, 1903, 1907, 1908, and 1911.

Holcomb's skill as marksman stood as a sure badge of distinction in an organization increasingly obsessed with accurate shooting. Holcomb won the individual world championship for long-range marksmanship at Ottawa, Canada, in 1902. He also represented the United States on a national rifle team at the Palma Trophy matches of 1902 and 1903. That first Palma match brought Holcomb international notoriety.[14] A Marine Corps official history explains that in 1902, "Holcomb, the youngest member of all the teams shooting, received a special gold medal for his outstanding performance. Even the British *Volunteer Service Gazette* noted his splendid performance when it characterized him as a 'brilliant young officer.'"[15]

Holcomb took much more than a few trophies and heightened prestige from these competitions. First, he realized that part of every Marine's training must include exhaustive practice with his rifle. "Marksmanship was a key part of his career. He believed in it," remarked his son, Franklin Porteous Holcomb, in an interview. This fit with the Corps' philosophy that every Marine should be first and foremost a rifleman.[16] Thomas Holcomb also became a stubborn devotee of the .30-06 caliber Springfield rifle Model 1903, the weapon he used in many of his competitive matches.

The attentiveness and patience so necessary in long-range shooting must have nourished Holcomb's calm demeanor. Later, when he ceased competitive shooting, he took up photography as a hobby.[17] Selecting the object, calculating the angles, and gauging the light for a perfect photograph required the same skills as determining wind speed, controlling one's breathing, and gently squeezing the trigger for that perfect shot on the rifle range. Being a crack shot and a good photographer required a certain temperament, which was neither impulsive nor wasteful.

Holcomb's years as a junior officer were marred by one tragedy. His younger brother Franklin died in a freak accident in 1907. Franklin, then serving on the USS *Connecticut*, went ashore with several other officers on a small boat. Later that evening, on his return to the warship during rough weather, his boat somehow got fouled in tow lines of moored ships in the harbor and capsized. Franklin and all hands on board drowned in this sad incident. His devoted older brother, who had sacrificed so much so that Franklin could attend the Naval Academy, was stationed far away in China at that time. Thomas was probably not even able to attend Franklin's funeral.[18]

TOUR AT HEADQUARTERS MARINE CORPS

In August 1914, peace ended when Europe plunged into the bloody First World War. That year, Captain Holcomb returned to HQMC in Washington to become inspector of target practice and aide-de-camp to Commandant George Barnett, who had remembered what an outstanding junior officer Holcomb had made in China. This tour at the Corps' nerve center made the young captain privy to the many inner workings of the Corps. He experienced firsthand the manifold challenges confronting a commandant and his staff: allocating limited manpower to far-flung stations, establishing roles for the service in strategic plans, recruiting physically fit men, and preparing for possible participation in the First World War.

Holcomb made lifelong contacts in the nation's capital. Among the civilians was Assistant Secretary of the Navy Franklin Delano Roosevelt, with whom Holcomb worked closely on Corps matters. Both men shared an interest in shooting: Holcomb the champion and Roosevelt the gentleman marksman. They enjoyed their hobby on a rifle range in nearby Winthrop, Maryland. They also formed a friendship that would last three decades and help see the Corps through its darkest hours. Just as important, Holcomb worked closely with the new assistant to the commandant, Colonel John A. Lejeune, and with the brilliant Marine strategist Major Earl H. "Pete" Ellis. The long-term influence of these two officers on Holcomb, in terms of both professionalism and patronage, cannot be overstated.[19]

When Lejeune became Barnett's assistant in 1915, he expanded the responsibilities of his new position by making himself the de facto chief of staff, responsible for all administrative activities internal to the Corps. Lejeune's management style was firmly rooted in the progressive movement of the late nineteenth century. He tried to create successful organizations run by professionals and centered on "rationality" and "efficiency," the two magic words and basic goals of progressivism.[20]

The American military slowly embraced progressive management principles in the aftermath of the Spanish-American War. Logistical problems were painfully apparent in that conflict, because many more American military personnel died off the battlefield than on it. Nothing short of an organizational revolution was necessary.[21] A social historian of the American military, Peter Karsten, notes that a new generation of progressive officers "and their more senior allies, often acting in such organizations as the Naval Officers Association, the Marine Corps Association, and the Infantry Association, were the prime organizers of the military revolution."

Karsten identifies these men as the "armed progressives."[22] Lejeune and other progressive officers such as future commandant John H. Russell realized that victory on the modern battlefield required careful planning and implementation, and that achieving those goals meant taking cues from the business world.

Although Holcomb absorbed Lejeune's ideas, he could not be considered the typical "armed progressive" in all respects. He did not graduate from the Naval Academy, as did Lejeune, or attend civilian college as had so many of his peers. Indeed, Holcomb's exposure to the business world came from his work as a clerk in a steel mill, an experience that should not be undervalued, because in it he observed how a large, complex institution functioned. Once in the Corps, Holcomb further developed his administrative skills doing staff work and by emulating examples set by Lejeune and other superior officers.

In addition to his organizational reforms, Lejeune believed in preparing for future conflicts. In 1915, he created an ad hoc war plans committee comprised of himself and three promising Marine captains at HQMC: Ralph S. Keyser, Ellis, and Holcomb. In an interview five decades later, an elderly Thomas Holcomb enthusiastically recalled what it was like working for Lejeune: "Those were exciting days. Ellis and I felt as though we were in the thick of things, with officers dropping in to discuss both official and personal matters with us or to pay their respects to the Commandant or the Assistant Commandant. Neither of us was designated as an aide to the Assistant Commandant, but we both worked for him on an as-available basis."[23]

Among other subjects, Keyser, Ellis, and Holcomb examined the Navy's evolving strategic needs and tried to determine how the Corps could best fulfill them. As early as 1900, the admirals on the Navy's General Board believed that the nation's territorial acquisitions after the Spanish-American War required U.S. power to be projected far across the Pacific Ocean. Strategists prepared a number of scenarios, with potential allies and enemies designated by colors. The U.S. Navy's planners focused much of their attention on the Pacific Ocean and on Japan, otherwise known as "Orange."[24]

All permutations of War Plan Orange over the next decades shared some tenets. American strategists anticipated that the Japanese would launch a preemptive strike, probably without the formality of a declaration of war. That attack would presumably be directed against such American bases in the Pacific as the Philippines and Guam. Following the initial Japanese onslaught, the U.S. Fleet would sortie from Hawaii and sail across the Pacific. Marine Corps units would provide essential support for that counteroffensive by seizing and holding islands until relieved by permanent Army units. Guam and American Samoa, for instance, became known as "advanced bases," and Wake and Midway would eventually be added to this group in the 1930s.

These roles represented a new dual mission for the Marine Corps from the turn of the century, and certainly by 1907. The newly captured bases would subsequently function as coaling stations, safe anchorages, repair facilities, and supply depots. The U.S. Fleet would either relieve besieged American forces in the Philippines or liberate the archipelago, if it already had fallen. As the fleet menaced the Japanese home islands, it was unquestioningly assumed in the Orange Plan that ensuing naval battles would result in a decisive American victory.[25] According to military historian Edward S. Miller, debates erupted between two groups of the Navy's strategic planners: those with a "cautionary" mind-set, who advocated a deliberate Pacific campaign by Navy forces against the Japanese; and those with a "thruster" outlook, who wanted to strike a single great blow against the Japanese in a climactic battle. Gradually, the strategic realities of Japanese control of so much of the Central and Western Pacific in the 1920s and 1930s would swing the advantage toward the cautionary approach, of which Holcomb was a proponent.[26]

Regardless of which side held the upper hand in naval war planning circles, Lejeune, Ellis, Russell, and Holcomb, together with other prominent Marine officers such as Eli K. Cole and Robert H. Dunlap, grasped the importance of this new dual mission for the Corps and worked to prepare the Marines to perform both halves of it. Marines could no longer expect to subsist in their traditional duties as shipboard security, legation guards, and constabulary troops. Doing so would have relegated the service to obscurity and possible extinction.[27]

By 1916, however, it was not the Japanese threat or amphibious operations in the Pacific that increasingly grabbed everyone's attention at HQMC. Instead, the conflict raging in Europe posed the more immediate threat. Working with Lejeune, Ellis, and others especially convinced Holcomb of the value of meticulous planning, not only to create realistic operational contingencies but also to ensure that the Marine Corps could firmly establish itself as an integral part of the nation's war effort. Holcomb and the committee also needed to prepare for the huge expansion that would occur if the nation entered the conflict.[28] "I performed a variety of tasks . . . but my principal work involved procuring officers for the war we all saw as inevitable. However, I took my target practice duties seriously," explained a retired Holcomb in an interview. "Until the turn of the century, Marine Corps' rifle training had been perfunctory, and the performance of our teams in national and international matches was disgraceful."[29] Even in the midst of strategic planning for a major conflict, Holcomb's emphasis on a Marine's most basic of skills consistently rang clear.

The United States maintained the appearance of neutrality in the First World War, from 1914 until 1917. Holcomb and the Marines watched as the United States entered the global conflict in April 1917. Just as the U.S. Army and Navy expanded rapidly in this national crisis, so did the Marine Corps. In early 1916, for instance, the Marines had counted only about 11,000 men in their ranks, but that figure increased to more than 75,000 in late 1918.

Attracting potential recruits was hardly a problem for the Corps; rather, it was the massive influx of men that overwhelmed the service's limited organizational capacity. From April 1917 through November 1918, nearly 240,000 men eagerly applied to join the Corps. Of these, fully 75 percent received rejections, mostly for medical reasons. Unfortunately, once the accepted applicants left recruiting stations, the Corps lacked housing facilities as well as sufficient numbers of commissioned and noncommissioned officers to train them. Despite all the difficulties of a haphazard expansion, the service grew by more than 60,000 men in the war's twenty months. Every bit as important, the mobilization process provided Marine officers like Holcomb with an example of how a small organization with a particular self-identity might dramatically expand, while simultaneously maintaining that identity and achieving combat readiness.[30]

As the possibility of war grew, a sense of urgency spread throughout the Corps in 1917. Marines from Commandant Barnett down the ranks worried that they might not be included among the ground forces destined for combat in Europe. Otherwise, they would remain marginalized as ships' guards or as constabulary troops in Central America. Barnett lobbied skeptics in the Navy and War Departments to grant the Marines a dispensation to join in the American Expeditionary Force (AEF). Successful in May, he ordered the first elements of the 5th Marine Regiment to France in June 1917. He also began assigning thousands of Marines for additional training at the newly established base at Quantico, Virginia, just 35 miles south of Washington on the western bank of the Potomac River.[31]

The recently promoted Majors Holcomb, Ellis, and Keyser begged Barnett to be assigned to command the battalions forming at Quantico in late 1917. Holcomb lacked combat experience; nor had he served any lengthy tours in Central America, where many thousands of his fellow leathernecks had earned their spurs in "small wars" in the early twentieth century. Barnett approved Keyser and Holcomb's requests, but he ordered Ellis to remain at Quantico, in part because of his recurring health problems.

Ellis eventually went to France as a staff officer but never commanded troops in combat. He would find himself increasingly seen as a strategic planner rather than a combat leader. For his part, in August 1917 Holcomb received orders transferring him from HQMC to Quantico, where he assumed command of the 2nd Battalion, 6th Marine Regiment. His battalion contained the 78th, 79th, 80th, and 96th companies and other assorted units, totaling approximately 1,050 Marines. Once at Quantico, Holcomb had his troops participate in intensive exercises that emphasized marksmanship as well as drill and discipline. No matter what they might do in France, he believed that accurate small arms fire would be essential.[32] His 1917 push to ready the 2nd Battalion for combat earned him a commendation that tendered "great credit to Major Holcomb for his notable contribution toward the excellent condition and high efficiency of the Battalion."[33]

Relatively small in stature and quiet in demeanor, Holcomb did not at first impress some of the Marines in his unit. A young Lieutenant Clifton B. Cates did not see anything outstanding about him: "When we first joined the battalion we didn't think much of him," Cates said. But in an interview, he recounted how his first impression had been incorrect in France. "We soon changed our opinion. After Soissons, he was tops with everyone."[34] Cates' initial assessment of Holcomb typified reactions on meeting him. However, just as Cates referenced the Battle of Soissons in July 1918, Holcomb would gain respect because of his calmness, competence, compassion, and intelligence.

Apart from the turmoil of the First World War, Holcomb's personal life was also fraught with changes during his three years at HQMC. The year 1916 was bittersweet for him. His father passed away, but thirty-eight-year-old Thomas Holcomb courted Beatrice Miller Clover, seventeen years his junior and a former Washington debutante. They met at a party thrown by bachelor officers. The attractive Beatrice came from a family with an impressive military heritage as well as significant wealth and social standing. Her father was Rear Admiral Richardson Clover of the U.S. Navy; and her maternal grandfather was John Franklin Miller, a Union major general during the Civil War and later U.S. senator from California. Thomas and Beatrice were married on November 11, 1916, in an Episcopal ceremony at St. John's Church, Washington, D.C.

The newlyweds enjoyed a little more than a year together before the U.S. entrance into the First World War and Thomas' deployment to France. Their union produced a son, Franklin Porteous, on October 13, 1917, just a few weeks before the elder Holcomb left for France.[35] As one of his cousins related, Thomas Holcomb "was a very devoted family man. He idolized young Franklin and spoiled him."[36] Doting treatment was not unusual in any father, but in this case, Franklin was the namesake of Thomas' beloved younger brother, who had drowned in a boating accident back in 1907. Thus the son also represented an emotional tie to that deceased sibling.

COMBAT IN THE FIRST WORLD WAR

Thomas Holcomb and his 2nd Battalion sailed on the American transport ship *Henderson* from New York City on January 24, 1918, arriving in France two weeks later. Holcomb's unit was one of the three rifle battalions, along with one machine-gun battalion, that constituted the 6th Marine Regiment. The 6th Marines, together with the 5th Marine Regiment, formed the 9,500-man-strong 4th Marine Brigade. The U.S. Army's Brigadier General James G. Harbord commanded the brigade from

May 6 to July 15, 1918. The 4th Marine Brigade, in turn, combined with the two U.S. Army regiments in the 5th Brigade to fill out the U.S. 2nd Division (Regular). In France, the Army's Major General Omar Bundy and then briefly Harbord commanded the 2nd Division. Finally, the Marine Corps' own Major General John A. Lejeune assumed command on July 29, 1918.[37]

The Marines of the 4th Brigade received rigorous training with French weaponry and conducted intensive infantry exercises for several weeks in the cold, damp farmlands at Bourmont, France, for much of February and March 1918. The leathernecks learned new French tactical doctrines that stressed flexibility of platoon- and company-level movements as well as concentration of force and firepower against key points in enemy lines. Holcomb and many Marines attended courses designed to help them understand the techniques of trench warfare, and Holcomb then himself taught classes on topics such as combat engineering to familiarize his troops with how to construct and assault trenches. He drove his men hard in the classroom and in the field, because he knew that preparation and conditioning would be keys to victory in the coming battles.[38]

Fellow Marines took notice of Holcomb and his style. Some concluded that his habitual use of last names when addressing subordinates, and his contemplative silences when considering problems, made him "distant," "aloof," "taciturn," and "austere."[39] In reality, Holcomb's crusty exterior hid a softer core. Whether as battalion commander or as Marine Corps commandant, he cared deeply about the welfare of his men. During one period of calm in France in 1918, for instance, Holcomb decided to bring in entertainers to provide the troops with an escape from the dreary and dangerous life in the trenches. When the entertainers did not arrive on schedule, he lost his temper because he did not want to see his men disappointed.[40] This episode corroborated the experience of other Marines such as James Roosevelt, an officer in the Marine Corps Reserve and son of the future president, who remembered that Holcomb was "very human and kind" and "remarkably friendly."[41]

In mid-March 1918, Holcomb and his Marines finally got their first opportunity to use their newly acquired combat skills, in the Toulon sector of the Verdun front. The Marines coordinated their infantry movements with artillery fire, and they conducted day and night patrols scouting for enemy advances. Although this sector was supposedly quiet, shells from a mustard gas barrage by German artillery did catch one company in Holcomb's 2nd Battalion unaware and killed 40 Marines. Nevertheless, the Marines gained confidence as they successfully repelled every German assault against their entrenched positions.[42]

Following a brief respite, the 2nd Division moved to the front lines near Belleau Wood (Bois de Belleau) and Château-Thierry village on May 31. For the next six days, American soldiers and Marines desperately tried to stop German forces driving toward the Marne River and the French capital, as Marine veteran Gerald C.

Thomas recalled.[43] The opposing battle lines became so confused that it was not clear who was attacking or retreating just west of the village of Château-Thierry. Reports trickling into the headquarters of the XXI French Corps, to which the 2nd Division was attached, said that the Marine lines had collapsed. The corps commander, General Jean Degoutte, sought confirmation. His desperate query wound its way through channels to the 4th Marine Brigade's commanding officer, Brigadier General Harbord, who tried to make contact with Major Holcomb of the 2nd Battalion.[44]

Finally Harbord succeeded in telephoning Holcomb to ask whether his Marines were holding or retreating. As the story goes, Holcomb snorted in reply to Harbord, "When this outfit runs it will be in the other direction. Nothing doing in the fall-back business."[45] The Marines of Holcomb's 2nd Battalion stubbornly held their ground and, as the accomplished marksmen they were, raked the advancing German troops with precise rifle and machine-gun fire. The Marines thwarted one enemy attack after another, from May 31 to June 5.[46] Holcomb's steady leadership prompted Commandant George Barnett to cite him because he showed "rare ability as a leader of troops and inspired his officers and men to unceasing efforts by his devotion to duty and fearlessness."[47]

The sixth of June marked that first chance for Holcomb and his unit to run "in the other direction," as he had told Harbord a few days earlier. Orders came down for the 4th Brigade to launch attacks against Belleau Wood and the nearby village of Bouresches at 5 PM. The shells and shattered remains of several dozen brick houses in Bouresches offered ideal cover for German machine gunners and snipers.[48] Holcomb wrote to Beatrice just one hour earlier that he and his 2nd Battalion would take part in the "greatest battle in history—a small part of it at least."[49]

While other Marines of the 5th and 6th Regiments made their bloody frontal assault against more than 1,200 German soldiers ensconced in Belleau Wood proper, Holcomb's 2nd Battalion proceeded toward Bouresches, which was occupied by several hundred Germans. Holcomb's unit formed the link between the Marines to the west entering the wood and others fighting south and east of the village. About 5 PM, the smart-looking 79th and 96th Companies of the 2nd Battalion began their advance in good order across several hundred yards of open fields of green wheat up to their waists. Sadly, these companies' attack against Bouresches was doomed from start, because poorly coordinated American artillery provided only an initial barrage and failed to support the Marines with rolling fire to keep the Germans' heads down during the Americans' march across the field.

The Marines quickly came under devastating fire from German machine guns. It was here that Captain Donald Duncan, commander of the 96th Company and close friend of Thomas Holcomb, was mortally wounded. All the Marines found themselves pinned down in the open, with no communications between them and Holcomb. Several junior officers and noncommissioned officers took charge of

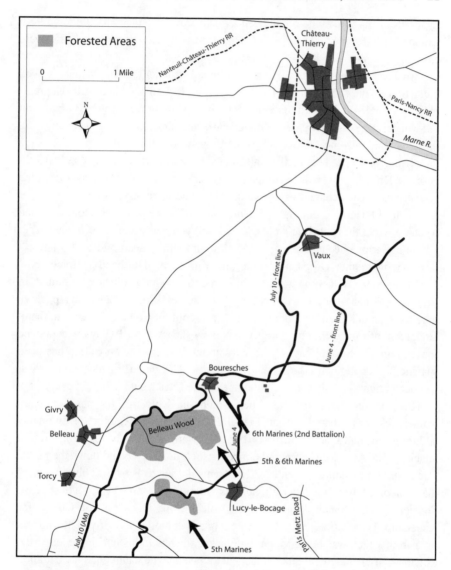

▶ Battle lines at Belleau Wood and Bouresches, June 4–July 10, 1918.

(Map by Michael J. Hradesky)

the situation and led the remaining Marines into Bouresches, where they secured the village.

Recognizing the significance of this village as a strong point to support further advances against the Germans in Belleau Wood, Holcomb moved all his available Marines to Bouresches. He also begged for and received additional reinforcements from Harbord. June 6 had been a costly day for Holcomb's 79th and 96th Companies. Of some 500 Marines who had led the attack, approximately 250 were casualties.[50]

Two days later, on June 8, Holcomb continued his letter to Beatrice that replayed the action on the two previous days: "As you know I am safe and well. The regiment has carried itself with undying glory, but the price was heavy. My battalion did wonderfully, especially dear old Duncan's company. There was never anything finer than their advance across a place literally swept with machine gun fire. They took [Bouresches] and held it through a never to be forgotten night and hold it still. Poor old Duncan, my favorite company commander was killed. You have seen the casualty lists. The behavior of the wounded was perfectly marvelous. There never was such self-sacrifice, courage, and spirit shown." Here Holcomb's tone softened when he wrote these closing words, "I will tell you many stories of it when I get you in my arms once again. . . . I love you with all my heart and soul. I haven't time to write mother. Drop her a line for me. Your devoted husband, T. Holcomb."[51]

On June 9, Holcomb again commented on some realities of combat in Bouresches in another letter to Beatrice. "My dearest girl," he began in a positive tone, "I write this from the front line. . . . We got out for a much needed rest, thank God. I am safe and well. I have not even had my shoes off for 10 days, except once for ten minutes. Several days I've been without food and my only sleep has been snatched at odd moments during the day time. . . . The whole brigade put up a most wonderful fight. We have been cited twice by the French authorities."[52]

The next few days in Bouresches would see Holcomb, the surviving 200 leathernecks of his battalion, and 175 soldiers of the 2nd Regiment of Engineers enduring repeated German artillery barrages while steadfastly repelling ground attacks.[53] The Americans garnered praise for their defense up and down the ranks. The man commanding the entire AEF, General John J. Pershing, bluntly stated that Holcomb's battalion "sturdily held its ground against the enemy's best guard division."[54] The French Army awarded Holcomb his first Croix de Guerre for leadership. The citation read: "Commanding a Battalion in a regiment of Marines on a front which was being violently attacked, thanks to his untiring energy, the exactness of his judgment and his tactical knowledge, he maintained his battalion on this line, later taking the village [of Bouresches] and repulsing a number of counter attacks."[55] Although Gerald Thomas was a sergeant in a different battalion at that time, he knew of Major Holcomb's "reputation as a very famous troop commander"[56] and a "good tactician."[57] Clearly then, Holcomb attracted the right kind of attention up and down the ranks.

A week later on June 13, Holcomb received orders to move his 78th and 96th Companies to relieve the exhausted Marine unit then fighting along the eastern edge of Belleau Wood. As Holcomb and his Marines made their way to that new position, they came under a violent artillery barrage—a "drenching bombardment," in translated German parlance—of 6,000 to 7,000 high explosive, mustard gas, and phosgene gas shells that started about midnight on June 14. A shocked Holcomb learned later that morning that the 78th and 96th Companies had lost a combined 31 Marines killed, and another 251 gassed or wounded, out of their total strength of 500. With a casualty rate nearing 60 percent, these two companies ceased to be effective combat units.[58]

In his daily report, Brigadier General Harbord succinctly assessed the situation of Holcomb's two debilitated companies: "General aspects of the day: Unfavorable to us." Harbord described the specifics of the artillery attack on the leathernecks. He concluded his report by stating, "I am very glad to report that notwithstanding their physical exhaustion, which is almost total, and the adverse circumstances of gas, the spirit of the [4th Marine] Brigade remains unshaken, but morale under such conditions is on pure nerve and is liable to snap."[59] So many Marines died that Holcomb could hardly reinforce, let alone replace, another unit. Nevertheless, the leathernecks held their position against all enemy incursions for the next three days, until relief forces arrived.[60]

Another fortnight of intense combat elapsed before a triumphant message went out to AEF headquarters on June 26 that "Belleau Wood now U.S. Marine Corps entirely." Thereafter, the French called the wood "Bois de la Brigade de Marine." Thus ended the defensive phase of the Aisne-Marne Campaign. While suffering grievous losses, American Marines helped break the momentum of the German drive toward Paris. Their courage earned them the nickname *Teufelhunden*, or "devil dogs," from their adversaries.[61] When chatting with Thomas Holcomb during an interview in 1964, Marine veteran and author Clayton Barrow Jr. observed that "Holcomb's eyes misted at the memory of Belleau Wood, where his 2d Battalion, 6th Marines—rechristened 'Holcomb's Battalion'—lost 21 officers and 836 men." This battle cost the entire 4th Marine Brigade more than 5,000 Marines killed, wounded, gassed, or missing out of 9,500. Of these, casualties on the sixth of June alone amounted to 1,087 Marines.[62]

After being relieved in early July, the 4th Marine Brigade enjoyed a few days away from the front line. The unit's all-too-brief rest ended on July 18, when Franco-American forces started the Aisne-Marne Campaign's offensive phase, in hopes of enveloping the German forces that had previously advanced to the Marne River. The 2nd Infantry Division was tasked with attacking east toward the village of Vierzy, just a few miles south of the town of Soissons. The Americans achieved initial success by killing, wounding, or capturing thousands of Germans, but by dusk the exhausted division dug in to a line just east of Vierzy. Holcomb's 2nd Battalion remained in reserve until the second day of the offensive. They then received orders that they should enter the fray that next day. Holcomb and the Marines would, hopefully, push the Germans back eastward beyond Vierzy and the Château-Thierry Road.[63]

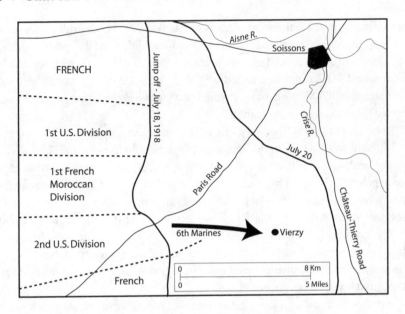

▶ The 6th Marines advance to Vierzy, July 19–20, 1918.

(Map by Michael J. Hradesky)

The entire 6th Marines moved up to the line about dawn on July 19. The 1st Battalion took the right, Holcomb's 2nd Battalion took the left, and the 3rd Battalion followed in support. Another officer in the 2nd Battalion, Robert L. Denig Sr., wrote to his wife about the ensuing advance by the Marine units: "At 8:30 we jumped off with a line of tanks in the lead. For two [kilometers] the four lines of marines were as straight as a die, and their advance over the open plain in the bright sunlight was a picture I shall never forget. The fire got hotter and hotter, men fell, bullets sung, shells whizzed-banged, and the dust of battle got thick."[64]

The Germans' devastating machine and artillery fire stalled the Marines' advance within two hours. All the while, Holcomb calmly gave orders and endeavored to maintain some semblance of command and control in the deteriorating situation. The supporting 3rd Battalion went into the line but to no avail, because that unit got chewed up by enemy fire just as had the 1st and 2nd before them. "At 10:30 we dug in; the attack just died out. I found a hole or old trench, and when I was flat on my back I got some protection. Holcomb was next [to] me," recounted Denig. "From then on to about 8 PM life was a chance, and mighty uncomfortable."[65] So vividly did Denig depict his combat experiences that his letter would eventually be reprinted in the *New York Times*.

At what become known as the Battle of Soissons, the citation for Holcomb's second Croix de Guerre in as many months depicted harsh combat conditions, yet pointed to his exceptional leadership: "Thanks to [Holcomb's] heroism, he led his troops across fields violently swept by concentrated machine gun and artillery fire. By his continued presence on the fighting line he inspired his marines to continue their advance in spite of heavy losses."[66] Of course, the last embellished phrase about the Marines continuing their advance conveyed little of the horrific realities of enduring German fire in open territory and losing so many officers and men.

More than 2,400 Marines had commenced that attack early in the morning of July 19. Then, a mere ten hours later, nearly half were killed or wounded. Those leathernecks still alive and unharmed were reduced to mere survival. Shortly after midnight, relief columns of French colonial troops arrived to replace the Marines, who evacuated and slowly limped back to their starting point, all the while under constant German artillery fire.[67] Nevertheless, Holcomb once again at Soissons proved himself to be a capable battlefield leader even in dire circumstances.

After the leathernecks went into reserve in the Marbache Sector in mid-August 1918, Holcomb relinquished command of his Battalion to Major Ernest C. Williams, to become the new assistant regimental commander at the rank of lieutenant colonel. Holcomb's responsibilities included overseeing intelligence and operations for the 6th Marines, which in turn introduced him to the U.S. Army's administrative staff organization. Modeled on the French Army's General Staff, this system incorporated the departments of personnel, intelligence, operations, supply, and training into a single structure. Each department fulfilled its requisite responsibilities and kept the officers commanding large formations informed about their activities. A division, corps, or army commander could then determine where and when to maneuver, attack, or retreat. The resulting efficiency and flexibility left a lasting impression on Holcomb as well as on John Lejeune, by then a major general and the 2nd Division's new commanding officer. Lejeune would restructure the staff at HQMC in a similarly progressive fashion as commandant in the 1920s.[68]

While the conflict dragged on into autumn 1918, the Marines saw more action in the Battle of Saint Mihiel in September, the Battle of Blanc Mont in October, and finally the Meuse-Argonne Campaign in November. Holcomb spent much less time in combat because, as assistant regimental commander, he analyzed intelligence reports and planned operations.[69] He did, however, occasionally venture into harm's way. His courage garnered much recognition from his superiors. In all, he received the Navy Cross, the Silver Star with three Oak Leaf Clusters, a Meritorious Citation, a Purple Heart, and three citations in general orders of the U.S. Army 2nd Division. The government of France awarded him the highly distinguished Chevalier de la Légion d'Honneur and, on three separate occasions, the Croix de Guerre with Palm. This list of medals ranked Holcomb among the most highly decorated Marines in the First World War.[70] Beyond his wartime accolades, Holcomb also received high praise from historians like Peter Owen in the following assessment: Holcomb's "tireless efforts at Quantico and Bourmont built his marines into a tough, well-organized, and highly spirited team. His rock-steady leadership through Belleau Wood and Soissons helped prevent the precious bond of esprit de corps and discipline from unraveling."[71]

Hindsight reveals that, although Holcomb and the Marines performed admirably on the battlefields of the First World War, their numbers were simply too small when compared with the more than one million American soldiers who decisively tipped the scales against Germany in 1918. Likewise, the Marines' employment as infantry did not provide them with a distinctive mission that would ensure the survival of the Corps. Nevertheless, the Marines achieved national recognition for their exploits. They created a new mystique for themselves as the "Old Breed."

The Marines' exploits at Belleau Wood and other battles made for great publicity and stimulated recruitment. Recruiters made a calculated appeal to young men's desires to serve a cause greater than themselves and to prove themselves on the battlefield, marking tangible passage into manhood.[72] So magnificent was the free advertising that cynical observers viewed the Corps' reputation as being little more than "an artificial concept—built, cultivated, and ceaselessly propagated by some vague but vast complex of press agentry."[73] These remarkable effects of favorable publicity on recruitment would not be forgotten by Holcomb or other Marines in subsequent decades and conflicts.[74]

Apart from the publicity bonanza, the First World War offered Marines like Holcomb opportunities to perform combat and staff duties on scales they had never previously imagined. He and three other future commandants—Clifton B. Cates, Wendell C. Neville, and Lemuel C. Shepherd Jr.—fought at Belleau Wood. Many other young Marines would don generals' stars in the Second World War, including Robert L. Denig, Roy S. Geiger, Charles F. B. Price, Holland M. Smith, Merwin H. Silverthorn, Gerald C. Thomas, and William A. Worton. They formed what amounted to a 2nd Division clique.[75] Holcomb maintained close contact with his fellow veterans after the conflict's end. Just as he was nurtured by his superiors, so he supported the careers of these younger officers.

The First World War ended with an armistice on November 11, 1918. Less than a week later, Lieutenant Colonel Holcomb and the war-weary leathernecks began their march 200 miles through Belgium and Luxembourg and across the Rhine River. They worried that the German troops might resist the Allied occupation or start fighting again, but no hostilities occurred during their several months of duty with the Army of Occupation. The miserable winter of 1919 melted into spring and then summer.

The Marines busied themselves with training, inspections, and sporting events. Morale also benefited from a generous leave policy. During the lengthy Paris Peace Conference, Assistant Secretary of the Navy Roosevelt and other dignitaries visited the Marine units in Germany. Holcomb doubtlessly renewed his friendship with the future president. Meanwhile, as was his wont, the lieutenant colonel assumed the duties of inspector of target practice and musketry training for the entire U.S. 2nd Division, in addition to fulfilling his responsibilities as the 6th Marine Regiment's assistant commander. So effective was his tutelage that the Marines and soldiers of the division dominated almost every marksmanship category in the AEF Competition and the Inter-Allied Championships held in Le Mans, France. Holcomb and the Marines finally left Germany in early July and sailed from Brest, France, on July 17, 1919. They arrived in Hoboken, New Jersey, three weeks later. After some celebratory parades, the Marines returned to Quantico and demobilized on August 13.[76]

THE CORPS UNDER LEJEUNE

During the 1920s, the former belligerent nations tried to return to a normal prewar existence. Most Americans, whether Republicans or Democrats, refused to support sizable armed forces, because they saw large militaries as precursors to involvement in future wars. The manpower and budgets of the U.S. armed services also sank back to prewar levels in a massive demobilization. For its part, the Corps shrank precipitously from 72,639 enlisted Marines in 1918 to 16,085 in 1920, while its officer cadre fell from 2,462 during the war to 962 in 1920.[77]

The prewar promotion process, which considered seniority as the primary consideration for an officer's advancement, returned with a vengeance. Any officer wishing to remain in the service faced a promotion bottleneck in which he could expect to remain at rank for fifteen years or more. Holcomb was immune to these problems. His record helped him advance in rank much quicker than other officers. On June 4, 1921, he attained the permanent rank of lieutenant colonel, and just seven and a half years later, he was promoted to colonel on December 22, 1928.

In the intervening years, Holcomb enjoyed the professional benefits of serving in key posts: chief of staff at Marine Barracks, Quantico, from 1919 to 1922; commandant of Marine Barracks, Guantanamo Bay, Cuba, from 1922 to 1924; student at the U.S. Army's Command and General Staff School in 1924 and 1925; head of Operations and Training Division at HQMC from 1925 to 1927; and commanding officer of the Marine Detachment at the American Legation in Beijing, China, from 1927 to 1930.[78] He rode the tides of reform initiated by John A. Lejeune, who in 1921 became the Marine Corps commandant.

Lejeune's eight years leading the Corps would require every bit of ability and creativity he possessed. He introduced several reforms in structures and procedures designed to improve the service's functions and capabilities. Lejeune personified managerial progressivism, with its goals of delegating authority to subordinates and coordination of their efforts, balancing vertical levels and the horizontal divisions with an organizational structure, cooperating with outside entities to determine and achieve common goals, and protecting the organization from threats and unanticipated variables.

Thomas Holcomb recalled that "Lejeune's postwar plans were clear: he would rebuild the Marine Corps with the framework of his three 'Es': economy, efficiency, and education. . . . I can add some Es that applied to Gen. Lejeune's Marine Corps. Enthusiasm and excitement and energy come to mind. And the adjectives most often applied to him by his admirers in Congress were ethical and earnest. They believed him and trust him implicitly."[79] All Lejeune's Es in the 1920s clearly left lasting impressions that would have positive effects during Holcomb's own commandancy. But his glowing praise betrayed a partisanship that tended to whitewash Lejeune. On at least one level this is easily understood, because Holcomb owed much of his success as an officer to Lejeune, who was both his mentor and role model, just as Holcomb would be the same for Alexander Vandegrift.

Lejeune streamlined HQMC by establishing the Division of Operations and Training, with sections devoted to Operations, Training, Intelligence, Material, Aviation, and Reserves. The commandant authorized the formation of a War Plans Committee in 1924. Later renamed the War Plans Section and moved to the Operations and Training Division, this committee worked to bring the Corps into line with the American strategic priorities outlined in War Plan Orange. Lejeune delegated the direction of the Operations and Training Division to the assistant to the commandant, who already supervised the Personnel, Education, and Recruiting Sections. The remaining Quartermaster, Paymaster, and Adjutant and Inspector Departments continued to be separate entities responsible for logistics, finances, and oversight.[80]

Many of the Corps' procedures and policies underwent review. For example, Lejeune believed that seniority should no longer be the primary criterion for promotion. Under his new selection process, officers could also rise on the bases of meritorious service and the possession of particular skills. As Lejeune noted in the *Marine Corps Gazette* in 1928, he hoped to create "an officer corps balanced between proven troop leaders and staff specialists."[81] Holcomb's advances in rank notwithstanding, Lejeune was not completely successful in instituting this reform. Most commissioned officers could still expect at best to retire as majors.[82]

In one of his most important legacies, Lejeune also expanded the Marine Corps Schools (MCS) in Quantico in 1920, by creating what would evolve into the Marine Corps Command and Staff College. Officers took courses designed to make them experts on advanced base defense, amphibious assault, or small wars. As time passed, the coursework focused increasingly on operational aspects of amphibious assault and base defense. Indeed, the doctrinal foundations for the Corps' eventual amphibious successes germinated in the 1920s at the MCS.

In this environment created by Lejeune, Holcomb and other officers, including Robert Dunlap, Earl Ellis, Alexander Vandegrift, Roy Geiger, and Holland Smith,

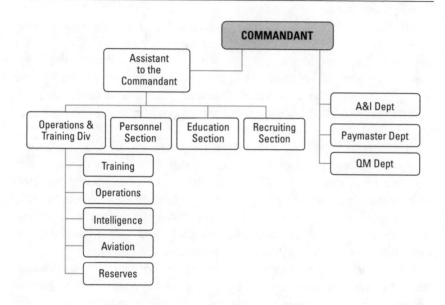

▶ Organization of Headquarters Marine Corps, 1920.

(Adapted from Condit et al., *Brief History of Headquarters Marine Corps*, 13)

developed into a close-knit cadre of professional officers with expertise in strategic planning and amphibious operations. Raising the professionalism and increasing levels of expertise were key characteristics of the progressive movement that so heavily influenced Lejeune.[83]

External to the Corps, outstanding Marine officers increasingly attended advanced schools operated by the Army and Navy and by foreign militaries. Lejeune tapped Lieutenant Colonel Holcomb to attend the Command and General Staff School at Fort Leavenworth, Kansas. His study of operational-level warfare added theoretical knowledge to his practical experiences on the bloody battlefields of France. Holcomb excelled in his coursework and graduated "with distinction" in 1925, ranking thirty-ninth in a class of 256 officers.[84] While highly intelligent and a natural learner, Holcomb worked very hard to earn outstanding grades. He spent little time with Beatrice and their young son, Franklin, because he attended classes all day and studied well into the night. For their part, Beatrice and Franklin found Leavenworth to be a "dreadful place."[85]

Aside from Commandant Lejeune's marked improvements in the Corps' organizational structures and policies, he also helped solidify its place in American naval strategy. At his behest, Major Pete Ellis authored two reports on amphibious operations in 1921. His definitive "Navy Bases: Their Location, Resources, and

Security" and "Advanced Base Operations in Micronesia" (OPLAN 712 D) predicted with remarkable accuracy the base defense and amphibious assault operations that characterized the coming war in the Pacific.[86] Because Japan was "the
only purely Pacific world power," Ellis saw it as the principal threat to the United
States. His report "Navy Bases" anticipated that Japan would take the offensive
and try to capture outlying American island bases. These would then form a strategic defense-in-depth. In Ellis' recommendations, he identified the Marine Corps
as the best force to recapture those bases.[87]

His other report, "Advanced Base Operations," stood as a companion work to
the first. It outlined a strategy for seizing and defending various Pacific islands,
including the Marianas, Marshalls, and Carolines, which the Japanese controlled
after the end of the First World War. Ellis specified targets for amphibious assaults
and anticipated certain sea battles. He suggested that Marines receive simultane-
ous training for the offensive and defensive components of their dual mission.
Both his reports cast the Corps in roles mandated by War Plan Orange.[88]

A dual mission was now the service's strategic raison d'être. Thomas Holcomb
directed the Operations and Training Division at this key point, when the Marines
achieved such significance in American war plans and began to contemplate how
best to fulfill their two roles in those plans. He thus gained intimate knowledge of
how the Marines could carve an amphibious niche for themselves in the nation's
strategies.[89]

Although the Corps' new dual mission was clearly distilled, obtaining the
resources to fulfill that mandate became Lejeune's primary goal in the final years
of his commandancy. The Corps needed new equipment and more manpower.
Reductions in budgets and personnel, however, persisted throughout the 1920s,
despite Lejeune's best efforts. Never during this decade did the Corps' strength rise
above 20,000 Marines.[90]

Following his duty in Operations and Training, Holcomb returned to China in
1927 for his last tour, this time commanding the Marine Corps detachment at the
American Legation in Beijing. Beatrice and Franklin accompanied him, and they
found those three years to be "very pleasant." The Holcomb's social life entailed
attending and hosting formal dinners, as well as attending and participating in
sporting events. The family's "life was built around polo" and "horse racing on the
weekends," recalled Franklin.[91]

Despite what seemed like an adventure to a boy of ten years of age, China in
the late 1920s could be a dangerous place because of the ongoing conflict between
regional warlords and nationalist forces led by Chiang Kai-shek, the titular leader
of the nation. Thomas Holcomb monitored this infighting as well as the rising tensions between the Chinese and the Japanese. As Franklin relates, his father made
"many trips into North China on intelligence missions but under cover of hunting

Holcomb loved to hunt, here in China c. 1928.

(Marine Corps University Archives, Holcomb Papers, Box 35)

trips."[92] With his language skills and knowledge of Chinese history and culture, Holcomb gathered much useful information to send back to Washington.

At the end of this tour in 1930, the Holcombs made a circuitous voyage home across the Indian Ocean, on to Egypt to see the pyramids, and through the Mediterranean Sea to southern France. They then took an overland trip through the French countryside, and Thomas took his son and wife to the great battlefields of the First World War. Franklin remembered, "We walked the ground at Belleau Wood and the wheat field." The landscape was still visibly scarred by the horrific fighting. Franklin learned how his father's unit inflicted severe casualties on their German adversaries at Bouresches. Thomas told his son how his Marines destroyed seven enemy regiments in that fight, "never to be reconstituted." In his oral history interview, Franklin talks of his father's extreme pride in the 2nd Battalion, 6th Marine Regiment.[93]

THE GREAT DEPRESSION

The same year of 1929 that Lejeune stepped down as commandant, the stock market crashed and sent the American economy into a downward spiral. The ensuing Great Depression had detrimental effects on American civil society, as unemployment skyrocketed from 3 percent in 1929 to more than 24 percent in 1933. The depression spurred ongoing military downsizing. The fiscal assault came at the hands of the isolationists, who believed that the United States had erred by entering the First World War and henceforth should remain insulated from military and political entanglements around the globe.

Leading isolationists included Senator Gerald P. Nye, Republican from North Dakota; Senator Henrik Shipstead, of Farm-Labor Party from Minnesota; Representative Hamilton Fish III, Republican from New York; and Representative Ralph E. Church, Republican from Illinois. Their message resonated with most Americans, who cared nothing about problems in Europe or East Asia when they could barely feed, clothe, and house themselves and their families. Congress responded to isolationism's political power by slashing personnel levels in the American military. Between 1931 and 1934, the Corps suffered a 25 percent reduction in manpower, and the Navy a 6 percent cut.[94]

The stock market crash set off a chain reaction that eventually plunged the world into economic depression in the early 1930s. Japan was no exception. Rising unemployment and the collapse of that Asian nation's export trade put pressure on its moderate government. The Japanese people reacted in 1930 by electing a new militarist government dedicated to an expansionist foreign policy. Because a thirst for natural resources heightened national ambitions, Japan invaded Manchuria in 1931. That subjugation of Manchukuo, as the Japanese called the puppet state they created there, violated principles of sovereignty espoused by the League of Nations. Japan's continental expansion likewise threatened the entrenched American policy of the Open Door in China. But with isolationism so strong, President Herbert Hoover only condemned Japanese aggression. Such inaction also meant that the United States had no clearly defined strategies to counter Japan in East Asia.[95]

During the lean years from 1929 to 1934, Commandants Wendell C. Neville and Ben H. Fuller labored to maintain the Corps' place in the nation's shrinking military establishment. They tried to portray their service as a positive good within it.[96] In an article in *Proceedings of the United States Naval Institute* in 1929, Neville proclaimed the Corps to be "versatile in the extreme" by furnishing the Navy with units capable of land and sea duty. He also outlined ways in which the Corps had increased its level of professionalism.[97] Although Thomas Holcomb's name appears nowhere in Neville's article, his experiences as a student at the Naval and Army War Colleges from 1930 to 1932 exemplified the type of professional development advocated by Neville. The Great Depression seemed to have no negative effects on Holcomb's career. Quite the contrary, it was then that he received some of his most stimulating assignments to date.

In the senior course of the Naval War College in Newport, Rhode Island, from June 1930 to June 1931 Holcomb completed the required studies of command, logistics, operations, strategy, policy, and international law. The college's curriculum increasingly focused on Japan—Orange—as the potential, if not probable, enemy of the future. Holcomb participated in war games that simulated War Plan

Orange, with all the components of fleet engagements, joint operations, and defense and interdiction of communication lines, as well as amphibious assault and base defense. Indeed, many of the strategic decisions and operational efforts in the Pacific a decade later were played out by students at the Naval War College. Holcomb's work in Newport raised his awareness of decision-making processes at every level of warfare, from tactics up through grand strategy.[98]

When Thomas was not studying, he and Beatrice maintained their usual active social calendar, attending and hosting parties. They also enjoyed sailing with Franklin in their cabin cruiser, the *Jeanette*. They made one long voyage that took them to the Hudson River,

Colonel Thomas Holcomb, early 1930s.

(Marine Corps University Archives, Holcomb Papers, Box 41)

the St. Lawrence River, and Lake Champlain before returning to Newport. The mother and father found such excursions to be relaxing respites from the everyday lives of an officer and his wife. Franklin remembered that in his early teens, boating "was a key influence" in his parents' lives; it was "their great hobby."[99]

Colonel Holcomb's next year at the Army War College, from June 1931 to June 1932, proved perhaps more valuable from a professional standpoint. He worked with other students to formulate plans for attacking enemy nations and their forces. Some scenarios were fabricated, while others were realistic. In one course project, Holcomb played the role of naval commander of an American force conducting an amphibious assault on Halifax, Nova Scotia. Among the students on his team of officers was the Army's Major George S. Patton, with whom the Holcomb family developed a close friendship and enjoyed their shared love of boating. The Nova Scotia assignment reinforced Holcomb's conviction that planning, down to the minutest details, was necessary for a successful amphibious operation.

On the more realistic side, analyzing German and Allied ground operations taking place in September 1914 in another course allowed Holcomb and his peers to cull lessons from good and bad decisions made during the First World War. He and so many other students also drew on their own experiences in the trenches and wheat fields of France.[100]

Additionally, while working independently at the Army War College, Holcomb prepared a special report titled "The Marine Corps' Mission in National Defense, and Its Organization for a Major Emergency." He asked an important question about the Corps: "What should be the most suitable organization for a major emergency?" Holcomb's answer outlined the principles of seizing and defending advanced bases, and he discussed all aspects of training and supplying Marine units. He averred that amphibious operations represented the service's future role in the nation's war plans. No longer did Holcomb see the Marine Corps merely as a constabulary force fighting small wars or "other minor operations," as he called them in his report.[101] His previous assignment at Operations and Training during the 1920s helped steel his arguments.

Few better examples of prescient thinking appear in Holcomb's report than his examination of the best force structure of a Marine division. Debates over divisional tables of organization erupted in the Army following the First World War. An American "square" infantry division in that conflict had numbered more than 20,000 men in two brigades. Both of those were then subdivided into pairs of regiments, each composed of approximately 4,000. The term "square" was derived from a division's four regiments. Field artillery, engineer, logistics, and administrative units were attached to each division. Experiences fighting the German Army revealed that such large square divisions lacked mobility and flexibility. Some Army officers argued for a smaller, more agile force structure capable of maneuvering in fast-moving, modern battles. Numbering between 13,000 and 16,000 men, this new "triangular" formation would contain three infantry regiments, directly responsible to the division commander. This effectively removed a brigade-level layer of leadership and made command and control that much easier. At the same time, a triangular division could maintain sufficient fighting power to function as an independent unit.[102]

During his year at the Army War College, Holcomb listened and undoubtedly weighed in on debates regarding the ideal divisional force. Not surprisingly, he rejected the square division because it was too cumbersome for successful amphibious operations, the Corps' mission priority for the future.[103] He stated unequivocally in his "Marine Corps' Mission" report: "The triangular formation in all organizations in the division, which increases maneuverability, is superior to the square formation."[104] A Marine division's three regiments should therefore each contain three battalions, and those would contain three companies apiece.

Although Holcomb's report drew on contemporary ideas and sources, its significance as a theoretical endeavor cannot be discounted. He anticipated the creation of the Fleet Marine Force (FMF) the following year, in 1933; the end of the Corps' constabulary duties in Central America in 1934; and the publications of doctrinal statements on amphibious assault operations in 1934 and base defense operations in 1936. He created a blueprint for the Corps' future that Marines could follow, and that he himself helped put into effect as commandant of the MCS and then as commandant of the Marine Corps.[105]

Holcomb graduated from the Army War College in 1932. His newly acquired knowledge made him the ideal choice for special duty in the Navy Department, where he served in the Navy's War Plans Division and offered advice on amphibious operations and strategic planning relating to War Plan Orange. While in the War Plans Division, Holcomb advocated what military historian Edward S. Miller sees as a "cautionary" strategy. The U.S. Navy would strike at Japanese forces across the Pacific using as stepping-stones island bases seized and held by Marine Corps units, rather than seeking a climactic single battle between the enemy fleets as a primary goal.

Japan's acquisition of the Pacific Micronesia Islands from the Germans after the First World War necessitated this more realistic and cautious strategic mindset.[106] Aside from the invaluable experience in the Navy Department, Holcomb placed himself firmly within the ascendant faction of the Corps' officers seeking a prominent place for their service in War Plan Orange. He would later be able to put the strategic ideas and concepts into practice in the Second World War. His time at the Navy Department gave him yet more and better understanding of the Navy's administration that would assist him in navigating that bureaucracy as commandant of the Marine Corps. This position also added to his already considerable visibility in Washington, because he rubbed elbows with many men who would later reach flag rank during the Second World War.[107]

While stationed in Washington, the Holcomb family continued boating on the Potomac and the Chesapeake on their newly purchased fifty-foot deckhouse cruiser, the *Slow Boat*. Thomas and Franklin hunted together in nearby Maryland. It was perhaps during these trips that the family saw the area near St. Mary's City, southern Maryland, that would become their home a few years later. The years 1932 to 1935 were not completely idyllic for the close-knit Holcombs, because Beatrice suffered from severe sinus problems and endured repeated surgeries that never offered permanent relief. She would be well for a year or two, and then what Franklin called "wicked headaches" would recur.[108]

THE ROOSEVELT ADMINISTRATION

When Franklin D. Roosevelt ascended to the presidency in the election of 1932, the Marine Corps' fortunes took an upward turn. A longtime friend now in the White House looked sympathetically on the plight of the Navy and Marine Corps. Because Roosevelt's popularity had long coattails, those two services gained two other powerful allies in Congress. First and foremost was Representative Carl Vinson, who assumed the chairmanship of the House Naval Affairs Committee in 1933.[109] In this capacity over the next four decades, "Uncle Carl" acted as legislative patron for both seaborne services. As a self-proclaimed "big Navy man," despite representing a district in rural Georgia, Vinson shepherded the 1934 and

1938 Naval Appropriation Bills into law and thus promoted the expansion of the Navy and Marine Corps.[110]

On the other side of the aisle was Representative Melvin J. Maas, a Republican from Minnesota and instrumental supporter of the Corps. As the ranking minority member on the House Naval Affairs Committee in the 1930s, he worked closely with Vinson to sponsor legislation to fortify island bases in the Pacific and continue reforms in the military's promotion system. Maas personified civil-military relations as a congressman and aviation officer in the Marine Corps Reserve. The latter two experiences gave him unique perspectives on the military. Maas took every opportunity in Congress, at the podium, and on the airwaves to alert the American people to the growing global dangers and the need for a strong military to protect American interests.[111]

Although Roosevelt, Vinson, and Maas recognized that the march of events increased the possibility of conflict in Europe and East Asia, domestic problems still demanded the lion's share of Americans' attention. Isolationists galvanized public resistance against reactionary foreign policies, and they helped pass the Neutrality Acts of 1935, 1936, and 1937. In the event of war, supplying American munitions or floating loans to belligerent nations would be prohibited, and American travel on belligerent ships would be forbidden. The isolationists also sought to obstruct Vinson, Maas, and Roosevelt as they worked to increase military preparedness.[112]

Despite the best efforts of the president and his congressional allies, the 1930s saw Marine Corps budgets slip to ever lower levels. Nevertheless, this decade also saw the flourishing of operational improvements, technological innovations, and doctrinal developments that easily surpassed those of any decade before or since in the history of the Corps. While commandant from 1934 to 1936, John H. Russell stated that the service must become "a striking force, well equipped, well armed and highly trained, working as a unit of the Fleet under the direct orders of the Commander-in-Chief."[113] The commandant's attempts to implement this mandate bore fruit in 1933, with the creation of the FMF. It was a modest unit, initially composed of two small elements based in Quantico and San Diego.[114]

With this amphibious force structure on paper, the Marine Corps needed to codify the amphibious doctrines to be employed by the FMF in future conflicts. Much work had already been under way at the MCS in the mid-1920s, when Brigadier General Robert H. Dunlap was the school's commandant. His ideas and efforts, as well as those of Ellis and others, formed the foundations for the *Tentative Manual for Landing Operations* (1934) and the *Tentative Manual for Defense of Advanced Bases* (1936) produced by the MCS faculty and students.[115] The two "tentative" surveys looked to the future, while a separate doctrinal study titled the *Small Wars Manual* (1935 and 1940) enumerated past lessons. These three manuals represented what Marine Corps Chief Historian Charles D. Melson has called the "holy trinity" of Marine Corps doctrine.[116]

Thomas Holcomb directly influenced significant portions of the doctrinal development during this decade, first as commandant of the MCS from 1935 through 1936 and subsequently as commandant of the Corps after December 1936. He was perfectly placed, as a Marine with combat service, war plans experience, and distinguished academic accomplishments, to mold the service into the modern force that would eventually be capable of amphibious operations in the Pacific War.

Prior to Holcomb's arrival, classes at the MCS were suspended from November 1933 through May 1934, so that faculty members and students could compile the *Tentative Manual for Landing Operations*. They completed their work in June. The resulting document not only outlined lessons learned from past amphibious operations but also anticipated challenges in future operations. Despite the British amphibious fiasco at Gallipoli during the First World War, for example, American Marines postulated that careful planning, adequate training, and proper equipment could overcome the tactical advantages enjoyed by an enemy defending a shoreline.

This document created a rational framework that would facilitate American amphibious assault operations in the Second World War. Nevertheless, the handbook made no detailed examination of the complexities of advanced base defense, the other half of the Corps' new dual mission. Two years later, in 1936, the *Tentative Manual for Defense of Advanced Bases* would fill that void, by providing a doctrinal foundation for advanced base defense that had been so intricately tied to the Marine Corps' strategic roles since 1898.[117]

In the meantime, Thomas Holcomb received his first star and became commandant of the MCS in February 1935. During the next twenty-two months of his tenure, the faculty and students made various revisions to the *Tentative Manual for Landing Operations* that would subsequently be folded into the U.S. Navy's *Fleet Training Publication (FTP 167)* in 1938. Holcomb also supervised the completion of manuals for base defense and small wars doctrine. If the documentation outlining the creation of the *Tentative Manual for Landing Operations* can be taken as an example of the educational process at MCS, then it was most likely the model emulated by Holcomb in the *Tentative Manual for Defense of Advanced Bases* and the *Small Wars Manual*. Because of his previous work on war plans and his military studies, Holcomb brought considerable knowledge of amphibious warfare to the writing of the Corps' new base defense manual. Just as he routinely conducted spot inspections in classrooms and on parade grounds at Quantico, it is reasonable to infer that he sat in on discussions about artillery placement or unit deployments and read drafts of the manual.[118]

Although no documents cite Holcomb by name, his tacit influence can be seen in the following lines in the *Advanced Bases* manual: "Defense of advanced bases will involve the combined employment of land, air, and sea forces. Depending on the nature of the hostile attacks against a base, one arm or service may play the major role, but in the event of a general landing attack, the land forces will constitute the basic element of the defense. In any case, the ultimate success of the defense will depend upon the closest coöperation and coördination between the naval defense forces, the shore defense forces, and the aviation forces."[119] This quote, highlighting the need to use combined air, naval, and ground forces to mount a successful defense, is markedly reminiscent of Holcomb's 1932 report at the Army War College. The base defense manual offered doctrinal visions for the Corps' future, tentative though they may have been.

Not only did Holcomb oversee the compilation of the *Advanced Bases* manual at the MCS, his tenure as the schools' commandant also overlapped the ongoing work on drafts and revisions of the initial version of *Small Wars* in 1935. Using questionnaires distributed to Marine officers serving in Nicaragua and experiences of those serving elsewhere in Latin American, the MCS's faculty and students gleaned lessons regarding a variety of roles, such as training indigenous forces, conducting counterinsurgency operations, supervising elections, providing disaster relief, and creating infrastructure. This process of systematic self-examination and self-criticism regarding practical lessons and experiences demonstrates the institutional adaptability that has been a defining trait of the modern Marine Corps.[120]

HOLCOMB CHOSEN AS COMMANDANT

While Holcomb supervised the crafting of doctrine at Quantico, Commandant John H. Russell reached the mandatory retirement age when he turned sixty-four in 1936. He had led the Marine Corps for only two years. Heralded as an effective leader and progressive administrator like Lejeune, Russell had spent his brief commandancy solidifying the Corps' place in American strategy and shepherding the growth of the FMF to fill the dual mission. Despite his best efforts, however, Russell failed to secure the necessary manpower as the Corps' strength dropped to its lowest point yet, in June 1936, at 1,208 officers and 16,040 enlisted Marines. The Corps' budget slipped to a correspondingly low level. To put this figure in perspective, New York City's Police Department contained more personnel than did the tiny Marine Corps.[121]

In the final weeks of his commandancy, Russell submitted his "Final Report of the Major General Commandant," which was also published in the November 1936 issue of the *Marine Corps Gazette*. It provides a snapshot of what the Corps looked like at that time. Russell summarized how he initiated reforms in the promotion process that preceding commandants had outlined. The "most efficient" officers, he declared, should not be forced to remain at rank for fifteen years or to advance in rank side-by-side with "mediocre officers." Russell claimed that the promotion process "is improved and Marine officers generally exhibit a keener interest in their profession and display eagerness to fit themselves for further advancement."[122] Nevertheless, he could not claim to have completely alleviated the Corps' promotion difficulties.[123]

The report discussed other severe problem areas requiring the next commandant's attention. The Corps needed more equipment and manpower to complete its new force structure and fulfill the dual mission of amphibious assault and base defense. Antiquated weaponry and dismal personnel levels would not suffice in 1937 or thereafter, let alone when hostilities erupted.[124]

The last section of Russell's report covered the timely topic of the "Selection of the Major General Commandant." He used this section as a forum to make his best argument for promotions based on merit: "Seniority should not be the controlling factor in the selection of the Commandant of the Marines. Whether the officer selected be the senior major general of the Corps or a brigadier general, efficiency should be the governing factor in his appointment."[125] Although Russell made no mention of Holcomb by name, he clearly had in mind an officer with Holcomb's credentials, temperament, intellect, and skill. Holcomb had the requisite command and staff experience for the Corps' highest position, but his leap over so many more senior officers to become the next commandant would surprise nearly everyone. Throughout 1936, no one was certain who would be named Russell's successor when he made his retirement announcement. In August of that year, one Marine officer stationed at HQMC wrote to Colonel Alexander A. Vandegrift, noting: "Rumors continue to fly around as to who the next Commandant will be but to be frank I don't think anyone knows and I can't even hazard a guess myself."[126]

Eight general officers stood above Holcomb in rank or grade. Of these, Major General Charles H. Lyman, Major General Louis McCarty Little, Major General James C. Breckinridge, and Brigadier General Hugh L. Matthews looked like the odds-on favorites to assume the commandancy.[127] Any one of them could have legitimately been so promoted. Internal politics also pointed to one of these four higher-ranking Marines. As early as May 1936, for instance, a retired John Lejeune threw his support behind Matthews in private letters to Secretary of State Cordell Hull. Lejeune touted Matthews as "able, forceful, unselfish, and a very efficient administrator."[128] He also enjoyed the advantage over the other highest-ranking Marine flag officers, in that he had seen action with the 4th Marine Brigade in the First World War.

Charles Lyman, another presumed front-runner, was certain that he would be the next commandant. He possessed a balance of command, foreign, sea, and staff duty. Yet he also had shortcomings. In addition to missing combat service in France during the First World War, Lyman's biggest weakness was his age. Already sixty-one, he could not finish the commandant's four-year term before mandatory retirement. Nevertheless, many other Marine officers also expected that Lyman would succeed Russell.

Lyman first heard the news of Holcomb's promotion from a friend's wife during dinner at the Marine Corps' Birthday Ball in early November 1936. The moment was all the more awkward because Holcomb, by this time aware of his impending promotion, was also in attendance. To Lyman's credit, he bore no grudge. In fact, Lyman became one of the new commandant's strongest supporters.[129]

Neither the official record nor personal correspondence explains precisely why Holcomb was elevated to the commandancy. Even Franklin Holcomb did not know the precise reason for which President Roosevelt chose his father over so many other flag officers. Not since 1864, when Major Jacob Zeilin was chosen as commandant over three more senior Marines, had an officer so junior in rank been named to the Corps' highest position.[130] With no concrete proof available, conclusions about this promotion must be drawn from circumstantial evidence and several relevant factors.

It was true that President Roosevelt had been a longtime friend of Holcomb's, going back to the First World War. As described earlier, Holcomb, then stationed at HQMC, had interacted on professional and social levels with Roosevelt, at that time the Assistant Secretary of the Navy. James Roosevelt, son of the president and a Marine Reserve officer, speculated that his father had consulted with Assistant Secretary of Navy Henry Latrobe Roosevelt (the president's distant cousin) regarding the selection process in late 1935 or early 1936. Henry Roosevelt apparently took the lead in consulting with Russell and choosing Holcomb.

Connections between Henry Roosevelt and the Marine Corps did exist, long before 1935. He received a commission in the Corps in 1896, saw action during the Spanish-American War, and later deployed to Latin America. He rose to the rank of colonel before leaving the service in 1920. With the Corps being so small and close-knit, Henry Roosevelt likely crossed paths with Holcomb during his twenty-four-year career and knew of Holcomb's excellent reputation. These points notwithstanding, assessing the degree to which Henry Roosevelt helped to choose Holcomb may also be obscured or limited because Henry passed away in February 1936. In any event, these inferences are not directly corroborated by other sources.[131]

There was more to the story behind Holcomb's selection. He fit a particular political profile inside the Corps that placed him in the ascendant clique. Holcomb favored the new dual mission of amphibious assault and base defense over the outmoded mission of constabulary security in small wars. Indeed, his interest in amphibious doctrine and strategic planning dated back twenty years, to his membership on Lejeune's ad hoc war plans committee in 1916. This made Holcomb an ideal candidate for Russell, who was one of the most fervent amphibious warfare advocates in the Corps.[132]

Holcomb's career track provides other concrete justifications for his promotion. In the first thirty-six exemplary years of his career, he climbed steadily through the commissioned ranks, gained valuable experience in the First World War, distinguished himself in the military's education system, demonstrated administrative skills in performing staff duties, supervised significant doctrinal developments at the MCS, and maintained cordial contacts with civilian and naval officials alike. Just as important, he enjoyed high levels of prestige as a China Hand, and as one of the Old Breed of the First World War.

Holcomb benefited from such high-ranking patrons as Lejeune and Russell, both of whom helped him into many key postings.[133] When news about Russell's successor become public, excerpts of the "Service News and Gossip" section of the *Army and Navy Journal* of November 14, 1936, offered the following observations about the unlikely Thomas Holcomb:

> The appointment of Brig. Gen. Thomas Holcomb to be Major General Commandant of the Marine Corps brings a real lover of the water to the highest post of the "soldiers of the sea." . . . Besides his brilliant war record, two other things stand him in good stead as Commandant—his wide knowledge of the Orient and his considerable reputation as a military student. . . . Considered a leader and a diplomat rather than a driver, General Holcomb will bring to his new post a knowledge of the administration of the Navy Department, having service in the Office of Naval Operations prior to taking over his present post.[134]

Holcomb was the right person in the right place at the right time to become commandant in 1935, just as he always seemed to be the right person for a given post throughout his career. Another compelling reason for this promotion was his well-known temperament. Political scientist Fred I. Greenstein terms this trait "emotional intelligence" and defines it as a leader's "ability to manage his emotions and turn them to constructive purposes, rather than being dominated by them and allowing them to diminish his leadership."[135] Holcomb rarely lost control of his emotions, and his facial expressions revealed few hints of enthusiasm or anxiety. He desired neither fame nor power beyond what was necessary to perform his duties. "He was a man of tremendous reserve," said son Franklin. "I've never seen him hesitate or worry or respond to pressure of any kind."[136]

When problems arose, Holcomb weighed evidence, considered perspectives, chose solutions, and moved on to the other matters at hand. Such outstanding American military leaders as General George C. Marshall, General Dwight D. Eisenhower, and Admiral Chester W. Nimitz shared with Holcomb this temperament, or emotional intelligence.[137]

Lastly and not of least significance was the fact that President Roosevelt had an uncanny ability for assessing leadership potential among his subordinates and placing those best suited in particular positions. Here Franklin Holcomb makes some germane observations in an interview in 1978. His father "had the confidence of the President," said the son. "Franklin Roosevelt loved to do things differently." And the elder Holcomb was "always an outstanding officer who attracted attention."[138] Roosevelt showed wisdom in choosing Marshall, Eisenhower, and Nimitz for high command, and the same went for his choice of Holcomb.

Just before noon on December 1, 1936, Thomas Holcomb raised his right hand and took the oath of office to become the seventeenth commandant of the United States Marine Corps.[139] At fifty-seven years of age, he did not project a striking presence as the battle-hardened leatherneck he was. He stood a stocky five feet, seven and a half inches tall, with thinning gray hair. Round steel-rimmed glasses obscured his most impressive feature—solemn blue eyes that seemed to look right through anyone on whom he focused his attention.[140] Many years later, retired Marine William Worton still recalled the exhortation that the outgoing John Russell gave to his successor. "Tommy, I give this to you," said Russell. "You keep the faith. This is our Corps."[141]

With Thomas Holcomb at the helm, Marines could view their future with guarded optimism, especially in operational and intellectual development. The Corps had a force structure capable of fulfilling its strategic dual mission under War Plan Orange. The Marines used their monopoly on amphibious warfare to develop unique tactics and technologies for the FMF. They established doctrinal principles for both the offensive and defensive portions of the Corps' strategic dual mission. Beyond all these, a new commandant, highly qualified for leadership and management of the service during the next years of the Great Depression and Second World War, had just assumed office. Holcomb would prove equal to the future tasks. His success was rooted in his diverse experiences during the First World War, in China, and at Quantico, which, according to Franklin Holcomb, affected his father's "whole orientation as a marine."[142]

CHAPTER 2

TAKING CHARGE
OF THE
STRUGGLING MARINE CORPS

December 1936–August 1939

Thirty-six years of command, staff, and educational duties gave Thomas Holcomb a solid foundation for beginning in December 1936 his tour as major general commandant of the Marine Corps. He went on to establish an efficient administrative system within the Corps that coupled effective horizontal and vertical communication with practical delegation of authority. Outside the Corps, he faced such challenges as isolationist sentiments, fiscal restraints, interservice rivalries, and limited resources. Overcoming these difficulties meant cultivating good relationships within the U.S. military establishment and with the Congress and American people. Added to Holcomb's worries was the uncertain military strategy in dealing with increasing international tensions that would explode in China in 1937 and in Europe in 1939.

FIRST MONTHS AS COMMANDANT

On the day after being sworn in, December 2, 1936, Holcomb sat for an interview with the *Army and Navy Journal*. The resulting front-page spread included some of the new commandant's comments: "I hope to see a Marine Corps that is more and more useful to the Navy, to which it belongs and which is the reason for its existence." The article summarized Holcomb's immediate calls for increased personnel and more money so that the Corps could achieve its greatest value to the Navy. Next the article turned to questions about leadership and management style, to which he responded, "I'm rather conservative and slow about making changes. . . . I always like to look over the machine and see how it is working before making any innovations."[1] Holcomb's self-portrayal as "conservative" and "slow" would be proven in a few isolated cases, but for the most part his words belied his innate ability to move quickly and decisively. True to form as a progressive manager, the new commandant would make thorough examinations of existing factors, procedures, or policies before deciding on "innovations."

Holcomb began his commandancy by soothing bruised egos among his fellow Marine generals. There was disappointment among certain senior subordinates who felt they should have been the next commandant. Holcomb avoided bad feelings by transferring officers to new posts where he believed they could best serve the Corps. He abolished the position of assistant to the commandant and sent its holder, Major General Charles Lyman, to San Francisco to assume command of the Department of the Pacific. Holcomb made this transfer so that Lyman, himself a contender for the commandancy, would not have to serve directly under the man who had bested him. The fact that no Marine generals resigned in protest reveals the respect Holcomb enjoyed among Marines of higher rank. His promotion was popular among lower-ranking Marines, many of whom knew him from classes at the Marine Corps Schools, tours of duty in China, or the trenches of France.[2]

Holcomb brought one of his closest confidants, Colonel Alexander A. Vandegrift, to HQMC to become his military secretary in June 1937. Together they initiated structural and functional reforms at HQMC. They sought more effective ways to integrate line officers from the FMF with staff officers in the administrative departments and divisions at HQMC. Previously, a two-tier system had existed. Miscommunications and misunderstandings had occurred because the line and staff officers competed with one another, rather than cooperating. Some Marines ensconced in staff assignments could never hope to get promoted out of these posts under a selection system that favored line officers; furthermore, their desk jobs did not provide them with practical command experience in the field. Resentment arose among those Marines who spent most of their careers at HQMC or at Marine barracks throughout the United States. Conversely, line officers could not or would not cycle into staff positions. This meant they neither lent their field expertise to the Corps' administrative machinery nor gained any understanding of logistics, finance, personnel, or other staff functions at HQMC.

Holcomb broke this logjam by rotating officers between field and administrative assignments. Line officers such as Vandegrift and Holland M. Smith understood bureaucratic functions; and, conversely, Merwin E. Silverthorn and Omar T. Pfeiffer with staff experience learned about command in the FMF. The resulting cross-fertilization would benefit the Corps during the Second World War.[3]

Beyond these administrative reforms, Holcomb attempted to translate into operational realities the doctrinal foundations for amphibious assault and base defense. He wanted to mold the FMF into a more viable combat formation, capable of either conducting successful assaults on enemy-held beaches or holding actions against enemy attacks on friendly island bases. Simulated amphibious assaults provided the best practice of the FMF. These drills occurred in the form of annual Fleet Exercises (FLEX). Beginning with FLEX 1 in early 1935 and FLEX 2 in early 1936, several U.S. Navy ships and thousands of Marines conducted practice assaults on islands in the Caribbean or off the West Coast of the United States.[4]

From January to March 1937, the Marines undertook FLEX 3 at San Clemente Island off the coast of southern California. About 2,700 Marines in the FMF and 800 soldiers from the Army's 1st Expeditionary Regiment, as well as more than twenty Navy warships, participated in these maneuvers. The Navy performed several types of long-range shore bombardment, including counter-battery and interdiction fire. The Marines tested existing equipment that they might employ in an actual amphibious assault, and they established a defensive position against possible counterattacks from land or sea.

The Marines discovered deficiencies in the Navy's landing craft. Only with great difficulty could Navy whale boats or motor launches transport troops from ships through the surf to the beach. These craft offered little protection to their occupants, moved too slowly, lacked seaworthiness in rough surf, and failed to traverse coral reefs. The Marines also found weaknesses in the Navy's warships and loading procedures. They would need to consider carefully how transport vessels might be packed so that equipment could be off-loaded more efficiently. It became abundantly clear that existing Navy warships, although absolutely necessary as weapons platforms, were not ideal for moving men or equipment.[5]

Although Holcomb did not observe FLEX 3, he kept abreast of the maneuvers via detailed reports from subordinates. He had long held a deep interest in all aspects of amphibious warfare, having watched its doctrine develop in the Corps throughout his career. He understood that finding effective landing craft represented one of his organization's greatest priorities. Holcomb paid special attention to the Marine Corps Equipment Board's tests of vehicles and weapons for amphibious operations. This body's recommendations then went to the appropriate Navy bureau for possible funding and adoption by the Corps. It took several years before the service found suitable landing craft and the money to pay for them.[6]

Many tasks beyond administrative reforms and amphibious assault preparations required Holcomb's attention. He needed to maintain good relations with Congress and the American people. During the first weeks of his commandancy, he immersed himself in the congressional appropriations process for the Corps' budget for Fiscal Year 1938. The draft budget that Holcomb inherited from Com-mandant John H. Russell included requests for manpower, uniforms, facilities, and research and development. This wound its way through the Budget Office to the Navy Department and finally to Congress, while Holcomb negotiated details in informal meetings at each stage. By the time of the formal congressional hearings, most of the significant decisions had been made. While on one level the hearings were pro forma, they did give Holcomb the opportunity to make public statements about the Marine Corps' integral roles in the nation's defense, a necessary gesture to counteract the isolationist environment of the late 1930s.[7]

Budget estimates dating from February 1936 highlighted the Corps' need for more officers and men for FY 1938. Those estimates called for acquisition of better equipment for the FMF's amphibious capabilities and expansion of education and training for active duty and reserve Marines. It fell to Holcomb to try to turn these requests into realities at the end of the annual budgetary process. Sitting before the House Naval Subcommittee of the Appropriations Committee on December 10, 1936, Holcomb argued that the FMF constituted an essential component of the U.S. Fleet. As such, it should possess a peacetime complement of 6,500 Marines, or 50 percent of the Corps' potential wartime strength of 13,000. By June 1937, however, the FMF's actual complement of 3,300 Marines represented only 25 percent of that.[8]

Holcomb's efforts yielded some positive results insofar as the Corps' authorized expenditures rose 5 percent, from $21,170,000 in 1936 to $22,276,000 in FY 1938. He did not, however, achieve his larger goals of increasing manpower, equipment, and training. Most Americans remained preoccupied with the Great Depression and committed to isolationism's foreign policies.[9]

It was not surprising that few Americans wished to increase military appropriations at a time when unemployment rates had risen from 16 percent in 1935 to almost 20 percent in 1937, during the period known as the Roosevelt Recession. Security threats in Europe and East Asia were either mistakenly assessed or ignored altogether. The isolationists' political power was nowhere more evident than in the passage of the Neutrality Act in May 1937. They tenaciously held onto the belief that a militarily strong and internationally active United States would provoke a future conflict. The latest Neutrality Act maintained most of the stringent restrictions of the previous 1935 and 1936 versions, such as bans on arms shipments and loans to belligerent nations. Consequently, large appropriations were hard to come by, not only for the Corps but also for the Army and Navy.[10]

As soon as Congress passed the 1938 budget, Holcomb and his subordinates immediately started preparing requests for FY 1939. According to Alexander Vandegrift, the commandant understood the "relationship between the members of Congress and the people they represented." Prior to any hearing, Vandegrift explained how Holcomb would lay the "groundwork very carefully by informal talks with certain Congressional figures," such as Representative Carl Vinson, Democrat from Georgia and chairman of House Naval Affairs Committee; and Senator David I. Walsh, Democrat from Massachusetts and chairman of the Senate Naval Affairs Committee.[11] Holcomb compromised when necessary, either trading appropriated funds from one project to another or bargaining for part of the appropriation in one year's budget while planning to obtain the balance in the future.

He requested only necessary funds and required subordinates to document every item in their proposed budgets. Holcomb had Vandegrift compile all those requests and justifications in a booklet, which he took with him to committee hearings and cited specific details during rounds of questioning. Vandegrift recalled that the straightforward commandant "never bluffed" when he could not adequately answer a congressional query. Instead, according to Vandegrift, Holcomb would state, "Gentlemen, I am sorry but I cannot answer that question now. I will, however, have the answer for you tomorrow morning."[12] In this way, Holcomb gained credibility with the members of Congress. He may have lost some budgetary battles during 1937 and 1938, but his "careful preparation and honest presentation" won him respect on both sides of the aisle.[13]

It was not enough, however, to cultivate good relations with members of Congress. Holcomb devoted many of the Corps' limited resources to maintaining a positive public image and enticing young men to enlist. Although ostensibly separate entities, the Public Relations Section and the Recruitment Division performed closely related tasks. Portraying the Corps in positive ways would help attract new recruits and more funding.[14] But, Vandegrift points out, Holcomb never stooped to seeking "cheap publicity." Rather, the commandant sought opportunities for "legitimate publicity," such as sending Marines to perform at community fairs or as reenactors in mock Civil War battles, even though such public engagements strained the Corps' limited manpower.[15]

In one example, in late 1937 forty-eight Marine aircraft flew from Quantico to Florida for the Annual Miami All-American Air Maneuvers. Aside from increasing flight hours, the official report on the Miami air show stated that the Marine pilots' tactical demonstrations "were very well-received" by audiences. Marine participation also proved financially feasible because the air show's organizers paid all lodging and fuel expenses.[16]

When Holcomb's busy schedule permitted, he made public appearances before supportive groups. On January 27, 1937, he spoke on "The Contribution of the Marine Corps to National Defense" at the Twelfth Women's Patriotic Conference on National Defense in Washington, D.C. In a short speech, he commented on the mounting global turmoil: "In many places mankind is ruled no longer by law but by man. Government is by decree and fiat. The rule of reason based upon precept, the collective experience of civilization, and the codified wisdom of past generations have been jettisoned for a more direct and arbitrary rule."[17] The commandant appealed to several fundamental tenets of democracy and freedom. Holcomb believed that the United States of America stood as a "bulwark" of order in a world "filled with anxiety and mistrust." He argued that the Marine Corps constituted an integral element of America's "first line of national defense."

Any future war would, he believed, begin as a naval conflict. Holcomb identified the defense and seizure of island bases as "axiomatic" and "vital" to success, especially in naval operations in distant waters. Although he underscored the Corps' defensive role, he skillfully suggested an offensive amphibious role for the Corps. Those bases could provide safe harbors and logistical support for American warships. As was standard procedure, the Marine Corps Public Relations Section then circulated his speech among newspapers for publication.[18]

Marines attempted to preserve their presence in other media, including cinema and radio. Throughout the 1920s and 1930s, such films as *Tell It to the Marines*, *The Leatherneck*, *Moran of the Marines*, *Devil Dogs of the Air*, *The Marines Are Coming*, *Flight*, and *Fix Bayonets* portrayed leathernecks fighting for their nation in jungles, trenches, and the air.[19] They were also permitted to sponsor commercial products in advertisements. Some caveats and limitations existed because, as Holcomb warned in a letter to a magazine advertising manager, the product and the ad could not "bring discredit or reproach on the Marine Corps."[20]

Radio broadcasts emerged as increasingly important publicity venues, because most American families owned radios and used them to keep current with the wider national, if not international, scene. Holcomb directed his subordinates to monitor the scripts and production of programs involving Marines. The Public Relations or Historical Section would, whenever possible, provide factual data to producers and writers so that the Corps could be presented in a favorable, yet accurate fashion.[21]

Holcomb recognized the need to assess the likes and dislikes of Americans, so he asked a fellow Marine veteran of the First World War, Samuel Meek of the J. Walter Thompson advertising agency in New York City, for a poll to determine "what most favorably impressed youngsters and their parents about the Marine Corps."[22] The service tapped the results to improve recruiting strategies that targeted not only young men as potential Marines, but also their families and hometowns as support networks. Recruiters bombarded regions with thousands of letters, newspaper clippings, and radio broadcasts, and they established personal contacts with high school principals and local businessmen.[23]

The rhetoric of Marine Corps recruitment continued to emphasize education, travel, adventure, and employment as viable options for young men otherwise destined for soup lines or railroad cars. As one student of Marine communications observed, the recruitment and publicity during the 1930s portrayed service in the Corps as fulfilling "an esteem need in the individual . . . aimed at the desires of the individual to attain status and prestige in relation to self and others."[24] Becoming a Marine offered the means to see the world and, more important, gain self-fulfillment. The young recruits needed some tangible means of legitimizing their status as adult males. Service in the Corps appealed on another level, because it provided an escape from the hardships of the Great Depression. On a practical level, the new recruits received food, clothing, shelter, and medical care that they often could not have obtained otherwise.[25]

Despite the Corps' effective publicity and popular appeal, it teetered on the edge of insignificance during the Great Depression. Brigadier General John C. Beaumont, who directed the recruiting effort, sent Holcomb a disheartening report on the "situation" in April 1937. According to Beaumont, the Corps stood 449 Marines below its authorized strength of 17,000 men. Enlistments of no more than 350 men per month accounted for this shortfall, despite the fact that Beaumont had established a monthly quota of 500 enlistments. These figures did not bode well for bringing the Corps up to its authorized strength. Beaumont anticipated another shortfall of 200 enlistments over the next three months—April through June—of FY 1937. This, he worried, would leave the Corps at a strength of a mere 16,350 men.[26]

The Marine Corps Recruiting Bureau's "Statement of Recruiting" for the first and second quarters of FY 1937 confirmed Beaumont's assessment of manpower deficits. More Marines had resigned, retired, or received discharges than had joined.[27] Beaumont believed that two factors caused those discouraging figures. First and foremost, a "skeletonized recruiting force" at an insufficient number of recruiting stations handicapped efforts to fill the ranks. From 1930 to 1937, the total number of "main stations" and "substations" dwindled dramatically, from 103 to only 17; and recruitment personnel dipped from 26 officers and 303 enlisted to 15 officers and 70 enlisted Marines.[28]

Second, Beaumont lamented that too many men were being discharged either before or during basic training due to "physical or other defects," such as flat feet, myopia, or other deformity or disease.[29] From among the 6,350 applicants for enlistment or reenlistment during the first three months of FY 1937, only 1,041— or 15 percent of that total—were accepted into the Corps with regular enlistments.[30] Once in basic training, 25 recruits received discharges because they were "physically unfit or otherwise not qualified for service."[31] Poor living standards during the Great Depression affected American health levels. Millions of young men suffered from beriberi and pellagra, caused by malnutrition. This, in turn, reduced the pool of physically qualified applicants for the Marine Corps.[32]

To solve the problem of insufficient recruitment resources, Beaumont recommended that additional stations with full staff complements be established in more cities across the country. Existing recruiting stations should have their staffs bolstered with additional personnel. But Beaumont could not offer any real solution to the high percentage of enlistment denials and recruit discharges. Lowering medical standards would lower the quality of men; this was no option, even if it would have solved the recruitment shortfalls. Instead, recruiters needed to find more productive ways to attract to the Corps more men of the highest caliber and the best medical condition.[33]

The "Daily Reports on Recruiting" indicated that Beaumont's glum predictions for the final three months of FY 1937 had been too pessimistic. By the end of June, the Corps' actual strength stood at 16,900 men and 17,132 by December. Increased enlistments made up for the shortfall. This represented good news, especially in light of the fact that medical and mental standards for enlistment had become stricter over time. Although no documentary evidence exists to show Holcomb's specific authorization, clearly he heeded Beaumont's recommendations, because newly established recruiting stations sprang up in Denver, Colorado; and Cincinnati, Ohio. This helped boost the number of enlistments in 1937.[34]

While Holcomb felt great pressures in his official duties and public engagements, his early years as commandant also included great emotional stresses in his household. Health problems frequently plagued his beloved Beatrice throughout their marriage. She sometimes seemed to be sick more that she was well. "She developed a series of illnesses which largely involved terrible headaches," lamented Franklin of his mother's condition and treatment. "They kept operating on her. Awful operations—frontal sinus operations. Antium operations. Just wicked. Because no one does those anymore. This is surgery gone mad. All this sort of developed in her medical history, which she kept having repeats for the rest of her life."[35]

Beatrice's illnesses weighed heavily on Thomas, and then their son also was stricken. In 1936, the teenage Franklin inexplicably fell ill with a severely debilitating fever that nearly killed him and left him bedridden, his muscles atrophied. His recovery required intensive physical therapy to strengthen his body. As it turned out, exercise in water provided the best means of muscular development, but the commandant's official residence in Washington had no pool.

To solve this problem, James Roosevelt, the president's son and a Marine Reserve officer, suggested to his father that Thomas bring Franklin to the White House. Franklin Roosevelt agreed. So during 1937 and 1938, Franklin Holcomb frequently visited the White House, swam in the pool, and rebuilt his muscles so that he could again walk and be fully active.[36] Aside from the extraordinary assistance rendered to Franklin, this incident indicates the high regard and close friendship that President Roosevelt must have felt for Commandant Holcomb.

RISING INTERNATIONAL TENSIONS AND SHIFTING AMERICAN STRATEGIES

During the first two years of Holcomb's commandancy, tensions in East Asia grew more acute. The Japanese consolidated their hold on Manchuria and extended their influence in Inner Mongolia north of the Great Wall. China, meanwhile, remained a nation divided between nationalist forces led by Chiang Kai-shek and communist forces led by Mao Zedong. The year 1937 represented a watershed in Sino-Japanese relations. A fragile truce collapsed in July at the Marco Polo Bridge, just south of the city of Beijing. Japanese and Chinese troops clashed over control of the bridge, and Chiang would not relinquish territory or sovereignty to the Japanese intruders. During the following months, the Japanese occupied Beijing and began pushing south toward Nanjing, Chiang's seat of government. This raised the risk of violent confrontations with Marine units stationed in Shanghai and several other Chinese cities.[37]

Within six months after the escalation of hostilities, in December 1937 the Japanese captured Nanjing. They committed unspeakable atrocities against civilian Chinese men, women, and children living in the city. From Nanjing, the

Japanese Army advanced farther inland up the Yangtze River, but failed to achieve a war-winning battlefield victory. The Chinese forces, now led by the uneasily and temporarily allied Chiang and Mao, stymied the Japanese invaders at almost every turn. They attempted to wear down their common enemy by attrition. Chiang withdrew his forces to Hankow and eventually to Chongqing, deep in China's interior. Mao, meanwhile, made use of his communist troops' high mobility and guerrilla tactics to attack the lengthening Japanese supply lines and widely dispersed troop formations.[38]

Thomas Holcomb took an active interest in Chinese affairs because, having spent so many years there and studied the language and culture, the commandant knew the nation and its people well. He received frequent reports from Marine officers stationed in China. The 4th Marine Regiment, stationed in Shanghai since 1927, held ringside seats for observing the Japanese in action. Colonels Charles F. B. Price and Joseph C. Fegan, successive commanders of the 4th Marines in the late 1930s, watched the Japanese troops execute amphibious landings, drill their troops, and fight the Chinese. They did not make a favorable impression on the two Marine officers, who believed the Japanese lacked the discipline and training to defeat the supposedly inferior Chinese; certainly they were no match for the Americans.[39]

Price also witnessed firsthand the Japanese mistreatment of China's civilian populace. One of his letters to Holcomb included photographs of their wanton destruction. It described their "raw but real" brutality as "undisciplined" and "barbaric" conduct by "a nation of drunkards." Lacing his observations with the cultural slur "Jap," Price clearly held America's future foes in low esteem, not only for ethical reasons but also because of the racial prejudice that was all too common at the time.[40]

Other Marines, such as Captain Evans F. Carlson, offered perceptive observations on the military situation in China. Carlson had come to Shanghai earlier in the 1930s to study Chinese language and culture. Once hostilities began, he left the comparative safety of that city's International Settlement and traveled to the battlefront to witness engagements between the Chinese and Japanese. As Carlson interacted increasingly with Mao and his communist followers, their methods left lasting impressions on him. The mobility, guerrilla tactics, and high morale of Mao's forces served as a model for Carlson when he later helped organize the 2nd Marine Raider Battalion in 1942.

Carlson's reports on China found their way back to Holcomb and HQMC in 1937 and 1938. Carlson also sent copies independently to President Roosevelt. His communications were not limited to American military or government officials. Because Mao, his followers, and their ideas influenced Carlson so much, the Marine officer sought out media outlets to tell the American people what he had learned. But his sympathetic portrayal of the communist cause elicited condemnation from many Marines, including Holcomb. The commandant silenced Carlson by ordering him to refrain from public pronouncements, and Carlson reacted by resigning in late 1938. He would later rejoin the Corps in 1941, when war with Japan was imminent and his knowledge of guerrilla tactics was *en vogue*.[41]

Meanwhile, when not monitoring the Japanese operations, the 4th Marines in Shanghai guarded the International Settlement and attempted to care for Chinese and European refugees who entered this area to escape the war-torn countryside. The Marines bided their time, waiting for the next crisis to erupt and drilling constantly to maintain high levels of military discipline and rifle marksmanship. Despite efforts to avoid confrontations, fistfights sometimes broke out between Japanese soldiers and American Marines in the streets of Shanghai. More serious incidents occurred that could have spiraled out of control into full-fledged conflict between the two sides. On December 12, 1937, for example, Japanese aircraft attacked and sank three Standard Oil tanker ships and the *Panay*, a U.S. Navy gunboat, on the Yangtze River. Three Americans were killed and thirty more wounded.

In response to the growing strains, Holcomb sent reinforcements to Shanghai in late 1937, bringing the 4th Marines' total strength to 2,536 officers and men. This figure amounted to 15 percent of the Corps' manpower. Once the *Panay* crisis subsided and the Sino-Japanese battlefront moved farther from Shanghai in 1938, the perceived threat to the Marines lessened, and Holcomb ordered that 1,000 leathernecks return to the United States to join the expanding FMF.[42]

In recognition of the Japanese threat, the U.S. government began sending financial and material aid to Chiang Kai-shek's Nationalist forces. The U.S. Department of State proclaimed a "moral embargo" against Japan, prohibiting that nation from buying American-manufactured military aircraft. This action inaugurated what diplomatic historian Akira Iriye calls a "cold war" between the two nations.[43] By the end of 1937, the Japanese declared a "New Order in East Asia" that rejected American influences in the region. Japan conquered larger tracts of China and took control of greater portions of that nation's economy. Yet the Japanese never decisively defeated the Chinese forces led by Mao and Chiang. The Sino-Japanese War cost the Japanese hundreds of thousands and the Chinese millions of casualties.[44]

Just as American anxieties about Japanese aggression rose, so too the future in Europe looked increasingly grim.[45] Nazi Germany annexed Austria in March 1938. Neither France nor Britain stopped Germany's territorial expansion. Instead they appeased the Germans at Munich in September 1938, allowing them to annex the Sudetenland and occupy the rest of Czechoslovakia early in 1939. The British and French acquiescence emboldened the German chancellor, Adolf Hitler, to move further toward dominating Europe. President Roosevelt harbored few delusions about Hitler. As early as 1935, he privately called the German dictator "a madman" and believed some of his advisers to be "even madder than he."[46]

The fluid situations in East Asia and Europe made the Orange War Plan obsolete in 1938. The new set of strategic realities dictated that the United States prepare for new scenarios, including conflicts with multiple allies and enemies.[47] Nevertheless, another version of the outmoded Orange Plan appeared in March. Some American strategists, especially in the Navy, remained locked in the mind-set that the United States would face Japan as a single adversary. Other assumptions in the 1938 version remained consistent with earlier Orange Plans. Several pages outlined the defense of the Alaska-Hawaii-Panama frontier. In the likely event of a Japanese first strike, American forces in the Philippines and on other islands in the Western Pacific would fight holding actions until the U.S. Fleet launched a counterattack and swept across the Pacific to relieve them.[48]

The Japanese, for their part, also planned for a possible war with the United States. They expected to capture American-held advanced island bases in the Western Pacific. The Japanese would then employ these and their own bases in the Marshalls, Marianas, and other Micronesian islands in offensive and defensive operations. Construction of airfields began on these islands as early as 1934, and limited military building programs took shape in 1940. The Japanese war plan to defeat the U.S. Fleet mirrored the American Orange Plan in many ways. It seems that each side was playing into the other's hands. Japan's strategy remained intact until 1940, when such priorities as natural resources and such realities as American naval expansion caused the Japanese to shift toward an offensive mind-set.

The outmoded American strategic plans did not affect the Marine Corps, which continued to play an important tactical and operational role in the last Orange Plan and in all subsequent war plans. The Marines kept their focus squarely on defending friendly island bases and attacking enemy-held island bases.[49]

Two important measures in 1938 and thereafter bore witness to the Navy's acceptance of the Marine Corps as its amphibious assault and base defense force. First, the Navy adopted the *Fleet Training Publication 167* (*FTP 167*) as its blueprint for amphibious operations. Marine planners had a hand in this new document, because Commandant Holcomb ordered that they modify the Corps' own *Tentative Manual for Landing Operations* of 1934 according to the Navy's needs. The resulting revision added broad strategic and naval perspectives to the Corps' tactical and operational focuses. Consistent with Navy regulations for operations consisting of both Marine and naval units, the new document also established unity of command by charging the senior naval commander with authority for all air, sea, and inland elements in amphibious operations.[50]

Second, Secretary of the Navy Claude Swanson appointed Admiral Arthur J. Hepburn to head a board of naval officers to assess the strategic roles of bases on Guam, Wake, Midway, and other islands in light of Japanese threats in the Pacific Ocean. In its report of December 1, 1938, this so-called Hepburn Board prioritized the advanced bases in the Pacific relative to strategic needs dictated by a given base's possible benefits for aircraft, submarines, and surface warships in a war with Japan. The board argued that Guam should become a "Major Advanced Fleet

Base" for operations in support of American forces on the Philippines and in the Western Pacific. Wake and Midway Islands should become patrol plane bases for reconnaissance or supply bases for defensive and offensive actions.

The Hepburn Board members believed that construction should be started as quickly as possible on those islands. In addition to their recommendations regarding the bases proper, their final report instructed the Marine Corps to organize "defense detachments" to hold those island bases against possible Japanese attacks in the opening stages of a conflict. Although it would take almost another year for these specialized Marine units to be organized, the board's call for "defense detachments" represented the realization of many ideas outlined in the Marine Corps Schools' *Tentative Manual for Defense of Advanced Bases* of 1936.[51]

While the Hepburn Board met in late 1938, the Corps undertook its own studies of the Western Pacific islands. Commandant Holcomb had long recognized that those islands in the Central and Western Pacific represented key strategic points for naval operations. In September, he received a report on the potential island defenses from the Division of Operations and Training at HQMC. Like other reports of this kind, it summarized the "problem involved," stated the "facts presented," outlined the "discussion," and suggested "recommendations" to solve the problem. The report listed the strategic and tactical requirements for the bases. The recommended estimates for manpower, weapons, and equipment figures fulfilled only barest necessities, although they certainly stretched the tiny FMF as it then existed.[52]

These reports helped to consolidate the Corps' place in naval strategy, not only in the offensive but also in the defensive phases. To expand their operational capabilities, Marines continued to train in exercises conducted with the Navy. FLEX 4 was conducted near Puerto Rico in the Caribbean from January through March 1938. Several thousand sailors, soldiers, and national guardsmen joined the 2,100 Marines in landing and defensive maneuvers. One exercise consisted of a daylight amphibious assault with live naval gunfire, and another entailed a nighttime attack from the sea. The air component emerged as an essential ingredient for any successful attack, because no assault or defense could be successful without first establishing tactical air superiority.

The Marines tested various experimental landing craft and tank lighters designed to carry tanks from ships to the beaches.[53] Holcomb received one report from an officer who called the exercises "a most complete success."[54] The Marines were optimistic that they could successfully land on enemy-held beaches. They also recognized their superiority over the Army and National Guard forces in seaborne operations. Yet FLEX 4 still suffered from two recurring deficiencies. First, the small number of Marine participants made any attack by a division-strength unit impossible to simulate. Second, finding effective amphibious landing craft for men and equipment continued to be the most critical problem. Without specially designed landing craft, amphibious assaults could be doomed to failure.[55]

Two American entrepreneurs provided the technological fixes for problems of ship-to-shore transportation during amphibious operations. Andrew Jackson Higgins built boats for trappers, loggers, and oil drillers in Louisiana. His "Eureka" boats easily navigated the backwaters and swamps near New Orleans. This environment required shallow-draft vessels that could maneuver on water of unknown depth, filled with hidden obstacles. The Eureka boat's spoonbill-shaped bow enabled it to run up on beaches or over sandbars. A tunnel stern protected the propeller, so that a Eureka could also extract itself from both beaches and sandbars. The boat was relatively fast, easy to maneuver, and carried a large payload. Just as important, the design had the attributes of simplicity and ruggedness, an undoubted benefit in combat situations.

Since 1934 Higgins had tried with little success to interest the Navy and the Marine Corps in his design; but meager budgets restricted even the smallest research and development projects in the sea services. After the fleet exercises convinced Marines of the need for effective landing craft, however, Higgins finally gained an audience with the Navy's Bureau of Construction and Repair in 1937, and with the Marine Corps Equipment Board shortly thereafter. The Navy awarded him a small contract to build a single prototype.[56]

The Marines discovered another landing craft design in Donald Roebling's "Alligator" amphibian tractor. He intended it as a rescue vessel to save downed aviators or hurricane victims in the Florida Everglades. The Alligator had no propeller; instead, it had dozens of metal paddlewheel treads not unlike those of a tank. The treads provided propulsion in the water and gave the vehicle the ability to climb onto land, over sandbars, and across coral reefs. The Alligator thus proved to be a truly "amphibian" vehicle.[57]

A 1937 *Life* article on Roebling's Alligator piqued interest among sailors and Marines. That article found its way from the Navy to the Corps and finally to Commandant Holcomb, who sent it to the Marine Corps Equipment Board for further investigation. The Alligator impressed everyone who saw it perform. After Holcomb personally observed its trials in 1938, he instantly grasped its great potential. "My God, this is the future of the Marine Corps. We can use something like this," exclaimed the commandant. "No more will we have to crawl on our bellies and swim ashore."[58]

Holcomb recommended that a prototype be built for the FLEX 5 maneuvers slated for early 1939. But the Bureau of Construction and Repair denied his request due to budgetary constraints. Undaunted by the setback, Roebling redoubled efforts to adapt his Alligator to the military's needs. Over the next two years, he spent his own money and a few thousand dollars scrounged by the Marines to rework his design and develop a viable amphibious assault vehicle for the Corps' needs.[59]

ATTRACTING RECRUITS AND
SWAYING CONGRESS

Back in Washington, Commandant Holcomb reacted to the rising international tensions by accelerating his preparations for a possible large-scale emergency mobilization. He and his HQMC staff started in early 1938 to lay the foundations for the intensification of positive publicity efforts and exploitation of good relations with Congress. Holcomb knew only too well how thinly spread his recruiters were, and how important it was to have skilled Marines assigned to such duties. According to a statistical report filed in January 1938, the recruitment and mobilization efforts during the First World War represented the only viable model for large-scale mobilization. Some 73,219 men enlisted in the Corps during 1917 and 1918; they joined the 11,000 Marines already in uniform. Four regional recruiting divisions produced those new enlistees in the following ratios: the Eastern Division with its headquarters in Philadelphia recruited 19,786 men (27 percent of the Corps' total enlistees); the Central Division, headquartered in Chicago, recruited 30,322 men (41 percent of the enlistees); the Southern Division, headquartered in New Orleans, recruited 10,017 men (14 percent); and the Western Division with its headquarters in San Francisco recruited 13,094 men (18 percent). Although this January 1938 report contained much statistical data, it offered no analysis of what the figures might mean for the future.[60]

Colonel Julian C. Smith, director of Personnel for Recruiting, completed a follow-up report titled the "Emergency Recruiting Plan" six months later, in June 1938. It provided sound recommendations for Holcomb regarding the Corps' future mobilization. Smith's introductory paragraph called "for the organization and training in time of peace, of an Emergency Recruiting Service for the Marine Corps, capable of operating immediately in case of war or national emergency, for the procurement of personnel to complete and maintain the Marine Corps Forces during such an emergency."[61] In the event of a national crisis, Smith anticipated Congress would authorize a manpower increase from the current 1938 level of 17,000 Marines to the statutory strength of 27,400. The number of recruiters would need to be expanded dramatically from its current strength of 83. This tiny cadre could barely maintain the peacetime quota of 500 enlistees each month, let alone add the 60 percent anticipated in Smith's report.[62]

Should an emergency arise, Smith called for a sharp increase to a total of 1,047 recruiters. The additional personnel would be divided among the four recruitment divisions according to the recruitment percentages mentioned earlier in his report. The Central Recruitment Division received the largest expected recruitment quota, and was thus allocated 322 recruiters.[63] The 1,047 Marine recruiters amounted to a twelve-fold expansion over the peacetime recruitment billets. If the growth of monthly enlistment quotas also increased twelve times, then 500 enlistees per month would grow to 6,000 for the duration of a national emergency.[64] Such a massive projected increase would prove to be more accurate in 1942 than anyone could have imagined four years earlier in 1938.

According to Smith's report, retired or reserve Marines could fill most of the new recruiter positions. He anticipated that the Corps would quickly reach its 27,400-man statutory strength and continue to pull more men into the Marine Corps Reserve. The reservists could then be called to active duty during a conflict or when Congress authorized an increase in the Corps' strength. Smith allowed for the possible passage of a new Selective Service Act. The "draft" would swell the manpower pool for the United States as a whole, but Smith cautioned that it would also make it difficult for the Corps to maintain the high quality of individual Marines, if the organization were forced to take draftees.

The image of the Corps as an elite, volunteer service would be challenged. Smith worried that the service might not attract the right types of draftees, those who were "qualified mentally, morally, and physically" to become Marines. To stave off these possibilities, he suggested that recruiters receive training about how to evaluate applicants. Finally, he supported the immediate creation of "a complete wartime publicity program for use by the Marine Corps Recruiting Service and for general publicity purposes."[65] Again, Smith's prognostications would be remarkably accurate for mobilization in the Second World War.

Even in peacetime, a direct connection between recruitment and publicity can be seen in official documents. Throughout 1938, the Corps continued its drive for a positive image, not only for the sake of recruitment, but also for popular support. Marines distributed literature containing conspicuous imagery that had changed little since the 1920s. One such advertisement touted the meaningful benefits of service in the Corps: "A Marine Corps Background—Thousands have found it a valuable asset—U.S. Marines: Travel, Education, and Career." The rhetoric of the recruitment and publicity continued to adjust to the nation's isolationist tendencies.[66]

In addition to distributing printed materials, the Corps invested as much manpower, time, and money as possible in public appearances. Commandant Holcomb chose carefully from many opportunities. He needed to maximize the effects of Marine participation at fairs, patriotic meetings, or other public functions with minimal cost incurred by the Corps. Two cases illustrate how his prioritization worked.

The first occurred in the spring of 1938, when organizers of the South Dakota State Fair invited the Marines to set up an exhibit. They hoped to raise awareness among their state's citizens about military affairs in general, and the Corps in particular. In an internal memorandum to the commanding officer of the Central Recruiting Division, Holcomb agreed that this opportunity might be "desirable" for "stimulating recruiting." He further acknowledged that an exhibit could "create good-will" or "stimulate recruitment in that area to some extent."[67] But he then stated that the idea had three drawbacks: far too little informational material on the

Corps was available in the areas of Chicago or Kansas City, the distance in transporting this material to South Dakota was too great, and the total cost exceeded the possible return in enlistments. Armed with these negative assessments, Holcomb regretfully declined the offer from the fair's organizers.[68]

The other case revealed that recruitment and publicity resources could be better spent in major public appearances where hundreds of thousands of people could learn more about the Corps. As early as December 1937, Marines planned to set up an exhibit at the Golden Gate International Exposition scheduled for January 1939. Holcomb actively participated in every stage of the process. He submitted an estimated budget of $4,400, together with a blueprint for the exhibit's design, to Chief of Naval Operations (CNO) William D. Leahy in March 1938. During the summer months, Holcomb delegated authority to make specific arrangements to the Marines in the Western Recruiting Division's headquarters in San Francisco. In September, that division requested $4,350 for 50,000 booklets and 350,000 folders to be distributed to people attending the exposition.[69] In October 1938, Holcomb directed that the eight enlisted Marines accompanying this exhibit should receive "careful indoctrination" in the recruitment process.[70] The publicity bonanza made the potential benefits well worth the costs. The populous western states, no doubt, added more value in recruitment to this public appearance.

Holcomb's efforts to maintain a positive public image and recruit qualified Marines helped generate support among the American people and in Congress. In December 1937, he appeared before the House Subcommittee on Naval Appropriations and presented the Marine Corps budget for FY 1939. Holcomb repeated his opening statement before the same body from eleven months earlier: the FMF continued to be "an essential component of the Fleet and must be maintained in a state of immediate readiness." The force remained barely half the size that Holcomb considered necessary to be in an "efficient state of readiness." He added some new material to his concluding remarks in 1937. It was his "considered judgment that the nation's defense requires that the Marine Corps have an orderly expansion of not less than 1,000 men per year until the year 1945, at which time, unless foreign relations dictate otherwise, it should be stabilized."[71] Holcomb won a victory because Congress agreed to this time line for expansion to 27,400 Marines, but he suffered a disappointing defeat because he did not receive the funds necessary to follow the time line.

For Holcomb, legislative victory often meant fending off reductions in the Corps' appropriations, if not obtaining increased appropriations. Throughout 1938, he lobbied Congress for passage of specific bills that benefited the Corps. He worked with Marine Corps advocates such as Senator Walsh, Representative Vinson, and Representative Maas. They provided critical support in introducing bills, negotiating budgetary line items, hearing testimony in committee, making modifications in standing committee, offering arguments in floor debates, hammering out compromises in conference committee, and ensuring final passage in both houses.[72]

A ranking minority member of Vinson's Naval Affairs Committee and a Marine Reserve officer, Maas in particular showed himself to be a great friend to Holcomb and the Corps. According to Franklin Holcomb, the feelings were mutual; his "father was very fond" of Maas, who often visited the commandant's residence.[73] Maas energetically preached to the American public the need for military preparedness. He cleverly cast that need as an essential component in maintaining America's defensive posture. Thus he defused some isolationist arguments. Maas wanted a U.S. Fleet large enough to protect both the Atlantic and Pacific Oceans. As a pilot in the Marine Corps Reserve, he likewise recognized that the Navy needed more aircraft, aircraft carriers, and advanced air bases.[74] He repeated statements in print or on radio broadcasts such as: "No strong nation with a powerful Navy has ever been attacked. . . . An adequate Navy will be far less expensive than a War which may result from having a weak Navy,"[75] and "There will be no surer way of guaranteeing our early participation in a war, and a disastrous war for us, than by weakening our naval defense."[76]

Events in early 1938 raised expectations for Holcomb and the Marines. Carl Vinson introduced H.R. 9997, otherwise known as the Personnel Bill or the Naval Selection Bill. Among other provisions, this bill, if signed into law, would rationalize the promotion process for Marine officers. Despite reform efforts by Lejeune, Russell, and Holcomb, they continued to spend decades in rank. The bill offered the means to retire officers who had spent an overly long time in rank. A colonel, for example, would have only two chances at promotion. If twice judged unsuitable for advancement to brigadier general, then he would be retired after a set amount of time in rank. The Naval Selection Bill thus expedited the promotion process by allowing, in theory, those "best fitted" Marine officers to move up the ranks in a less-stagnant environment.[77]

The Naval Selection Bill included several more provisions that could potentially benefit the Corps. It called for raising the service's statutory strength to one-fifth of the U.S. Navy, expanding the percentage of privates first class from 25 to 50 percent of the Corps' manpower, and increasing the ratio of officers to enlisted men from 4.75 to 6 percent. At 10:00 AM on April 7, 1938, Holcomb appeared alone before the House Naval Affairs Committee. In a cordial exchange, Chairman Vinson allowed him a lengthy opening statement in which he outlined the Corps' most pressing needs.[78]

Holcomb argued that the Corps' current allotment of 1,181 officers would be insufficient for the many tasks assigned to his service once it expanded to the approved strength of 27,400 Marines by 1945. To attain the 6 percent figure, the commandant asked the Naval Affairs Committee for more than 400 additional officers. Some 300 of these new officers would be assigned to the FMF, which currently possessed only 280 officer billets in the spring of 1938. Under no such circumstances could the FMF be considered in a state of readiness. Holcomb pointed to other units, such as aviation, that also suffered from officer shortages. To rectify these problems, he requested an annual increase of 60 new officer billets per year until the cadre reached 1,640 officers. This total represented the ideal 6 percent ratio of officers to enlisted Marines for the 1945 expansion.[79]

During hearings on the bill, Vinson asked Holcomb about the additional cost per year for those 60 additional officers. The commandant candidly replied, "This will increase the cost—I have here approximately, but I believe it is essentially correct—the estimated increased cost for the first year would be $64,344."[80] Vinson, Maas, and other supportive committee members then pitched Holcomb several easy questions that allowed him to make logical points about the procurement of new Marine second lieutenants.[81] Only Ralph E. Church, an isolationist Republican from Illinois, made serious inquiries during the hearings. "What possible need can there be for the 14 general officers over and above the heads of staff departments and additional numbers in grade?" he asked. The Corps currently had 11 active-duty general officers, three billets less than Holcomb was requesting.

The commandant cited a need for five more generals in his answer by stating, "I can tell you what we would do with five, if we had them. I am not asking for them; I know that we cannot get them." He then listed the five flag officers' billets: assistant to the commandant, director of aviation, director of the Marine Corps Reserve, director of the Division of Operations and Training, and assistant commander of the FMF. Holcomb also pointed to the need for an additional general's slot: "There is another force called the base defense force which might very well indeed have a brigadier general," referring to a sixth billet upon which he then elaborated. One of the high-ranking billets—assistant to the commandant—did not even exist in 1938; and colonels occupied the other five. For Holcomb, officers in those six positions should wear generals' stars, as opposed to colonels' eagles, because the attendant responsibilities were so weighty. He repeated in closing: "There are five jobs for brigadier generals. We are not going to get them, so most of them will have to be done by colonels."[82]

Later that same day, April 7, the usually dispassionate Holcomb gleefully wrote to a close friend and fellow First World War veteran, Lieutenant Colonel Gilder D. Jackson, about the good news regarding manpower. The hearings on the Naval Selection Bill "went off beautifully," according to the commandant. "The attitude of the Committee was most friendly and helpful. We are definitely on the bill, including the provision to use the same percentage of officers to enlisted men that the Navy has, or hereafter may have; that is [4.75 percent], and this bill proposes to make it 6%. The bill also carries the provision that the authorized strength of the Marine Corps shall always be 1/5th the authorized strength of the Navy."[83]

By late April 1938, the Naval Selection Bill had passed both houses of Congress. The next step involved the ever-delicate joint conference committee meetings in which senators and representatives struck compromises on their houses' respective versions.[84] Holcomb vacillated between optimism and pessimism about this process. Such was his existence during the first lean years of commandancy. A week before the conference committee's vote on the Naval Selection Bill, he complained that the measure for which he had worked so hard was "apparently dead," as he wrote to Major General Louis McCarty Little, commanding general of the Fleet Marine Force, San Diego.[85]

Then, to Holcomb's great surprise, on June 14, 1938, the conference committee agreed to a slightly modified Naval Selection Bill, and it passed the House and the Senate the next day. His desired goal of a 6 percent ratio of officers to enlisted Marines had not survived the deliberations, but the bill's final version included a still-considerable increase to 5.5 percent. The Naval Selection Bill also raised the number of privates first class from 25 to 40 percent of the Corps' total manpower. The bill's biggest disappointment was its failure to appropriate the necessary funds to make these positive developments into realities.[86] Nevertheless, the upbeat commandant proclaimed about June 14, "This has been a big day."[87]

Thomas Holcomb proved his skills as an advocate as he laid the groundwork for the Corps' future growth.[88] Major General Charles Lyman paid him the supreme compliment for his effective dealings with Congress: "There was no Commandant between [George] Barnett and Holcomb who could have achieved the result of the past six months—I take off my hat."[89] Barnett's commandancy had dated from 1914 to 1920. In the interim, such giants as John A. Lejeune and John H. Russell had served. Lyman knew these men personally and could speak with authority about their skills relative to Holcomb's. His praise was all the more impressive because Holcomb had jumped over him on the seniority list to become commandant almost two years earlier. Lyman's comments revealed that he had become one of Holcomb's most avid supporters, which was a tribute to the latter's leadership and character.

However, despite Holcomb's best efforts and hard-won partial legislative victories, the first eight months of 1939 looked like they would be no easier for the Marine Corps or other branches of U.S. military. Because the United States faced potential foes on two continents, President Roosevelt wished to allow himself more flexibility in dealing with those threats. Yet his hands remained tied both legally and politically. In no way could he get tough with Hitler other than uttering a few public denouncements of the latter and his policies.[90] Isolationism embodied in the Neutrality Acts still held sway over American military and foreign policies. Pushing through Congress any legislation, let alone military appropriations increases, would prove nearly impossible in early 1939. Roosevelt nevertheless began to promote military preparedness, barely hidden behind the facade of national defense. The political climate prevented him from requesting a military capable of offensive strikes across oceans, but he did argue for increasing capabilities to help defend the nation and the Western Hemisphere.[91]

It was in these international and domestic environments that Thomas Holcomb labored to prepare the Corps for a future conflict. He once again appeared in January before the Naval Subcommittee on Appropriations of the House of Representatives. He pleaded for more money for FY 1940. His prepared statement cataloged the many "fundamental tasks" that the Corps was expected to perform. These included maintaining the FMF in a state of readiness for service in fleet operations, protecting American lives and interests around the globe, providing security on board ships and at naval installations, and preserving Marines' education and morale. The commandant's statement asserted that the past year's addition of 1,000 Marines had proved inadequate to fulfill all the Corps' responsibilities.[92]

Nowhere were manpower needs more desperate in 1939 than in the FMF, which included amphibious assault and base defense units. According to Holcomb in his testimony: "Immediate readiness implies that, upon the occurrence of a national emergency, the FMF will be able to perform its allotted tasks without any delay due to lack of adequate equipment, strength, or training."[93] Reality fell far short of this desired level. He told the subcommittee members that the FMF stood at only one quarter of its manpower complement for training, nowhere near the level necessary for wartime deployment. Other elements, such as the Marine Corps Reserve and Marine Corps Aviation, stood at similarly low levels of readiness.[94] Holcomb concluded his statement by expressing his "firm conviction that the present strength of the Marine Corps is inadequate for the efficient performance of its fundamental tasks."[95] He hoped that Congress would authorize an additional increase of 4,000 men, bringing the Corps from 18,000 to 22,000 Marines. This hope, like so many of Holcomb's previous requests, went largely unfulfilled.[96]

Holcomb and other Marines expected better results later in the spring of 1939, when the Naval Appropriations Bill worked its way through the Naval Affairs Committees in the House and Senate. The committee chairmen, Representative Vinson and Senator Walsh, respectively, helped pass some beneficial legislation in May 1939. The Corps received authorization for 1,000 more Marines, a fraction of what Holcomb had requested. The service's strength rose from 18,000 to 19,000 Marines in FY 1940. Still, this legislation also included $750,000 for replacing some buildings recently destroyed by fire at Marine Barracks in Quantico. These increases represented small gains, but they were gains just the same.[97]

In addition to cultivating congressional support, public relations and increasing efforts to attract recruits occupied much of Holcomb's time. He saw to it that the Corps was marketed to the American people as an elite service in which opportunities for employment, adventure, travel, and education abounded. Marine publicity stressed that this service afforded a recruit the rite of passage into manhood.[98]

Recruitment numbers held steady during the first half of 1939. The Corps' authorized strength stood at 18,000 Marines, and actual strength at 17,546. By the close of the fiscal year in June, recruitment numbers rose, and the Corps' actual manpower strength exceeded that authorized strength by 14 marines. The total strength of the Reserve also increased from 14,467 by almost 500 men to 14,964 during the same six-month period. These gains were all the more impressive because the four regional recruiting divisions only received between $150 and $200 each month to produce literature and purchase advertising. Holcomb did his best to sustain the Corps' public visibility throughout 1939, given his budgetary limitations. He delivered commencement speeches at colleges and participated in patriotic meetings. At these venues, he raised public awareness of threats abroad, advocated increased military preparedness, and marketed the Corps as an ideal first-line defensive force. But he refused to get bogged down in political partisanship. Holcomb resisted the temptation to pass judgment on the Roosevelt administration's decisions regarding foreign affairs and military appropriations, even when he may have had strong personal opinions about those or when the Corps' interests could have been advanced by some politically motivated statement.[99]

The sometimes hectic travel schedule that Holcomb's job demanded became even more burdensome in early 1939, when Beatrice, his wife of twenty-three years, underwent a serious surgery and a lengthy convalescence. Holcomb sometimes skipped public engagements to care for her. Her poor health was common knowledge among high-ranking officers in the Corps, a service in which everyone knew everyone else.[100] Major General Louis McCarty Little, the commanding officer of the FMF, expressed his concern in a note to the commandant: "Only today I have heard of Beatrice's operation. It seems as if she has had almost too much pain in her life and I feel almost resentment that such things can come to one who is always so gay and cheerful."[101]

Although Beatrice still suffered with intermittent illnesses, Franklin had recovered sufficiently from his sickness of 1936 to start attending Georgetown University in Washington. The healthy son lived with his parents at the commandant's residence while he prepared for a career in the foreign service. Franklin sometimes drove his father's car to campus, dropping him off at HQMC in the Navy Department en route. Franklin Holcomb graduated from Georgetown in May 1940, took a commission in the Marine Corps, and entered the Office of Naval Intelligence. He would eventually post to North Africa and participate behind the scenes in Operation Torch in late 1942. Still later, Franklin went on to coordinate counter-intelligence operations in France as part of the Office of Strategic Services.[102]

CARVING A STRATEGIC NICHE FOR
THE MARINE CORPS

Military threats in Europe and East Asia compelled American strategists to revise the irrelevant War Plan Orange by taking into account the possibility of multiple allies, adversaries, and theaters of operation. No clearly defined connection between President Roosevelt's foreign policies and American military strategy existed in 1939. This situation left American planners with too many questions about who the country's adversaries would be, where conflict would most likely be, what the aims of any war might be, and how it might start. Answers to these strategic questions were not forthcoming because of a cautious Roosevelt administration and an isolationist Congress and American public.[103]

Even though there was a dearth of diplomatic or grand strategic direction, the Joint Planning Committee convened to create new plans that offered more flexibility than did the Orange War Plan. Three Army and three Navy officers from their services' respective War Plans Divisions served on this committee. They formulated the more realistic Rainbow Plans during early 1939. Its five versions addressed the variety of unsavory wartime circumstances that might confront the United States.

In Rainbow Plan 1, the United States alone would defend the Western Hemisphere north of the Caribbean and Panama Canal Zone. American forces would not become involved with conflicts in Europe or East Asia. Rainbow Plan 2 anticipated that the United States, Britain, and France would concentrate their offensive striking powers in the Pacific against Japan. Europe, meanwhile, would remain a secondary strategic priority. Rainbow 3 echoed the basic tenets of the Orange War Plan, in which the United States would fight a unilateral and offensive war against the Japanese in the Western Pacific. Neither Britain nor France would be involved in any meaningful way. Rainbow Plan 4, building on Rainbow 1, expected that the United States would alone defend the Western Hemisphere and the Atlantic Ocean against enemy incursions from Europe and East Asia. Lastly, Rainbow 5 envisioned American, British, and French offensive operations to defeat Germany as decisively and quickly as possible. The United States, meanwhile, would stand alone on the strategic defensive in the Pacific against Japan until Germany's defeat. Once this occurred, all available American and Allied forces would be redirected against Japan.[104]

The U.S. Army reoriented its strategic emphasis toward defense of the Western Hemisphere and war in Europe, and away from Japan and the Pacific Ocean. East Asia held little or no interest among Army planners, except for those who agreed with General Douglas MacArthur's delusional belief in the defensive viability of the Philippines in a war with Japan. This left Navy and Marine Corps strategists to plan for possible conflicts of varying levels of concentration in both the Atlantic and Pacific Oceans. Unlike the Army, the seaborne services needed to prepare for all five Rainbow Plans.[105]

All the new plans projected the Corps to play an active operational role in the Pacific. The recently released Hepburn Board Report reiterated the Corps' contributions as an integral part of Navy strategy and policy. It mattered little whether the American forces undertook a strategic defense or offense. If the U.S. Fleet initiated an offensive campaign against the Japanese, then Marine Corps units would capture enemy bases in support of the fleet, and they would defend them against possible counterattack. Conversely, if the fleet stood on the defensive, then the Marines would also be called upon to hold American bases and recapture any bases taken by the Japanese.[106]

Marine planners at HQMC, according to Brigadier General Alexander A. Vandegrift, could therefore devote themselves to "*real* military planning" in several areas.[107] Gaining practice in amphibious operations proved to be one of the Corps' most critical needs. Early in 1939, Marines began participating in more maneuvers in the Caribbean. Meantime, back in Washington, Holcomb worked to acquire the best landing craft available. He further streamlined HQMC by instituting a series of reforms to improve efficiency levels.

Marines joined soldiers and sailors in FLEX 5, another round of joint amphibious maneuvers from January to March 1939. More than 2,000 Marines led by Brigadier General Richard P. Williams continued to perfect their amphibious assault techniques. Williams' leathernecks made several landings on Vieques and Puerto Rico. They fought simulated battles against Army and National Guard units holding those islands. Marine units sometimes switched roles and defended islands against attacks. Although Holcomb did not attend the maneuvers, he frequently received reports from Marines on the scene. These gave him details about the personalities, equipment, performance, and conditions of the maneuvers. The reports indicated an intimacy between Holcomb and his subordinates as well as providing proof of Holcomb's familiarity with amphibious operations.[108]

The FLEX 5 maneuvers constituted the most realistic and successful simulations to date. In his role as the Marines' chief umpire for the exercise, Brigadier General William P. Upshur wrote to Holcomb how the Navy and Marine personnel interacted "smoothly and efficiently."[109] The helpfulness and professionalism of the sailors and naval officers in the Atlantic Squadron impressed the Marines. The Navy made marked improvement in its efforts to supply Marines ashore with rations and ammunition in a timely manner. For the first time in an amphibious exercise, the naval commander assigned warships to the specific duty of gunfire support. The ensuing shore bombardment drills gave his gunners valuable practice in pre-assault and counter-battery fire. The rough surf gave the Marines exposure to the realities of seasickness as they approached the beaches in small craft. Once ashore, they contended with mosquitoes and other tropical insects. The bites became so bothersome that the simulated battles were suspended to allow relief from this unexpected onslaught. Such experience added not only new solutions but also new wrinkles to amphibious operations.[110]

Perhaps most important, FLEX 5 included various tests of Andrew Jackson Higgins' Eureka boats. Upshur again reported to Holcomb: "The Higgins boats seem to be the best of all the types we have tried out—on standardization runs they have made 15 knots only, instead of 18, but none of the others can make more— the Jacobs-Peterson, Luters (I think), and Seabright skiffs are not as good—the Higgins will turn on a dime, like a tank, and they can come off a beach under their own power and get out, even without a stern line."[111] Marines at HQMC like-wise favored Higgins' design as the best choice. Colonel Holland M. Smith, then directing the Marine Corps' Operations and Training Division, showed particularly strong support for the Eureka boats.

These otherwise ideal landing craft did have one weakness: Marines disembark-ing by climbing over the boats' sides or their bows completely exposed themselves to enemy fire. Nevertheless, Marines such as Smith and other officers making decisions on the Equipment Board preferred the Eureka boats because they were sturdy and practical.[112]

While the Eureka boat underwent testing at FLEX 5, Donald Roebling pushed his Alligator boat as another possible amphibious assault vehicle. As described earlier, the tracks of this light but rugged little vehicle could be used as paddles in the water, or as tank treads on land. In May 1938, Holcomb had requested a prototype of the versatile amphibian tractor for assessment, and the Marine Corps Equipment Board had concurred with his request. But gaining internal approval was not the problem. The real obstacle came in convincing the Navy's Bureau of Construction to fund the project. Budgetary restrictions continued to hobble both seaborne services. Roebling could not acquire seed money to adapt his boat to military needs, so he again absorbed costs and built a modified model in hopes of gaining a future opportunity to demonstrate its value. His chance would occur soon enough.[113]

As Marines honed their amphibious assault techniques in the Caribbean, the other half of the Corps' dual mission also began to take shape on paper in early 1939. The Navy Department, consistent with the Hepburn Board's recent report, recommended a $287 million building program on several islands in the Pacific. Guam stood out as the most important, because naval planners considered it "the cornerstone of America's Pacific Defenses."[114] Representatives Carl Vinson and Melvin Maas tried to get the full amount through Congress, but their colleagues would only authorize $53 million for building projects at several American bases. Guam, perhaps the most essential base needing construction, received none of this money because of political sentiment rather than strategic necessity. To isolation-ists, building a base on Guam seemed too much like an offensive or preemptive action vis-à-vis the Japanese, who held the nearby island of Saipan also in the Marianas Islands.[115]

Not all the news in 1939 stood as setbacks or partial victories for the Corps, however. The Hepburn Board had also called for the service to establish "defense detachments" capable of defending American island outposts against an amphibious, sea, or air assault.[116] CNO William Leahy concurred with the board's recommendations and announced plans to send modified Marine antiaircraft units to Wake, Midway, Unalaska, and Guantanamo to function as base defense forces. Holcomb eagerly embraced this new means of fulfilling the service's time-honored mandate. The antiaircraft detachments represented the reincarnation of the Marine Corps Advanced Base Force of the early twentieth century. Holcomb based his support on several intertwined factors. He recognized that the U.S. Fleet and the FMF needed base defense units to augment their operational capabilities. Whereas the anticipated war with Japan might be offensive or defensive at the strategic level, either way there would be a need for Marines to hold islands.[117]

During the spring and early summer of 1939, Holcomb and his planners labored to turn the defense detachments into an operational reality. In July he unveiled the "defense battalion." Approximately 1,000 leathernecks filled this unit's ranks. Holcomb designated the FMF's 1st and 2nd Battalions of the 15th Marine Regiment as the "nuclei" of the first two defense battalions.[118] As outlined on paper in mid-1939, these 1,000-man units boasted an impressive array of weapons: twelve Navy 5-inch artillery pieces for coastal defense, twelve 3-inch antiaircraft artillery guns for air defense, forty-eight .50-caliber machine guns for either antiaircraft or beach defense, and forty-eight .30-caliber machine guns for beach defense.

All units would receive additional equipment, including high-intensity searchlights and radar systems. Some defense battalions might even receive larger 7-inch artillery pieces. The proportion of Marines per heavy weapon far exceeded that of the Corps' typical light infantry unit. Indeed, the firepower rivaled that of an infantry regiment or even one of the Navy's light cruisers. Depending upon the location and size of a given island base, Marine infantry units could augment the defense battalions. Once ensconced on a fortified island base, defense battalions provided the American naval or aviation forces with self-sufficient bases of operations. These units became part of the FMF and complemented the amphibious assault units therein.[119] As one retired Marine officer declared: "Whereas the function of the marine divisions is to attack and seize, the Defense Battalions are designed to dig in and hold on."[120] They helped satisfy the Navy's strategic needs in all the Rainbow Plans.

These battalions carried significant strategic merits, but Holcomb and other Marines also recognized the huge political and publicity benefits of touting the Corps as part of the nation's first line of defense. Heretofore known for projecting force across the globe, the service could now be portrayed as a protective force. The commandant followed CNO Leahy's sage admonition: "Whatever you do, make yourselves look defensive." Leahy liked the idea of making an advanced island base into "an unsinkable aircraft carrier" that could support fleet operations. He went so far as to remark in 1939: "Defense Battalions. Now that's what I call real war planning." [121]

The units fit the mold perfectly. Holcomb believed he could generate support for the defense battalions and thus increase his requests for manpower and equipment from the Navy and from Congress. The strategic need and clever publicity spin neutralized the faction of isolationists who refused to support America's military preparedness. This did not mean that Holcomb neglected the offensive role of amphibious operations. He merely balanced the offensive and defensive mandates as he sculpted the Corps' image. [122]

Meanwhile, the evolving strategic priorities and operational requirements exposed shortcomings in the Marine Corps' administrative structure. The marines at HQMC could hardly react or adapt fast enough to those changes. In undertaking reforms to boost efficiency, Holcomb demonstrated a clear understanding of effective management. He drew on his years of service under Commandants John A. Lejeune and John H. Russell, both of whom employed progressive management principles to create a more efficient line and staff system. The administrative system of the U.S. Army in the First World War also influenced Holcomb's efforts to make the Corps more rational in its structure and more practical in its functions.

Two elements constituted the policy-making process at HQMC. Both needed to be reformed. First, the Operations and Training Division was responsible for formulating policies. This task might entail determining the best possible distribution of new Marines to various duty stations or debating the efficacy of replacing the 1903 Springfield rifle with the newer M1 Garand rifle. The Operations and Training Division would then suggest the best courses of action to meet the challenges. In April 1939, Holcomb reorganized HQMC by combining the responsibilities of the Operations and Training Division with those of several other offices into the Division of Plans and Policies. He modeled this new entity on the War Department General Staff. This division, nicknamed "Pots and Pans," included five sections: M-1, Personnel; M-2, Intelligence; M-3, Training and Operations; M-4, Supply; and M-5, War Plans. The Plans and Policies Division did not, however, have the authority to supervise or execute policy. [123]

The second element at HQMC, the administrative staffs, entered the process after Holcomb had made policies. Implementation was the responsibility of the Quartermaster Department, the Paymaster Department, the Department of the Adjutant and Inspector, the Division of Reserves, the Division of Personnel, the Division of Recruiting, and the Division of Aviation. Officers at the rank of colonel or higher led these divisions and departments. More often than not in practice, the entire frustrating process resembled robbing Peter to pay Paul, because the

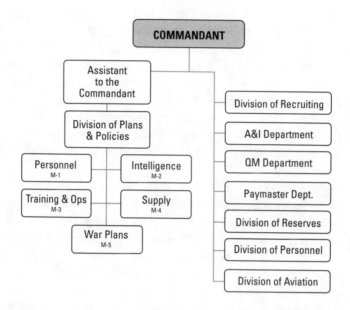

▶ Commandant Thomas Holcomb's organizational reforms of Headquarters Marine Corps, 1939.

(Adapted from Condit et al., *Brief History of Headquarters Marine Corps*, 13)

Corps so rarely had enough resources to solve problems completely. The assistant to the commandant coordinated the implementation process, both the planning and administrative elements, assuming the de facto role of the commandant's chief of staff. Alexander Vandegrift served in this position from 1937, when it was known as the military secretary to the commandant, until 1940, when the title assistant to the commandant was restored.[124]

Holcomb's reforms represented positive steps, but they did not yet translate into operational readiness in 1939. Despite the fact that global war appeared more likely, the United States' armed forces remained ill-prepared for any conflict. During the summer of that year, the Navy conducted a detailed self-assessment to answer the question, "Are We Ready?" A negative answer came on August 31 in the final report submitted by Admiral Harold R. Stark, the recently promoted CNO.[125] Both seaborne services, according to Stark, suffered from numerous and "critical deficiencies" in manpower and equipment. Of relevance to the Corps was "the lack of Pacific bases west of Hawaii." Stark further cited the inability of the Navy or the Marine Corps to seize any island bases or protect them once they had been captured. The CNO saw it as his major task to alleviate these deficiencies, and he spent his next thirty months in office trying to do so.[126]

Rarely did the Marine Corps enjoy a better advocate than Admiral Stark. When Holcomb heard in early 1939, that Stark was going to be promoted to CNO, he wrote him an ebullient letter stating that "the President could not possibly have made a better choice and I assure you that the appointment has received enthusiastic approval not only from us marines but so far as I can see by everybody around the [Navy] Department. I wish you every success and look forward with keen pleasure to seeing you back here in the Department and in the key position."[127] For his part, Stark also held Holcomb in the highest esteem and recognized the commandant's good judgment.

The two officers had much in common. Both unexpectedly received their promotions over the heads of many senior officers. Each made the most of line, staff, and educational opportunities during their earlier military careers. Lastly, like Stark, Holcomb proved himself during his rise as a competent, modest, diligent, judicious, and tactful officer. The two service chiefs forged a close professional relationship built on mutual respect and common purpose. Stark's unfailing support for the Corps could be felt immediately upon his promotion on August 1, 1939. He began deploying Marines to island bases in the Pacific, and then the new CNO directed Holcomb to organize four full defense battalions.[128]

As international events spiraled out of control, many positive advances had occurred for the Marine Corps and for Commandant Thomas Holcomb. The service's well-oiled publicity and recruitment machines attracted the goodwill of the American people and drew young men to recruiting centers. Under Holcomb's able direction, the Corps' amphibious capabilities drew closer to the expectations outlined by amphibious doctrine. Marines also secured an important place in American strategy. The Corps remained too small by half to fulfill its many responsibilities, but momentous events in September 1939 in Europe would do much more to spur the mobilization of the Corps and the American military as a whole. Holcomb's new challenge became getting enough well-trained Marines with enough weapons, ammunition, and equipment in the field as fast as possible.

CHAPTER 3

HOLCOMB AND
THE MARINE CORPS TRANSITION
FROM PEACE TOWARD WAR

1939–1941

T he period between September 1939 and December 1941 marked several shifts in the Corps' situation. After war erupted in Europe, a conspicuous change in American military policy occurred, in a slow transformation from that of an isolationist nation at peace to one capable of waging global war. As American strategic plans evolved in reaction to new threats and contingencies, Commandant Thomas Holcomb gradually enlarged the Corps. He divided his time between external relations—with Congress, President Roosevelt's administration, the other armed services, and the American people—and internal activities such as strategic planning, technological innovation, manpower mobilization, and equipment procurement. But despite his best efforts, the Corps always remained at least six months behind its manpower and material requirements for preparedness.

EFFECTS OF WAR IN EUROPE

When German forces rolled over the Polish border on September 1, 1939, the governments of France and Britain promptly declared war on Germany. The Soviets then shocked the world again by invading Poland later that month. President Roosevelt understood all too well the gravity of these events. The situation in Europe required him to be more proactive. On September 8, he declared a "limited national emergency" with two goals in mind: "safeguarding" American neutrality and "strengthening our national defense within the limits of peacetime authorizations."[1]

Over the next few weeks, Roosevelt worked diligently to alter the Neutrality Act of 1937 to give himself more latitude in dealing with threats to the nation's security. He rejected the existing law's strict policy of impartial neutrality and wanted fewer restrictions on aid to Britain and France. Reaching across ideological and partisan lines, Roosevelt cobbled together a coalition of northeastern Republicans, northern Democrats, and southern Democrats in Congress that supported military preparedness. In so doing, he successfully drove a wedge between moderate isolationists in Congress who favored a strong national defense, such as Senator David I. Walsh, Democrat from Massachusetts; and more extreme isolationists such as Representative Hamilton Fish III, Republican from New York, who opposed any military buildup under any circumstances. Roosevelt won passage of a less stringent revision of the Neutrality Act and signed it into law on November 4, 1939.[2]

War in Europe likewise affected American strategic planning, because it made Rainbow War Plan 2 the newly applicable response. In the event of entrance into conflict, the United States would focus its resources against Japan in the Pacific, with some help from Britain and France. Europe could remain a secondary priority because these two allies would concentrate their presumably ample resources on defeating Germany.[3]

The Marine Corps reaped numerous benefits from these shifts in the domestic and international landscapes in September 1939. Roosevelt unilaterally authorized an increase in personnel from 18,500 to 25,000 Marines. This alone represented a 35 percent expansion and gave Commandant Thomas Holcomb and the Corps a much-needed boost in manpower that would help fill all the new roles and duties necessary to fulfill the Corps' mission. To further swell ranks, for example, plans were made to call Marine reservists to active duty. At HQMC, Holcomb also redoubled the Corps' publicity and recruitment efforts to meet these personnel needs. Marines in the Public Relations Section courted the American media in hopes that the Corps might receive some free, yet legitimate, publicity. They used news periodicals, motion pictures, and other information outlets such as the Golden Gate International Exposition and New York World's Fair. The Marines meticulously screened public exposure. If a magazine article or advertisement gave short shrift to the Corps, the HQMC staff or occasionally Holcomb himself contacted the organization to ask for a more balanced portrayal of Marines as essential to the nation's defense. That organization would often release additional materials that contained positive images or texts.[4]

The Public Relations Section and Recruitment Division worked hand in hand to sculpt a reassuring image for the American people. Variations of the slogans "Defend America" and "National Defense" figured more prominently in Marine publicity and recruitment messages and supplanted previous emphases on opportunities for adventure, education, and employment. Likewise, the concept was for Marines to exhibit the best qualities of American citizens, to be seen as the guarantors of American safety. Overall, the Corps' publicity and recruitment energies were primarily directed at Caucasian Americans, the only group who could achieve manhood and perform the many duties required of Marines. Sadly, the Corps snubbed some minority groups, dismissing them as unworthy of service in the country's elite military organization.[5]

Because of an authorized increase to 25,000 Marines, annual enlistment quotas climbed above 2,500 recruits. Additional Marines received orders to become recruiting officers. Whereas only eighty acted as recruiters nationwide in July 1939, at least sixty-nine Marines served with each of the four regional recruiting divisions by the year's end. The Eastern Recruiting Division alone boasted 101 Marine recruiters.[6] By November, Marine reservists began filling the gaps when they were appointed "emergency recruiting officers."[7] These Marines augmented the existing recruitment stations or worked at newly opened substations. Multiple recruitment substations sprang up in cities such as Philadelphia, Los Angeles, and Chicago. New substations appeared in Nashville, Tennessee, Pittsburgh, Pennsylvania, and Des Moines, Iowa. Remote cities like Ogden, Utah, and Pocatello, Idaho, were also targeted because the Corps received "very favorable" and "very good" ratings on public relations surveys in those cities.[8]

Thanks to the added resources, the year's enlistments and reenlistments of 6,885 Marines far exceeded reductions of 2,298 men due to "ineptitude," "desertions," "retirements," "deaths," or "medical status." The Corps experienced a net gain of 4,587 Marines to reach a total strength of 22,600 by January 1, 1940, only four months into the limited national emergency declared by President Roosevelt the previous September.[9] These numbers represented good news for Holcomb, who received copies of every "Daily Report on Recruiting." The Corps continued its steady expansion throughout 1940. It actually surpassed the authorized strength of 25,000 by July 1, 1940, when it contained 26,369 officers and men.[10]

Holcomb did what he could on his own to reduce restrictions on enlistment. He sought greater latitude in waiving applicants' medical and health qualifications. Various maladies or physical conditions restricted many otherwise capable men from joining the Corps. Among existing medical standards was the requirement that men be rejected because of "marked malocclusion"—a severe overbite or underbite. Medical officers in the Recruiting Divisions believed this process had "become too meticulous" in applying an inexact standard. They did not know how much of a bite problem constituted "marked malocclusion." Medical personnel pointed out that this standard needed to be revised.

Such changes could benefit the Corps in two ways: it would mean a more judicious dental evaluation process as well as a larger applicant pool.[11] Holcomb believed this to be a valid policy change, so he appealed to the Navy's Chief of the Bureau of Medicine and Surgery, who approved the reform. An applicant could now move through the recruitment process if his dental condition, malocclusion or otherwise, did not affect his "general health."[12] Moreover, assuming an applicant had at least twenty teeth and required no immediate dental treatment, any such problems could be waived as an enlistment requirement. Secretary of the Navy Charles Edison approved this change in light of the "the present emergency."[13]

Holcomb was mindful, all the while, that his reforms in age and health standards for enlistment had to be reconciled with his more absolute need for physically, mentally, and morally eligible recruits. Shortcomings in these areas accounted for the rejection of 48,609 out of 61,723 applicants in 1940. The remaining 13,144 successfully enlisted—winners in a winnowing process that eliminated 79 percent of the competition. Basic training, the first stage in the recruit's life after enlistment, remained rigorous enough to filter out any men unfit to wear the globe, eagle, and anchor.[14]

Even with the growth in manpower, the Corps remained perpetually too small to fulfill its ever-expanding military responsibilities. As ever, qualified officers and senior enlisted Marines were in particularly short supply. Looking back to Holcomb's statement before the House Naval Subcommittee on Appropriations on November 3, 1939, the commandant echoed his past statements regarding the Corps' critical missions and activities. He then deluged committee members with details about how thinly spread his Marines were at home and abroad. This time his pleas sounded more urgent. The FMF could not be deployed as an independent fighting unit. This amphibious assault force languished at one-quarter of its required wartime strength.

Of the 22,000 Marines in the Corps that November, some 1,500 served in China alone, and more than 3,200 Marines saw duty on military vessels. Newly commissioned aircraft carrier or battleship required three Marine officers and seventy-eight enlisted men. Holcomb concluded his testimony by asking that the Corps be enlarged still further, so its duties could be performed efficiently.

Bad news overseas did indeed help speed the mobilization process more than any of Holcomb's efforts. Following months of inaction, on May 10, 1940, German forces attacked France through the Ardennes region in Belgium. A few weeks thereafter, the Germans pushed the British forces off the continent. The French and Germans signed an armistice on June 22, giving Adolf Hitler effective control over Western Europe.[15]

This outcome prompted defense-minded legislators to join President Roosevelt in firming up foundations for American mobilization. Senator Edward R. Burke, Democrat from Nebraska, and New York Republican Representative James W. Wadsworth cosponsored the Selective Service Act of September 1940, which created a pool of sixteen million American men who could be drafted into military service. The debate, passage, and signing of this bill revealed the degree to which strict isolationists were weakened as the European situation became more alarming. But effects on the military's manpower shortages were not immediate because of a dearth of training facilities.[16]

Dismal defeats in Europe also encouraged Congress to authorize expansion of the Corps' budgets as well as those of all the nation's armed forces. In May 1940, naval and Marine officers testified in more hearings before the House Naval Subcommittee on Appropriations. It was here that Representative James A. Scrugham, its chairman, proved most supportive. He asked questions designed to allow Marine officers the opportunity to make their best cases for more money.

During late May, for example, Scrugham's subcommittee considered supplemental appropriations for the Corps totaling $22 million for FY 1941. This figure amounted to a 67 percent increase over the $33 million in expenditures for the previous fiscal year. Among the largest allocations were $2,344,000 for salaries for 4,500 additional enlisted Marines, $1,933,000 for more uniforms, $3,591,000 for more equipment, $4,500,000 for new building projects, and $4,600,000 to arm two additional defense battalions.[17]

No sooner had the Corps' supplemental needs for FY 1941 been approved than the Marines began preparing their budgetary requests for FY 1942. Once estimates were completed, the Marines sent them to the Navy Department's Bureau of the Budget and subsequently to congressional committees. Marine officers giving testimony before committees could often expect friendly queries and supportive comments.[18] When Holcomb appeared before the House Naval Affairs Committee in September 1940, Congressmen Vinson and Maas worked together in a seemingly choreographed exchange with the commandant. Vinson led off with several dozen questions about the most pressing needs in manpower, equipment, and funding that plagued the Corps. His queries were short, such as, "What about your officer personnel?" or "What is the officer strength?" Vinson then allowed Holcomb to craft his answers in ways that made the Corps' further expansion to 50,000 Marines seem reasonable. The commandant explained how he had initiated an emergency-recruitment program modeled on the Emergency Recruiting Plan of early 1938. He just needed funding to put it into full effect.[19]

After Vinson finished, he yielded control of the hearing to Maas, the committee's ranking minority member. He asked even more pointedly leading questions: "General, your permanent future needs for the Marine Corps will never be less than 50,000 from now on under the authorizations that Congress has passed for the expansion of the fleet?" Holcomb replied, "I am sure that it will always be 50,000 at least, if not more." Maas' follow-up question to that was more sales pitch than query. "I can foresee," he speculated, "where it will probably be considerably in excess of that permanently from now on. We all feel the permanent Navy is going to be between 400,000 and 500,000 when we have our two-ocean navy, which . . . would bring the Marine Corps up to between 80,000 and 100,000. So we need have no hesitancy about authorizing 50,000 now." Holcomb could answer truthfully, "I think that is very conservative."[20]

These types of exchanges occurred frequently when the commandant appeared before the Naval Affairs Committee, led as it was by two of the Corps' most zealous advocates. Later in 1940, for example, Holcomb wrote to Mass: "I know that I can count on your continued assistance to get for the Corps those things so badly needed, and it is a great source of satisfaction to me to know that the Senior Minority Member of the Committee is not only a strong personal friend of mine but is such a true friend of the Corps."[21]

Only the most adamant isolationists in Congress refused to support supplemental budget authorizations for the nation's defense in late 1940, following the fall of France and the near demise of Great Britain. Their faction represented a fast-shrinking majority. Several public opinion polls in 1939 and 1940 indicated that more and more Americans came to see Germany, Italy, and Japan as threats to the American way of life. Their sentiment nonetheless did not translate into overwhelming calls for American entrance into the conflict. It did, however, give greater credence to the middle option of making the American military better prepared to defend the nation. Congress passed tax increases in June 1940 totaling almost $1 billion in revenue, to pay for larger defense expenditures. Meanwhile in East Asia, the United States attempted to discourage Japanese imperialism with commercial sanctions and to assist the Chinese with millions of dollars in loans.[22]

The election in November 1940 bore witness to the groundswell that now supported a strong national defense. Franklin Roosevelt won reelection to an unprecedented third term. His popularity, having waned by 1938, rebounded. He had helped his cause by promising to keep the nation out of war. International tensions ensured his victory, because Americans wanted to keep their trusted leader in the White House. Roosevelt had shepherded the United States through the Great Depression years, and now he would guide the nation through new crises. Roosevelt's reelection thus augured well for the Corps' future. He ordered that the already activated Marine Corps Reserve be integrated into regular Marine units in December 1940. This action alone added 15,000 men to the Corps' manpower pool and raised its ceiling to 38,000 by year's end.[23]

HOLCOMB'S REAPPOINTMENT
AS COMMANDANT

The close of 1940 marked another milestone in Thomas Holcomb's distinguished career. His first term as major general commandant of the Marine Corps was to expire on November 30, and he could have stepped down after having done yeoman's work for the previous four years. Holcomb was conflicted about what to do. On the one hand, he preferred retirement and the life of a gentleman farmer over more military service. On the other, however, duty demanded that he set aside his personal desire to serve his nation. In a note in November 1940 shortly before President Roosevelt made his decision, Holcomb confided to CNO Stark: "Naturally, since you and the Secretary [of the Navy] have recommended me, I hope very much to be reappointed. Should I not be, possibly the President will ask my advice; in which case I am asking you to do your best to have [Holland M.] Smith appointed."[24] In addition to Holcomb's first choice of Smith, several other flag officers such as Philip Torrey, Alexander Vandegrift, or Charles Barrett could have become the next commandant. Holcomb respected all of them and judged that any could perform the commandant's duties. But of the four Marines, he favored Smith for his experience, competence, and age.[25]

All available fitness reports on Holcomb offer concrete evidence of how highly acclaimed his performance as commandant had been, and why he could justifiably be reappointed to that post. On his September 1939 report, Secretary of the Navy Charles Edison praised Holcomb as "the outstanding man in the Marine Corps and he performs his duties as Maj. Gen. Commandant in a highly credible manner."[26] For the months from October 1939 through June 1940, Edison gave Holcomb the highest possible "outstanding" rating in the following areas: regular duties, administrative duties, executive duties, attention to duty, initiative, intelligence, force, loyalty, presence of mind, general value to the service, and judgment and common sense. Holcomb received next highest rating, "excellent," for six other areas. When the second fitness report of 1940 asked of Edison to consider "the possible requirement of the service in war" and "indicate your attitude toward having [Holcomb] under your command," Edison checked the most favorable response: he would "particularly desire to have" Holcomb as commandant during wartime.[27]

Edison's successor as Secretary of the Navy, the able Franklin Knox, rated Holcomb's performance as commandant in the "excellent" range in eleven areas from late June through September 1940.[28] Later in November, Knox made even more complimentary observations about Holcomb while his reappointment as commandant was being considered at the Navy Department and White House. "I have just discussed with Admiral Stark the reappointment of General Holcomb as Major General Commandant of the Marines and both join in a recommendation to you in favor of his reappointment," wrote Knox to President Roosevelt. "[Holcomb] has carried on the rather arduous task of organizing a much enlarged Marine Corps with great industry and intelligence. Thus far I have encountered no one among the highest ranking officers in the Marine Corps whose appointment as Commandant would be more advantageous to the Corps than the renewal of Holcomb's command."[29]

It is worth noting that both Edison and Knox assessed Holcomb so highly in 1939 and 1940 using terms and concepts with remarkably similar connotations to leadership qualities of political scientist Fred Greenstein. First, Holcomb's fitness reports rated him excellent or outstanding in leadership, defined on all fitness reports as "the capacity to direct, control, and influence others and still maintain high morale." This official definition in 1939 and 1940 equates to Greenstein's analytical category of "organization capacity," which, he explains, is a leader's "ability to rally his colleagues and structure their activities." Next, Holcomb received high marks in using judgment and common sense, defined as "the ability to think clearly and arrive at a logical conclusion." This calls to mind Greenstein's "cognitive style," which he describes as a leader's capacity to process "advice and information that comes his way."

Last and perhaps most significant, Secretaries Edison and Knox believed that Holcomb possessed and would continue to exhibit proper presence of mind, defined as "the ability to think clearly and act promptly and effectively in an unexpected emergency or under great strain." Holcomb's strong presence of mind was, to use Greenstein's term, high "emotional intelligence" or a leader's "ability to manage his emotions and turn them to constructive purposes, rather than being dominated by them and allowing them to diminish his leadership."[30] Holcomb had developed these leadership qualities throughout his career, whether in combat commands in France or as a protégé of great leaders including John A. Lejeune and John H. Russell.

Returning to late 1940 when President Roosevelt was considering the decision about Holcomb's future, official assessments of Holcomb's fitness reports were not the only positive acclamations. *Time* featured him on the cover of its November 11, 1940, issue, with caption reading "Holcomb of the Marines—In foreign parts, in troubled times." Inside, a lengthy article described the commandant's performance as well as discussing the Corps' history, weapons, and contemporary activities. Apart from celebrating the service's birthday, the piece painted in glowing terms Holcomb's effectiveness and success as commandant.[31]

With such a leader already in place and so much riding on effective execution of the commandant's duties, it made no sense to replace Holcomb. Also at that time in the 1940s, there was no term limit for commandancies by either mandate or tradition. President Roosevelt therefore decided to reappoint Thomas Holcomb to a second term as commandant of the Marine Corps on December 16, 1940. In an internal White House memorandum, Roosevelt made the pragmatic decision "in view of the present emergency and of the necessity for continuity in policy and expanding Marine Corps activities."[32] Holcomb would be expected to serve until September 1943, when he would reach mandatory retirement at sixty-four years of age. Indeed, he would be the last commandant to serve so long—almost two full four-year terms.

Numerous politicians and military officers offered Holcomb their congratulations on his reappointment and expressed continuing confidence in his skills, intelligence, and temperament. Lieutenant Colonel Gilder D. Jackson, one of Holcomb's closest friends, wrote what was likely the universal sentiment in the following note: "I am thankful that our Corps will have your hand at the helm until this emergency, or worse, is over."[33] The reappointment did not unequivocally please Holcomb, however, as evinced in his wistful reply to retired Commandant John A. Lejeune: "I am deeply flattered at having been reappointed, but I cannot help regretting that the world situation has made it impossible for me to retire at the end of my four years as I had always planned."[34]

Previously during the summer of 1940, he and Beatrice had purchased Rose Croft, a working farm on the shore of the Chesapeake Bay near St. Mary's City, approximately seventy miles south of Washington, D.C., along scenic Route 5. The Holcombs would have very much enjoyed spending more time there or cruising on their yacht, *Slow Boat*, on the Chesapeake or Potomac. Thomas could have gardened, hunted, and cared for Beatrice, who was so often afflicted with physical maladies.[35]

THE MARINE CORPS, STRATEGY, AND OPERATIONAL PREPARATIONS

Events in late 1939 and through 1940 cast ever more frightening shadows over humanity. Germany dominated Europe and, on the other side of the globe, Japan sought to consolidate its hold over large segments of China. Whether the United States would mobilize its resources and prepare for conflict ceased to be a major question. The new seminal questions concerned how much and how fast the nation could move toward these ends. President Roosevelt adopted a short-of-war strategy. He moved the U.S. Pacific Fleet to Pearl Harbor, Hawaii, to act as a deterrent to further Japanese expansion; and he initiated embargoes on the sale of scrap iron and aviation fuel to Japan. These actions represented conspicuous steps away from isolationism and neutrality.[36]

On the strategic level, Rainbow War Plan 3 replaced the irrelevant Rainbow 2 in early 1940, and called for American forces to concentrate on defeating Japan. When France fell in June, American planners immediately adopted Rainbow 4. The situation degenerated to a point that only the beleaguered Great Britain stood against the Axis powers. This fourth contingency plan reduced the United States to defending the Western Hemisphere against potential enemy incursions.[37]

The Marine Corps exercised no significant influence over the changes in war plans at the strategic level. Holcomb realized in 1940 that the Corps could hardly field a viable force in one ocean, let alone two. The Corps lacked all types of weapons, ammunition, and equipment necessary for deployment in wartime. The FMF possessed only 54 percent of the number of .30-caliber machine guns required for combat readiness; and only 45 percent of the necessary .50-caliber machine guns, 24 percent of 81-mm mortars, and 50 percent of 3-inch antiaircraft guns. The Corps' ammunition stockpiles looked worse yet. For projectiles of all types larger than .50 caliber, only 2.5 units of fire (a generic designation for the number of rounds needed for a single day of combat; the exact number varied from weapon to weapon) were on hand. Combat readiness required 22.5 units of fire.[38] Compounding these ammunition deficiencies was the discouraging fact that delivery dates for required weapons, equipment, and ammunition stretched from three months to twenty-four starting in August 1940. The Corps could not hope to mobilize quickly enough to keep up with any of the Rainbow Plans' timetables.[39]

Nevertheless, Holcomb and the Marines did what they could to enhance their amphibious assault and base defense capabilities after the outbreak of war. With this in mind, in early 1940 Marine units participated in FLEX 6. The simulated attacks showed great improvements and achieved the highest levels of realism to date.[40] Brigadier Holland M. Smith wrote years later how "Fleet Landing Exercise No. 6 was the turning point in the development of landing tactics."[41] He could make this assertion from firsthand knowledge because he commanded 2,244 troops of the 1st Marine Brigade and the 1st Marine Aircraft Group participating in FLEX 6.

These two units comprised almost half of all personnel in the entire FMF. More than twenty naval vessels, including battleships and submarines, accompanied the Marines. The naval elements took part in the landing, gunfire support, and reconnaissance portions of the maneuvers. Repeated assaults occurred over the nine-week period. The Marines approached beaches laced with underwater and shoreline obstacles. Once ashore, they established defenses against a potential enemy counterattack. They kept Commandant Holcomb apprised of progress by describing to him in detail all activities, conditions, and personalities.[42]

Throughout FLEX 6, several landing craft were put through their paces. Andrew Jackson Higgins' Eureka boats and Donald Roebling's Alligator boats proved themselves once again as superior to all competitors. So well did each perform, as far as Holcomb, Smith, and members of the Marine Corps Equipment Board were concerned, that they pushed the Navy Department to award contracts to both entrepreneurs to construct several hundred landing crafts. Passing these bureaucratic and budgetary hurdles represented major victories in improving amphibious preparedness.[43]

Amphibious assault forces were not the only beneficiaries of increased budgets. Marine defense battalions also took shape as the Corps' island base defense forces, the other half of the Corps' dual mission. Commandant Holcomb coordinated his efforts with CNO Stark to secure more ammunition, weapons, and equipment from the Army during late 1940. They hoped these resources would help bring several defense battalions on line to be stationed in island bases in the Pacific Ocean. The materials earmarked for these battalions legitimized the units as high priorities for the Corps. Defense battalions finally began deploying across to Midway, Wake, and Guam, which in Rainbow 5 were deemed the most critical advanced bases in the Pacific. Additionally, islands such as Palmyra, Johnston, and Tuitila, also in the Pacific, were slated to be garrisoned by defense battalions.

It would be 1941 before these deployments and even longer before construction projects on all these island bases would move forward. Whether on Wake, Midway, or other islands, Marines had few weapons and very little equipment. Whereas these modest advances represented some good news for Holcomb and the Corps, funds took a long time to get disbursed to contractors, and the manufacturers procured new materials at an interminably slow pace. This sluggish process vexed Holcomb.[44]

To factor these shortcomings into the changed strategic situation, CNO Stark completed an assessment of the United States' options in his so-called Stark

Memorandum of November 12, 1940. The CNO had to balance the Navy's strategic emphasis in the Pacific with the crisis in the Atlantic and Europe. "The present situation of the British Empire is not encouraging," observed Stark. "I believe it is easily possible, lacking active American military assistance, for that empire to lose the war."[45] This set the stage for the rest of the twenty-five-page report in which Stark quelled internal differences among naval officers, persuaded President Roosevelt to take a stand on the nation's grand strategy, and stated his own preferences for new strategic priorities. Stark grappled with the following question: How could the United States sustain war efforts of epic proportions against Japan in the Pacific and against Germany and Italy in Europe? His answer sketched out four unappealing scenarios.[46]

Plan A called for a unilateral American defense of the Western Hemisphere similar to that of Rainbow 4. Plan B mandated an offensive war by the United States concentrated against Japan in the Pacific, not unlike the antiquated Orange War Plan. Plan C prescribed equally strong American military efforts in the Atlantic and the Pacific. Lastly Stark laid out Plan D, known as Plan Dog and resembling Rainbow 5. Stark's Plan Dog rested on two realistic assumptions: American entrance in the war was all but inevitable, and Europe constituted the more immediate threat to the United States. It called for American forces to concentrate on defeating Germany and Italy in Europe first.

American forces in the Pacific would stand on a strategic defensive. Only after Europe was secure would they turn to a concerted effort against Japan.[47] Plan Dog's endorsement conceded what the Army's strategic planners wanted. The war in Europe would be dominated by the Army, leaving the Navy in a subordinate role. The seaborne services would play a larger, albeit defensive, role in the Pacific against Japan. Plan Dog did eventually form the nucleus for American strategy.[48] Indeed, according to military historian Louis Morton, the Stark Memorandum with its Plan Dog stood as "perhaps the most important single document in the development of World War II strategy."[49]

Marines only observed the creation process of this plan, but that hardly meant CNO Stark ignored the Corps as irrelevant. Plan Dog dealt with strategic and national goals that concerned the Corps in terms of mobilization timetables and resource allocation but mattered very little to it in terms of its dual missions. Both base defense and amphibious assault were indispensable to Plan Dog's operational requirements. With help from the Marines, the U.S. Navy would hold the defensive perimeter against Japanese incursions, from Alaska to Hawaii to Central America. American forces were also expected to preserve the logistical lifeline through Australia to British-held Malaysia.

Stark hoped advanced bases on Wake, Midway, and other islands could be maintained during wartime operations. Japanese-held island bases would have to be assaulted, and the captured areas defended in turn. Any American islands taken by the Japanese would need to be recaptured. These operational activities were not strategic offensives; on the contrary, the Navy would conduct limited operations using its fleet as well as Marine forces to maintain the strategic status quo in the Pacific. After the defeat of Germany, the nation could turn its full weight against Japan. Herein lay the significance of Plan Dog and its successive plans for the Corps: Marines could expect to play active roles in both base defense and amphibious assault, whether supporting offensive or defensive operations.[50]

Hard on the heels of the Stark Memorandum, American strategists met with their British counterparts to formulate coalition war plans in what became known as the ABC-1 Talks. They discussed specific factors and means to achieve the goals that Stark had outlined a few weeks earlier. The joint American-British-Canadian staff conversations during February and March 1941 represented a substantive change in American postures. The resulting strategic plans affected the Marine Corps in both positive and negative ways. Meanwhile, Commandant Holcomb found himself experiencing an embarrassment of riches: larger appropriations and greater responsibilities, yet insufficient time to absorb the money or expand the Corps accordingly.[51]

The British military and naval representatives met with Americans in Annapolis, Maryland, from January through March 1941. Rear Admirals Robert L. Ghormley and Richmond Kelly Turner and three other officers represented the U.S. Navy.[52] Marine Lieutenant Colonel Omar T. Pfeiffer joined the American delegation as a last-minute replacement for one naval officer. But his participation was no accident. After graduating from the Naval War College in 1937, he served with the Corps' own War Plans Section at Quantico until January 1941. While at this post in 1939, he prepared plans for possible American military operations in North Africa. Pfeiffer's knowledge and experience thus qualified him to offer advice to the Navy's delegates on "purely military proposals" relating to amphibious and ground operations, as opposed to fleet operations.[53]

Stark kept abreast of progress at the talks and advised American delegates, but he did not participate in any planning sessions. This he left to Ghormley and Turner, both of whom boasted impressive records commanding warships and serving the Navy's War Plans Division.[54] Of the two admirals, Pfeiffer recalled, Turner emerged as "the most forceful and dominant personality and dominated the conversations despite the fact that Ghormley was his senior."[55] Turner did not fear alienating his colleagues nor interrupting the proceedings to get answers to his questions. He even acquired the nickname "Terrible" Turner. Omar Pfeiffer later described him as a "very very gifted" officer yet a "stubborn, self-opinionated, conceited" person.[56]

The Anglo-American delegates hammered out the strategic priorities in fighting a potential war against Germany, Italy, and Japan. The final report of March 27, 1941, revealed how closely Anglo-American conclusions echoed Plan Dog in the Stark Memorandum of the previous November. Although no documentation reveals what exactly Commandant Holcomb knew about the ABC-1 Talks, Pfeiffer undoubtedly supplied him with pertinent information about progress. Later during the Second World War, Holcomb frequently stopped by Pfeiffer's office in the Navy Department to talk about issues facing the Corps. Holcomb relied heavily on him to obtain cooperation from the Navy. With this in mind, it is reasonable to assume that Holcomb also consulted with Pfeiffer about how the ABC-1 Talks would affect the Marine Corps during 1941.[57]

Following the end of the ABC-1 Talks, American planners updated Rainbow War Plan 5 to conform to new Anglo-American strategic goals. This revision did not relegate American forces to a purely static defense from the Panama Canal to Hawaii to Alaska. The plan allowed much latitude in interpreting what "strategic defense" actually meant at the operational and tactical levels.[58] As part of limited offensive operations, Marine amphibious assault units would move from San Diego to Hawaii and "make preparations and train for landing attacks on Japanese bases in the Marshalls for purposes of capture or demolition, with particular emphasis on plans for the capture of Entiwetok."[59] Marine defense battalions would hold bases on Wake, Midway, Palmyra, Johnston, Samoa, and Guam against potential Japanese attacks, or alternatively they would bait the Japanese into battle over their control.[60] The U.S. Pacific Fleet could react to Japanese operations in these or other areas, effectively using the bases to lure the Imperial Japanese Navy into a decisive battle.

Admiral Husband E. Kimmel, newly promoted commander in chief of the U.S. Pacific Fleet (CINCPAC), recognized the possibilities for offensive operations under the modified Rainbow War Plan 5. The fifty-nine-year-old officer brought a workaholic's obsession and a warrior's spirit to headquarters at Pearl Harbor.[61] Kimmel, contends military historian Gregory J. W. Urwin, "knew the best defense was an offense—even a limited one. Rainbow 5 offered him a loophole through which he could assume a more active part in the coming struggle. At the first sign of war, Kimmel intended to hurl his fleet at the Japanese Mandates and seize them." As soon as the situation allowed for more aggressive operations, these islands, according to Urwin, would then become "a stepping-off point for further advances."[62]

Kimmel knew he needed someone with amphibious expertise on his planning staff. To fill this post, Commandant Holcomb chose Omar Pfeiffer, who had recently been promoted to colonel. Holcomb considered him to be "a very fine officer" and promised he would prove to be "a valuable assistant" to Kimmel "in the event of any landing operation."[63] Pfeiffer went from being a member of the American delegation to the ABC-1 Talks to Fleet Marine Officer with the U.S. Pacific Fleet. Ordinarily, the Fleet Marine Officer oversaw the Marine detachments assigned to warships, but Pfeiffer made himself invaluable to Kimmel by helping to translate new strategies into operational possibilities.[64] As Pfeiffer remembers it: "Initially, my main duty was to answer questions on the Rainbow Plans until the written plans arrived." He eventually assumed a more active role on the Pacific Fleet's War Plans Section as "someone educated and trained in assault and defensive military action."[65]

Just like his superior officer CNO Stark, Admiral Kimmel remained the Corps' advocate until he was relieved of command shortly after the attack on Pearl Harbor. But even though the Corps' participation was integral to successful operations and Kimmel's support was steadfast, the Marine units remained under-equipped and undermanned. The admiral complained to Congress, for example, that the defense battalions lacked antiaircraft artillery and light and heavy machine guns as well as sufficient ammunition for these weapons. All available scarce resources were being moved from coast to coast or region to region in a strategic shell game that ultimately short-shrifted the Marine units in the Pacific.[66]

Events beyond Kimmel's or Holcomb's control hobbled the Corps, when in 1941 Iceland required immediate garrisoning by troops. This key Anglo-American outpost in the North Atlantic flanked the sea lanes on which supply convoys sailed between North America and the British Isles. The conquests of Norway and France by Germany made possession of Iceland all the more critical, because warships or aircraft based on the island could control these lines of transportation. By mid-1941, some 25,000 British troops occupied Iceland to stem the rising German tide in the North Atlantic. British Prime Minister Winston Churchill asked that the United States provide replacements to defend Iceland. In so doing, he did have an ulterior motive. The shrewd Churchill wished to secure a greater American commitment for Britain's war in Europe.[67]

Because no U.S. Army troops were prepared for this deployment, President Roosevelt decided to send Marines. High-ranking officers in the U.S. Navy opposed this assignment as a waste of offensive amphibious forces, but Roosevelt insisted. Brigadier General John Marston's 1st Marine Brigade (Provisional), totaling 4,095 men of the 6th Marine Regiment and 5th Defense Battalion, arrived in Iceland on July 7, 1941. Once there, the Marines served as mobile ground and air defense forces in "mutual cooperation" with the British. Several months later, available U.S. Army units began arriving as well. Marston's Marines were ordered to detached duty with the Army, and they found themselves under the Army's control.

Commandant Holcomb vehemently objected to the Marines being subsumed into an Army unit, but CNO Stark directed him to follow orders. The Marines found converting to Army regulations an unpleasant process.[68] They feared they would be sidelined permanently on Iceland, as revealed in Marston's message back to HQMC: "I believe that the Marine Corps and the Navy Department should be advised of the efforts which I am convinced are being made to retain [the 1st Marine] Brigade indefinitely in Iceland. As I see it, it is a simple solution to [the

U.S. Army] of their problem of landing enough regularly enlisted men to fill the Iceland requirements. Indeed, four thousand Marines had practically landed in their lap."[69]

The 1st Marine Brigade (Provisional) remained on the island until March 1942, when elements rotated back to the United States or shipped to the South Pacific. In any event, deployment to Iceland meant yet another requirement that Holcomb added to the ever-burgeoning obligations of the Corps. Moreover, attaining a level of readiness to support any large-scale operations in the Pacific eluded Holcomb.[70] One Navy Department report in June 1941 outlined the Corps' many shortages and the problems causing them: "Landing Force Boats and Engines, Paravanes and Paravane handling gear, Life Rafts, Tank Lighters, Artillery Lighters, Amphibian Tractors, Standard Boats, Rubber Boats, Support Landing Craft, and Airplane Rescue Boats totaling about $13,000,000 are held up for procurement because of lack of funds. Procurement of this material should be started immediately, in order that it may be available for equipping vessels to be taken over under Rainbow."[71] The tank and artillery lighters were especially critical deficiencies, because only with these boats could heavy vehicles and weaponry be deposited directly onto the beach where they could support the Marines. The new challenges confronting Holcomb, Stark, and Kimmel in 1941 were ones of volume and time—how much and how fast materials could be made ready for war.

HOLCOMB'S SUCCESSES IN EXPANDING THE MARINE CORPS

More and more Americans recognized the growing threats as Germany launched offensives in North Africa and against the Soviet Union. In the Pacific Ocean, meanwhile, neither America's deterrents nor its punitive economic sanctions discouraged Japan's further expansion into Southeast Asia. President Roosevelt recalled the retired Douglas MacArthur to active duty in the U.S. Army and placed under his command all American and Filipino military forces in the Philippines. Roosevelt hoped these actions would create uncertainty or dread among the Japanese and thus give the United States more diplomatic leverage. But the hardening American line failed to elicit these intended effects on the Japanese.[72]

Commandant Holcomb and other realists in the American military could see that war between the United States and Japan was increasingly likely. They only puzzled over matters of when and where hostilities would start. Holcomb and his staff redoubled their efforts to get men and materiel ready for the coming conflict.[73] On February 13, 1941, Holcomb testified to the Naval Affairs Subcommittee of the Senate Appropriations Committee on the Corps' needs for FY 1942. He began with a brief assessment of his service's current personnel and procurement conditions. The commandant then conceded that the Corps had "experienced no difficulty" in recruiting men for enlistment during most of his commandancy. In the current crisis, he told committee members: "It is essential that we be permitted to continue recruiting in an orderly manner and with full utilization of recruiting and training facilities until at least a strength of 100,000 enlisted is attained."

Holcomb reminded the senators that as of February 1, 1941, the Corps had stood at 45,111 enlisted Marines. An authorized expansion to 50,566 by July 1 required an authorization for more money. The Marines would need to increase their officer corps accordingly by July 1, from 2,265 to more than 3,000. Procurement and delivery of weapons and equipment may have been "satisfactory," but these items failed to match the actual needs of the Corps in 1941. And the situation was bound to worsen as the organization continued to grow.[74]

Holcomb also pointed out that too many leathernecks served in detachments on naval vessels, on guard duty at naval installations, and as protectors of American lives and property overseas.[75] These missions drained manpower that could be employed in other missions. Holcomb asserted that the FMF, as a prime example, could not be utilized as a rapidly deployed strike force by the Navy, because of a galling manpower shortage of 30 percent, or 8,000 Marines. Nor could the FMF be quickly expanded, because the Marine Corps Reserve had already been mobilized.[76] Siphoning Marines away from other duties provided the only means for raising the FMF to wartime strength. The Navy's shipboard detachments required 3,400 Marines, and protecting American lives and property overseas demanded another 3,800. The senators needed to know that every new warship launched and every new overseas station established meant a requisite "reduction in the contemplated strength of the FMF" and consequently a decline in operational capabilities.[77]

As the new Navy Appropriations Bill followed the legislative process, Holcomb worked behind the scenes to make sure that his "most pressing needs" were understood before he ever took the stand. On one occasion, he sent a "personal and confidential" memorandum to Representative Vinson on the House Naval Affairs Committee. Holcomb used phrases like "tragic shortage," "vitally necessary," and "impossible situation" to highlight the Corps' dearth of manpower, ammunition, training facilities, and transport vessels. The figures that the commandant cited resembled those in his aforementioned Senate testimony.[78]

Holcomb's interactions with military and civilian leaders demonstrated his political gamesmanship. Henry I. Shaw Jr., former chief historian of the Marine Corps, pays the commandant this compliment: "A respected colleague and friend of the admirals who commanded the Navy, Holcomb was equally at ease and a friend to the politicians who controlled the military budget."[79] Knowing everyone of importance in Washington and carrying himself like a consummate military professional gave Holcomb credibility.

As Congress ceased to be as tight-fisted as it had been during the first four years of his commandancy, effective relations with the House and Senate alike paid dividends for the Corps throughout 1941. Holcomb took greatest satisfaction when, on February 15, Congress approved the establishment of "a really fine combat training area" at New River, along the coast of Onslow County, just outside Jacksonville, North Carolina.[80] Funds totaling $14,750,000 for purchase and construction of a base at New River passed through Congress as part of a Supplemental National Defense Appropriations Act later in April. The seven miles of beach and one hundred square miles of adjacent land offered an ideal setting for amphibious training.[81]

Holcomb's other long-term effort to bolster defenses on island bases in the Pacific finally started to bear fruit on March 23, when President Roosevelt signed a bill that allocated $4.7 million to fortify Guam and Samoa as advanced bases. Moneys were subsequently authorized and timetables set for construction projects on other island bases across the Pacific. This good news coincided with deployments of defense battalions to Midway, Samoa, Palmyra, and Johnson Islands. An advanced base on Wake Island, though not yet occupied by Marines, also received some support when Admiral Kimmel and CNO Stark agreed in February that fortifying and manning this island should occur as soon as possible.[82]

Federal largesse ensured the Corps' expansion, but Holcomb and the Corps experienced severe growing pains. Permission to spend money did not speed the process of incorporating raw recruits into the Corps, procuring more equipment, or constructing defenses on far-flung island bases.[83] The "speed of attainment" for weapons and equipment on order for the most essential Marine units—the two divisions and six defense battalions—ranged from four to sixteen months.[84]

As 1941 progressed, many events caused still more problems in the Corps' mobilization. One of the most dramatic occurred on March 11, when Roosevelt signed H.R. 1776 into law. Debate had raged across the United States about this so-called Lend Lease Bill. Ardent isolationists insisted that Lend Lease gave the president carte blanche to make America an unofficial belligerent and provide material support to the British. They believed that a war declaration was the next logical step, but they lost their bid to stop the bill. American opinion gradually became more sympathetic to the British cause. After all, the bill's supporters pointed out that Germany and Italy already controlled Western Europe and menaced the British Isles. Later in March, Congress passed the bill by healthy margins. This measure represented a defining moment in the national debate over preparedness and marked the steep decline of isolationism's influence. By year's end, the isolationists could only argue against the United States' entrance into the war. All other nuances about neutrality withered away.[85]

The Lend Lease Act affected the Marine Corps in a significant, albeit negative, way because it drained off thousands of potential volunteers who might otherwise have enlisted in the Corps. Britain was spending billions of pounds sterling, and the U.S. government was funneling billions of dollars into industry and agriculture to support Britain, Greece, China, and eventually the Soviet Union. Lend Lease's initial $7 billion budget allocation and subsequent funding sent millions of Americans back into new manufacturing jobs with good pay. Alternatively, joining the Marine Corps looked less appealing to many American men.[86]

Consequently, a problem heretofore unknown to the Marines cropped up in the spring of 1941. The Corps' recruitment numbers declined and remained lower than hoped for throughout the year. Because the Navy Department had ordered the Marines to cease active recruitment in late 1940, the assigned monthly quotas for February and March looked dismal, with respective 328 and 300 enlistee quotas. Recruiters could not even meet these modest goals, when in March 1941 they attracted only 288 first-time enlistees.[87]

In the meantime, the United States lurched ever closer to conflict. During one of President Roosevelt's normally calming Fireside Chats, on May 27 more than 80 million Americans listened to the radio as their leader declared a state of "unlimited national emergency."[88] Thereafter, the Navy Department lifted recruitment restrictions, and in June 1941 the Marine Corps' experienced a dramatic improvement of 1,905 first-time enlistments. Even so, this influx failed to reach June's much higher monthly quota of 3,100 enlistments, nor did the Corps make up for the previous several months of shortfalls.[89]

The service's seemingly impressive expansion from 38,648 to 50,087 Marines in 1941 can mostly be credited to the influx of 8,700 reservists called to active duty, first-time enlistments at Marine Corps bases, and reenlistments from the Corps' own ranks or from the Army or Navy, as opposed to enlistments at recruiting centers. These gains notwithstanding, the crisis forced Marines to do soul-searching about how to boost their enlistments, as well as how to improve their publicity efforts. As Holcomb stated in a blunt self-assessment in June: "We need all the honest publicity we can get. My recruiting is picking up but not as fast as I would like and we need every means available to keep the Marine Corps favorably before the people."[90] Other Marines inside and outside of recruitment recognized these problems and suggested solutions. Their ideas filtered through the Corps' chain of command and resulted in substantive reforms.[91]

One analysis came in March 1941 from Colonel Thomas S. Clark, commanding officer of the Eastern Recruiting Division. In a report submitted to the Adjutant and Inspector General, Clark fixed some of the blame for shortfalls on external factors. Candidly summarizing the first quarter's recruiting in 1941, he stated that the new applicants were "generally poorer physically, indicating that the 'cream of the crop' have already enlisted or have secured civilian employment."[92] Clark also linked poor recruitment to factors inside the Corps. He believed that recruiting efforts were "handicapped by lack of efficient publicity."

The quantity and quality of publicity had slipped from what it had been in earlier years. Clark pointed out that fewer opportunities existed for "free publicity" on billboards or street cars, because advertising agencies wanted to charge for the use of such media. He directed some of his criticisms at the Marine Corps Publicity Bureau, because this office had not produced new theatrical trailers or radio spots in many months. Although he conceded that Marines in the Publicity Bureau worked diligently, he lamented: "The fact remains that the Marine Corps is using amateurs in an endeavor to compete with [the Army's] professional publicity agents, without much success."[93]

To solve these problems, Clark wanted to change the messengers and their messages being sent to the American people. He called for wholesale transformations of publicity and recruitment activities. He advised that more recruiting stations be opened throughout the nation, and that additional Marines be assigned to those offices. Next, Clark recommended that the Corps hire "a qualified publicity man to give a needed impetus to Marine Corps publicity."[94] This idea was consistent with progressivism's approach to problem-solving—which, among other tenets, called for the use of experts. Finally, Colonel Clark argued that the Corps' image and message should shift from old publicity cultivating public approval and encouraging recruitment to new methods acknowledging that most Americans favored a stronger Marine Corps as a defensive measure.[95]

Commandant Holcomb recognized the need for improvements in publicity and recruitment. He was privy to internal communiqués such as Clark's about these issues, and he took several steps to bolster recruitment and improve publicity. Holcomb expanded the four recruitment divisions, reformed the public relations apparatus, generated media coverage, and created new images of the Corps. He almost doubled the service's manpower detailed to recruitment duties, from 364 Marines in January 1941 to 669 in December. Simultaneously, many new recruiting districts and substations were opened in Utah, Colorado, and Montana.[96]

The most significant improvement occurred on July 1, 1941, when Holcomb created the Division of Public Relations. It would supervise all publicity activities, including those related to recruitment, in ways reminiscent of Colonel Thomas Clark's report three months earlier.[97] The Division of Public Relations represented yet another example of Holcomb's willingness to listen to his subordinates, his ability to discern a need for structural reform, and his wisdom in determining the right way to institute that reform.[98] Holcomb's solution likewise calls to mind what political scientist Fred Greenstein calls "organizational capacity." Holcomb exhibited this quality, which, according to Greenstein, was evident in his "ability to rally his colleagues and structure their activities effectively."[99]

Holcomb recalled retired Brigadier General Robert L. Denig Sr. to active duty and made him director of the new division.[100] The Division of Public Relations absorbed the still-extant Marine Corps Publicity Bureau, and supplanted the Adjutant and Inspector's office "as the agency responsible for the Censorship and release of photographs, movie pictures, new articles, and advertising which relate to the Marine Corps."[101] Always the rational manager, Holcomb thus centralized all publicity activities into a single office at HQMC. The selection of Denig as director astounded no one more than Denig himself. Commissioned in 1905, he had seen action with Holcomb in France in the First World War. When Holcomb asked him in June 1941, "Well, Denig, what do you know about public relations?" Denig replied, "I don't know anything about it. I never heard of it before. What is it?" Holcomb responded, "You'd better learn because that's what you're gonna be."[102] The closest Denig had previously come to doing publicity had been in 1918, when the *New York Times* had published his letter to his wife describing the Battle of Soissons.

Taking Holcomb's order to heart, Denig immediately began educating himself about the principles of public relations and recruitment. Later in July 1941, he participated in a conference for Navy public relations officers. His presentation contended that the Marines needed to get themselves in print more prominently. He believed that not enough Americans had general knowledge about the Corps, other than reminiscences about the glories of the First World War or duties in China or Central America. He argued that the people had to learn the "who, what, when, where, how and why" of the Corps, and that his division had to make them understand the service's significant contributions to the nation's defense. This could be done by plugging new storylines and images into advertisements. Increased advertising budgets would further help Denig promote the Corps' positive image in all broadcast and print media.[103]

The Division of Public Relations made its presence felt almost immediately. Marines began producing new images on everything from posters to bubblegum cards. These told stories about the Corps, as Colonel Thomas Clark had previously recommended. One poster showed a Marine manning an antiaircraft machine gun silhouetted against a city's buildings. A spotlight beam swept through the night sky. The words read "Always on the alert at sea, on land, in the air. U.S. Marines." This imagery both glamorized life in the Corps and reminded viewers of the dire need for a strong national defense.[104]

Furnishing men and materials for exhibitions or other public forums represented yet another important function of Denig's division.[105] One such venue was the National Defense Program Exhibition Train, which wound its way around the United States from September through November 1941. The displays on board the eleven railroad cars promoted the need for better-prepared military forces. The train departed from the nation's capital, chugged through the South to the West Coast, and took a northern route through the Rockies, Great Plains, Midwest, and back to New England. The Marine Corps shared the fifth car with the Navy and Coast Guard. Recruitment photographs in the Corps' section told the story of a Marine's life, from everyday uniform inspections to more exotic duties around the globe. Stylized paintings of leathernecks in combat appeared in the exhibit.

Themes of elite status, martial virtue, and unit pride played out in these images, all of which were calculatedly designed to appeal to young men. Although the exact number of visitors is not recorded, many thousands of Americans certainly saw the Corps' exhibit during three dozen stops along the train's 7,000-mile route.[106]

Denig and the Division of Public Relations received help from Holcomb and many other sources. Holcomb reached out to his many press contacts to generate positive coverage. He maintained close contacts with staff at *Time* and *Life* magazines, and he worked hand in hand with his fellow "Devil Dog," Samuel Meek of the J. Walter Thompson advertising firm.[107] More help for this blitz also came from a retired Marine officer, John H. Craige. He spotlighted the Corps in his book, *What the Citizen Should Know About the Marines*, appearing in 1941. Craige outlined the Corps' two main contributions to the nation's naval strategy: "the function of the marine divisions is to attack and seize" enemy island bases, and "the Defense Battalions are designed to dig in and hold" onto island bases.[108] Prior to 1941, no popular publication could have mentioned America's offensive military capabilities without drawing crippling criticism from isolationists.

Ideas like Colonel Clark's and efforts by Denig and Holcomb to craft a more vivid public image yielded positive results.[109] For example, in a 1994 survey of seventy-nine veterans who served in the 7th Marine Defense/Antiaircraft Artillery Battalion during the Second World War, twenty-eight had enlisted in the Corps before December 7, 1941. Respondents cited many reasons for their choice. "Patriotism," "duty," and "employment" motivated twenty-five; six specifically recalled the desire "to be Marines" as their main reason for enlisting.[110]

Public relations specialist and retired Marine officer Fred C. Lash averred that the Corps' advertisements tried "to influence, persuade, and 'sell' a consumer." Young men represented the consumer who might purchase the product by enlisting in the Corps. Lash offered a careful clarification of this dynamic between product and consumer: The main purpose of advertising "was not so much to generate the 'sale,' but rather to create conditions which precede the sale. The actual sale depends primarily on the recruiter. Put in other words, [advertising] must create the right 'climate' within the community and for the target audience."[111] This approach to publicity was consistent with contemporary advertising practices in the civilian world.

Advertisers endeavored to turn a product's image into perceived reality. Marketing historian Daniel Pope draws on the ideas of another historian, Daniel Boorstin, to explain this phenomenon: "Twentieth century advertising is often neither true nor false. The omnipresent image no longer either mirrors or distorts an underlying, more tangible reality. The advertising image itself dominates and becomes the reality, cast adrift from the physical products it sells. Credibility becomes the central issue, and the older moral problems of truth and falsity are not so much resolved as bypassed."[112] Although neither Pope nor Boorstin had the Corps in mind, they accurately summed up the essence of the service's marketing efforts.

HOLCOMB'S IMPACT ON AMPHIBIOUS PREPARATIONS AND INNOVATIONS

As so much political, diplomatic, and strategic maneuvering occurred in 1941, Commandant Holcomb kept the Marines focused as much as possible on perfecting amphibious capabilities, for both the offensive assaults and base defense. Admiral Royal E. Ingersoll, the Assistant CNO, had instructed Holcomb in January to "take the necessary steps to provide for the organization and equipment of six (6) additional Marine Defense Battalions, the project to take first priority after the completion of the organization of the two Marine Divisions."[113] To meet the challenges of overseas operations in 1941, the Navy's General Board produced a plan for expansion of the Marine Corps that concurred with Ingersoll's order that the FMF's divisions and defense battalions should receive first and second priority, respectively, over all other aviation, garrison, and shipboard units.[114]

Because naval campaigns would require divisional-strength amphibious assault units, Holcomb received authorization to create more viable, larger force structures of approximately 18,000 Marines capable of seizing enemy-held islands. The creation of two divisions on paper as part of the FMF occurred in early February 1941, but both remained under strength in reality. The 1st Marine Division expanded from the 1st Marine Brigade. After years of moving from place to place on the East Coast and in the Caribbean, these self-proclaimed "raggedy-assed" Marines eventually took up permanent residence at New River, North Carolina, in the spring of 1941. Meanwhile on the West Coast, the 2nd Marine Division expanded from the 2nd Marine Brigade and integrated a hodgepodge of units including Holcomb's old 6th Marine Regiment from the First World War.

The division's personnel were nicknamed the "Hollywood" Marines because they made war films as part of their training. The 2nd Marine Division began the year at the Marine Corps Base in San Diego, California. The division outgrew these confines and moved later in the year to the newly constructed "Camp Holcomb" near Kearny Mesa, California. The commandant bridled at the name, feeling that only deceased Marines should have bases named after them. He demanded that the camp's name be changed, and thereafter, it became known as Camp Elliott.[115]

The two divisions required structural modifications when compared with a standard division in the U.S. Army. Holcomb recognized the value of the triangular division's basic configuration then being adopted by the Army. A pragmatic reformer, he decided that the division model should be modified to fit the needs of an amphibious assault unit and that a "triangular strength reinforced" division should be created. Like the Army's triangular infantry one, Holcomb's division consisted of three infantry regiments supported by artillery and tank units. Unlike the Army's design, however, a Marine division fielded more riflemen per regiment. The Marine version also included heavier artillery and larger combat engineer components, both of which were integrated into each infantry regiment to form three independently functioning assault forces. Holcomb also added the all-important landing-craft elements to his division.[116]

The commandant could rightfully claim some credit for designing the Marines' triangular-strength reinforced division, because he had long ago outlined a similar table of organization and equipment in his forward-looking report, "The Marine Corps' Mission in National Defense, and Its Organization for a Major Emergency," written as a student at the Army War College almost a decade earlier, in 1932.[117]

As had been done for several years during the winter, Marines went to Culebra and Vieques in the Caribbean for maneuvers. Elements of the 1st Marine Division joined elements of the Army's 1st Infantry Division in FLEX 7 in February 1941. Major General Holland Smith, commanding officer of the 1st Marine Division, also took command of the 1st Infantry Division. A large naval contingent, including three battleships, four cruisers, two aircraft carriers, and five destroyers, participated. Additional aircraft for close air support came from the 1st Marine Aircraft Group. At long last, a sufficient number of transports took part in the simulated amphibious assaults. Ernest J. King, just promoted to admiral and named commander in chief of the U.S. Atlantic Fleet in February, held unified command over all participating forces.[118]

Because coordinating thousands of men on beaches, in the air, and on the ocean represented a major hurdle in FLEX 7, all participants from the three services gained experience in combined-arms landing operations involving air, land, sea, and amphibious components. Though successful on some levels, FLEX 7 was far from perfect. To call it a divisional-strength exercise was in reality a misnomer, because three Marine battalions combined with two battalions from the Army to make brigade-strength landings. Their equipment remained inadequate to the task of amphibious assault. Obsolete radios and inexperienced radio operators wreaked havoc on communications between the ships and the troops ashore. The large number of transport vessels needed modification to carry ample landing craft, amphibian tractors, and tank lighters.[119] Smith and King complained about these shortcomings to Commandant Holcomb and CNO Stark back at the Navy Department in Washington. For his part, Holcomb made recommendations to Stark for improvements in landing craft and transport vessels that same month.[120]

Problems also occurred between FLEX 7's two ranking officers. Admiral King and General Smith bickered over mundane things like who would first read the only available copy of a newspaper at breakfast. More substantive clashes erupted because King wanted to choose the beaches to assault and direct troop movements on shore, as granted to him in his capacity of over commander in the Navy's existing *FTP 167*. But Smith believed these decisions should be his prerogatives, as the assault force commander and the more experienced amphibious practitioner.[121] Military historian Allan R. Millett illuminates the two men's personalities when he observes: "Notorious in the Navy for his brilliance, drinking, meanness, and womanizing, King had a wide knowledge of carrier operations and surface warfare, but no amphibious experience. Holland Smith had an ego and temperament to match King, along with hard-learned practical experience as commander of the 1st Marine Brigade."[122]

The two officers eventually worked together well enough to make the maneuvers worthwhile. King, for his part, learned much about amphibious operations and came to appreciate the capabilities of Smith and his Marines.[123] The unity of command difficulties, nonetheless, would remain unresolved until late 1942 during the campaign for Guadalcanal.

As FLEX 7 came to a close, it became clear that the 1st Marine Division needed more space and a better locale for future amphibious training. Holcomb bemoaned the fact that the division's Marines did "not have good training facilities at Guantanamo and it is a terrible place for the men."[124] Parris Island, the major East Coast recruit depot in South Carolina, was bursting at the seams with enlistees undergoing basic training. The Marine Corps Base at Quantico barely kept pace with burgeoning officer education needs. No room at either base could be made for the thousands of leathernecks of the 1st Division. Construction of a base at New River rectified this situation by providing everything that a division could want to conduct advanced training in all aspects of amphibious warfare.[125]

As soon as enough tents, washrooms, mess halls, and storehouses were erected, the New River base went operational. The 1st Marine Division arrived in June 1941, and the Army's 1st Infantry Division joined it shortly thereafter. There the two divisions formed the I Corps (Provisional), U.S. Atlantic Fleet, under the command of Holland Smith. One month later, this force was redesignated as the 1st Joint Training Force, U.S. Atlantic Fleet.[126] Some 16,500 soldiers and Marines of the two under-strength divisions subsequently took part in small unit exercises on shore as well as in limited regimental or battalion-strength amphibious landings. These prepared them for the Joint Training Force Landing Exercise (JTF-1), which was a full dress rehearsal that August.[127]

Army, Navy, and Marine Corps elements participated in ship-to-shore movement, antiaircraft artillery target practice, coastal artillery target practice, inland maneuvers, parachute training, and tank and antitank training. Although JTF-1 suffered from many logistical, communication, and equipment problems, the participating Marines and soldiers learned what not to do.[128] Military historian Russell F. Weigley posits great value in this problem-solving process: "Simply by defining the specific problems into which amphibious operations divided themselves, the

This Higgins "Eureka" boat was tested at New River, North Carolina, on July 7, 1941.

(Marine Corps University Archives, Holcomb Papers, Box 38)

Marine Corps made it evident that the problems most likely were not insoluble; and the Corps went on to delineate many of the solutions."[129]

Beyond the doctrinal and organizational lessons learned, JTF-1 provided a laboratory for more testing of new assault craft. Although Andrew Jackson Higgins' Eureka boats were seaworthy and maneuverable, the Marines on board needed to climb over the vessel's four-foot sides and drop into the surf or onto the sand. Disembarking this way would expose them conspicuously to enemy fire. Remedying the problem required designing a new bow that could allow them to exit without undue danger or delay. The idea for the new bow did not come from the Marines themselves or even from Higgins. Rather, it originated with the Japanese.

While observing a Japanese amphibious assault across the Yangtze River in China in 1937, a young Marine first lieutenant named Victor H. Krulak took a photograph of a Japanese *daihatsu* boat with a bow ramp that could be lowered so troops could run directly onto the beach or shallow surf. It struck him as "exactly what the Marines had been looking for—sturdy ramp-bow-type boats."[130]

Krulak gave his photograph as well as a miniature model of the ramp-bowed *daihatsu* to Holland Smith later in 1937. A duly impressed Smith passed along both items to Commandant Holcomb, who recognized the design's great potential, and in turn he made the Marine Corps Equipment Board and Higgins aware of the ramped-bow design. The idea floundered for several years for want of funding. But by early 1941, after good showings in several FLEX exercises, the Eureka

From left: Major General Holland M. Smith, Commandant Thomas Holcomb, Secretary of the Navy Franklin Knox (with binoculars), and Colonel Theodore Roosevelt Jr., of the 1st Infantry Division, observe amphibious exercises at New River, North Carolina, July 7, 1941.

(Marine Corps University Archives, Holcomb Papers, Box 39)

emerged as the best landing craft available. Brigadier General Emile P. Moses, then chairman of the Marine Corps Equipment Board, dusted off the ramped-bow design and gave Higgins the go-ahead to build prototypes using his Eureka boats. In no way did this hinder the Eureka's ability to retract itself from the beach once troops had disembarked.[131] The testing results impressed everyone. "The Ramp Bow Boat embodies a splendid principle," gushed an enthusiastic Smith in his final report on JTF-1, "and though models used during the exercises demonstrated numerous faults, none was organic and it is believed that all can be, or already are remedied."[132] An equally pleased Commandant Holcomb informed CNO Stark that "the tests were considered highly successful."[133] The modified Eureka boats would be officially christened landing craft, vehicle, personnel, or LCVP.[134]

The LCVP and several ramped-bow variants joined Donald Roebling's highly regarded Alligator amphibious tractor, known as a landing vehicle, tracked (LVT), as the transportation mainstays of future amphibious assaults.[135] The development of these vehicles demonstrated the degree to which the Marine Corps had what Allan Millett aptly describes as "a foundation in institutional commitment, and an organizational embrace of a new mission."[136] Millett's comments ring true because the Marines enjoyed efficient vertical lines of communication, from junior officers in the field up to the commandant, as well as efficient horizontal lines of communication between the commandant's office, Equipment Board, and Marines participating in exercises. That Lieutenant Krulak's proposal for a ramped-bow landing craft could find its way up the chain of command to Commandant Holcomb's desk attested to an organizational culture where forward-looking ideas could become realities.

Holcomb rightly deserved praise for recognizing and embracing the innovations in effective landing craft designs, but he did not adopt every innovation just as easily. He could be a technological conservative, as evinced in the eventual replacement of the .30-caliber Model 1903 Springfield rifle with the M1 Garand. The Marines had first begun using the bolt-action Springfield in 1908. With its five-round capacity and charger-loaded box magazine, this rifle featured superb accuracy and exceptional reliability. Armed with this weapon, then-Captain Holcomb led the Marine Corps Rifle Team to a national championship in 1911. The Springfield became the standard-issue Marine rifle during the First World War and would remain so through 1942. It acquired a legendary status as a marksman's tool among Marines over the intervening three decades.[137]

Despite the enduring popularity of the Springfield in the late 1930s, the Army and Marine Corps considered upgrading to a semiautomatic rifle, which fired one bullet for every trigger pull, after which the spent casing was automatically ejected from the rifle breach by gas-propelled backward recoil. Both services tested several designs. Because there was no bolt mechanism to work by hand, the semiautomatic's rate of fire was many times that of the Springfield. Furthermore, the shooter could keep his eye on the target as he expended his rounds without having to reacquire it after every shot.

Two new rifles emerged as the best weapons in the competition. Marine reservist Melvin M. Johnson Jr. developed the Johnson semiautomatic rifle in the mid-1930s. It held ten rounds of .30-caliber ammunition in a box magazine. The other was the M1 Garand. Named for its inventor, John Garand, this rifle first appeared in 1937. It held eight rounds dispensed by a top-loaded clip. The Army and Marine Corps put the Johnson and Garand rifles through exhaustive field testing. The Garand fared better, while the Johnson had too many design complexities and functional problems to be effective in combat.[138]

Holcomb kept abreast of results of the rifle tests. He acknowledged that although it was a "fine semi-automatic rifle," the Garand was "unnecessarily expensive, that the lack of interchangeability of parts was a serious drawback and the requirement that it be kept lubricated, together with many other minor disadvantages might render it unsuitable for landing operations where it is inevitable the rifles will be wet with salt water and may well get sand in them."[139] As a marksmanship purist, the commandant still preferred the Springfield to either the Garand or the Johnson. Holcomb seemed to ignore the benefits of increased firepower. Although stubborn resistance to adopting newer semiautomatic rifles delayed the procurement process, the Corps eventually followed the Army's lead and accepted the Garand as its standard-issue rifle in 1941. It would be early 1943 before the new weapons became available in large quantities. Marines in combat came to respect them as easily maintained, rugged weapons with firepower superior to that of the Japanese bolt-action service rifles.[140]

COUNTDOWN TO PEARL HARBOR

By autumn 1941, Thomas Holcomb had struggled for nearly five years to expand the Marine Corps for an oncoming conflict. His fitness report for the period between April 1 and September 30 testified to his efforts, because Navy Secretary Franklin Knox affirmed Holcomb as a "splendid organizer and administrator."[141] The growth in the Corps' manpower during 1941 represented an especially significant step forward. The Marines moved closer to creating viable amphibious forces as doctrinal principles found their way into practice during training exercises. Yet every time Holcomb made gains, still more chronic shortages of updated weapons, equipment, and trained personnel plagued the Corps. To the great credit of many Marines, morale remained high even among those stationed on far-flung islands in the Pacific. Such positive attitudes started at the top with Holcomb, and flowed downward and outward.[142]

The years of his labors took their toll on the exhausted commandant. "I am now the oldest man in the Department among the officers at least," confessed Holcomb to his friend retired Admiral William D. Leahy, in late August, "and sometimes feel as if I would like to step aside and let a younger man take my place." Holcomb did not retire because of his sense of duty and, as he explained, "I have a grand crowd here with me including Charlie Barrett and they manage to keep me on the track most of the time."[143] Along with Barrett, Holcomb's inner circle of advisers included several exceptional officers: Alexander Vandegrift as assistant to the commandant; Robert Denig as director of the Division of Public Relations; Emile Moses as chairman of the Marine Corps Equipment Board; and Seth Williams as quartermaster.

While his "grand crowd" minded the store at HQMC, Holcomb found some relief from the stresses as commandant by relaxing with his family at Rose Croft. "I think it is the loveliest location I have ever seen, standing as it does on the point between St. Mary's [River] and St. Indigoes [Creek]," remarked Holcomb. "We thought it well to own some land and a home. We expect to spend our leaves and weekends there as much as possible until my retirement and then go there to live."[144] The commandant relished the days he could spare to stay in the rambling farmhouse, sail on the Chesapeake, and pursue his passion for photography. Beatrice spent her time on the farm convalescing, looking after the house, and canning vegetables for the winter.[145] Other Marines appreciated what the brief respites at Rose Croft meant to the Holcombs. "The house is comfortable and the ground beautiful," observed Vandegrift. "They seem to be enjoying themselves immensely and as it is close enough to Washington for weekends I feel it will do them both a tremendous amount of good."[146]

Opportunities for restfulness would become all the more rare and precious, because relations between the United States and Japan deteriorated precipitously in the final weeks of 1941. President Roosevelt attempted to deter Japanese expansion into resource-rich Southeast Asia with economic pressure and military intimidation. He hoped that Japan might negotiate some settlement of differences with the United States regarding China and Southeast Asia. But nothing worked, and both sides grew more intractable in their stances.[147]

On November 3, Admiral Isoroku Yamamoto, commander in chief of the Japanese Combined Fleet, approved a plan for a massive air attack on the U.S. Pacific Fleet based at Pearl Harbor. He believed this preemptive strategy represented the only chance to cripple American naval capabilities. Yamamoto knew all too well from his visits to the United States that Japan could not stand a lengthy war of attrition with a nation so rich in industrial potential. The attack would be one of several coordinated strikes against American, British, and Dutch territories across the Pacific Ocean. Yamamoto's new "bite-and-hold" approach thus replaced Japan's long-standing "wait-and-react" strategy.[148]

Meanwhile, Secretary of State Cordell Hull issued a series of demands to the Japanese government on November 26. The "Hull Note" proposed that Japan agree to a *status quo ante bellum* on the Asian mainland that turned the clock back to before the Manchurian Incident in 1931. Japanese acquiescence would be tantamount to surrendering all territorial gains over the last decade. But the Hull Note had the effect of quickening Japanese intentions to strike the United States first.[149] That same day of November 26, 1941, a massive naval strike force departed in secret from Japan and began its long voyage to an attack position north of Hawaii.

One day later, CNO Harold Stark warned Admiral Husband Kimmel at Pearl Harbor and Admiral Thomas C. Hart, commander in chief of the U.S. Asiatic Fleet on station in the Philippines, that hostilities could break out at any time. Similar warnings went out to island commanders in the Pacific. Stark ordered his subordinates to make preparations to initiate the defensive components of Rainbow War Plan 5. Then the Japanese government fatefully decided to make war on the United States, Great Britain, and the Netherlands on the first of December. Less than a week later, the Japanese ambassador to the United States, Kichisaburō Nomura, was directed by his superiors in Tokyo to deliver a memorandum to Secretary Hull on December 7, 1941, that stated Japan was terminating negotiations. Although it was not a declaration of war, Nomura's memorandum made conflict a fait accompli.[150]

Throughout November and the first week of December, Holcomb was unaware of some details, but his tasks were nevertheless straightforward. Could he move enough men, weapons, ammunition, and equipment to Pacific outposts before hostilities erupted? Could he make up for lost time after waiting so long to establish bases of operations? The answers to both questions were the same: No.

The process of moving Marine units from one place to another resembled a global shell game. The 4th Marine Regiment in Shanghai evacuated to Manila in the Philippines by November's end. Back in the United States, as soon as recruits could be trained and materiel procured, the men and equipment were rushed into the divisions or defense battalions for deployment to the Pacific. Fully manned defense battalions, for example, were split into halves to form the foundations for two new units. As soon as defense battalions could be shifted from the West Coast to Hawaii, the personnel and equipment already there were relocated to advanced island bases on Wake, Midway, Palmyra, Johnston, or Guam in the Pacific. Elements of the 1st Defense Battalion were scattered on four different islands.[151]

Admiral Kimmel worked tirelessly, but only with partial success, to garrison fully those bases. Beyond procurement problems facing Holcomb and Kimmel, some blame for the plodding movements of Marine units rested on Admiral Claude C. Bloch, commandant of the 14th Naval District at Pearl Harbor. Although he managed one of the most complex districts in the Navy, incorporating Hawaii and outlying Pacific island bases, Bloch was slow in expediting transfers of Marines, ammunition, and equipment requested by Kimmel. Resentment apparently fueled Bloch's foot-dragging, because Kimmel had leapfrogged him to take charge of the Pacific Fleet. Not only was Bloch senior to Kimmel, but the former had been commander in chief of the entire U.S. Fleet in the late 1930s.[152]

Because Wake Island would become a primary target for Japanese attack, it can be used as a case study in America's last-minute prewar preparations. Construction of defensive fortifications had just started in the summer of 1941. By December, additional reinforcements brought the 1st Defense Battalion on Wake to a total strength of 388 Marines and Navy medics—still less than half the allotted personnel of a full-strength defense battalion. The Marines could not man all the artillery batteries on the island, and those they did operate were handled by under-strength gun crews. They did not yet possess the promised early-warning radar. One of the few encouraging developments occurred on December 4, just three days before war broke out. A dozen Grumman F4F-3 Wildcat fighters arrived on Wake and gave the advanced base a modicum of air power. The same day, Marines unloaded a large cache of ammunition, including 10,000 artillery shells, 1,245,200 machine-gun rounds, and 599 bombs and depth charges. These would help the otherwise short-handed and outgunned Wake Marines put up a stubborn fight when called upon to do so a few days later.[153]

Meanwhile, Japan and the United States jockeyed for position during the first week of December.[154] Saturday, December 6, 1941, dawned cold in Washington and grew colder all day. Commandant Holcomb remained in the nation's capital for the weekend.[155] He may have worked several hours that day in his office at Headquarters Marine Corps. He did not, however, expect to work on Sunday because, as he later confided to General George C. Marshall, "I never work on Sunday unless there is a real emergency. What I cannot accomplish during regular working hours has got to be done by my staff who probably do it much better."[156] There was more than work that kept Holcomb from relaxing at Rose Croft during that final day of peace. Beatrice was slowly recuperating from another surgery in November, and she could not travel easily or far. When in Washington, Holcomb preferred to spend quiet evenings with her at the commandant's residence. They attended dinner parties or official functions only when necessary. Although evidence is unavailable, the Holcombs probably dined together at home on Saturday, December 6, before retiring about 9:30 PM, as they usually did.[157]

Although suspicious of Japan's recent movements, other key American leaders did not anticipate the next day's tragedy. President Roosevelt conferred with advisers about the situation in the Far East and entertained guests at the White House until almost midnight. CNO Stark attended a play with his wife and some close friends. That evening, Roosevelt and Stark spoke on the phone briefly but inconclusively about Japan's aggressive behavior. Only Admiral Kimmel out at Pearl Harbor showed any real concern on Saturday. He worried about Japanese expansion into Southeast Asia. He did not, however, act on his feelings and sortie his warships. Doing so would have caused an uproar among servicemen and civilians alike in Hawaii, and Kimmel lacked the carrier-based air cover to patrol for Japanese submarines. He instead attended a dinner party but called it an early night, because he looked forward to playing golf the next morning with Lieutenant General Walter C. Short, his friend and the commanding officer of the U.S. Army's Hawaiian Department.[158]

Just 220 miles north of Hawaii in the morning darkness of December 7, six Japanese aircraft carriers made final preparations to launch an attack against the American warships and shore installations at Pearl Harbor on Oahu. These ships had spent the previous ten days running silently across the rarely traveled Northern Pacific Ocean. The carriers turned east into a strong wind at 5:50 AM Hawaiian time. In the next twenty minutes, 183 Japanese planes lifted off their decks and flew south toward the unsuspecting Americans. A second wave of another 200 aircraft followed them an hour later.

Between September 1939 and December 1941, the Marine Corps had made great strides toward preparedness under Commandant Thomas Holcomb's able direction. Manpower levels increased significantly, as did the procurement of new weapons and better equipment. The Marines moved closer to creating viable amphibious forces as doctrinal principles slowly found their way into practice during training exercises. More and better publicity and recruitment activities set the stage for the Corps' exponential expansion in 1942. The service's place in American strategy remained secure, because no one could doubt its potential contributions to naval operations in a future conflict with Japan. Nevertheless, this race for preparedness would not be won no matter how hard Holcomb and others tried. Onrushing events of December 1941 would do for Holcomb and the Corps what they could not have completely achieved on their own.

CHAPTER 4

MARINE MOBILIZATION
IN THE
FIRST SEVEN MONTHS OF WAR

December 1941–June 1942

Thousands of unsuspecting sailors, soldiers, and Marines awoke on what should have been a routine Sunday morning at Pearl Harbor on December 7, 1941. Then Japanese bombs started dropping and torpedoes splashing at 7:55 AM. The noise of war disrupted the serene setting as general quarters sounded, air raid sirens whined, explosions erupted, and pandemonium ensued. Minutes later a desperate call went out over the airwaves in unencoded English: "Air raid, Pearl Harbor. This is no drill." Nearly 400 Japanese airplanes spent the next two hours wrecking American military installations on Oahu and sinking warships moored in the harbor. They left the Pacific Fleet and Army and Marine Corps forces in shambles.[1]

Five time zones away on a wintry Sunday in Washington, D.C., the telephone rang about 1:40 PM in President Franklin D. Roosevelt's office. Secretary of the Navy Franklin Knox told Roosevelt that Japanese aircraft had just attacked Pearl Harbor. A few minutes later, CNO Harold R. Stark reported to Roosevelt that the fleet had suffered serious damage and many American lives had been lost. Although shaken by the tragic news, the man who struggled with polio and paralysis and who had led the United States during the Great Depression now would energize the nation in war. He immediately met with his closest advisers to discuss the situation in Hawaii. Later Sunday evening, Roosevelt drafted a war message he would deliver to Congress and the nation the following day.[2]

Commandant Thomas Holcomb also learned about the Japanese attack early Sunday afternoon and drove to HQMC in the Navy Annex. Marines occupied only one section of this large converted warehouse overlooking Arlington National Cemetery. The remaining sections housed the leadership of the Navy Department, including the Secretary of the Navy and the Chief of Naval Operations. Holcomb entered the Navy Annex at the same time as many other Marines hurriedly returned from a luncheon with their wives. An announcement of the attack had come over the radio while those men ate, and most had frozen in place and listened in stunned disbelief.[3] By late afternoon, the Navy Annex was abuzz with activity as sailors and Marines scurried from one office to another. According to one officer, the scene resembled "an ant hill with the top kicked off."[4]

When asked decades afterward if Holcomb was a "steady rock in the storm of confusion" on that fateful Sunday, his aide-de-camp, Major Austin R. Brunelli, answered unequivocally, "He certainly was, yes."[5] Another Marine, Colonel William W. Rogers, recounted how the commandant ordered the Corps' Division of Plans and Policies "to break out the war plans and see what we were supposed to put into effect. So we put the Rainbow War Plan into effect and notified everybody in code to go ahead with the war."[6] By late Sunday afternoon, Holcomb had walked down the hallway to the Secretary of the Navy's office for a high-level conference with Knox and his staff. Barred from the meeting, Holcomb's aides milled around outside that office, wondering what had actually happened at Pearl Harbor and what would happen next.[7]

Throughout Sunday night and into the next morning, distressing reports kept rolling in. The Japanese had launched coordinated attacks against American forces stationed across the Pacific Ocean. Japanese bombers took the Marines on Wake Island by surprise and destroyed most of their fighter aircraft on the ground. American advanced bases on Guam, Midway, Johnston, and Palmyra endured naval and aerial bombardments. Japanese bombers successfully annihilated most of General Douglas MacArthur's Far East Air Force on the ground in the Philippines. Back in Hawaii, rumors ran wild that Japanese troops had landed on Oahu or that saboteurs had poisoned the island's water supply. Fear and paranoia reigned at Pearl Harbor. Americans fully expected another air strike, but a second Japanese attack never came.[8]

A little after noon on Monday, President Roosevelt addressed Congress and the entire nation with these stirring words, "Yesterday, December 7, 1941—a date that will live in infamy—the United States was suddenly and deliberately attacked by naval and air forces of the Empire of Japan." He laid out an argument for Japan's treachery and united the nation. Roosevelt concluded his speech by asking Congress for a declaration of war.[9] This he received within the hour. With the exception of one dissenter, even the staunchest isolationist senators and representatives voted for war.

The first days of the United States' involvement in the Second World War brought little hope to the nation. Defeat followed defeat. American units still in China surrendered. Guam fell without a fight on December 10. Within a week, Japanese troops landed in the Philippines to begin their conquest of that archipelago. Then, quite unexpectedly, several hundred outgunned Marines of the 1st Defense Battalion on Wake Island raised the nation's morale with their stubborn resistance against Japanese attacks on that tiny atoll. Commandant Holcomb's report to Secretary Knox on December 11 caught the mood of the moment:

A cheery note comes from Wake and the news is particularly pleasing at a time like this. The island with its small garrison was attacked four times by enemy bombers and nine of the twelve Marine fighting planes were lost. Then, they were attacked at dawn yesterday by several enemy light vessels. In spite of materiel and personnel losses which they had suffered and, as I said, with only three fighting planes remaining, they were able to report sinking one enemy light cruiser and one enemy destroyer. Enemy transports with cruiser and destroyer escort were sighted in the vicinity and unquestionably a landing will be attempted. However, Wake, with its weakened forces is still resisting and the general tone of the dispatch indicates the sort of determination to do their job which we like see.[10]

In actuality, the Wake Marines sank two Japanese destroyers and damaged several other enemy vessels. Victory, albeit a momentary one, was theirs.[11]

The Navy Department released to the press a slightly redacted version of Holcomb's report, which in turn helped focus attention on the Marines' courageous stand against overwhelming odds. During a press conference on December 12, President Roosevelt likewise praised them for "holding out" and doing "a perfectly magnificent job."[12] Suddenly the Wake Marines dominated the news wires with their heroic actions. Headlines read "Marines Keep Wake." The nation's confidence and resolve soared to renewed heights. Americans, who previously had not known that Wake existed, now anxiously awaited more reports from the island. Holcomb made use of that coverage to bolster national will to fight and, of course, to increase the Corps' visibility and boost recruitment. More men chose to enter the service in three weeks of December than in the entire six months before the attack on Pearl Harbor.[13]

Admiral Husband E. Kimmel, commanding what remained of the Pacific Fleet at Pearl Harbor, wanted to help the beleaguered Marines on Wake. On December 15, he launched a relief expedition consisting of air and ground reinforcements. Kimmel next received word from Roosevelt that he would be relieved of command two days later. His temporary successor, Vice Admiral William S. Pye, questioned the viability of the Wake relief operation but allowed it to proceed.[14]

Then a second, more determined Japanese invasion force made an amphibious assault against the Marines on Wake on December 23. Bitter fighting raged all that morning on the island. A message sent early that morning from Wake to Pearl Harbor summarized their situation with brutal honesty: "Enemy on Island Issue in Doubt." This report was enough for the hesitant Admiral Pye, who canceled the relief effort and ordered those forces back to Pearl Harbor. He did not wish to risk losing more of his battered fleet or especially his precious aircraft carriers, and no help reached Wake. Prudent or not, Pye's decision drew criticism from Thomas Holcomb and other Marines of all ranks.[15]

One of the strongest indictments came from someone very close to Pye at Pacific Fleet Headquarters. "I call this the blackest day in the history of the U.S. Navy," lamented Colonel Pfeiffer. "The only excuse I ever heard given by Admiral Pye was that we could not afford further losses at this time after the losses we had suffered at Pearl Harbor. That was a decidedly negative and defeatist view. . . . At least, we could have kept the faith with our pitifully inadequate forces on Wake, to whom we had promised aid in case of need."[16]

Wake's valiant Marines fought for several hours on December 23, but to no avail because the Japanese were too resourceful and determined. Word of their surrender on that same day filtered back to the United States. Far from causing discouragement, Americans found hope that a few hundred Marines could have held off the Japanese forces for so long.[17] Holcomb and the Corps culled many benefits from the heroic defense of Wake in the months ahead. A new rallying cry went up: "Remember Wake!"[18]

Despite defeats and disappointments, no hint of frantic desperation can be found in Holcomb's correspondence in the days and weeks after Pearl Harbor and Wake Island. Urgency yes, but not frantic desperation. Holcomb showed his mettle; even the most discouraging news had no visible effect on him. The commandant knew that the public example of his own behavior would help to steel the resolve of his Marines. Around close friends and staff at HQMC, Holcomb also maintained his composure, sitting quietly at his desk in the Navy Annex, making hard decisions about the war effort, and puffing on one of his favorite pipes.[19] Throughout the early weeks of the conflict, he drew upon what political scientist Fred I. Greenstein calls "emotional intelligence."[20] The commandant controlled his emotions and refocused his energies toward preparing his Corps to fulfill its dual mission of base defense and amphibious assault.

In addition to Holcomb's affirmative public statements, his personal correspondence contained quiet assurances of success. He had seen combat at its most horrific in the First World War, and he knew the resilience and spirit of the American troops. One example illustrates his state of mind. On December 27, 1941, Holcomb read an article titled "Alone, Unaided, and Unrelieved" in the *Washington Post*. That same day he wrote its author to "take exception" to "the note of discouragement" in the article. "I deplore the fact that you envisaged the loss to the enemy of our position at Midway. It seems to me that writers in this country must do everything in their power to discourage a spirit of defeatism," scolded Holcomb.

Perhaps your thought is that the people should be prepared for the worst in order that the reputation of the defenders might not be sullied if over-powering force defeats them. If such is your thought, it was I am sure prompted by kindly motives but permit me to say that Marines expect no one to apologize for them and I am sure that this applies equally well to our sister services, the Army and the Navy.

I know that the Marines on Midway are not sorry for themselves; that they are not anticipating defeat; that they have resolved that Midway shall not be taken.

Closing his letter, Holcomb scribbled in his own hand that "with God's help, and with the confidence of their countrymen, they will succeed."[21] The commandant's words could have been applied to Marines stationed anywhere in the Pacific.

Brigadier General Alexander A. Vandegrift, recently assigned as assistant commander of the 1st Marine Division, shared Holcomb's growing confidence as the initial shock wore off. He spoke for many Marines when he said: "To us the real meaning of Pearl Harbor lay in the psychological transformation of our troops and those recruits who joined us by the thousands. From this time, no one held the slightest doubt that we would ship out, fight and win. Lethargy vanished, never returned."[22] Holcomb, Vandegrift, and other Marines recognized that they needed to redirect their energies toward planning and preparing for the coming operations in the Second World War, rather than pining away about past defeats and mistakes. This statement was as relevant for the Marine Corps as it was for the Army and Navy.

While the dramatic events played out in December 1941, members of the Joint Board of the U.S. Army and Navy met to discuss the nation's options. Their prewar plans had never anticipated so many successful Japanese attacks across the Pacific.[23] They held their first conference at 2:45 PM on Monday, December 8, barely two hours after Roosevelt's speech ended. Among those attending were CNO Stark, Chief of Staff Marshall, and their respective deputies and war plans directors. An excerpt from the minutes encapsulates the nation's grim situation in Hawaii, in the Philippines, and on the West Coast: "Navy members announced that in view of the losses in the Hawaiian battle, the Navy would not be unable to carry out the tasks assigned in the existing war plan."[24] Its members concluded that a defensive posture represented United States' best option.

The Joint Board met five more times over the next two long weeks and decided that the country would establish a defensive perimeter running west from the Panama Canal to Hawaii and then north from Hawaii to the Alaskan coast. American naval forces would also protect sea lanes between the United States and Australia. Pearl Harbor remained the linchpin for this defensive posture and the springboard for any offensive operations in the very distant future. Meanwhile, the Joint Board ordered that reinforcements, including Marine Corps air and ground units, be rushed to the Pacific as soon as possible, because the strategic situation called for containment of Japanese expansion and consolidation of American forces in the Eastern Pacific. This situation looked more like the unilateral defense of the Western Hemisphere outlined in Rainbow War Plan 4 than the robust strategic defense of the Central Pacific envisioned by Rainbow 5.[25]

By late December 1941, Commandant Holcomb assumed a more prominent place in the decision-making and strategy-formulating processes. He received word that Congress would authorize his permanent promotion to lieutenant general, a higher rank commensurate with the rapidly expanding size of the Corps and with his growing responsibilities as its commandant. He would be the first Marine in history to wear a third star. Meanwhile, the service quickly surpassed its largest First World War manpower levels, and there seemed to be no upper limits to the manpower requirements the Corps might soon need to meet.[26]

Other American flag officers assumed new positions during December 1941. Admiral Chester W. Nimitz replaced Pye as CINCPAC at Pearl Harbor. Back in Washington, President Roosevelt elevated Admiral Ernest J. King from his previous assignment as commander in chief of the Atlantic Fleet to the newly created position of commander in chief of the U.S. Fleet, CINCUS for short. This was quickly changed to COMINCH because the original version sounded too much like "sink us." This new post made King a potential competitor to Admiral Harold Stark, the titular head of the Navy as CNO.

Stark avoided conflict with King by stepping aside in early 1942, when he left for London for his new assignment as commander of U.S. Naval Forces in Europe. Roosevelt then named Admiral King as the new CNO on March 7, 1942, in addition to his position as COMINCH. This dual-hatted appointment made King one of the most powerful admirals in American history, because he exercised both strategic command of the fleets at sea and administrative control of the Navy's bureaucratic structure. He spent the war in the nation's capital serving on the Joint Board and subsequently on the Joint Chiefs of Staff.[27]

Holcomb worked closely and effectively with King for the remainder of his commandancy. He went to King's office to attend daily conferences on important strategic, logistical, procurement, and manpower issues. Holcomb did not, however, enjoy the close friendship with King that he had maintained with Stark.[28] Others noticed animosity between King and Holcomb. According to one of Holcomb's aides-de-camp, Major Frederick Roy, the commandant's personal relationship with the COMINCH-CNO was "not what I would call overly cordial." Roy explained that "if the telephone would ring in our office and I would answer it, they'd say, 'This is Admiral King's office. He would like to speak with General Holcomb.' I'd go in and say, 'General, Admiral King's office is on the line. The Admiral wants to speak with you.' I could hear him mumbling under his breath, 'What the - - - - does he want?' So I knew that there was no great love between them."[29]

They clashed because their temperaments were so dissimilar. Holcomb remained calm regardless of the situation. He cultivated goodwill and confidence in people, whether they were his subordinates, other senior military officers, or members of Congress. He accomplished many of his goals by cooperating with those contacts.[30] But King's temperament was markedly different. He exuded neither charm nor goodwill. What respect he instilled in others was founded not on admiration but fear and intimidation. King was, according to historian David M. Kennedy, "a gruff man" whose "choleric manner masked an incisive strategic intelligence, possessed of qualities that perfectly fitted him for senior command." Kennedy goes on to list King's traits: "the ability to anticipate, the capacity for penetrating analysis of his adversary's predicaments, an unerring grasp of the reach and limits of his own forces, and a pit bull's determination to seize the initiative and attack, attack, and attack."[31] It is, therefore, not hard to see why retired general Gerald C. Thomas claimed that Holcomb "hated" King, yet Gerald Thomas also averred the Commandant and the COMINCH-CNO respected each other's ability and judgment and thus "got along" for the higher purpose of winning the war. In any event, King certainly recognized the Corps' integral operational contributions to his strategic plans.[32]

Evidence of Holcomb's newfound importance could be seen even before his promotion to lieutenant general became official on January 23, 1942. The commandant joined King, Stark, President Roosevelt, Secretary Knox, and Army Chief of Staff George C. Marshall on the American delegation that in late December 1941 attended the Arcadia Conference. "That's the first one of these really high-level ones that [Holcomb] was invited to participate in," declared his aide-de-camp Austin Brunelli.[33] Arcadia resembled the prewar ABC-1 Talks in early 1941. British and American military and naval staffs discussed joint plans at sessions held almost every day. They felt compelled to adopt a hold-and-build strategy in the Pacific in which the Navy and Marine Corps would defend a perimeter running from Alaska to Hawaii and on to the Panama Canal. Holcomb offered expert advice on amphibious operations that might be undertaken in the Pacific.[34]

Although Alexander Vandegrift did not attend the conference, he fully grasped its ramifications for the Marine Corps. "Our task now became holding what we could with no thought of immediate offensive action," observed Vandegrift. "Arcadia confirmed the earlier strategy of keeping Europe the primary theater, but it also gave the United States primary responsibility for the Pacific theater."[35] Marines would play significant roles, not only in defending far-flung Pacific island bases like Midway, Samoa, and New Caledonia, but also in preparing for amphibious assaults in the Marshall and Solomon Island chains, both operations for which the Marine Corps had been preparing for several decades.[36]

The months that followed the adjournment of the Arcadia Conference in January 1942 saw Japanese forces continue to ride a wave of victories. They occupied Bougainville and in January captured Rabaul on the island of New Britain. They slowly squeezed American forces in the Philippines into surrender. And during April and early May, Japanese troops landed on Guadalcanal and started to cut a landing strip out of the jungle. Transliterated as *Gadarukanaru* in Japanese and translated as "cactus" in English, this island rested at the southeastern end of the Solomons chain. Suddenly Guadalcanal began to draw the attention of Americans.[37] The longer that COMINCH-CNO King watched these events, the more he grew impatient with the Navy's defensive posture. On March 2, 1942, he called for a new strategic plan that would allow American forces "not only to protect the line of communications with Australia, but, in so doing, set up 'strong' points from which a step-by-step general advance can be made through the New Hebrides, Solomons, the Bismarck Archipelago. It is to be expected that such a step-by-step general advance will draw Japanese forces to oppose it, thus relieving pressure in other parts of the Pacific—and that the operation will of itself be good cover for the communications lines with Australia."[38] King herein sketched an island-hopping strategy that American forces would follow for the next two years. Guadalcanal would be the starting point.

Replacing the old Joint Board, the newly formed Joint Chiefs of Staff (JCS) met on March 14 and approved King's proposal. In this scheme, the Pacific Fleet could conduct limited offensive operations against Japanese naval forces and island bases. The Navy's War Plans Division, under Rear Admiral Richmond Kelly Turner, inserted four stages into King's strategic framework. The first entailed assembling and training the necessary forces in the Southwestern Pacific to defend American bases and prepare for future offensive operations. In the second stage, presumably starting in early 1943, American and Allied forces would fight their way northwest through the Solomons and along the coast of New Guinea. The latter two stages would take place later in 1943 or thereafter, in campaigns in the Central Pacific and the Philippines, respectively. King and Turner fully expected to employ Marine defense battalions to safeguard newly American island bases in all four stages, and to use Marine divisions to conduct amphibious assaults in the latter three stages.[39]

King's own experiences during the JTF-1 exercises in August 1941 gave him confidence in the Marines' ability to fulfill both responsibilities. The Marine Corps thus remained an integral part of the Navy's new Pacific strategy, just as it had been during the prewar years. The Corps' central role in operations also guaranteed that Holcomb would be relevant in the high-level decision-making process in Washington.

The first American counterattacks would be launched from New Zealand under Nimitz's overall control, and with his subordinate Vice Admiral Robert L. Ghormley exercising operational command of naval and Marine forces in the area. He brought vast sea and shore experience to his new post, including stints as director of the Navy's War Plans Division and head of the American delegation to the ABC-1 Talks in 1941. More recently he had returned from duty as special naval observer in London. Ghormley departed for his new headquarters in Auckland, New Zealand, in early May 1942, arriving at the end of the month. Rear Admiral Richmond Kelly Turner joined Ghormley's staff in June and assumed command of all amphibious forces. Like his superior, Turner's naval career had been impressive. He had served as director of the War Plans Division in 1940 and then chief

▲ The plan for an American counterattack beginning on Guadalcanal was laid in spring 1942.

(Map by Michael J. Hradesky)

of staff to Ernest King during the first months after Pearl Harbor. The always-assertive Turner clashed first with Ghormley and later with Vandegrift, who was now promoted to major general and named to command the 1st Marine Division.[40]

During Ghormley's month-long junket from Washington to New Zealand in May 1942, momentous events transpired. The U.S. Pacific Fleet scored strategic victories against the Japanese Combined Fleet at the Battle of the Coral Sea in early May, and again at the Battle of Midway in early June.[41] These two actions halted the enemy's heretofore uninterrupted expansion into the Southwestern and Central Pacific, respectively. For Japanese historian Saburō Ienaga, Midway constituted a "catastrophic" defeat. "Japan's offensive capability was blunted," wrote Ienaga. "The Allied counteroffensive was under way far faster than anticipated."[42] American forces could now switch from defending the Eastern Pacific and initiate limited offensive amphibious, air, and naval operations to capture the Solomon Islands. During June and July 1942, King's strategic plan from earlier in March evolved into Operation Watchtower, the code name given to the American conquest of the Solomons and subsequently Rabaul on New Britain.[43]

Back in Washington, the need to balance American manpower and materiel between the Pacific and European theaters caused much anxiety for Commandant Holcomb and his staff. Allocating resources to launch Operation Watchtower in the summer of 1942 needed to be reconciled with assigning resources to Operation Bolero, the Allies' presumed cross-channel assault against German-occupied France. Following much debate, the JCS struck a compromise in early July. Bolero lost its strategic urgency when the JCS scrapped the cross-channel strike in favor of a smaller, more practicable invasion of North Africa later in 1942. This compromise allowed additional American troops and resources to be sent to the Pacific. It also dictated that Commandant Holcomb expand the Corps as quickly as possible to fulfill its wartime responsibilities.[44]

HOLCOMB MOBILIZES THE MARINES: PROGRESS YET PREJUDICE

Dissension among Americans over their country's possible involvement in the war had evaporated after the attack on Pearl Harbor. The groundswell of nationalism could be felt in every region of the nation and all segments of society. Isolationist groups either disbanded or shifted their support to winning the war.[45] On the evening of December 7, the America First Committee's national headquarters issued a formal statement urging "all those who have subscribed to its principles to give their support to the war effort of this country until the conflict with Japan is brought to a successful conclusion."[46]

As a result of Pearl Harbor, Commandant Holcomb now experienced no difficulties in acquiring funds. By January 1942, he summarized his relations with

Congress in a half-serious, half-humorous way: "We were before the [Senate] Appropriations Sub-committee day before yesterday and it was a love fest. I considered asking for a personal grant for my living expenses of a million dollars but eventually decided not to do so. I might have gotten it."[47] Four years of cultivating good relations were now paying the greatest dividends. In fact, key congressional leaders such as Representative Carl Vinson, still the powerful chairman of the House Naval Affairs Committee, sought out Holcomb to determine what additional resources the Corps might need. Just days after the United States entered the conflict, Vinson asked Holcomb if he wanted an emergency authorization raising the Corps from its strength of 51,000 to 200,000 Marines.

Holcomb declined Vinson's offer because he wished to maintain the Corps' statutory one-fifth manpower ratio with the Navy and, more important, he needed time to put additional recruits through basic and advanced training. Instead, the commandant requested a somewhat more manageable increase to 150,000 Marines. This early in the conflict, the Corps' training facilities could hardly accommodate so many new recruits. Besides, Holcomb expected that the service would expand to 220,000 in another year's time.[48]

One hearing before the House Committee on Appropriations in May 1942 demonstrated the trust between Congress and Holcomb. In what may have been a deferential tone, Representative Clarence Cannon, Democrat from Tennessee and the committee chairman, asked: "Of course it is too much to ask that you be able to meet all your objectives, but to what extent are you keeping up with the schedule?" Holcomb replied in his usual candid manner that "so far as equipment and procurement go, practically everything which the Marine Corps procures under its own appropriations is coming along all right. In the matter of material which we do not have to procure directly, that is, ordnance, ammunition, and that sort of thing, which are procured through other agencies, there are still serious shortages, as everyone knows."[49] Herein the commandant alluded to the Corps' awkward relations with the Army and the Navy, as well as its competition with them for the nation's limited industrial resources.

Despite problems caused by interservice rivalries, dollars flowed easily from congressional coffers. The Marine Corps received more than $155 million in supplemental funding in January 1942, for the remaining six months of FY 1942. This figure amounted to 60 percent of the Corps' expenditures of $242 million for the entire fiscal year. The appropriation and its various supplements for FY 1943 totaled $493 million. Contrasting these figures with the Corps' expenditures in the earlier years of Holcomb's commandancy revealed the extent of the wartime windfall: $23 million in FY 1938, $24 million in 1939, $33 million in 1940, and $67 million in 1941. This exponential influx notwithstanding, the Corps' expenditures represented a miniscule fraction of the Navy's entire expenditures of $8 billion for FY 1942 and $20 billion for 1943.[50]

In addition to benefiting from good relations with Congress, Holcomb and the Corps remained popular with the American people. As Marine first lieutenant George W. Killen recalled, Holcomb "was aware of the favorable public image of the Marine Corps and adroitly exploited it."[51] The commandant actively participated in the public relations process. On one occasion, he granted to a *Family Circle* journalist a twenty-minute interview that formed the basis for an article on the Marine Corps that reached some 2 million readers.[52]

Holcomb could not devote too much of his own time to public relations while still fulfilling his countless other responsibilities as commandant. Progressive manager that he was, he handed over the daily coordination of all the Corps' publicity activities and recruiting efforts to Brigadier General Robert L. Denig Sr. and the Division of Public Relations. Denig and his small staff corresponded with sponsors, reporters, producers, and writers regarding the content of news articles, radio broadcasts, newsreels, and commercial advertisements. In the war's early stages, the Division of Public Relations contained very few officers, but all boasted substantial experience in the media and marketing as civilians. Captain William P. McHill, for instance, held a degree in journalism and had worked previously for the Associated Press. Several enlisted Marines and civilian clerks rounded out Denig's tiny cadre. Experienced photographers, cameramen, and correspondents joined his division over time. They entered the Corps as reserve sergeants, or sometimes Denig's subordinates plucked promising recruits from basic training. Even at its largest in 1945, only 256 Marines served in the Division of Public Relations, yet the level of their output far exceeded their small numbers. Their dedication made up for their small numbers, and the use of such experts represented yet another exhibition of progressivism in Corps.[53]

At Holcomb's specific suggestion, Denig established several wartime policies regarding publicity that the Corps could accept. Marines could appear in advertisements for non-military products as long as two criteria were observed: "The individual concerned is not identified," and the Marine should not "become involved in undesirable publicity."[54] Denig added additional provisions governing the use of images of Marines. The advertisements must be factual, but the advertised product could not be currently tested by the Corps. Consistent with prewar policy, textual and visual materials had to receive sanction from his division. Last and most important, none of the Corps' public representations could be contrary to its values of courage, duty, or patriotism for which leathernecks were known.[55]

The Division of Public Relations presented an astounding amount of information about the Corps in several media venues. According to statistics on Marine Corps publicity gathered by the National Association of Broadcasters, in March 1942 alone, radio stations across the United States broadcast 31,450 live spots, 1,050 fifteen-minute scripts, and 1,160 fifteen-minute transcriptions. In a report updating Holcomb on the division's efforts, Denig added two important comments regarding these figures. First, the Corps' programming "is being accepted to an extent equal with and in some respects more than that of the Army and the Navy." Second, the number of live spots, scripts, and transcripts had increased "almost 1000%" over radio broadcasts back in August 1941.[56]

The Corps' publicity efforts achieved high quality as well as great quantity. Denig actively pursued the "type of advertising calculated to have an inspirational effect upon American men."[57] The service's claim of providing a legitimate means for American boys to achieve manhood remained a primary method of attracting recruits. Intricately linked with this selling point were appeals to patriotism. A literal conversion of boys into men occurred during basic training, where skinny, uncoordinated enlistees gained height and weight and increased their strength and stamina. They also underwent mental and emotional transformations as Marine drill instructors broke down their civilian values and inculcated in them the Corps' ideals of toughness and selflessness. Enlistees learned to obey orders without question, and the discipline instilled in them would enable them to fight, kill, and die in combat.[58] Thus, the recruitment and training processes, according to military historian Craig M. Cameron, played central roles in the self-identification among Marines as "warrior representatives of their country, a kind of American samurai class."[59]

Nowhere can the Corps' slogans, myths, themes, and symbols be better understood than in an examination of recruitment posters.[60] Marrying the idea of storytelling to the Marines' defense of Wake Island represented an obvious subject for posters. Their bravery and sacrifice remained very much in the public's mind in 1942 and thereafter. Posters cited Franklin Roosevelt's praise for the Wake Marines beneath an ominous sea of bayonets. Other posters dealt with aspects of the Corps' contributions to the war effort. Two Marines could be seen hunting for an unseen Japanese enemy in tropical jungles with the slogans "Let's go get 'em!" and "U.S. Marines." Particularly dramatic were the recruitment posters targeting potential pilots. One depicted an American eagle ripping a Japanese airplane apart in midair with its beak and talons. The Marines' signature globe, eagle, and anchor loomed large in the background. Across the top ran the words: "Wear the 'Fighten'est' wings in the service." And along the bottom of the poster ran, "Fly with the Marines." Most also included an urgent plea to young men to "apply, or write, to the nearest recruiting station."[61]

The activities of the Division of Public Relations fit into a national publicity campaign directed by the U.S. Office of War Information, which media historian George H. Roeder Jr. heralds as the "government's primary wartime propaganda agency." It coordinated public and private organizations to create "the most systematic and far-reaching efforts" in American history and "shape the visual experience of the citizenry."[62] The influence of this agency extended from news reporting and popular print media into the motion picture industry. The Office of War Information's own Bureau of Motion Pictures worked with the armed services and movie studios to make such wartime films as Paramount's *Wake Island*, released in 1942. Its script was drafted even before the battle for the island had ended. Unlike the real Marines on Wake who faced Japanese prisoner of war camps after their surrender on December 23, 1941, the onscreen leathernecks courageously fought to the last man. The American people found this fictional ending reassuring, because in it they could take heart, rise from defeat, and win the war. Not coincidentally, *Wake Island* reinforced racial stereotypes of the Japanese as a brutal, if not inferior, enemy.[63]

Films, newsreels, posters, and other media encouraged droves of young men to try to join the Corps. A 1994 survey of veterans of the 7th Marine Defense Battalion/ Antiaircraft Artillery Battalion gives evidence about the effect on recruitment of the Corps' publicity efforts. Of the seventy-nine veterans responding to the survey, fifty-one Marines had joined the Corps after the attack on Pearl Harbor. Twenty-seven of these cited "patriotism," "flag waving," "duty," or the "war with Japan" as their motivations for enlisting. Their reasons for becoming Marines in the Second World War strikingly resemble the motivations of the Devil Dogs and Old Breed a generation earlier in the First World War. Many of the 7th also recalled feeling the need to join the service as a proof of manhood.[64] Although the passage of time and the desire to reconstruct the past in a positive way may have affected these responses, the majority of their answers indicate that the media's pro-war, pro-American blitz did play a significant role in motivating them to become Marines.

The best summary of the publicity and recruitment process comes from Craig Cameron: "The images created and disseminated by recruiters, public relations men, and correspondents, while serving the institutional needs of the Marine Corps by bolstering recruitment and individual standards, also took on a life of their own, establishing standards and expectations inside and outside of the service that affected all that followed."[65] The number of enlistments skyrocketed from 2,000 for all of November 1941 to an astounding 6,834 between December 8 and year's end. This total included 6,253 first-time enlistees. The new recruits were on average nineteen years of age and hailed from all regions of the United States.[66] The Marine Corps Reserve also experienced rapid growth, from 11,905 reservists on active duty in November 1941 to 15,306 by year's end.[67] These numbers swelled still further because married men were granted eligibility to enlist as reservists, rather than be drafted. The Marine Corps Reserve allowed this concession "to fill its ranks with desirable men."[68]

On December 31, 1941, the total strength of the Corps stood at 55,598 Marines. This figure needed to be nearly doubled to reach the Corps' newly authorized strength of 102,000 men for FY 1942, or tripled to meet the expectations for a still larger Corps of 150,000 men. Attaining the 100,000-man plateau by February 1, 1942, meant that the service should attract some 5,000 recruits every week, not including applicants rejected at some point in the process. Commandant Holcomb recognized the extreme challenge, so he issued "Letter of Instruction No. 61" on December 28, 1941, and "Letter of Instruction No. 71" on January 20, 1942. They called for processing and training recruits as well as identifying and training those with potential to become noncommissioned, warrant, or commissioned officers. Any letter of instruction emanating from the commandant's office carried the equivalent weight of an administrative or executive mandate.[69]

Even when the initial shock of Pearl Harbor subsided in subsequent months, tens of thousands of young American men continued to apply for enlistment in the Corps. The monthly average in all of 1942 stood at 14,000 enlistments, or 3,500 per week, which apparently stretched the Corps' recruitment and training processes to their limits. Because of the massive influx of applicants, Holcomb restored high recruitment standards, which had been relaxed during 1941.[70] The Marines could now afford to be highly selective in their screening process. Rejections occurred because medical examinations exposed such physical defects as "heart murmurs," "flat feet," "molar occlusion," or "defective vision." Other applicants were deemed "physically unfit" for service because they suffered from certain diseases, malnutrition, or, quite rarely, obesity.[71]

Following the physical examination, applicants received a psychiatric evaluation designed to weed out would-be Marines with deviant sexual or moral behavior patterns. They might be diagnosed with the following "abnormal" psychological problems: neurasthenia, psychasthenia, depression, instability, anxiety, psychoneurotic behavior, or sexual psychopathy.[72] The latter two were code words denoting homosexual tendencies or behaviors. What was seen as cutting edge diagnostic methods of the 1940s actually betrayed a systemic bias, the foundation of which portrayed homosexuality as a disease. In early 1942, however, few applicants received rejections because they failed to meet standards of moral and emotional stability.[73]

Yet not all Americans of the requisite patriotic zeal, physical capability, mental acuity, and moral uprightness were allowed to join the Corps. Holcomb, as an unquestioning product of the Jim Crow era, personally tried to ensure that selected minority groups would be barred from the Corps' ranks. The commandant believed these groups might lower the overall effectiveness of his service—which was composed mostly of Caucasian males. Enlistments by selected Hispanic and Native Americans represented two exceptions to the Corps' standing policy.[74]

Holcomb's efforts to maintain racial and ethnic exclusivity dated back to the summer of 1941, when President Roosevelt had established the Fair Employment Practices Committee under his Executive Order (E.O.) 8802. According to media historian George Roeder: "Balancing needs to correct and protect customary social arrangements, a persistent challenge to Americans, was given new urgency by the war. President Roosevelt, in addition to his role as commander-in-chief, served both as corrector- and protector-in-chief of American society."[75] The president charged this agency with ensuring that all Americans, regardless of color, race, creed, or nationality, be allowed to participate in national defense, whether they served in the military proper or worked for government contractors. Roosevelt believed that the national manpower crisis could be alleviated by the new employment policy, and that existing race relations could be made more equitable for African Americans and other minorities.[76] Holcomb appointed an officer to represent the Corps' interests on the new committee but otherwise opposed enlistment of non-Caucasian males into the Corps.

Although in technical violation of E.O. 8802, Marine Corps recruiters nevertheless routinely turned away men who were not white. One example of the Corps' exclusivity occurred a few days after Pearl Harbor, when seventeen-year-old Filipino American Louis C. Padillo Jr. attempted to enlist. He passed the physical examination at a recruiting station in Binghamton, New York. But when the recruiter learned that Padillo was of Filipino descent, he flatly rejected his application. Like so many Americans of that era who felt a close connection with their president, Padillo wrote directly to Roosevelt to appeal that decision. His letter of December 11, 1941, made an eloquent argument against the Corps' enlistment practices. "I cannot see why any boy who is an American citizen, and is willing to fight for his country, cannot enlist," protested Padillo. "I was also told that if I was allowed to join, a lot of Filipinos would come to this country, join some branch of military service, then ask for transportation back to the Islands. I don't see where that has anything to do with me, as I am an American citizen, and they aren't." Padillo concluded with a passionate plea to be allowed to join the Corps and fight for "this great democracy of ours."[77]

When Padillo's letter arrived at the White House, it is highly unlikely that Roosevelt read it because he received tens of thousands of letters every week from the public. He never read or answered more than a few of them. Instead, the White House's postal staff forwarded his letter to HQMC for action, as was policy. A major from the Division of Recruiting named W. E. Burke reviewed and denied Parillo's appeal on December 29 with this explanation: "It has long been the custom of the Marine Corps to accept for enlistment only men of the Caucasian race because of the limited size of the Marine Corps and the diversified duties performed by its members. To make an exception to this policy in your case is not deemed practicable. . . . We regret that a more favorable reply cannot be made."[78] Even in late 1941, people of Filipino descent still carried with them the stigma of being savage natives that Americans had subdued in 1902. Some saw them as effeminate domestic servants or dangerous criminals, both of which made Filipinos anathema to the Marines' desire to attract recruits with proper moral uprightness and masculine traits. Such unenlightened and unprogressive biases meant that Padillo, despite being an American citizen by birth and physically and mentally fit for service, could find no place in the Corps.[79]

The Corps' policy of accepting only Caucasians had not, of course, originated with someone of Major Burke's middling rank. It came from much higher in the command structure at HQMC. No evidence can be found to determine whether Thomas Holcomb read Louis Padillo's particular appeal. Nevertheless, the commandant had to have established recruiting policies based on race, ethnicity, gender, and age, such as the one Burke cited.

Along with other minority applicants, African Americans faced resistance in the Corps when they tried to enlist. In January 1942, Holcomb testified before the Navy's General Board that "there would be a definite loss of efficiency in the Marine Corps if we have to take Negroes."[80] In this case, his use of the term "efficiency" denoted progressive management principle in a rational organization. Holcomb ostensibly worried that the Marines would lose combat effectiveness if blacks, like Filipino American applicants, were permitted to join the Corps. In actuality, his testimony revealed his other fears that training and supervising African American units would sap his short supply of qualified officers and noncommissioned officers. If understood in the context of the 1940s and especially of Holcomb's progressive managerial vision for the Corps, with smooth-running structures and clearly defined functions, his objections to African American Marines were logical, albeit indefensible when examined several decades hence.

Holcomb closed his remarks to the General Board by stating that "the Negro race has every opportunity now to satisfy its aspirations for combat in the Army—a very much larger organization than the Navy or the Marine Corps—and their desire to enter the naval service is largely, I think, to break into a club that doesn't want them."[81] Holcomb thus argued African Americans would dilute the Corps' status as a small, elite organization. He likewise questioned their motivations for joining as less than honorable, because he felt they were only doing so for the sake of attaining membership in an exclusive group.[82] Taken with Major Burke's above-mentioned defense of racial selectivity in Padillo's case, Holcomb's testimony pointed to a pattern of restrictive policies in the Corps in the opening months of the Second World War.

Opposition to the inclusion of African Americans pervaded the seaborne services. Secretary of the Navy Knox and members of the Navy's General Board, for example, believed blacks should be restricted to serving as stewards in naval officers' messes, duties they were then performing.[83] Indeed, the General Board stated on February 3, 1942, that "the enlistment of negroes for unlimited general service is inadvisable. . . . The nation is now at war and the induction into the Navy of increasing numbers of negroes in the wider field of activities cannot fail to increase the difficulties of preparing for war and distract the attention of the Navy from concentrating all of its efforts toward winning a complete victory."[84] Even after blacks finally were admitted into the Corps and Navy, the General Board agreed that they should not see combat because "their value generally for field service is gravely doubted."[85] These words resembled Holcomb's assumptions that African Americans might somehow hurt efficiency.

President Roosevelt read the General Board's findings and quickly responded on February 9 with unapologetic bluntness: "This report of the General Board I regard as (a) unsatisfactory and (b) insufficient." He continued: "It is my considered opinion that there are additional tasks in the Naval establishment to which we could properly assign an additional number of enlisted men who are members of the negro race."[86] As the commander in chief, Roosevelt's "considered opinion" had to be taken as an order by the Navy and Marine Corps.[87] Roosevelt resolved the matter officially in May 1942, when he signed legislation authorizing the inclusion of African Americans in the Navy and Marine Corps. The Navy was to begin the following month recruiting 1,000 blacks each month for shore and sea duty. The decision also mandated that the Corps form a complete battalion of 900 African American Marines during the summer of 1942. While not prepared to defy the president, Knox, Holcomb, and the members of the General Board did win some small injunctions. All newly organized African American units would be segregated and led by Caucasian officers.[88]

Holcomb chafed at the new requirement. In an oral history interview in 1978, retired Lieutenant General Gerald C. Thomas makes some unflattering claims regarding the commandant's racial attitudes during the Second World War. Gerald Thomas recalled that the usually calm Holcomb lashed out at COMINCH-CNO Ernest King after hearing that "negroes" would be forced on the Corps. Purportedly Holcomb grunted at King, "I would form a black guard and put it right on your battleship."[89] This statement probably said as much about Holcomb's dislike for King as it revealed about the commandant's attitudes about race. But despite his aversion to black Marines and his dislike for King, Holcomb's personal feelings were immaterial, because the commandant recognized that President Roosevelt expected him to make their addition as successful as possible during the coming months.[90]

That race-based discrimination figured so prevalently in the Marine Corps in 1942 and thereafter should come as no surprise. Racism thrived in both the American military and civilian sectors. However, labeling these attitudes of Holcomb and the Corps, as several historians do, simply as products of their time belies the complexity of the issue.[91]

Marine Corps historian Heather Pace Marshall dissects the complicated racial views among Marines. She finds that hierarchies existed in the Corps, and Marines believed that the world likewise functioned on the basis of hierarchies. Many Marines, for instance, viewed people of color, including those of Hispanic ancestry, as inferior to the white race. These assumptions had become part of the Corps' cultural fabric when leathernecks had served in Central America, China, and the Philippines earlier in the twentieth century. The Marines saw the guerrilla wars they waged in Central America as part of the process of civilizing that region. In the context of the early twentieth century, the word "civilized" entailed forcing Central Americans to adopt the political practices, religious beliefs, and business practices of the United States, and keeping those newly civilized people in subservient and dependent positions relative to the United States.

According to Marshall, the Southern upbringing of 40 percent of all Marine officers in the 1920s exacerbated the feelings of racial superiority that permeated the Corps throughout the first half of the twentieth century. A disproportionately large percentage of the officer corps hailed from a region with a fraction of the nation's total Caucasian population. Indeed, hierarchies based on social, cultural, religious, gender, or racial status underpinned Marines' self-identification as masculine warriors and protectors of Anglo-Saxon civilization.[92] Thomas Holcomb, as evinced in his upbringing and his wartime attitudes, fit the mold.

A striking illustration of the Corps' complex views on racial hierarchies can actually be found in one exception. Individuals of Native American descent had enlisted successfully in the Corps before the attack on Pearl Harbor. Caucasians had long viewed them as warriors, albeit of a savage sort. In the whites' eyes, the red race did not necessarily share the characteristics of indolence, effeminacy, or cowardice that people of black, brown, or yellow color exhibited.[93] That Indians were seen in this way begs the question of whether racial stereotyping, positive though it may have been, remained prejudice just the same.

Then, early in 1942, Holcomb decided to recruit actively among young Indian men to fill a particular need. It became apparent in combat exercises that the Corps had no reliable means for relaying coded radio messages between ground units and naval support vessels. Because the Japanese could decipher conventionally designed codes, Holcomb wanted to find an unbreakable one. Major General Clayton B. Vogel, commanding officer of the Amphibious Force, Pacific Fleet, suggested that Holcomb consider the Navajo language as a possible solution to the dilemma, because it "is completely unintelligible to all other tribes and all other people, with the possible exception of as many as 28 Americans who have made a study of the dialect. This dialect is thus equivalent to a secret code to the enemy, and admirably suited for rapid, secure communication." With this in mind, Vogel recommended that the Corps enlist 200 Navajos. They would, as Vogel readily conceded, need to exhibit sufficient "linguistic qualifications in English" and meet the Corps' "physical qualifications."[94]

Colonel Allen H. Turnage, then director of the Division of Plans and Policies at HQMC, agreed that this novel approach was worth trying. He recommended only that the initial recruiting goal be reduced to thirty enlistments, a more manageable number for an experimental program. Holcomb liked the idea and decided that thirty Navajos should be recruited, trained, and deployed with the Corps' amphibious units. He ordered that more studies be conducted to determine the effectiveness of the Navajo language as a secure code, leaving open the possibility for further growth of what would eventually become the very successful Navajo code talkers. Nowhere in the correspondence were criticisms raised by Holcomb, Vogel, or Turnage because the Navajos were not Caucasians.[95]

Commandant Holcomb's resistance to accepting non-white males into the Corps could be tempered by operational necessity in the case of Navajo, or ended by political necessity in the cases of African Americans and, eventually, women. In May 1942, the foundation for opening the Corps to women was already laid in Congress. Representatives Edith Nourse Rogers and Margaret Chase Smith, both Republicans from Maine, helped pass legislation that created the Women's Army Auxiliary Corps. Despite Holcomb's objections, it would only be a matter of time before similar legislation for the Marine Corps would follow.[96]

HOLCOMB MOBILIZES THE CORPS: UNITS, TRAINING, AND MATERIEL

In the spring of 1942, it was not yet certain whether Marines would fight only in the Pacific Ocean, or if their unit deployments would be divided between the Pacific and Atlantic Oceans. The United States had already committed substantial Corps manpower to the Atlantic and on the East Coast. The 4,095 men of the 1st Marine Brigade (Provisional) remained on station in Iceland. The 1st Marine Division at New River, North Carolina, could be used in amphibious operations in North Africa or Europe. Out on the West Coast, the 2nd Marine Division at Camp Elliott near Kearny Mesa, California, prepared for operations against Japan. Neither division rated better than half-trained and ill-equipped.[97]

As Major General Charles F. B. Price, commanding the 2nd Marine Division, reported to Holcomb in March: "If these men can be supplied adequately with proper weapons and with a liberal allowance of ammunition so that they may learn to use them, they can lick their weight in wildcats of any description."[98] Even if the divisions could be made combat-ready, however, the Navy's logistics system in the Pacific Ocean could not provide the Marines with sufficient supplies or transport capacity. Similar deficiencies in equipment and preparedness plagued defense battalions that were scattered across the Pacific, on Samoa, Midway, Johnston, Palmyra, and the New Hebrides. Six months of receiving cannibalized equipment and reassigned personnel did not rectify these units' shortcomings.[99]

Admiral Nimitz likewise apprised Holcomb of the existence of similar needs on Midway Island: "Procurement difficulties are recognized but the fact remains that the tanks for Midway, Johnston, and Palmyra are for use in the zone of actual combat operations. Garrisons at these bases must have the most modern combat equipment. Recently an effort was made to borrow tanks from the Army in Hawaii but none could be obtained. At this moment Midway should have tanks and it is earnestly recommended that they be immediately provided with at least one platoon of light or medium tanks."[100] Nimitz knew full well that the Japanese would soon attack that island, and he wanted its leatherneck defenders to be as well prepared as possible.

For his part, Holcomb faced the Herculean task of expanding the Corps from 55,500 Marines in December 1941 to more than 143,000 by July 1942. Structural turmoil reigned as the service tried to absorb the multitude. The recruit depots in San Diego and Parris Island overflowed with "boots," the nickname given to would-be Marines in basic training. The number of recruits in basic passed the 12,000 mark by mid-1942.[101] One historian used terms such as "hurried," "improvisational," and "potentially disastrous" to describe the Corps' training program during this period.[102]

Limited time and subpar instruction were at the root of these problems. In an effort to push recruits through as quickly as possible, the prewar seven-week course was reduced to six in December 1941, and then further slashed to five weeks in early 1942. Experienced noncommissioned officers from the Marine divisions, and enlisted Marines who were otherwise qualified for Officer Candidate Class, filled some of the vacancies. Outstanding graduates of basic training courses immediately cycled back into the process as assistant drill instructors in subsequent courses. This quick fix, in turn, deprived combat units of noncommissioned officers. No completely feasible solution was found during the Second World War.[103]

And yet two bright spots could be found in the process: superior recruits and effective marksmanship. Even though it was available only to a portion of the population, the elevated qualifications meant that only the best, most highly motivated enlistees were accepted and entered basic training.[104] Brigadier General Charles D. Barrett found this to be true during his inspection of Parris Island in January 1942. "Officer and non-commissioned officers speak in the highest terms of the quality of the recruits received since war was declared, and from what I have seen they are a splendid looking lot," reported Barrett to Holcomb. "This shows still further the wisdom of your decision to keep recruiting going full blast—we not only got the numbers but probably a better type than will ever be available again."[105] The outstanding recruits also received superb weapons training, even in the shortened basic training courses. Marine recruits routinely achieved high levels of proficiency with their rifles. This was consistent with the premium that Holcomb, a champion marksman himself, placed on the most basic of combat skills.[106]

The newly minted "Pearl Harbor" Marines filled defense battalions and divisions at home when their existing personnel were transferred to units that were newly activated or deployed overseas. The constant manpower turnover had detrimental effects in both the commissioned and noncommissioned ranks. The few experienced Marines found themselves strewn among units before proper replacements could be found. The 1st and 2nd Marine Divisions in particular seemed to be manpower clearinghouses.[107] Holcomb remarked to Charles Price of the 2nd Division: "I know how distressed that you must be in seeing your division torn apart. I think it is one of the most tragic things that can happen to a command."[108] Major General Alexander Vandegrift, lately given command of the 1st Division, also felt the pinch from this scramble for trained personnel during March and April. "Headquarters ordered us to flesh out the 7th [Marine Regiment] and one battalion of artillery with the best men, weapons and equipment we possessed. These units," according to Vandegrift, "would form the 3rd Marine Brigade to sail immediately for Samoa. General Holcomb telephoned me to make these units as combat ready as possible, so I stripped other units mercilessly."[109]

The specialized defense battalions, barrage balloon battalions, parachute battalions, and raider battalions benefited most from the constantly shifting personnel. These units fulfilled specific military assignments that those of typical Marine riflemen presumably could not undertake. Because of the higher demands for performance, many highly skilled and well-trained Marines served in them. Among the four units, only two participated in several combat operations. Defense battalions served an important strategic purpose because they secured island bases against Japanese attacks or counterattacks. Marines of the 1st Defense Battalion had proven their tactical value at Wake, and those of the 3rd Defense Battalion successfully repelled Japanese air attacks on Midway. Other battalions would continue to play supporting roles in future amphibious operations, most notably Guadalcanal.[110]

The raider battalion stands as another case study in the process of Marine development. Its creation had been the subject of debate at HQMC since 1940. The raider concept caught the fancy of President Roosevelt and his son James, as a Marine Corps version of elite British commandos and German *Fallschirmjägeren* (paratroopers). The president's interest was piqued during discussions with Marine Lieutenant Colonel Evans F. Carlson, who had observed Mao Zedong's successful guerrilla tactics during combat in China; and with presidential adviser William J. Donovan, who wanted to create American units capable of infiltrating enemy-occupied territory and assisting resistance groups. Major General Holland M. Smith also encouraged the formation of lightly armed hit-and-run Marine units. He believed they could land on enemy beaches prior to large-scale amphibious assaults proper, clear those beaches of enemy forces, perform reconnaissance missions, and secure key points inland against enemy counterattacks.[111]

But Holcomb saw no need for so-called special units like the raider battalions, let alone the parachute or balloon barrage battalions. The raider battalion's status as a special operations force would make it elite. This was redundant in the Marine Corps—already an elite organization, as far as Holcomb was concerned.[112] Historian Robert D. Heinl's notes from a postwar interview with the retired commandant reveal that Holcomb believed "any properly trained and led Fleet Marine

Force rifle battalion should be capable of conducting raider operations."[113] Since both interviewer and interviewee shared biases against Evans Carlson and his raider concept, their objectivity was clouded. Still, their sentiments reveal why Carlson faced the resistance that he did. Nevertheless, Holcomb's misgivings about the raider program proved futile by 1942. He conceded "that the main reason why he had been forced to go along with what he considered an unsound approach . . . was the White House backing enjoyed by Carlson. Admiral King insisted on raider battalions, doubtless under pressure from F.D.R."[114]

Holcomb ordered that two raider units be organized in February 1942. The 1st Marine Raider Battalion fell under Lieutenant Colonel Merritt A. Edson's command at Quantico; and Carlson commanded the 2nd Raider Battalion stationed near Camp Elliott in southern California. Both units sapped highly qualified and intelligent Marines from the Corps' limited pool of manpower.[115] Especially hard hit were the two divisions then training on each coast. Vandegrift of the 1st Division complained that "Edson's levy against our division, coming at such a critical time, annoyed the devil out of me, but there wasn't one earthly thing I could do about it."[116]

The raider concept rankled Holcomb even after the units were formed, and the maverick Carlson particularly irritated him. Carlson focused entirely on training his raiders in guerrilla tactics of hit-and-run ambushes or nighttime infiltrations. He dispensed with the formalities and privileges of rank. Every Marine in his battalion could speak his mind in the decision-making process, and each could choose his own weapons and equipment. During his sojourns in China in the 1930s, Carlson had adapted his raider battalion's battle cry—"Gung Ho"—from a Chinese term meaning "work in harmony" or "working together." His mentality and methods were a strange combination of communism, individualism, and democracy that some Marines worried could not make an effective fighting force and probably constituted subversion of the Corps' values.[117] Heinl's interview notes again indicate that Holcomb "showed evident distaste for [Carlson's] concept of raider operation. . . . He concluded by pointing out that as far as actual combat participation or results were concerned, Carlson had accomplished virtually nothing."[118]

The stories behind the creation of the defense battalion and the advent of other special units like the raider battalion illuminate Holcomb's opposing reactions to change. He could be innovative or at least pragmatic on the one hand, but on the other he sometimes stubbornly held onto tradition. He had embraced the defense battalion concept, specialized in mission and costly in manpower though it may have been, because it satisfied important strategic and political needs.[119]

Meanwhile, during this period of flux in 1942, the two Marine divisions continued intensive amphibious training. At New River, leathernecks in the 1st Division built large wooden boats on the intercoastal waterway, to practice loading and unloading equipment as quickly and efficiently as possible. The Marines took advantage of other opportunities to hone their skills. Elements of the 1st Division conducted simulated landings at Lynnhaven Roads, Virginia, in January; and Solomons Island, Maryland, in March and April. While valuable in terms of experience, these left much to be desired in the operational sense, just as had so many other exercises during the 1930s. Little coordination and communication existed between the naval and Marine officers. Unit integrity broke down as Marines from one unit became entangled with those from another. Landings occurred at the wrong places at the wrong times.[120]

The poorly equipped Marines in the divisions nonetheless maintained good morale in 1942. The 2nd Division's Charles Price appreciated leading "this very fine group of men here, both officers and enlisted, who have given me such splendid support. I never worked with more intelligent, energetic and zealous young people and it has been a real joy."[121] Holcomb did his part to keep the Marines' spirits high. As was his habit throughout his career, he liked to make inspection tours of bases. He recognized that a visit from the commandant could bolster the morale of those whom he saw. He made one such inspection in the spring of 1942, when he visited the 1st Division at New River. The commandant "came out to see us one afternoon," recounted a young and impressionable Private William White. "He spoke of the good work we were doing and of how our firing exercises had that touch of professionalism sought by many and attained by few. For this, he said, we deserved a hearty 'Well Done.' . . . He was not a particularly good speaker, but he knew how to talk to young men. He was a major general yet still one of us. You knew he had been in situations just as bad as ours. His talk was well received. We felt proud of being told that we were doing so well with so little."[122] Cloistered at HQMC most of the time, Holcomb also needed to gauge for himself conditions of the readiness and morale of his Marines.

Holcomb made his presence felt in other ways. He actively participated in decisions about transfers of colonels and generals from unit to unit. Not unlike President Roosevelt, he had an innate ability to assess accurately which officer would be best suited for a particular position. A given officer's skills, temperament, intelligence, and record played roles in personnel decisions.[123] One of the most significant command changes occurred on March 23, 1942, in the 1st Division. Long dissatisfied with Major General Philip Torrey's leadership, the higher-ranking Major General Holland Smith decided to relieve him as division commander. Smith felt that Torrey did not execute orders as directed, or work well with subordinate officers. With Holcomb's sanction, he replaced Torrey with the younger and more competent Alexander Vandegrift. Although they were none too friendly with one another, Smith respected Vandegrift as an able leader. This confidence augured well for the new commander's future.[124]

Vandegrift worked to raise the strength of the division from a low of 7,389 Marines in December 1941, but he still did not reach the 10,000-Marine plateau by April 1942.[125] "My fear that I had inherited a training division and would spend the war at New River preparing battalions and regiments for overseas duty proved short-lived," said a relieved Vandegrift.[126] At that month's end, he learned what would be his division's first wartime deployment. As part of the Navy's multiple-stage campaign laid out two weeks earlier by COMINCH-CNO King and Admiral Turner, Thomas Holcomb ordered that the 1st Marine Division go to Wellington, New Zealand. Unfortunately, the 2nd Marine Division, already stationed on the West Coast, did not have sufficient manpower, because several thousand of its Marines were just returning from their eight-month stint on Iceland.

Although the 1st Division numbered fewer than 10,000 leathernecks, it had to be split into halves and sail in two separate convoys. Too few American transport ships were available to carry the division in a single trip in May 1942. Vandegrift sailed with the advanced echelon of some 6,000 Marines from Norfolk on May 20, and the rear echelon departed by rail for California shortly thereafter. Vandegrift and his Marines arrived in New Zealand on June 14 after an exhausting, yet uneventful, 10,000-mile voyage.[127]

Once on the island, the 1st Division continued its training efforts because, as Vandegrift reported to Holcomb, it had "not yet attained a satisfactory state of readiness."[128] New Zealand's beaches made it possible to simulate sufficiently realistic amphibious assaults, though it should be remembered that the under-strength division also lacked its full complement of weapons, equipment, ammunition, and other supplies. The division's rear echelon, with its 4,000 additional Marines, set sail on June 22, 1942, from San Francisco. They joined their fellow leathernecks in New Zealand on July 11. Vandegrift anticipated having six months to bring his division up to full combat readiness. He likewise expected to receive more landing craft, artillery, and rations. Only then did he expect that the 1st Marine Division would be thrown into the fray, early in 1943.[129]

Those expectations were dashed less than two weeks after his arrival. On June 26, Vice Admiral Robert Ghormley, new commander in chief of the South Pacific Area (COMSOPAC), called Vandegrift to his headquarters in Auckland. When they came face to face, Ghormley gave the Marine general a top secret dispatch from COMINCH-CNO King, setting the Guadalcanal D-day for August 1, 1942.[130] Vandegrift explained the gist of the dispatch in his memoir: "It directed Ghormley to confer with MacArthur concerning an amphibious operation against two enemy-held islands, Guadalcanal and Tulagi, in the Solomon Island chain northwest of us. This was to be a naval task force including my division and we were to land on August 1—less than 5 weeks away." The initial counteroffensive would be part of Operation Watchtower. An incredulous Vandegrift gasped, "I could not believe it."[131]

For his part, Ghormley was equally surprised. He had just arrived in New Zealand a week earlier, on June 19, and had received King's dispatch on June 25. Ghormley, Vandegrift, and their staffs suddenly needed to push their training timetable forward by five months. Operation Watchtower, otherwise christened

Operation Shoestring by tongue-in-cheek Marines, stood as a major operational and logistical undertaking with precious little time for planning or preparation.[132] Commandant Holcomb's precise role in those deliberations cannot be determined from the existing evidence, but it can be assumed that he found the accelerated timetable to be as disconcerting as did Vandegrift.

Thomas Holcomb and the Marine Corps had weathered the first seven months of the Second World War. The commandant proved himself as a manager, strategist, and publicist in years of plenty as well as famine. Holcomb was a "splendid administrator" with "high personal character," wrote Secretary of the Navy Franklin Knox on his six-month fitness report ending on March 31, 1942.[133] As the war dragged on, Holcomb jockeyed to improve the Corps' position relative to that of the Army, Navy, Allies, and American industry. Congress, the Roosevelt administration, and the American people may have been sympathetic to the service's needs, and the nation's resources may have been enormous, but obtaining the necessary manpower and materiel to fulfill the Corps' amphibious assault mission proved no easy task. The only blemish on Holcomb's otherwise strong record came in his restrictive policies regarding recruitment of certain non-Caucasians.

CHAPTER 5

▼

GUADALCANAL:
THE FIRST BIG TEST FOR HOLCOMB
AND THE MARINE CORPS

*July 1942–February 1943**

Following the decisive victories in the Battles of the Coral Sea in May 1942 and Midway in June, the United States could finally launch Operation Watchtower in August. The Marine Corps emerged as the only American service capable of landing a division-strength force on Japanese-held Guadalcanal so soon after Pearl Harbor. Although myriad problems plagued the operation at all stages, Commandant Thomas Holcomb worked closely with Major General Alexander A. Vandegrift over several months to achieve victory. Their interactions reveal the respect and trust that had developed between the service chief and his field commander. During a trip to Guadalcanal in October 1942, Holcomb toured the combat zone and ensured that reforms in amphibious command relations would make the Corps (and the Army) more effective in future amphibious operations. These changes constituted one of Holcomb's most important contributions during the Second World War.

PLANS AND PREPARATIONS FOR OPERATION SHOESTRING

The genesis of the first American counteroffensive against the Japanese occurred in February 1942, when initial planning began at the behest of Admiral Ernest J. King, then COMINCH, but not yet appointed CNO. The key to success of what evolved into Operation Watchtower lay in controlling Guadalcanal. Capturing the airfield on this island would deny the Japanese its use as a means of disrupting American supply lanes to Australia, while giving American forces a base from which to start their drive northwestward up "the Slot" through the Solomons toward the large Japanese base at Rabaul on New Britain. The final planning took place in Wellington, New Zealand, in July 1942. Major General Vandegrift, commanding the 1st Marine Division, and his staff worked with Rear Admiral Richmond Kelly

*Adapted from author's article published in *War & Society* 28 (October 2009): 113–47.

Turner and his staff to iron out details of the amphibious assault. They expected the 1st Marine Division to seize the nearly completed airfield on Guadalcanal and occupy nearby islands of Tulagi, Florida, Gavutu, and Tanambogo. The Navy, meanwhile, would ferry in supplies, reinforcements, and aircraft to those islands and help defend them against Japanese counterattacks.[1]

Holcomb watched the planning and preparations for Operation Watchtower with great interest. The commandant knew all the personalities involved, whether in the Marine Corps or the Navy. He also had long held a firm grasp of the ins and outs of amphibious operations, dating from his work as a student at the Army and Naval War Colleges and his years as commandant of the Marine Corps Schools in the early 1930s.[2]

Vandegrift's 1st Division included the 1st and 5th Marine Regiments, already in Wellington, and the 11th Marine Artillery Regiment that arrived later in July. The 1st Marine Raider Battalion, 1st Marine Parachute Battalion, and 3rd Marine Defense Battalion would further augment the division in early August. The fact that Vandegrift as division commander and Holcomb as commandant cobbled together this force only eight months after Pearl Harbor stands as a tribute to their efforts. Nevertheless, the 1st Division was not combat-ready. Its logistical situation could be considered fragile at best.

No sufficiently large caches of ammunition existed for an extended campaign, and there was not enough cargo space on the Navy's transport. In theory, the 18,134 leathernecks required at least 100,000 metric tons, or 4 million cubic feet, of supplies for combat. This allowed for sixty days of rations and gasoline, with 22.5 units of fire. In actuality, however, the twenty-three transoceanic transport vessels that the Navy had allocated to support the Marines could carry a maximum of 50,000 metric tons, or half the cargo needed for a division going into combat. The most worrisome supply shortage was ammunition, of which the few Navy transports could carry only ten units of fire.[3]

To make matters worse, planning and preparations in New Zealand hit many snags throughout July and early August. Poor intelligence, inadequate supplies, inefficient command relations, and personality conflicts made Watchtower a gamble. Neither the Navy nor the Marine Corps had accurate hydrographic data on Guadalcanal. Some information about the island came from old issues of *National Geographic* and Australian plantation owners, British colonial officers, and missionaries who had lived on the island before the Japanese occupation. Reconnaissance aircraft took aerial photographs in July, but the Marines could not obtain them until after the initial landing, due to poor communications.[4] Vandegrift found the "hit-and-miss" process of intelligence-gathering to be disconcerting, and he worried that these many shortcomings portended disaster.[5]

In the weeks leading up to the actual invasion of Guadalcanal on August 7, 1942, Vandegrift kept Holcomb up to date on the evolving situation. Years of friendship

▲ This map shows Marine objectives on Guadalcanal and nearby islands in August 1942.

(Map by Michael J. Hradesky)

and trust made their working relationship effective. Reports by Vandegrift and his subordinates relayed the state of the division's combat readiness, evaluations of amphibious exercises, status of supply stocks, and relations with naval officers.[6] Try as Holcomb might, though, he could do little to improve the division's situation some 10,000 miles away. He could not wring supplies from either service without working through official channels at the Navy and War Departments. A mountain of requisitions needed to pass through channels before movement across the Pacific Ocean. Because so much equipment had not yet been manufactured, the procurement process took more time than otherwise would have been needed. It was little wonder that Marines and sailors cynically nicknamed this undertaking Operation Shoestring.[7]

Beyond the intelligence and logistical shortcomings inherent in Operation Watchtower, command structures and personality conflicts exacerbated all other problems. Vice Admiral Robert L. Ghormley exercised strategic control as COMSOPAC but refused to interject himself into the operational planning process.[8] Below Ghormley was Vice Admiral Frank Jack Fletcher, the expeditionary force commander. Fletcher's Task Force 61, including three aircraft carriers and one new battleship, would provide air cover and naval support for Major General Vandegrift's Marine landing force on Guadalcanal and protect Rear Admiral Turner's transport vessels. Fletcher was thus superior to Turner, who was in turn superior to Vandergrift.[9]

As outlined in the Navy's *FTP 167*, the ranking naval officer in charge of the amphibious force directed not only the amphibious assault proper but the Marine forces ashore. This command structure would be applied in Watchtower.[10] The ranking naval officer in charge would be Turner, who, as Vandegrift related later in August, might advance some "half baked idea" about amphibious operations because Turner "thought he knew all about it, when he did not even know the terms."[11] Vandegrift found himself hamstrung by the command structure and beset by senior naval officers who either did not support Watchtower or did not fully grasp the complexities of amphibious warfare. He had little autonomy or flexibility above the tactical level.[12]

Skepticism and pessimism could also be found among other American leaders. Vice Admiral Ghormley and General Douglas MacArthur opposed the operation because they considered it the "gravest risk" based on their "gravest doubts."[13] Even as late as July 8, 1942, Ghormley and MacArthur urged the JCS to postpone Watchtower to a much later date or cancel it altogether, but the JCS denied their request. The invasion of Guadalcanal would go forward, but the fact that the 1st Marine Division would not be ready by the planned invasion date of August 1 could not be ignored. Thus the JCS agreed to postpone D-day for six days, until August 7. Unlike Ghormley, whose attitudes negatively affected his actions, Vandegrift's doubts never metastasized into defeatism. And, to Admiral

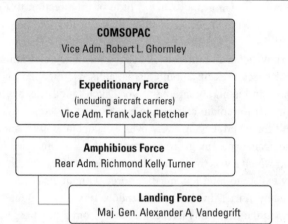

▶ Command structure during Operation Watchtower in 1942, as outlined in *FTP 167* (1938).

(Adapted from Miller, *Guadalcanal*, 23, 29)

Turner's credit, he believed that the gamble should be taken and that the assault on Guadalcanal should proceed. After all, he had been the architect of the specific details of King's multiple-stage strategic plan earlier in the year.[14]

Despite all these problems and setbacks, American naval and Marine forces finally got under way on July 22, 1942, and departed from Wellington, New Zealand. They rendezvoused with Fletcher's Force 61 several days later near Koro, one of the Fiji Islands. Fletcher immediately called a conference with Vandegrift, Turner, and their respective staffs on his flagship to discuss details of the invasion. Nowhere were the command structure problems and personality conflicts more apparent than in this meeting. According to eyewitnesses and historians alike, the discussion degenerated into a shouting match between Fletcher and Turner over how many days it would take to disembark the Marines and their supplies and how many days Fletcher would keep his aircraft carriers nearby to provide air cover for this process. Turner wanted five days to land the Marines, and Vandergrift concurred that several days would be necessary for these tasks. An unmoved Fletcher denied Turner's request and instead granted carrier-based air cover for only two days.

Fletcher stated his warships lacked the fuel to remain off Guadalcanal any longer, and he did not wish to remain vulnerable to Japanese air attacks. But another factor doubtlessly influenced Fletcher's decision. He had lost aircraft carriers in the Battles of Coral Sea and Midway, and he did not want to lose more. Making matters more problematic was the fact that Watchtower's overall strategic commander, Vice Admiral Ghormley, offered little or no direction to Fletcher in the planning phase or later in the heat of battle. In fact, he did not even attend this July 27 conference.[15]

For his part, Vandegrift fumed at Fletcher's obstinacy and ignorance regarding the tactical necessities of amphibious assaults. He recalled his real feelings many years later in his autobiography: "My Dutch blood was beginning to boil but I forced myself to remain calm while explaining to Fletcher that the days 'of landing a small force and leaving' were over. This operation was supposed to take and hold Guadalcanal and Tulagi. To accomplish this I commanded a heavily reinforced division which I was to land on enemy-held territory, which meant a fight. I could hardly expect to land this massive force without air cover—even the five days mentioned by Turner involved a tremendous risk."[16] This quote indicates that Vandegrift joined the ranks of Fletcher's critics. From a practical standpoint, the Marine general's hands were tied, however, because of his position of weakness in the command structure.

With no other alternatives and as the dutiful subordinate, Vandegrift held his tongue and took all discouraging news in stride. Like his old friend Thomas Holcomb, he had considerable reserves of emotional intelligence—which leadership scholar Fred Greenstein sees as fortitude and facility for making the best of bad situations.[17] Vandegrift's outlook filtered down the 1st Marine Division's ranks, creating what military historian R. R. Keene dubs a "can-do" attitude in his division. Vandegrift would need every bit of that determination and resilience in the months ahead.[18]

Over the next three days, the 1st Division participated in a large-scale amphibious assault rehearsal at Koro. Although the leathernecks' performance was poor, Vandegrift solved several problems, such as malfunctioning landing craft engines and uncoordinated naval gunfire support, in time for the actual D-day on Guadalcanal.[19] Finally, the seventy-five American warships and transport ships left Koro on July 31 and sailed to Guadalcanal, roughly 1,200 miles to the northwest. Low-lying clouds and rainstorms concealed their approach from the watchful eyes of Japanese pilots flying reconnaissance missions, so the American forces would achieve total tactical surprise. The 18,000 jittery leathernecks appeared off Guadalcanal on August 6, the night before D-day.[20]

Meanwhile back at HQMC, Commandant Holcomb eagerly awaited news. Much was at stake for the prosecution of the war effort—for the Marines making the assault proper, for Vandegrift commanding them, and for the commandant who had so long billed the Corps as the ideal unit for amphibious operations. Yet, in early August, no one observing Holcomb's demeanor could sense the gravity of the occasion. He spent the weeks before the invasion attending innumerable meetings, smoking his ubiquitous pipe, and following his daily routine.[21] "General Holcomb carried his lunch in his little tin pail and drove his own little Chevrolet convertible car," explained Lieutenant Colonel James P. Berkeley of the Division of Plans and Policies. "He had no chauffeur to drive him back and forth; he ate lunch at his desk, otherwise he would have eaten in the cafeteria with everyone else."[22] The commandant methodically worked through problems facing the Corps. His calmness bred confidence among his subordinates. Berkeley described life under Holcomb: "We did work long weekends; we worked every Saturday and Sunday, or halfday Sunday, and . . . every now and then we'd get a whole Saturday or Sunday off. We had gas rations so we didn't go anywhere anyway, but at least you got a breathing spell. There was not too much pressure around the place."[23]

Holcomb's own words confirmed Berkeley's observations, as evinced in one exchange with Army Chief of Staff George C. Marshall. He wrote Holcomb on August 4 to wish him a happy birthday and applaud the Marine Corps for its contributions to the war effort. Marshall also expressed concern about the mounting wartime stress levels being experienced by his fellow service chiefs.[24] Holcomb's response on August 7 said much about his state of mind:

> I have managed to keep in good physical condition so far and my recipe is as follows: out of bed at 6:30, fifteen minutes of setting up, one and one-half miles of vigorous walk, no overtime work except in case of real emergency, no night parties that can possibly be avoided and to bed by 9:30 if in any way possible. I get to the office at a few minutes past 8:00 and invariably leave at 4:35 and I take every other Saturday off to spend a long week end at our place in Southern Maryland and I never work on Sunday unless there is a real emergency.[25]

No hint of anxiety can be detected in this note, even if Holcomb realized full well the momentous events far across the Pacific Ocean. He had clearly found coping mechanisms to manage the ups and downs of wartime leadership—another proof of the commandant's enormous emotional intelligence.

GUADALCANAL: AUGUST TO OCTOBER 1942

D-day, August 7, arrived at long last. Just after 6:00 AM, an American naval and aerial bombardment of Guadalcanal lit up the early morning, sending shells screaming across the sky and igniting fires of exploding ordnance on shore. Marines climbed down cargo nets to the amphibious assault craft and made their runs into the beaches. Some 10,900 leathernecks made the main landing just east of Lunga Point on Guadalcanal proper. They faced negligible resistance from the small Japanese garrison, who quickly fled into the jungles.

The Japanese on Guadalcanal may have been surprised, but the enemy elsewhere in the Solomons wasted no time in reacting to the American landing. The first of daily air attacks began as aircraft struck the American forces and dam-

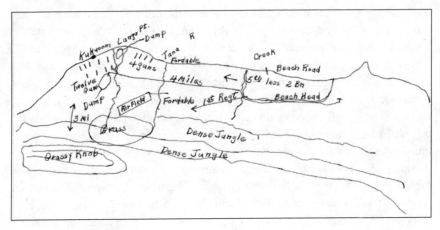

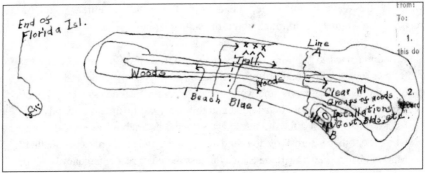

▶ Major General Alexander A. Vandegrift sent these hand-drawn maps of D-day on Guadalcanal and Tulagi, August 7, 1942, to Commandant Thomas Holcomb on August 11, 1942.

(Marine Corps University Archives, Holcomb Papers, Box 24)

aged several ships. Meanwhile, another 6,900 Marines landed on Tulagi, Florida, Gavutu, and Tanambogo islands about twenty miles north across Sealark Channel from Guadalcanal. They secured these islands only after several days of very bloody fighting against an outnumbered but determined Japanese foe.[26]

According to one of Vandegrift's many reports to Holcomb, his Marines' initial landing "proceeded with the smoothness and precision of a well-rehearsed peacetime drill. All boat formations crossed lines of departure promptly and moved inshore toward assigned beaches with all boat groups in good order and under excellent control."[27] Once ashore, Marine units moved inland toward the airfield. What actually slowed their advance to a crawl was not enemy opposition but the heavy packs they carried through oppressive heat and thick vegetation. Meanwhile, American landing craft ferried additional Marines and supplies to the island. The first few hours of off-loading went almost flawlessly, but difficulties increased that afternoon as the narrow beach became congested with supplies and equipment. By midnight, all ship-to-shore movements ceased for the next ten hours to clear the clutter. Off-loading efforts broke down thereafter, as sheer exhaustion overcame the shore and pioneer parties and the Marines assisting them.[28]

On D+1, as the next day of August 8 was designated, the Japanese enemy remained so quiet that Vandegrift quipped: "I'm beginning to wonder whether there's a Jap on the whole damned island."[29] Once again, however, Japanese aircraft returned for another attack. This time, despite the stubborn defense by American carrier-based aircraft and shipboard antiaircraft gunners, the enemy sank a transport ship. This loss added to Fletcher's growing paranoia that all the ships, and especially his three aircraft carriers, were vulnerable to future strikes by enemy land-based or carrier-based aircraft.[30]

On Guadalcanal, late that afternoon the Marines advanced southwestward and occupied the airfield south of Lunga Point. They subsequently took up a defensive position on the eastern side of the Lunga River. At the airfield, as an elated Vandegrift informed Holcomb, the Marines discovered an abandoned Japanese camp with these essential items: "a power house, an alternate one, a radio receiver station with six sets with remote control to a sending unit 3 miles away, innumerable pieces of machinery such as generators, engines, pumps, etc. 9 Road Rollers, over 100 trucks so far found of the Chev 2 ton types, Anti-aircraft guns, loaded and locked—can you beat that. Tons of cement, some fifty or sixty thousand gals. of gas and oil and double that much destroyed by bombs."[31] The nearly completed runway stretched 2,000 feet, and hangars stood ready to house aircraft. Just as fortuitously, the Marines found large amounts of rice and canned fish, which would prove a godsend in the coming weeks. Because the American assault caught the Japanese soldiers and Korean construction workers completely off guard, they fled westward so quickly that they neglected to destroy these supplies, as was standard military procedure when evacuating a base.[32]

Late in the evening of D+1, Vice Admiral Fletcher informed the dumbfounded Turner and Vandegrift that he would withdraw his three aircraft carriers immediately, citing aircraft losses and low fuel. Neither eyewitnesses nor most historians fully believe the admiral. Both have leveled harsh criticisms at the supposedly gun-shy Fletcher for putting his carriers' safety ahead of the Marines' success in ongoing operations on Guadalcanal.[33] Turner, for example, supposedly grumbled about Fletcher: "He's left us bare arse."[34]

One of Fletcher's only apologists is naval historian John B. Lundstrom. In his recent biography, Lundstrom skillfully defends the admiral on grounds that he withdrew because the risk to his carriers was not justified by the potential damage to be inflicted on Japanese forces. From a logistical perspective, Fletcher did indeed have to be concerned with fuel shortages because, for instance, his larger warships were refueling his destroyers off Guadalcanal. Furthermore, Lundstrom argues that the loss of more than twenty American fighters—20 percent of Fletcher's total force of carrier-based fighters—in two days constituted a severe setback. Beyond these factors, Fletcher had no hard intelligence regarding the location of Japanese carriers, and he correctly expected counterattacks by land-based enemy aircraft. Consequently, while causing much consternation, his decision to depart on the evening of D+1 looked reasonable.[35]

Irrespective of historical debates, neither Turner nor Vandegrift could expect air cover to oppose Japanese aerial attacks, and only American and Australian cruisers and destroyers would remain in Sealark Channel to screen those transports against possible surface attacks. Their worst fears about another enemy strike became reality early in the morning of D+2, August 9, when several Japanese cruisers slipped unnoticed by Savo Island into Sealark Channel. The enemy ships unleashed deadly gunfire and torpedo attacks on unsuspecting American and Australian ships on patrol, sinking or irreparably damaging four Allied cruisers in minutes while losing not a single vessel themselves. This stunning tactical coup, known to history as the Battle of Savo Island, gave the Japanese cruisers a clear shot at Turner's vulnerable transports less than 20 miles away off Lunga Point. In an instant, they could have destroyed the Marines' tenuous foothold on Guadalcanal. But the Japanese did not strike, for fear of exposing themselves to reprisals from American carrier-based aircraft. Instead, because they had no idea that Fletcher's carriers had left the area just hours earlier, the Japanese cruisers reversed course and retired to the northwest before sunrise.[36]

On D+2 Turner's position became completely untenable, with no large warships, let alone air cover, to protect his transports. Vandegrift could not stop his superior officer from leaving. Turner withdrew that same day, leaving the hapless Marines on Guadalcanal with barely enough ammunition for four days of combat and just thirty-seven days of food.[37] The desperate situation led one Marine officer to christen his abandoned unit the 1st "Maroon" Division.[38]

Reports of severe losses at the Battle of Savo Island and withdrawals of American aircraft carriers and transports alarmed some civilian and military leaders back in Washington.[39] But nothing discouraged Thomas Holcomb. He continued to portray the war effort in positive terms. In one radio broadcast on NBC on August 12, he stated: "The Marine Corps is proud that once again its men are taking part with the Navy, Army, and the forces of our Allies in offensive action. I share with you the anxieties of the hour, but I share them with the firm conviction that though there may be many anxious moments in the days to come, the righteousness of our cause and the valor of our forces will prevail."[40] Holcomb also tried to buoy Vandegrift's spirits in a note written two days later, on August 14. The commandant expressed similarly positive sentiments in congratulating him. "You have certainly done a fine job. I hope you soon have complete control of everything. Everyone here is tremendously proud of the work of the division," beamed Holcomb. "It is perfectly grand that the first operation was such a success. The Division should be hard to stop now."[41]

Like Holcomb, Vandegrift never lost heart throughout the campaign on Guadalcanal. He immediately set his division to fortifying a 9,000-yard defensive perimeter against future ground attacks, creating artillery emplacements against any naval attacks, moving supplies inland from the beaches, and finishing the runway as part of what became known as Henderson Field. The airfield, named for a Marine pilot killed in action during the Battle of Midway, was the key target of all subsequent Japanese air, naval, and ground attacks. Holding onto Henderson Field became the leathernecks' primary mission on Guadalcanal.[42]

Holcomb's pronouncements and Vandegrift's determination notwithstanding, the Marines experienced extreme hardships. For one, those next few days from August 9 through August 20 would be "twelve days in limbo."[43] The Japanese continued daily air raids almost like clockwork. Vandegrift recorded the effects of one attack in a note to Holcomb: "Just ducked in the side of a hill as six Jap Zeros came sailing by at low altitude, guns blazing, no casualties. I wonder why we (U.S.) are the only ones with shortages of short-range fighters. These [Zeros] come from 450 miles away. They climb and maneuver well. When the bombers came down the other day, 44 of them, they had fighters over them."[44] The Japanese aircraft tried unsuccessfully to destroy Henderson Field and damage the Marines' defensive positions on the northern coast of the island.

Finally on August 20, the Marines on Guadalcanal witnessed the first encouraging event since D-day, when elements of Marine Aircraft Group 23 (MAG 23) landed.[45] A relieved Vandegrift wrote to Holcomb: "We at least have planes on our field and now do not feel so helplessly blind."[46] These American fighters and dive-bombers gave much-needed air cover against daily bombing raids, close air support against enemy ground forces, and strike capability against Japanese warships. More and more American aircraft followed, allowing the so-called Cactus Air Force to maintain a consistent strength of eighty planes or more. Marine Brigadier General Roy S. Geiger arrived in early September to take command of the burgeoning air unit. Under his aggressive leadership, American aviators shot down more than 400 Japanese aircraft and sank ten ships, losing only 100 aircraft themselves.[47]

Just one day after aircraft from MAG 23 arrived, on August 21 the first serious ground engagement between American and Japanese forces erupted in the Battle of the Tenaru River, which was actually Alligator Creek but American maps were inaccurate. In what would be a complete victory, leathernecks of the 1st and 2nd Battalions, 1st Marine Regiment, supported by American tanks, enveloped and annihilated the enemy force of 900 men.[48] While fighting "was pretty thick until daylight," reported Vandegrift to Holcomb, "the men are fine, in good spirits and thank God still in good health. The youngsters are the darndest people when they get started you ever saw."[49] Such excerpts of correspondence demonstrate that although thousands of miles away, the commandant remained well informed about the situation on Guadalcanal.

The Marines' victory at the Battle of the Tenaru River helped weaken the myth of Japanese soldiers' invincibility, which they had acquired by defeating the British at Hong Kong and Singapore, and the Americans on the Philippines and Wake Island.[50] A newer, more disturbing myth of suicidal fanaticism replaced the old one. "I have never heard or read of this kind of fighting," a stunned Vandegrift wrote to Holcomb in late August 1942. "These people refuse to surrender. The wounded will wait until men come up to examine them and blow themselves and the other fellow to pieces with a hand grenade."[51] Here was an enemy who validated all the fears and prejudices against the yellow Asian peril that had been burned into the Caucasian-American psyche. Yet this enemy could be beaten, as Vandegrift later explained in a 1943 interview. "Our people are as able as they," he said simply, but quickly appealed to Americans' own sense of racial superiority: "We have something the Jap does not have—native intelligence higher than theirs, the ability to work as an individual."[52] These contemptuous attitudes portrayed the enemy as vicious fighters who made a formidable opponent but were still, after all, an inferior race little better than animals.[53]

The next major ground combat test for the Marines occurred on September 12, when roughly 3,000 Japanese soldiers attempted to capture Henderson Field by attacking northward from the inland jungle. Some 1,250 leathernecks of the 1st Raider and 1st Parachute Battalions under Lieutenant Colonel Merritt A. Edson fought along the spine of a low-lying ridge line just south of Henderson Field. For three days, until September 14, the Japanese slowly gained ground against the Marines' tenacious defense, but then the exhausted and bloodied Japanese retreated. Later dubbed the Battle of Edson's Ridge, this engagement cost the Marines more than 250 casualties. The Japanese suffered much worse losses: 600 soldiers died in the fighting, and another 600 wounded soldiers came to grief in the jungle.[54] Vandegrift explained to Holcomb what had transpired in the hotly contested battle. He also praised Edson, who would receive the Congressional Medal of Honor for this engagement, as "one of the finest troop leaders I have ever seen."[55]

Vandegrift's frequent reports enabled Holcomb in turn to serve as his advocate for more or better support. The commandant appealed to Rear Admiral Turner through one of his Marine staff advisers in the following message: "I want to impress on you most strongly that I feel that we at this end, 6,000 miles from the theater, would be extremely negligent if we did not supply a division with everything (supplies, weapons, transportation, ammunition, etc.) needed for any operation they might be called upon to perform."[56] Turner listened to Holcomb's entreaties about the Marines' desperate situation and agreed, as did Admiral Chester W. Nimitz at Pearl Harbor. Over time, the irascible Turner evolved into an expert logistician and genuine supporter of the Marines on Guadalcanal, though he could occasionally interfere too deeply in ground operations and in Corps force structures.[57]

Unlike Nimitz and Turner, Vice Admiral Fletcher continued to hesitate to commit completely to the ongoing campaign, and the skeptical Vice Admiral Ghormley developed a defeatist attitude. Of the two, Ghormley drew the most criticism and caused the most consternation, even though it was Fletcher who had abandoned the Marines. Whereas Ghormley was acknowledged as a gifted strategist and effective administrator, he failed to provide inspired or inspiring leadership once the Marines had landed on Guadalcanal. Sadly, Ghormley also apparently suffered from exhaustion from ten months of tiring work since Pearl Harbor, which may have dulled his decision-making abilities. In his unpublished memoir written after the war, the admiral attempted to justify his decisions and actions as COMSOPAC. All of his protestations, however, have fallen on deaf ears among his contemporaries and historians alike.[58]

On the other hand, the assistance that Admirals Nimitz and Turner rendered to the Marines on Guadalcanal took many significant forms. Both admirals toured the island in September and gained a firsthand appreciation for the vexing stresses of combat. The low levels of food, fuel, and ammunition took on real meaning for these men, rather than as abstract statistics in recurring pleas for more supplies by Vandegrift or Holcomb. When Turner and Nimitz departed, they pledged to do whatever they could to provide Vandegrift with more supplies, aircraft, and manpower. And help they did.

Nimitz propelled Ghormley into action, who in turn ordered Fletcher and Turner to plan and execute more seaborne supply runs. The 4,200-man strong 7th Marine Regiment arrived on Guadalcanal in September; and 3,000 soldiers of the U.S. Army's 164th Infantry Regiment joined the fray in October. On thirteen out of that month's thirty-one days, Turner's transport ships arrived and off-loaded their invaluable cargoes. By mid-November, arrivals occurred daily. In the meantime, the U.S. Navy fought very costly duels with the Japanese Navy to ensure that supplies kept flowing to the Marines.[59]

Whereas Holcomb, Nimitz, and Turner continued to help the Marines, President Roosevelt remained anxious from August into November about the uncertain outcome on Guadalcanal. The challenge of balancing American resources in the Pacific and Atlantic posed serious strategic and logistical challenges for the president and his advisers. Simply not enough men or materiel existed to support extended campaigns in both theaters, let alone provide truly substantial resources to one. Roosevelt's anxiety did not, however, extend to the point of defeatism or skepticism.[60]

Holcomb never showed any hint of low morale, but he benefited from the occasional lift, especially during the first months of the campaign. One of these came in August 1942, from a retired Navy captain who congratulated Holcomb on the leathernecks' accomplishments on Guadalcanal. "I know the difficulties of such a conquest," wrote Captain W. D. Puleston. "I also know how faithfully the Marine Corps prepared its officers and men for the special operation. Years of patient preparation at Quantico in the 'Ship to Shore' School laid the foundation for this brilliant achievement." Puleston closed his note by praising the service as being "capable of the utmost in amphibious warfare."[61]

Apart from the positive tone of this letter, substantive compliments came through clearly in the captain's words. Holcomb recognized these as validations in his reply to Puleston, written the next day: "You are the first to mention the part that the Quantico schools played in this matter,—which was naturally very pleasing to me because I believe that our schools more than any single agency contributed to our success. . . . It is really a wonderful thing for us that our first amphibious attack was so successful. It will give the 1st Division and also other units confidence in our training methods, in our procedure and in their ability to meet the Jap and deal with him."[62] The initial landings and ongoing operations on Guadalcanal could indeed be traced back to the two doctrinal treaties, *Tentative Manual for Landing Operations* and *Tentative Manual for Defense of Advanced Bases*, both of which were written at the Marine Corps Schools during the 1930s.

Meanwhile on Guadalcanal during the first fortnight in October, the Japanese, reinforced by 15,000 troops, fought several bloody engagements with American troops, but the American forces held firm. In addition to repeated enemy ground, naval, and aerial attacks, the rainy season brought torrential downpours that soaked the men and muddied their quarters. Tropical diseases incapacitated more than 2,000 Marines in October, and 3,200 the next month. American morale on the island reached its lowest ebb in mid-October.[63]

Then, Vandegrift and his Marines and soldiers finally received a much-needed emotional boost on October 18, due not to any military victory but to a high-level command decision. With so much at stake, word came down from Admiral Nimitz that Vice Admiral Ghormley would be replaced as COMSOPAC by Vice Admiral William F. Halsey. This promotion surprised everyone, including the cantankerous Halsey himself. Nicknamed "Bull" because of his offensive-mindedness, the fifty-nine-year-old sailor brought to his new position those traits that Ghormley seemed to lack. The new COMSOPAC would aggressively take the fight to the enemy. Fear of potential American losses during naval combat did not trouble Halsey.[64]

Everyone from Vandegrift down to the enlisted ranks breathed a collective sigh of relief when they learned of Halsey's promotion. Vandegrift made a measured assessment of the two commanders, old and new, in the following: "I held nothing personal against Ghormley, whom I liked. I simply felt that our drastic, imperiled situation called for the most positive form of aggressive leadership at the top. From what I knew of Bill Halsey he would supply this like few naval officers."[65] Others were not so forgiving nor restrained in their reactions.[66]

As soon as Halsey assumed his new command, he called a meeting of his principal subordinates, Major General Vandegrift and Rear Admiral Turner, for October 23 at Noumea. Halsey wanted current, candid assessments of their situations in the theater. Not coincidentally, Commandant Holcomb, then en route to Guadalcanal, would also attend this momentous meeting. Halsey would prove to be both supportive and cooperative, here and in future combat operations.[67]

HOLCOMB'S GROUNDBREAKING TOUR OF GUADALCANAL

Thomas Holcomb had been planning his visit to Guadalcanal for several weeks before he actually departed Washington on October 8, 1942, for his month-long, 25,000-mile round trip. The commandant had stated his intention to visit the island in mid-September. "I am counting on reaching you," wrote Holcomb to Vandegrift, "if we can't, the trip will be a bit pointless. If we can possibly get through to you, we ought to come back better able to organize, train, equip, supply and otherwise serve the forces in the field."[68] Clearly then, Holcomb was cognizant of the logistical problems and wanted to get as many reinforcements and as much equipment as possible to Guadalcanal. Two weeks later the commandant's itinerary, including his inspection of the island on October 22, was set. Excited about his upcoming visit, Holcomb told Vandegrift, "There are a thousand things I want to talk about. . . . We ought to get a lot of useful dope. Hope you and your gang will have your thoughts organized, so we can get the most out of it."[69]

Among the most important topics to be discussed would be revising *FTP 167* to give a Marine commander more autonomy and authority during the planning stage and later during inland operations on the ground. Rear Admiral Turner, for instance, saw it as his prerogative to direct troop deployments on Guadalcanal, as well as to alter the tables of organization of Marine Corps units under his control. In one striking example of his meddling, he decided that a conventionally organized Marine division would be too large and unwieldy to fight the types of fluid jungle combat that Vandegrift's men experienced. Turner came to believe that the raider battalion model provided a more flexible structure. He likewise saw many benefits from small unit operations behind enemy lines, such as the marginally successful raid on Makin Island by Lieutenant Colonel Evans F. Carlson's 2nd Raider Battalion on August 17, 1942. Consequently, Turner decided he wanted all available Marine units, including the 2nd Marine Division then stationed in New Zealand, to be retrained and reorganized as raider units. He did not seek any advice from Vandegrift on this matter. Instead, Turner sent his recommendation directly to Nimitz, who in turn forwarded it to Holcomb for his reaction, as any reasonable superior officer should do.[70]

Both Holcomb and Vandegrift opposed Turner's idea of creating more raider battalions. The Marine generals and an equally dubious Admiral Nimitz believed that any properly trained Marine unit could perform tasks of infiltration or ambush when necessary. Moreover, because Turner had no expertise in ground warfare, the two Marine generals thought his recommendation was founded on faulty assumptions. Nimitz eventually sided with them and rejected Turner's proposal. At stake was a more important issue to the Corps than this particular controversy. Holcomb and Vandegrift believed that naval commanders should not interfere with the way Marine commanders structured their forces and fought their land battles. With these considerations in mind, it should be little wonder that Holcomb wanted to meet with Nimitz and eventually with Halsey to prevent Turner from further interfering and to resolve the more critical problem of command relations during amphibious assault operations.[71]

Holcomb and several key HQMC personnel finally left Washington on October 8, 1942. Of the various accounts of the trip, Brunelli's oral history interview, conducted in 1984, is the most complete and valuable.[72] Holcomb and his staff arrived in San Francisco on October 10. The next day they took an overnight flight to Pearl Harbor. During an eight-hour layover in Hawaii, Holcomb met with Nimitz, who informed the commandant of the impending relief of Ghormley by Halsey. Holcomb and Nimitz also began hammering out possible revisions to the existing command relationships between Marine and naval officers conducting amphibious operations. Nimitz was open to the potential changes that Holcomb and the Marines hoped to make.[73] "At that time, it was a blank," explained Brunelli. "Nobody was sure when and where everything stopped, where the command stopped, when who took over, and who did what to who."[74]

Later that evening of October 11, the Marine brass started to hop from island to island across the Pacific, flying from Pearl Harbor to New Zealand. They conducted brief inspections of installations. Holcomb and his tired staff landed in Wellington on October 17, but almost immediately departed to fly to Guadalcanal.[75] They risked being attacked by Japanese aircraft during this last 500-mile leg to the embattled island. Holcomb and his entourage found themselves sharing space with equipment and ammunition on two American cargo aircraft. As Austin Brunelli recalled of that flight: "I think there was a little, yes, there was a section of fighters flying shotgun on us on the way up to Guadalcanal. I spent my trip up there sitting astride a 500-pound bomb. . . . Any place you could find that you could sit, you sat. That looked like as good a place as any."[76] Such cramped travel accommodations even for the commandant of the Marine Corps were the realities of Operation Watchtower's logistical demands.

Holcomb, Brunelli, and the staff finally landed on Henderson Field at dusk on October 21, 1942. A Japanese artillery barrage welcomed the visitors, giving Holcomb an abrupt inkling of the stress endured by the Marines for the past ten weeks. Morale among the leathernecks soared because of the arrival of the commandant, who was himself a highly decorated combat veteran of the First World War. Vandegrift and his staff were especially delighted to see him on the island.[77] "It was a great thing to have General Holcomb come and spend a day or two with us. He's always been an inspiring figure," recalled Colonel Gerald C. Thomas, the division's chief of staff. "We talked a lot. We talked about his problems and his problems with Turner, the amphibious doctrine which Turner was violating, the relief of the Marines and what not by the Army and all, and we sat with Holcomb a long time at night talking to him."[78]

Seeing the poor conditions and inhospitable climate, the sixty-three-year-old commandant gained an appreciation for the strains of the situation there as he experienced firsthand the bombing raids by day and artillery barrages around the clock. He inspected the Marines' defensive perimeter that protected Henderson Field. Holcomb walked the ground where Edson's leathernecks had fought so hard in September against the Japanese. The commandant intently listened to the Marines on the island, because he wanted to learn as much as he could about their activities and needs.[79]

In his memoir, Vandegrift described Holcomb's demeanor: "As usual he spoke only when necessary, his eyes alert behind his steel-rimmed glasses. He was most interested in the descriptions of the various actions and paid numerous compliments to officers and men. I was pleased when he offered his impressions. 'Vandegrift, I think you've done a good job. I don't see how you could spread

From left: Commandant Holcomb, Lieutenant Colonel Merritt A. Edson, and Major General Alexander A. Vandegrift walk the ground on Guadalcanal, October 21–23, 1941.

(Marine Corps University Archives, Holcomb Papers, Box 39)

Holcomb (left front), pipe in hand, tours Guadalcanal with Vandegrift (left back) and Edson (right back), October 21–23, 1941.

(Marine Corps University Archives, Holcomb Papers, Box 43)

yourself out to cover any more territory than you have with what you have."[80] Vandegrift's description of the commandant's tone, activities, and words of praise were corroborated by a letter from Holcomb to Beatrice on October 24. "We talked half the night yesterday. We went over the whole position and met everyone," wrote Holcomb of his interactions with Vandegrift and his staff. "It was most interesting and they have done wonderful work. Things are rather quiet at the moment, except for the daily air raid, which didn't amount to much yesterday. I think everyone is looking wonderfully well, considering the circumstances."[81] Holcomb also mentioned to his wife that he kept photographs of her and Franklin near his bed. This month-long trip to Guadalcanal was likely their longest separation since he had become commandant. The trip definitely ranked as the most dangerous. Holcomb surely made light of the air raids to allay Beatrice's fears about her husband being in the hotly contested combat zone.

Holcomb's visit to Guadalcanal proved so worthwhile in part because Vandegrift's many reports coalesced with what the commandant now surveyed on the island. All of this presented a more accurate picture of this phase of Operation Watchtower, the complexities of which did not overwhelm the commandant. Vandegrift recalled that "General Holcomb easily took in all the details."[82] He calmly absorbed everything going on around him. Colonel Gerald Thomas averred that Holcomb "always had control of the situation."[83] In this way, he continued to demonstrate his strong "cognitive style," which, as Fred Greenstein writes of effective leadership, is that capacity to process a large amount of information and employ that data in solving problems and making decisions.[84]

Vandegrift also showed a considerable cognitive style, which carried him through the toughest months on Guadalcanal. This trait made Vandegrift, in Holcomb's mind, ideal for a still higher post in the Corps. After dinner on October 22, he spoke with Vandegrift in a private conversation. The commandant told his long-time friend and successful field commander that he intended to retire by his sixty-fourth birthday, the following September 1943. He had consistently applied this regulation to other Marines and did not wish to exempt himself, unless President Roosevelt ordered him to remain on active duty as commandant. As Vandegrift recalled in his memoir, Holcomb "studied me for a moment, then dropped a real bomb. 'If [Roosevelt] wishes me to retire, I am going to recommend you as my successor.' Brushing aside my thanks he continued, 'If he approves, I promise to keep you fully informed before you take over.'"[85]

Vandegrift was the most logical choice to be the next commandant of the Marine Corps. No other high-ranking Marine had led so many in combat. No one else displayed the combination of calmness and decisiveness that Vandegrift had on Guadalcanal. No one else boasted as much staff experience at HQMC as did he, including four years as Holcomb's military secretary and subsequently assistant to the commandant, from 1937 to 1941. Among possible competitors, only Major General Holland M. Smith, then commanding an amphibious corps and the Fleet Marine Force in San Diego, could stake a legitimate claim as Holcomb's successor.

But Holcomb did not like Smith as a person.[86] As he confided to Vandegrift, Smith would "not be very cooperative. He is becoming more impossible all the time. He was most humble and devoted until he got another corps; but now he owns the world and is getting condescending. I live and learn."[87] Holcomb made some legitimate observations about Smith's temperament. Ego and obstinacy did not detract from Howlin' Mad Smith's potential as a battlefield commander, but these traits could be liabilities as a commandant. Maintaining congenial relations with civilian and military leaders in Washington could never be Smith's forte. Commanding Marines in the field and sparring with admirals like Richmond K. "Terrible" Turner over amphibious operations suited Smith much better. Conversely, Vandegrift's temperament and bearing fit the requirements necessary to deal with the press, politicians, and officers from other services in Washington.[88]

The next day, October 23, Holcomb prepared to leave Guadalcanal to attend the planned conference with Admirals Halsey and Turner at Noumea. Holcomb and Halsey wanted Vandegrift to join them, because they believed the division commander could speak best for himself and his troops about conditions on Guadalcanal. Holcomb also doubtlessly wanted Vandegrift on hand to add weight to his attempt to revise the command structure in existing amphibious assault doctrine. Although Vandegrift did not want to leave the combat zone, where he expected an imminent ground attack, he conceded and flew with Holcomb to Noumea. Marine Brigadier General Roy Geiger assumed temporary command of the American forces on Guadalcanal, only to face the most serious and concentrated Japanese strike to date.[89]

The Noumea conference lasted two days and resulted in major successes for the Marine Corps. First, Holcomb and Vandegrift reiterated to Halsey what he already knew. Supplies of all sorts remained chronically short. The Marines' health levels were low due to infectious disease, limited medical care, and poor (and reduced) diet. The Navy had to do more to help the American forces on Guadalcanal.[90] In one key exchange, Halsey bluntly asked Vandegrift: "Can you hold?" Vandegrift replied: "Yes, I can hold. But I have to have more active support than I am getting."[91] Turner declared that the Navy was already doing all it could to help the Marines, which was true enough from his perspective. Halsey ended the discussion when he promised: "You go back there, Vandegrift. I promise to get you everything I have."[92] This unqualified pledge on behalf of the Navy constituted one major success, and Halsey would make good over the next weeks.

Second and more important in the long term, the Marine and naval officers successfully forged an agreement that reformed existing Navy-Marine command relations during amphibious operations. One controversy had centered on whether Vandegrift, as landing force commander, or Turner, as amphibious force commander, should exercise authority over the ground and air components on Guadalcanal. According to *FTP 167*, Turner held sway over Vandegrift at every stage of operations. This principle proved, however, to be impractical.[93]

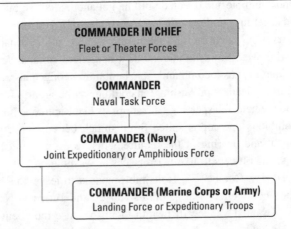

▶ Command structure during ship-to-shore movement, as drafted by Commandant Holcomb in October 1942 and later outlined in *FTP 143a* (1944).

(Adapted from Henry, "Historical Review of Command Relationships," 64)

After dinner and drinks on the second evening of the conference, Holcomb helped broker a solution to this problem, and he ghostwrote a reform in the command structure. He envisioned several new operational principles. During the planning stage for an amphibious operation, the naval expeditionary force commander and landing force commander would exercise equal authority. Then, on the voyage and during ship-to-shore movement stages, the naval commander would control all seaborne forces, including landing force units. After a successful landing had been made and a beachhead established, Marines would presumably begin moving inland.[94] It was of this last stage, according to Austin Brunelli, that Holcomb wrote: "The landing force commander should be on the same command level as the naval task force commander and should have unrestricted authority over operations ashore."[95]

Halsey and the officers at the conference then considered these reforms.[96] As Brunelli remembered the conversation, the admiral concluded, "It sounds to me like the way it ought to be," and he endorsed the revisions in draft form.[97] Halsey sent Holcomb's proposal by dispatch up the command chain to Admiral Chester Nimitz at Pearl Harbor. Meanwhile, the COMSOPAC and commandant of the Marine Corps agreed that the document would remain one step ahead of Holcomb during his return trip to Washington. That way he could field any questions along the way and guide the reforms through the Navy's bureaucracy.[98]

After this productive conference ended, Commandant Holcomb and his staff left on October 26 for their long journey home. They stopped for three days at Pearl Harbor. Holcomb met with Nimitz, who had received Halsey's dispatch with

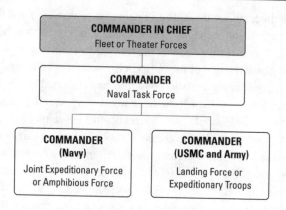

▶ Reform in command structure during inland operations, as drafted by Commandant Holcomb in October 1942 and later outlined in *FTP 143a* (1944).

(Adapted from Henry, "Historical Review of Command Relationships," 67)

the proposed revisions to *FTP 167*. Nimitz asked for Holcomb's opinion, and the commandant affirmed what he and Halsey had already said. In his capacity as CINCPAC, the ever-supportive Nimitz subsequently approved the changes.[99]

Only one more hurdle was left before they could be made official doctrine and new policy. Nimitz forwarded Halsey's COMSOPAC Dispatch 312126 to Admiral Ernest J. King in Washington. As both COMINCH and CNO by late 1942, King would have the final word. This dispatch with Nimitz's endorsement included several salient points of great significance to the Marine Corps: "Establish Corps commander on same echelon of command as commander amphibious force. . . . Joint planning between two commanders under control COMSOPAC. . . . When deemed advisable after conclusion of landing phase of an operation a task organization for the shore phase of operation will be established, or the Corps units will revert to the Corps, when and as directed by COMSOPAC."[100] Although not identical to the way Brunelli recalled the commandant's written words at Noumea, the phrases and concepts in COMSOPAC Dispatch 321216 were similar enough to Holcomb's that this lends credence to Brunelli's oral history interview and helps confirm Holcomb's contribution at Noumea and Pearl Harbor.

Also on November 3, 1942, Nimitz sent his follow-up CINCPAC Dispatch 030201 to King. This second missive read: "Recommend approval COMSOPAC 312126 but request final action be withheld until return LT General Holcomb Washington."[101] This dispatch provided still further evidence that Holcomb was in fact the author in concept, if not in precise wording, of the revisions in amphibious doctrine as previously established in *FTP 167*. It also substantiates what other sources say about his active role in guiding the reforms through the Navy's bureaucracy.

In the meantime, Holcomb left Pearl Harbor on November 5 and finally arrived in the nation's capital on the eighth. On his return, he met with King at the Navy Department, and once again examined the now-familiar revisions. At King's query about what Holcomb thought of them, Brunelli quoted the commandant as saying, "That is the way a landing operation ought to be conducted."[102] Holcomb's reply echoed Halsey's words back on Noumea. King concurred and accepted the policy changes. No more would naval commanders control the amphibious planning process, nor would they prescribe the employment of ground and air assets following the establishment of a beachhead and movement inland. Holcomb had, thus, successfully shepherded the reforms up the chain of command in remarkably short order. He showed himself to be especially adept at working within that system. In so doing, he helped to streamline future amphibious operations.[103] It is also worth noting that Holcomb could not have moved so quickly without the openness of Halsey, Nimitz, and King to the proposed revisions.

Available evidence proves that the basic tenets of Holcomb's prescribed reforms did occur in policy and later in practice. Wordings and concepts akin to those of his suggested revisions and of COMSOPAC Dispatch 312126 can also be found in *Fleet Tactical Publication 143a: War Instructions, United States Navy, 1944.* Admiral King approved and authorized *FTP 143a* in late 1944, and it essentially superseded *FTP 167.*[104]

The fourteen chapters in *FTP 143a* set forth the Navy's stances on various aspects of seaborne operations. Of particular interest was the final chapter, titled "Amphibious Operations."[105] It covered definitions, organizations, command relations, group tasks, plans, and training of the naval, aerial, and amphibious forces participating in an amphibious operation, otherwise known as a "joint expeditionary operation."[106] The most important part of *FTP 143a*'s last chapter was the third section, "Command Relationships": "A joint expeditionary force, or attack force, is under naval command until the troops are established ashore at the objective. . . . [Then] the commander expeditionary troops, or landing force, assumes command of the forces ashore. . . . Marine forces organized as landing forces perform the same tasks as stated for the Army in Joint Action of the Army and Navy, whether operating with the Navy alone or in conjunction with Army and Navy in an amphibious operation."[107] The shift in command in this passage for *FTP 143a* closely resembles reforms to *FTP 167* that Holcomb had proposed, and that had been subsequently enumerated in COMSOPAC Dispatch 312126 in late 1942.

Beyond winding their way through bureaucratic channel onto paper, Holcomb's reforms found applications in practice. The new command relationships took effect at Bougainville, Tarawa, and subsequent amphibious operations in the Pacific and European theaters of operation, in which naval commanders and their Marine Corps or Army counterparts shared responsibility. They greatly enhanced the efficiency of the Navy–Marine Corps and Navy-Army coordination as forces landed, established beachheads, moved inland, and secured objectives.[108] Holcomb's reforms in command relationships reverberated through decades thereafter in the establishment of the Marine Air-Ground Task Force during the Cold War.

Apart from meeting with King at the Navy Department, the commandant also confidently reported to Roosevelt and the American people that progress was being made on Guadalcanal. In an interview for the *Army-Navy Register* appearing on November 14, 1942, Holcomb stated: "The boys on Guadalcanal are tired. . . . There is no doubt about that. They have been under fire now for three months, twice as long as any division remained under fire at the front in France during the last war. Anybody else would be tired, and some of them break down and have to be evacuated, but the condition of that division is surprisingly good when you consider how long they have been in the line."[109] He then offered an assessment of the American troops relative to the Japanese, none too subtly tinged with racism: "The fighting has proved that the young American marine and the American soldier are individually superior to the Jap soldier in all respects—we had feared it might be otherwise, but it is not."[110]

No longer could the cynical epithet Operation Shoestring be applied to the Marines of Guadalcanal. Indeed, Holcomb fully expected an American victory.[111] He responded to one citizen who had written directly to Roosevelt expressing reservations about conditions on the island. The White House staff had forwarded the letter to HQMC. "You may be assured that everyone in authority is constantly considering the welfare and comfort of our armed services. High ranking officers representing our President are keeping him advised of the trend of affairs in the Pacific area," wrote Holcomb reassuringly. "The undersigned, accompanied by other high ranking Marine officers, has recently completed an inspection of the South Pacific areas, flying over 27,000 miles in 25 days. I can assure you that our forces are doing magnificent work."[112]

Back in the South Pacific, Admiral Halsey provided his promised support to Vandegrift. The aggressive admiral committed all available resources to the defense of Guadalcanal. President Roosevelt and the JCS made Halsey's task easier by making victory on Guadalcanal a major priority. They ordered more resources fed into Watchtower to ensure its success. Vandegrift's Marines subsequently received regular supply shipments as well as reinforcements, including sizable elements of the 2nd Marine Division and the Army's Americal Division.[113] The rest of October and November, however, saw more difficult trials as the Japanese ground, air, and naval forces desperately tried to dislodge the Americans from the island, but to no

Commandant Thomas Holcomb smiles while showing the 5-to-1 ratio of Japanese aircraft losses to those of the Americans on Guadalcanal, c. November 1942.

(Marine Corps University Archives, Holcomb Papers, Box 42)

avail. The four days of November 12–15, 1942, doomed the Japanese to defeat. In a series of running engagements known collectively as the Naval Battle of Guadalcanal, American ships and planes not only devastated Japanese naval forces but also demolished an already moribund logistical system.[114]

Finally, Vandegrift and the exhausted 1st Marine Division were relieved and left the island for some much-needed recuperation in Australia on December 9, four months almost to the day since D-day on August 7. Shortly before his departure, Vandegrift wrote to Holcomb: "This has been a memorable experience for me and one I will always cherish. . . . The comradeship and respect that I have gained for the American boy in adverse conditions under trying times makes me confident that they will carry on until and after this thing is over."[115] Sporadic yet vicious fighting dragged on another two months before the Americans could declare the island secure on February 9, 1943. Victory in the six-month campaign for Guadalcanal went to the Americans. Never again would the Japanese maintain any sustained offensive operations, nor would they stem the tide of the grinding American onslaught.[116]

In a speech to Marine students in Quantico on December 18, 1942, Commandant Holcomb may have touted Guadalcanal as a victory, yet he cautioned his audience against over-optimism:

The outlook is far more encouraging now than it has been since the start of the war. Axis aggression has been stalled by the rise of power of the allied forces but we do not, we dare not, be misled by the trend of present events. We must guard against the idea that this is the point at which the enemy will give up and collapse. Far from it, they will fight more intensely. Let us have no illusions. We know that the time of victory is not just around the corner. . . . If good leadership and good soldiering have brought us to the turning point, the best of both will bring us to final victory.[117]

Thomas Holcomb had performed many essential duties in support of Alexander Vandegrift and his Marines desperately fighting on Guadalcanal. He had navigated bureaucratic channels to initiate critical reforms in command relations that would help ensure successful amphibious operations in the future. For his part, Vandegrift provided inspiring and effective leadership for the leathernecks on Guadalcanal facing a fanatical enemy. Together Holcomb and Vandegrift worked to overcome obstacles and challenges in strategy, logistics, personality, and bureaucracy. Their teamwork could not be said to have been sufficient cause for the American victory, because too many other factors and people had also affected the overall outcome. Nevertheless, Holcomb and Vandegrift both made necessary contributions that worked toward victory at Guadalcanal. They also left lasting legacies in amphibious doctrine, policy, and practice.

CHAPTER 6

PREPARING THE CORPS
FOR A
NEW COMMANDANT

July 1942–December 1943

A lthough the American victory on Guadalcanal represented a strategic watershed, Commandant Thomas Holcomb could not focus his attention entirely on that campaign in late 1942. He needed to further enlarge the Marine Corps' force structure, streamline the service's organization, and exploit every victory to generate publicity and maintain recruitment. Having yielded to pressure to allow African Americans into the Corps, Holcomb would find himself forced to accept women. However, he consigned these two groups to noncombatant support roles or segregated units. Meanwhile, the American counteroffensive took shape with the Marines making significant contributions in the amphibious assault on Tarawa and ongoing operations in the Solomon Islands. After serving seven years as commandant, Holcomb would finally retire in December 1943, bequeathing a modern fighting force of 385,000 Marines to his successor, Alexander A. Vandegrift.

Official portrait of Commandant Thomas Holcomb, 1943.

HOLCOMB STREAMLINES THE MARINE CORPS

Maintaining logistical support for combat units on Guadalcanal while at the same time expanding the Marine Corps to meet future operational requirements proved almost insurmountable tasks for Commandant Holcomb. Although manpower, materiel, and organizational problems hampered his efforts to manage the service's continuing expansion, he succeeded in bringing new combat units on line and initiated several reforms in organizational structure at HQMC. September 1942 saw the activation of the 3rd Marine Division under Major General Charles D. Barrett at Camp Elliott, California. Plans were being laid to add still more divisions in 1943 and thereafter.

With the 1st and 2nd Marine Divisions, each numbering some 18,000 Marines, already deployed in the Pacific theater by autumn 1942, it became obvious that Holcomb needed larger corps-strength formations composed of at least two divisions and attendant units. Otherwise, he worried that the existing Marine divisions might be absorbed into one of the U.S. Army's corps. Holcomb's fears did not come to fruition, because he helped lay the foundation for two amphibious corps. Most Marines had never dreamed of seeing such large units composed of two or more divisions.[1]

The 2nd Joint Training Force (2nd JTF) on the West Coast, under Major General Clayton B. Vogel, had potential to expanded into corps-sized unit. Originally an under-strength formation dedicated to preparing Marines for amphibious operations, it was impractical as a combat unit. Holcomb decided that Vogel's 2nd JTF should be redesignated in April 1942 as the more battle-oriented Amphibious Corps, Pacific Fleet. Still commanding the new entity, Vogel bore administrative responsibility for all Marines stationed in the Southwest Pacific Area, including all logistical and personnel matters affecting combat operations.

But because these duties did not suit Vogel, Holcomb replaced him with Major General Holland M. Smith in September 1942. Smith had languished on the East Coast, where he had conducted endless landing exercises and trained amphibious units since Pearl Harbor nine months earlier. As the new commander of the Amphibious Corps, Pacific Fleet, the more capable Smith would lead Marines in future amphibious assault operations. The unit would be redesignated as V Amphibious Corps in August 1943.[2] One month after being replaced by Smith, Vogel assumed command of the second corps-sized unit, the I Marine Amphibious Corps (IMAC) established in October 1942. This new entity did nothing, in the short term, to resolve command relations that overlapped on the West Coast and in the Pacific, causing more confusion in reality than on paper. Planning and directing amphibious operations stretched the pessimistic and hesitant Vogel's capabilities to their breaking point. At any given moment during 1942, Smith, Vogel, or Vandegrift on Guadalcanal shared functional authority in a disunited command structure that gave Vogel nominal seniority but made decision-making problematic, because the chain of command was neither clear nor clean.

Vogel's shortcomings, common knowledge in the Pacific, were also recognized at HQMC. In 1943, Vice Admiral Halsey asked Holcomb to replace him in IMAC with Major General Vandegrift, then preparing to assume the commandancy. Holcomb agreed; and, despite his long friendship with Vogel, the commandant removed him a second time and appointed Vandegrift in July 1943. As it worked out in 1944, IMAC was redesignated as III Amphibious Corps (IIIAC), an independent force with a commander able to make decisions and receive resources with minimal outside interference.[3]

Back at HQMC, Holcomb tried to alleviate endless problems expanding the influence of the Quartermaster Department and the Division of Plans and Policies. The effective Major General Seth Williams, serving as quartermaster general since 1937, managed the logistical process and ensured timely release of moneys for wartime expenditures. Of course, Williams worked from the same position of weakness that affected the commandant and the entire Marine Corps. The service depended on the Navy, Army, and commercial sources for most of its resources. The Corps procured only 5 percent of its weapons, equipment, and supplies internally, whereas 70 percent came from the Army and Navy, and 25 percent from commercial sources.

The Division of Plans and Policies, otherwise known as Pots and Pans, also performed well under its director, Brigadier General Keller E. Rockey. He established regulations governing enlistment practices in the Corps and timetables affecting troop rotations between the Pacific and the United States. Rockey did not, however, exercise any authority over putting these policies into practice. This left him and his division at an administrative disadvantage.[4]

Implementation could be even more problematic because of duplicated effort and overlapping authority plagued the Adjutant and Inspector's Department (A&I), the Division of Personnel, and the Division of Reserve, which were collectively known as the HQMC's administrative staff. A&I maintained the Marines' individual records. Personnel supervised tour assignments, annual leaves, and medical surveys. Reserve bore primary responsibility for officer procurement in that most newly minted Marine officers received reserve commissions before being called to active duty.

The Personnel Division's failure to coordinate its record-keeping process meant that individual Marine reservists with particular training and expertise might not be directed to those units requiring troops with their skills. HQMC, at least in terms of manpower, thus suffered from a haphazardly decentralized structure. Making matters more complicated was the fact that other departments and divisions kept their own internal personnel records, separate from Personnel, A&I, or Reserve. This arrangement clogged HQMC with unnecessary paperwork documenting troop transfers, new duty stations, annual leave requests, retirements, and even parking space assignments. If Holcomb had questions regarding these matters, he might have to contact four different directors, each with his own fiefdom, and their answers could be contradictory. This convoluted arrangement made almost impossible Holcomb's attempts to manage a war with tens of thousands of Marines scattered across the Pacific. HQMC needed to be restructured.[5]

The reforms in 1943 stood as yet more examples of Holcomb's "organizational capacity" that political scientist Fred Greenstein sees as an intangible quality of a leader who structures subordinates' activities in efficient ways. Holcomb's efforts likewise embodied his most dynamic attempts at reconfiguring HQMC, the results of which looked very much like the progressive managerial solutions advocated by classical organizational theorists Max Weber and Chester Bernard. It must be noted that no documentary connections exist between Holcomb and these progressive thinkers, but this does not mean that the commandant was not indirectly or tangentially influenced by their principles of rationality and efficiency.[6] His considerable leadership and managerial strengths notwithstanding, reforming HQMC challenged Holcomb in at least two ways.

First, the commandant needed a clearly defined organizational structure that minimized duplication of effort and maximized creative problem-solving. Ever the progressive, Holcomb requested an expert evaluation of HQMC by the Navy Department's Management Engineer's office. Beginning in August 1942, this office spent five months examining all structures and functions of Holcomb's staff. The study found that a lack of accountability, coordination, and information management severely hampered the staff's efficiency. The Management Engineer's final report, completed in January 1943, suggested a variety of improvements that could streamline HQMC. Most important of these was the creation of a new centralized entity to deal with all personnel issues. Holcomb accepted the recommendations and established the Personnel Department on May 1, 1943. It absorbed the old A&I Department and Divisions of Personnel, Reserve, and Recruitment. Holcomb thus consolidated all functions regarding recruitment, training, assignment, discipline, promotion, and records.[7] In so doing, he achieved key progressive managerial goals of balancing vertical levels and horizontal divisions within his organizational structure.

Holcomb's second distinct challenge entailed extending control over all communication, decision-making, and implementation processes to ensure accountability at all levels. The logistical and operational problems he had seen during his trip to Guadalcanal in October and November 1942 made restructuring the HQMC organization all the more urgent. When problems arose, unit commanders should be able to request assistance directly from HQMC, where Holcomb or his senior staff could determine which division, department, or section should handle the request. This was in keeping with the practice Holcomb had established early in his commandancy. He wasted little time with what he saw as endless conferences, because he believed that a single office should have the authority and responsibility to solve problems. Once that office had recommended solutions, Holcomb issued a brief Letter of Instruction that stated the new policy and offered a brief justification.

In this way, Holcomb used his prerogative as commandant to effect needed changes, whether they involved seemingly mundane decisions like determining

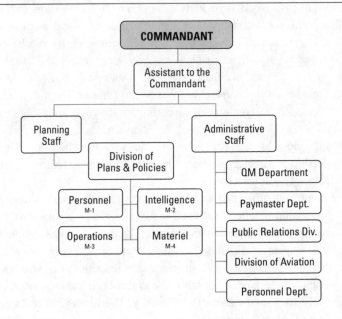

▶ Commandant Holcomb's second organizational reforms of Headquarters Marine Corps, 1943.

(Adapted from Rottman, *Marine Corps Order of Battle*, 41–43)

ice cream consumption quotas for Marines or much more serious ones such as establishing promotion procedures for African American Marines. His Letters of Instruction circulated widely among Marine officers and helped to put into practice the new policy or decision. This system proved decisive and effective, at least in cases where internal solutions could be found.[8] Colonel James P. Berkeley of Plans and Policies claimed that Holcomb's reforms worked well: "Once we knew of the need, we responded as rapidly as possible."[9]

Beyond Holcomb's attempts to initiate progressive administrative reforms throughout the Corps, he could solve some problems simply by providing solid leadership. Writing to a friend in 1943, Holcomb explained that "even if it has an ideal chart, any large organization, to be successful, must be headed by a personality; one possessed of those qualities of leadership which command respect and loyalty; which inspires in all hands the determination, and which is more important, the compelling desire, to work together for a common end." For Holcomb, even the most carefully conceived structural reforms could fail because "no graph or chart, no rules and regulations, or other printed works, can replace such leadership."[10]

Shortly after his retirement in December 1943, Holcomb pinpointed the traits of an effective leader for some newly commissioned Marine officers. "You officers will be leaders in our future operations," he said. "Leadership is not easy, is not automatic. You must be possessed of these qualities of leadership which command respect and loyalty—which inspire in all hands the determination—and more important—the compelling desire to work together for a common end."[11] These statements were two of the very few explanations of this kind that Holcomb offered. They hinted at the decades of his growth as a leader and manager, both through observing others in action and through developing his own style by trial and error.

HOLCOMB'S PUBLICITY AND RECRUITMENT SUCCESS AND SETBACKS

In late 1942 and throughout the following year, the Marine Corps' publicity and recruitment activities continued to portray Marines as the finest, toughest, most elite warriors in the U.S. military. Maintaining these favorable images for the American people remained a major priority for Brigadier General Robert L. Denig Sr., still director of the Division of Public Relations. The importance of his efforts was lost on no one, neither inside nor outside the Corps.

"Public relations includes not only official communication with the public media," as Secretary of the Navy Franklin Knox explained in July 1942, "but, broadly, all contact between naval officers and the public in connection with operations, activities, or projects, whether of naval origin or not, that are a subject of public interest or in connection with which naval participation in publicity is proposed."[12] A Letter of Instruction from HQMC replicated Knox's statement verbatim and made it Denig's mission. Civilian support proved essential in a long conflict such as the Second World War. Denig adopted a motto stressing that reality: "If the public becomes apathetic about the Marine Corps, the Marine Corps will cease to exist."[13]

Apathy was not a problem once the war had begun. Media outlets working with the Office of War Information willingly accommodated the needs of the Corps and the military as a whole.[14] "Advertising has become a fighting weapon in this way," as William L. Chenery, publisher of *Collier's*, proudly wrote to Holcomb. "Informing all of the people simultaneously so that we can all cooperate is the service that advertising has been able to render."[15] Even so, the Marine Corps lacked a mechanism to make the experience of combat real for the public. Holcomb wished, for instance, that the American people could have heard the real story of Wake's Marines, rather than learning about the doomed atoll's dogged defense from fragments of radio messages or idealized motion pictures.

Denig agreed wholeheartedly and created an innovative publicity program in the summer of 1942.[16] "We conceived the idea of enlisting young reporters and training them to be full-fledged Marines," recalled Denig years later. "They would be designated combat correspondents on the side to [join] Fleet Marine Force units and air wings. Their purpose would be threefold: to compile historical data for this Corps, to send back news and feature stories to our Headquarters for public consumption, and to help civilian correspondents in any way they could."[17]

Denig started this program by recruiting two civilian journalists, James Harblut and Herbert C. Merillat, into the Marine Corps Reserve. They immediately went on active duty and proceeded to the Southwest Pacific to join the 1st Marine Division destined for Guadalcanal. Harblut and Merillat, alongside civilian correspondents like Richard Tregaskis, reported on the war back to the home front. They gave accounts of conditions on the island, took photographs, and interviewed Marines with whom they served. Stories of the outnumbered, yet victorious Marine raiders on Edson's Ridge made for great copy. These fighting leathernecks were quickly immortalized in Marine folklore, taking their rightful place with the Devil Dogs of the First World War.[18]

If the Navy would not accept the Corps' combat correspondents' stories for some reason, the Division of Public Relations mailed copies directly to news services, radio stations, or publishers. The correspondents thus performed important functions in the publicity process and quickly became a fixture in public relations.[19] Military historian Allan R. Millett pays them an eloquent tribute: "The correspondents found their way into the early waves of each landing, bled and died beside infantry on the front lines, and wrote wartime prose reminiscent of Stephen Crane and Ernest Hemingway. . . . If the central Pacific campaign was the supreme test of amphibious doctrine, it was also a media event of unparalleled drama for American war reporting. And it was the Marine version of that war that largely dominated the press."[20] News from these reporters and other media outlets stirred up patriotism. The civilian populace began to identify with Marines in combat. Writing directly to Commandant Holcomb in late 1942, the mother of one Guadalcanal Marine stated, "I believe I am almost as much a Marine as any of you, only I can't talk the Recruiting office into giving me a uniform or sending me to 'Boot Camp.' I write to several Marines, bake cookies regularly for at least eight Marines, and am 'seeing' a boot through boot camp with candy bars and cigarettes each week."[21] The Marine thus became the nation's every-son.

The Corps' publicity efforts also helped promote the American war effort as a whole. A transition in the media's messages, however, occurred in 1943. Earlier in the conflict, popular reports had minimized the costs of lives and materials for fear of demoralizing Americans. But as the months dragged into years, political and military leaders worried that perhaps the American people would lose interest or became too overconfident. The tone of news circulating in the United States grew more realistic in 1943 than before. Marine combat correspondents, it should be noted, drove the leading edge of this move toward authenticity. The war's brutality in words and images steeled the nation's commitment to victory. The new realism filtered down to the people.[22]

Holcomb understood how closely linked with recruitment were the public image of the Corps and war. As he neared retirement in December 1943, the commandant told journalist John G. Norris of the *Washington Post* what traits those men should display. "We must have men," averred Holcomb, "who feel a sense of responsibility for their country, a sense of responsibility which makes them willing to take chances to risk their lives if necessary, in dangerous and difficult tasks." He then laid out more ideal characteristics for Marines: "We must have men who want to learn; men who realize that discipline is essential for the best results, who recognize that they have a responsibility to men under them as well as to those above them. We must have men who realize the teamwork is important, that it pays dividends. And finally, we must cultivate ingenuity, inventiveness, for the occasion when those qualities are required."[23] Holcomb wanted mature, adult men in his Corps. This fit perfectly with the public image of the service that was presented to potential recruits and the American people.

Good publicity had positive effects on the Corps' growth. New enlistments averaged 16,500 per month from July 1942 until the year's end. Holcomb's amiable relations with a sympathetic Congress, especially the ranking members of the Naval Affairs Committees in both houses, made this authorization process quick and easy. Holcomb and Vandegrift offered testimony about the Corps' expected needs in early 1943. They formed an effective team as the able commandant and his battle-hardened field commander.[24] They made "progress" in what Holcomb termed the "Battle of Washington."[25] For example, the service received congressional authorization in September 1942 to expand to 223,000 enlisted men plus officers by July 1943. Enlistment figures exceeded this figure by January 1943, six months ahead of schedule.[26]

The Marine Corps' massive recruiting surge of 1942 receded the next year, when a heretofore unfamiliar dilemma emerged. President Franklin Roosevelt's E.O. 9279 on December 5, 1942, caused a sea change in recruiting efforts. The new mandate forced Marines to cease their recruitment of volunteers and instead use those men drafted under the Selective Service Act of 1940 and its subsequent extensions and modifications. The changes sent tremors up and down the ranks of the Corps. Marines worried that they could maintain neither the image nor the reality of an elite force of volunteers with more rigorous physical standards for enlistment than the Navy or the Army. Such anxieties were not without foundation, because a huge percentage of those 46 million male registrants were classified "IV-F," or unacceptable for military service. They failed to meet the minimum physical and medical fitness for general "induction," the term used for men drafted into any of the armed services. The rejection rates of unfit draftees in all services reached 50 percent during 1942, and 65 percent in 1943. Only 10 million draftees of the pool of registrants met or exceeded standards for military service, and this in turn reduced the pool from which Marines might draw.[27]

Possible reductions in medical and physical qualifications of drafted men represented a major crisis for the Corps and the other services. In May 1943, eight military medical, personnel, and recruitment officers from the Army, Navy, and Marine Corps met at a conference to negotiate new standards for physical and medical fitness under the Selective Service system. They agreed that height standards should be uniform throughout the U.S. military.[28]

In cases of dental hygiene and venereal disease, all three services concurred that consistent standards should be adopted. Multiple missing teeth, severe malocclusion, or dental disease would disqualify inductees, because these indicated possible malnutrition, among other health problems. Some venereal diseases, such as acute or uncomplicated gonorrhea, would not necessarily disqualify an inductee. But a diagnosis of syphilis would be grounds for immediate rejection. Induction standards for hearing and vision proved to be points of contention. Soldiers attending the conference called for the Navy to reduce its requirements in these areas to levels that were lower than the sailors and Marines were willing to admit.[29]

The Army and Navy representatives articulated two different plans to change U.S. military medical and physical standards. The sailors and Marines suggested that only a few fitness levels should be lowered, while others remained at their current higher levels; but the soldiers attempted to maintain more existing lower fitness levels and conceded that others could be raised. The conferees submitted for further deliberation a joint report with their respective recommendations to the Army Service Force's Personnel Division and the Navy's Bureau of Naval Personnel.[30]

Throughout 1943 and thereafter, Marines fought running bureaucratic battles with the Selective Service Administration, Navy, and Army over the degree to which Marine inductees should be responsible for fulfilling the more rigorous standards that the Corps had consistently demanded of new recruits. Well aware of the service's tenuous position, Commandant Holcomb weighed in on the matter. In June, he penned a strongly worded letter to the Chief of the Bureau of Naval Personnel. After conceding that the Corps would take its allotment of manpower from the Navy's designated percentage of Selective Service inductees, Holcomb cited the fact that "currently the Marine Corps is receiving but one man out of every fifteen designated for Naval service and in the future will receive men on an even smaller ratio, as it is understood that the Navy's [manpower] requirements are to be stepped up."[31]

The commandant then reminded the personnel chief that "the Marine Corps has been given a definite mission by the Joint Chiefs of Staff, which mission requires the vast majority of its personnel to be fit for combat service. . . . All men designated for combat duty by the Marine Corps should in all instances be capable of firing a rifle with accuracy under any and all circumstances. Ability to meet this requirement is largely dependent on good eyesight."[32] Marines with poor eyesight would be less effective in combat. With this in mind, Holcomb worried that the "combat efficiency of the Marine Corps" would be detrimentally affected if vision standards were lowered; he asked that inductees with visual acuity of at least 15/20 binocular vision and a minimum of 6/20 in their weaker eye "be allocated to the Marine Corps from the group allotted to the Naval forces at the Induction Centers."[33]

Holcomb only partially succeeded in preserving higher vision standards. When he received the final verdict from the Navy, he circulated to all Marine officers at induction centers and recruiting districts a memorandum listing the new standards. Marines would be required to have at least 6/20 vision in one eye and at least 10/20 in the other, without benefit of glasses. Holcomb could not, however, ensure that 15/20 binocular vision was among the new requirements for inductees' visual acuity. Marines found themselves subject to the Navy's slightly lower standards— which coincided with the Army's slightly higher standards.[34]

Although Marine inductees first received their Selective Service notices in late 1942, they did not have to answer those calls until February 1943. Holcomb successfully argued that a two-month grace period was necessary to avoid any break in recruitment, volunteer or draftee. During this window, the Corps did boast an impressive 18,083 enlistments for December 1942; but the numbers then dropped off to 9,584 in January 1943, due in part to the difficult transition from the Corps' all-volunteer recruitment process to an all-draftee induction process. Beginning in February, Holcomb submitted monthly requests to Secretary Knox for certain quotas. Knox sent those requests through the civilian bureaucracy to the Selective Service Administration, the director of which examined the Navy Department quotas for the Navy, Marine Corps, and Coast Guard, balanced them with the War Department's quota request for the Army, and finally established proportionate induction ratios for all the services.

Newly inducted Marines received the designation USMCR-SS (Selective Service) and became known as "selectees." Enlistments did rise thereafter to a monthly average of 13,000 for the remainder of 1943, but this plateau remained about 25 percent lower than the recruitment quotas for drafted manpower. The Corps' induction numbers finally reached the established quotas in June 1944.[35]

Marine recruiters and raw recruits alike took several steps to circumvent the Selective Service Act while still following policies in the letter, if not the spirit, of the law. Across the nation, recruiters carefully cultivated good relationships with local Selective Service Boards, and they worked to find creative ways of attracting the best-qualified inductees. At induction centers, recruiters successfully delayed the induction of men worthy of and interested in becoming Marines until vacancies opened up in quota requests during the following month or two. Marine recruiters also watched for drafted inductees who might be willing to be discharged and then reenlisted as regular or reserve Marines. This reenlistment option proved popular among inductees, because they could drop the dubious SS designation from their service status and avoid any negative stigma attached to being a "selectee." Still, of the 224,323 inductees entering the Corps from 1943 through 1945, some 70,000 Marines retained the SS status.[36]

Try as they might, Marine recruiters could not reach the authorized personnel levels under Selective Service procedures. To close the gap between inductions and the Corps' actual manpower requirements, the service extended age limits in the cases of recruits and retirees with specialized skills. Seventeen-year-olds were targeted, and attracting some 59,000 young men from this demographic group helped the service meet its manpower requirements. The boys voluntarily enlisted in the Marine Corps Reserve and immediately went on inactive status. As mandated by Holcomb, in no way would these seventeen-year-olds be subject to lower physical standards in the Selective Service system. This guaranteed a pool of highly qualified recruits from which to draw. Once they turned eighteen, these reservists received their calls to active duty and entered basic training.[37] The Corps' time-honored selling points of proof of manhood, patriotic duty, and elite status continued to appeal to young (overwhelmingly Caucasian) Americans. Recalling his motivations decades later, Warren Ferguson told of how he had enlisted one day before his eighteenth birthday because voluntary enlistments were "closed to all except 17 year olds" and he "felt it was the proper course to join and the Corps was the only branch."[38]

HOLCOMB'S EXCLUSIONARY PERSONNEL POLICIES

The inclusion of African Americans caused consternation in the Corps' highest echelons in 1942 and afterward. The idea of allowing women into their service would add still more irritation. Holcomb and many other Marines saw no place in their elite organization for either group, even if the service did need more recruits and inductees. Holcomb knew he had no choice but to bow to the presidential mandate to add unwanted blacks and women into the Corps. He did not make their entrance into a Caucasian male institution smooth or simple. If they were not rejected outright, these would-be recruits faced serious obstacles to enlist.

Back in May 1942, Congress had helped create the Women's Auxiliary Army Corps, which in turn had laid the foundation for establishing women's components in the Navy, Marine Corps, and Coast Guard.[39] A furious Holcomb demanded of one of the Corps' most steadfast congressional patrons, Representative and Marine Reserve Lieutenant Colonel Melvin J. Maas: "Do you know that we have to take women into the Marine Corps?" Maas responded, "Yes, I introduced that legislation." The commandant shouted into the phone, "The Marine Corps will be ruined!" He told Maas, "Our friendship is over." Holcomb eventually calmed down, and in fact he gradually grew to value the women's contributions to the Corps.[40] This was one of several spats between the commandant and the Marine reservist-congressman. They fought over Maas' candid and sometimes embarrassing reports to Congress on such matters as Marine Corps relations with the Navy.

After Maas helped push the legislation through Congress, President Roosevelt signed Public Law 689 on July 30, 1942. This act authorized the establishment of the Navy Women's Reserves (Women Accepted for Voluntary Emergency Service, WAVES) and the Marine Corps Women's Reserve (MCWR). Women could henceforth become Marines over any and all objections in the Corps.[41]

Always the pragmatist, Holcomb shrewdly decided to make the most of this situation. He needed more personnel to fill the Corps' burgeoning logistical and administrative duty stations and, of course, the places opening up in combat units. Civilians, reactivated retirees, and inductees otherwise unfit for combat could perform some of these tasks, but sufficient numbers in these groups could not be found.[42] "There are many positions which could be adequately filled by women," wrote Holcomb to Navy Secretary Knox in October 1942. "In furtherance of the war effort, it is believed that as many women as possible should be used in non-combatant billets, thus releasing a greater number of the limited manpower available for essential combat duty. The Marine Corps feels that it can procure, train and assign to duty about 6,000 women every six months." Gradually warming to the idea of female Marines, the commandant concluded with a request that "for budgetary and planning purposes the Women's Reserve of the Marine Corps be authorized a strength of 1,000 officers and 18,000 enlisted by 30 June 1944."[43] Holcomb received President Roosevelt's approval for these short- and long-term goals a few weeks later.[44]

Holcomb liked neither acronyms used in the Army and Navy nor clever nicknames like "femarines" or "marinettes," as women serving the Corps had been known in the First World War. He resisted pressure to give members of the MCWR any name that set them apart. In an interview for *Life* in 1944, Holcomb unequivocally stated: "They are Marines. They don't have a nickname and they don't need one. They get their basic training in a Marine atmosphere at a Marine post. They inherit the traditions of Marines. They are Marines."[45] Although this statement may have connoted a degree of gender equality in theory, the reality was different up and down the ranks of the Corps. Many Marines unofficially gave the women the derogatory label of BAMS, for "broad-ass marines."

On an official level, Holcomb restricted women's activities and mobility within the Corps. Nevertheless, when the announcement of the MCWR creation took place on February 13, 1943, women flocked to recruiting stations.[46] The Division of Public Relations appealed to potential women recruits' sense of patriotism and desire to "Be a Marine. . . . Free a Marine to Fight."[47] Those who were interested and of the requisite age and educational background took aptitude tests as part of the application process. Some questions assessed vocabulary, such as choosing antonyms for "good," "sedate," and "profound"; or finding the links between "bulldog" and "fox" to "tenacity" and "slyness." Other questions assessed mathematical abilities in number sequencing, word problems, and logical puzzles.[48] The aptitude-scoring thresholds for female applicants far exceeded all screening requirements for the average Caucasian male. Holcomb accepted only the most outstanding women into his elite Corps. Throughout the conflict, the Corps experienced no trouble in maintaining its recruitment numbers in the MCWR.[49]

Holding women to higher recruitment and behavior standards than men of equal rank occurred in all U.S. armed services during the Second World War. Women were expected to show the moral qualities of ladies. Only then could they not lose their femininity or, worse still, take on aggressive masculine traits. Women without good morals might yield to the temptation to become lesbians, or female homosexuals, as they were sometimes known in the 1940s. Whereas people in the Women's Army Corps fell victim to public witch hunts and smear campaigns regarding purported lesbianism in their ranks, Marines received no such institutional maltreatment or negative publicity. Actual instances of female "sexual deviance" in the Corps were handled quickly and discreetly.[50] In any event, few women Marines received "psychiatric" or "pregnancy" disqualifications from service. Among 4,448 recruits examined for active duty from July 15 to October 14, 1943, only forty women were disqualified for psychiatric reasons and twelve for pregnancy.[51]

Once women enlisted in the Corps, the Naval Reserve formed the conduit through which they passed. They took their basic training alongside the Navy's female recruits at Hunter College in New York City or at Mount Holyoke and Smith Colleges in Massachusetts. Later in 1943, the Corps set up its own facility at Camp Lejeune, North Carolina. MCWR recruits learned military etiquette, discipline, and organization, as well as Marine Corps history. Following boot camp, the newly minted women Marines received advanced training preparing them for a wide variety of assignments. Letters of Instruction Numbers 382 and 426, emanating from Commandant Holcomb's office, set the policies for how they would be chosen for particular assignments and employed at their duty stations.

Some tasks, predictably, included clerical work such as auditor, clerk, and stenographer. Yet women Marines soon added many more duties to their repertoire, including those of storekeeper, parachute rigger, aviation machinist mate, aerial photographer, radio operator, purchasing agent, and control tower operator. All of these slots required between eight to twenty-one weeks of additional training. Women eventually held 225 assignments in the Corps, most of which were also performed by their male counterparts. Some 23,000 women served in the Corps by war's end, just as Holcomb had requested back in October 1942.[52]

Whereas Holcomb and many other Marines accepted women in the Corps only grudgingly, they resented the idea of African American Marines. Never before

1942 had blacks served in the Corps. According to Holcomb's only other biographer, John W. Gordon, "the commandant's opposition reflected both his own background as well as his assessment of the practical problems arising from having to provide special segregated training arrangements for black marines. On balance, Holcomb's views on race were those of an officer corps still largely, 'drawn from an old-family, Anglo-Saxon, Protestant, rural, upper-middle-class background.'"[53] Gordon quotes from Morris Janowitz's sociological study *The Professional Soldier*, which describes the socio-cultural lens through which most Marines viewed the world. In their Corps, they tolerated no challenges to their racial hegemony. Only under duress from President Roosevelt had the tradition-bound Holcomb acquiesced to including blacks.[54]

Recruitment of African Americans remained slow throughout 1942. Potential recruits found it easier to join the Army because, among other things, the Corps' demanding aptitude tests turned away many of all races, let alone African Americans. Less than half the desired total of 1,200 recruits had enlisted by September 1942. And after blacks did enter the Corps, they encountered institutionalized racism. They went through a segregated boot camp called Montford Point at Camp Lejeune, after which they served in all-black defense battalions, depot companies, and ammunition companies. Those units were officially relegated to garrison or logistical duties far behind the front lines in the Pacific War, although in practice many black Marines saw combat in the lengthy Central Pacific battles of 1944 and 1945. At no time during the conflict, however, did an African American become a Marine officer or receive command of Caucasian troops.[55]

African American Marines performed race-specific duties, as summarized in a memorandum from HQMC in December 1942. Those deemed less intelligent or less capable were assigned to "the type of duty which could be best performed by colored personnel and at the same time disturb the Marine Corps as little as possible," including assignments as messmen, chauffeurs, messengers, clerks, and janitors.[56] Those demonstrating greater intelligence and ability might advance to noncommissioned-officer rank and be transferred to duty with a Marine unit. The 1942 memorandum concluded with a defense of its policies: "The latter provision will largely tend to do away with the charge of race discrimination, as every Negro is placed in position for advancement as rapidly as he can so qualify."[57] Holcomb thus employed bureaucratic language to keep his Corps as free as possible from what he believed would be the detrimental effects of allowing blacks to become "real" Marines.[58]

By war's end, some 3,000 African Americans had volunteered and succeeded in becoming Marines, while 16,000 more entered the Corps through Selective Service. With very few exceptions, they served their nation and their Corps well.[59] Nevertheless, negative attitudes about blacks remained deeply embedded in the service. Colonel Samuel A. Woods Jr. explained to Holcomb what it was like to command the segregated basic training at Montford Point: "There have been obstacles and struggles. At times things have been humiliating for my family and for myself. Unfortunately, these unpleasant things have come from white people who should know better. However, they did not know and they have not thought."[60] Plaintive in its tone, Woods' letter understated the reality of institutional prejudice in the Corps. Holcomb's reply is not available, so any justifications he might have offered cannot be known. But elsewhere, his feelings about race and gender can be gleaned from the candid comments he directed to Major General Charles F. B. Price in May 1943: "Our three new projects—the colored folk, the women, and the dogs—are coming along satisfactorily. It will be difficult to carry out our work with such a large proportion of the first group mentioned, but we have got to do the best we can. The women are fine. We are getting a very high grade, and those on clerical duty are extremely efficient. The dogs are apparently quite a success."[61] The commandant's note revealed much about how he envisioned the Corps' cultural hierarchy.

Although defeated on the gender and racial fronts, Holcomb maintained what he considered to be standards of moral uprightness. The new influx of personnel meant that unfit and unworthy men might slip into the Corps, thus depriving his elite institution of its mystique and combat effectiveness. These possibilities worried the Marines, so they tried to build more bureaucratic hedges around themselves to stop any tainting of their service by recruits.[62]

So great were the manpower shortages that men with criminal records and jail time enlisted in the armed services. The Army accepted felons by the tens of thousands without disastrous results. In the case of criminals from Illinois, for instance, nearly 90 percent performed their duties well enough to receive honorable discharges. But the Marine Corps rejected volunteers or selectees with records.[63] In one case in October 1942, the father of a young applicant appealed directly to President Roosevelt. He requested that his son, implicated in an automobile theft and briefly incarcerated, be allowed to volunteer as a Marine. The father passionately wrote that his son now knew "that crime does not pay and has repented his folly. He has also promised me with tears in this eyes to make the military his life's work and to die for his country if need be. Is there any way you could intercede for him in order that he may enter the service of his country? He is so sincere that I know he will make good. Please Mr. President let us not keep him down."[64]

The White House post office again forwarded this father's letter to HQMC for action. Just as he had done in the past, W. E. Burke, now a lieutenant colonel in the Division of Recruiting, produced a reply in less than a week, rejecting the appeal in another form letter: "One of the strongest appeals of the Marine Corps to young men and their families is the fact that it does not accept, knowingly, men with police records. To make an exception in a case of this kind would discredit our claim to this appeal and would also establish a precedent which is not desired by the Marine Corps. While this ruling may work a hardship in certain individual cases of young men who earnestly desire to rehabilitate themselves, it is considered in the best interest of the services to adhere to the character requirements in all cases."[65] As with earlier appeals to waive the Corps' recruitment standards, Commandant Holcomb likely did not read this particular letter, but the policy cited by Burke emanated from high echelons at HQMC.

The Corps' strict policies regarding moral behavior did not stop with criminal activities. Beginning in 1942 and intensifying in early 1943, would-be Marines underwent careful screening for deviant sexual behavior. Applicants first received a medical examination assessing their physical fitness and health levels. Assuming they met minimal standards, they then endured psychiatric evaluations to determine mental and emotional stability. The second page of the "Report of Physical Examination," officially designated NMS Form Y 1939, contained a line item reading "Abnormal Psyche (neurasthenia, psychasthenia, depression, instability, worries)" followed by two blank lines for the examining doctor's explanation of the applicant's state of mind.[66]

Psychiatrists at the Menninger Clinic in Topeka, Kansas, consulting with the armed services and Selective Service Administration, used terms such as "psychoneurotic behavior" or "sexual psychopathy" to denote homosexual characteristics or tendencies. This paranoia continued in basic training and in the Pacific, where superior officers and physicians watched for any signs of sexual deviance among active duty Marines.[67]

In the historical context of the 1940s, the psychiatric community increasingly saw homosexuality not as immoral or criminal, but instead as a mental disease or behavioral maladjustment of unfit people. Within military circles, it was thought, homosexuals might prey on younger men or recruit them into their gay troupes, thus spreading their lifestyle to more and more people. This could hurt not only the morale but also the combat performance of the Marine units to which they belonged. Any Marine under suspicion could face extended investigation and adjudication processes. The final decisions and summary details wound their way from Marine units to HQMC for Holcomb's endorsement. He was, thus, privy to the details of all the cases.[68]

The assumptions and attendant policies regarding homosexuality left open too many possibilities for false or mistaken allegations that could lead to hazing incidents, tarnished personnel records, courts-martial, dishonorable discharges, and incarcerations. As cultural historian Beth Bailey argues: "Even though a system of moral absolutes had been replaced by a much more flexible system of evaluation, the two systems remained enmeshed, with the new 'scientific' evaluation often used to support old 'moral' claims." She concludes: "'Mental Illness' was the moral equivalent of sin. Thousands of men rejected by or discharged from the armed forces on psychiatric grounds during World War II returned home with official documents (requested by all prospective employers) labeling them 'sexual deviants.'"[69] Strong applicants and good Marines, regardless of sexual orientation, were doubtlessly victimized by what is homophobia in twenty-first-century parlance, and what in this context could be defined literally as the fear of homosexual behavior. Later in 1944, then-Commandant Alexander Vandegrift and the Navy's Neuropsychiatric Service initiated legal reforms that made investigation procedures confidential and more judicious.[70]

CHANGING PACIFIC STRATEGY AND MORE AMPHIBIOUS ASSAULTS

The significance of Guadalcanal's capture in February 1943 cannot be overstated in terms of either strategic importance or morale. The courageous Marines, soldiers, and sailors had penetrated the outer ring of Japanese defenses and maintained their foothold. Holcomb's brimming optimism can be felt in this letter to one of his cousins: "We will win this war, be sure of that, but I am afraid it is too much to hope that we will win it in 1943. But we must all do our best."[71] Indeed, the struggle on Guadalcanal represented the entire war in the Pacific writ small: American logistical resources and military power slowly overcame the Japanese fighting spirit, and American ingenuity and aggressiveness took full advantage of the enemy's mistakes and weaknesses.[72]

U.S. forces could now start rolling back enemy forces, and the Orange War Plan could finally be put into action. The theater-level situation in the Pacific seemed clear enough. The second and third stages of COMINCH-CNO Ernest King's strategic plan of April 1942 could progress toward the invasion of New Guinea and isolation of Rabaul in the Southwest Pacific. Meanwhile, the Americans could commence executing King's third stage by neutralizing and occupying key Japanese bases in the Marshall and Gilbert Island chains in the Central Pacific. Nevertheless, no clear directives existed for allocating national resources between these Pacific counteroffensives and ongoing Allied operations in Europe and the Mediterranean theaters. To solve this problem, President Roosevelt, Prime Minister Winston Churchill, and the Combined Chiefs of Staff met in Casablanca, Morocco, in January 1943. Intense debates erupted as the Allied commanders attempted to justify some strategic needs relative to others. The British representatives argued for all-out concentration on winning the Battle of the Atlantic and completing the conquest of North Africa and Italy. The Americans, especially Ernest King, desired a balance between the two theaters.[73]

Commandant Holcomb did not attend the Casablanca Conference, but he surely paid close attention to its outcomes. He recognized continuing opportunities, not only for the United States to exercise the strategic initiative against Japan, but also for the Marine Corps to fulfill its ongoing dual mission of seizure and defense of advanced bases. The Corps' place in Pacific strategy solidified still further at the

Pacific Military Conference in March 1943, and then at the Trident Conference later in May. American forces would island-hop and leapfrog their way to Japan in a two-pronged offensive. Marine divisions in IMAC would participate in Operation Cartwheel in the Solomons under General Douglas MacArthur's Southwest Pacific command. Meanwhile, the 2nd Marine Division would be trained and equipped in anticipation of Operation Galvanic in the Central Pacific under CINCPAC Chester W. Nimitz. As positive as the American situation looked just eighteen months after Pearl Harbor, nagging equipment shortages and inefficient logistical coordination between the Army and Navy, and excessive numbers of untested replacement troops plagued all U.S. combat units in the Pacific.[74]

Beginning on June 21, 1943, several U.S. Army units, augmented by Marine Corps raider and defense battalions, landed on New Georgia. This was the next large island up the Slot in the Solomons, just northwest of Guadalcanal. The Americans fought for several weeks before seizing the key Japanese airfield near Munda Point in northern New Georgia. American aircraft could subsequently use this base to provide air support for the next movements up the Slot toward Rabaul and the northern Solomons.[75] The next step in the island-hopping campaign came with the assault and capture of Bougainville, the last major island in the Solomons standing between American forces and the major Japanese base at Rabaul. Admiral Halsey tapped IMAC to make the assault on Bougainville.

Meanwhile, on September 15, Vandegrift, newly promoted lieutenant general and temporary commander of IMAC, handed the reins over to Major General Charles D. Barrett. IMAC appeared to be in good hands when Vandegrift departed on a theater-wide inspection tour before returning to HQMC to replace Holcomb as the next commandant. But tragedy struck on October 8, when Barrett fell from a balcony to his death. Holcomb ordered Vandegrift to rush back to complete IMAC's preparation for the coming attack on Bougainville.[76]

When the 3rd Marine Division (Reinforced) landed on Bougainville on November 1, 1943, Vandegrift proudly reported to Holcomb that the assault "went off beautifully and was one of the best examples of coordinated amphibious effort that I have seen so far. The timing was perfect. The air, both fighter and bombardment, was superior."[77] Soon thereafter, on November 10, Vandegrift left IMAC a second time, to make his way to Washington. The competent Major General Roy S. Geiger replaced him as commanding officer of IMAC. Elsewhere, the 1st Marine Division landed on New Britain at Cape Gloucester, in the northern Solomons. Operations on the island helped isolate the Japanese base at Rabaul, which was never attacked directly by American ground or amphibious forces.[78]

The Marine Corps' most difficult amphibious assaults in the Second World War began in November 1943, on Tarawa Atoll in the Gilbert Island chain. As part of Operation Galvanic, attacking Tarawa represented the first of many stepping-stones leading across the Central Pacific to the Japanese home islands proper.

Planning for the actual attack on Tarawa Atoll, with its airfield on the island of
Betio, began in earnest in August 1943. Major General Julian C. Smith, commanding general of the 2nd Marine Division, and Vice Admiral Raymond A. Spruance,
commander of the Navy's Central Pacific Force, met secretly in New Zealand to
discuss the most practical way to seize the atoll. The 2nd Division's operations
officer, Lieutenant Colonel David M. Shoup, accompanied Smith to provide added
amphibious expertise. He concluded that attacking from the north looked like the
best approach. This meant that amphibious assault craft would move into Tarawa's
interior lagoon before hitting the northern shoreline of Betio.[79]

Despite the great care taken in the planning stage, the actual amphibious assault
on Betio Island on D-day, November 20, 1943, nearly ended in disaster. The pre-
invasion naval and aerial bombardment did not sufficiently soften up Japanese
defenses. During an unexpectedly low tide, the LCVPs, as Higgins' modified
Eureka boats with bow-ramps were known, ran aground on the coral reef inches
below the water's surface. Marines disembarked from these useless boats and
waded several hundred yards to the beaches under constant enemy fire. Too few of
the 125 LVTs, Roebling's Alligator amphibian tractor design, were able to transport Marines across the reefs to the beaches, because so many were destroyed or
damaged by the defenders' gunfire.

Once ashore, Marines could barely breach the Japanese defenses at the water's
edge. Ship-to-shore communications broke down, because radios malfunctioned.
The narrow beaches left no space for additional equipment and reinforcements to
be off-loaded. Of the 5,000 Marines in the assault on D-day, about 1,500 lay dead
or wounded or went missing. This had been the costliest day for the Corps since
June 6, 1918, the Battle of Belleau Wood.[80] A message summarizing the situation
went out from Julian Smith up the chain of command to Admiral Nimitz at Pearl
Harbor, and on to Holcomb at HQMC: "Issue remains in doubt."[81]

On the next day, D+1, thousands more Marines landed and slowly expanded
inland, taking control of nearly the entire western half of the island by nightfall.[82]
That evening, Shoup radioed a more encouraging message to Smith: "Casualties
many. Percentage dead unknown. Combat efficiency—we are winning."[83] Shoup's
optimistic statement proved true on D+2, when the Marines secured the western
half of Betio; and on D+3, when they swept eastward and eliminated all organized
enemy resistance. As snippets of reports seeped back to HQMC, Holcomb offered
these encouraging words on D+4 to Julian Smith: "My heartiest and most sincere
congratulations to you and the gallant officers and men of the Second Division on
the splendid outcome of the Tarawa operation. This was our first atoll attack and
the sort of operation that we have always been planning, and your success is therefore particularly gratifying."[84]

Japanese losses on Betio reached 97 percent of their garrison, or more than
4,800 combatants killed in action. Fewer than 200 Japanese surrendered. They

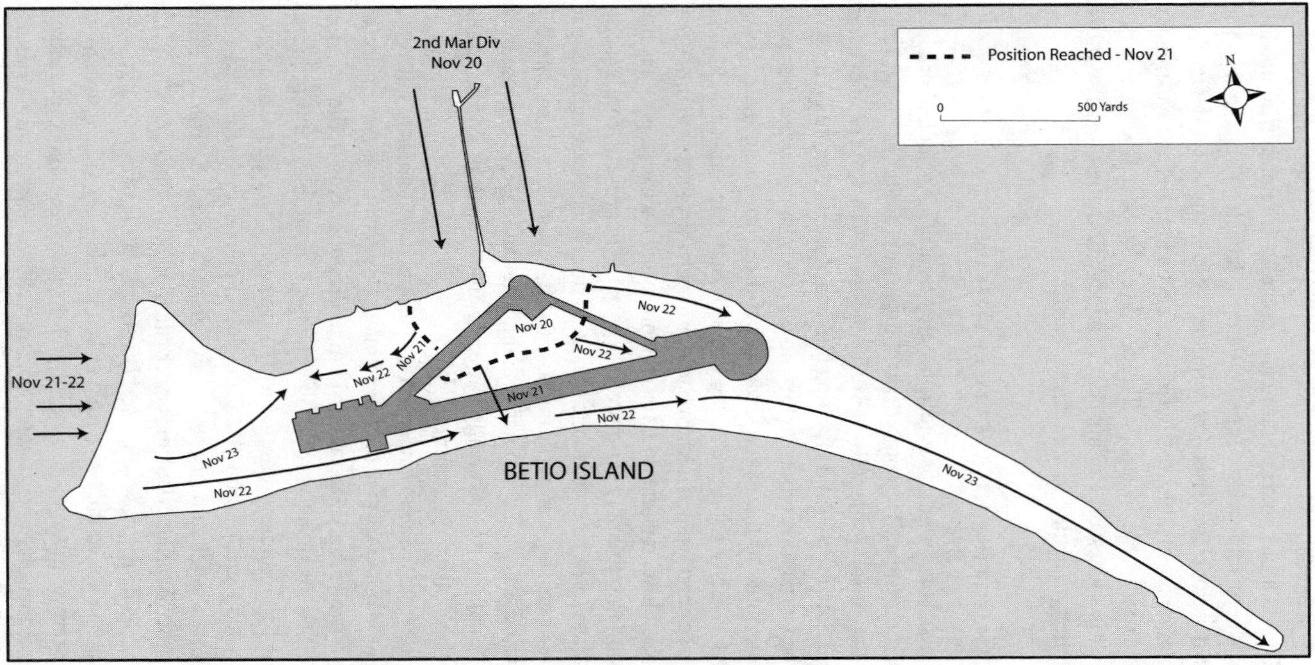

▲ This map shows D-day and subsequent operations on Betio Island, November 20–23, 1943.

(Map by Michael J. Hradesky)

BETIO ISLAND

2nd Mar Div
Nov 20

Nov 20

Nov 21

Nov 22

Nov 22

Nov 22

Nov 22

Nov 23

Nov 23

Nov 21

Nov 22

Nov 21-22

Position Reached - Nov 21

0   500 Yards

N

exacted a heavy toll on the 2nd Marine Division by killing 997 Marines and wounding 2,233 more. These casualty rates caused an uproar on the home front back in the United States, where some viewed the battle as a debacle. The fanaticism of the Japanese caused serious concerns that American forces might not defeat them without experiencing unreasonable losses. Congress even initiated an investigation to determine the causes of the losses on Tarawa. Over the next few weeks, first Holcomb and then his successor, Commandant Vandegrift, made good use of the Marine Corps' publicity machine to allay these fears.[85]

TRANSITIONING TO A NEW COMMANDANT

Even with the problems on Tarawa, prospects for the Marine Corps looked bright at the end of 1943. Commandant Holcomb derived great satisfaction in his service's wartime accomplishments. President Roosevelt even flirted with the idea of keeping Holcomb on special duty in 1944 and elevating him to a place on the Joint Chiefs of Staff. As the Marine Corps' first representative on that body, the president believed, Holcomb could contribute to the nation's war effort. But two sitting members of that body, COMINCH-CNO King and Army Chief of Staff Marshall, blocked the move. Neither service chief wanted a Marine to share such lofty status on the JCS.[86]

As 1943 drew to a close, it came time for Holcomb to leave the service. He had been looking forward to retirement for more than a year. After seven years as commandant directing the Corps in its dramatic transition from peace to war, he longed to spend more time at his shore-front farm, Rose Croft, in southern Maryland. He wanted to devote more time to his hobbies of sailing, gardening, and photography. His beloved wife, Beatrice, so frequently suffering from health problems, could also enjoy more of her husband's attention.[87]

In June 1943, Holcomb wrote to Undersecretary of the Navy James E. Forrestal, "I feel it is for the good of the service to have a younger man who has demonstrated his qualifications to take over. Reluctant as I am to drop the reins in the midst of a great war, should the President agree that a change is desirable, I am prepared to submit a request for voluntary retirement. This would be as of 31 August, the month in which I reach the age of 64."[88] Although still physically fit for a man his age, Holcomb believed he should not serve any longer because he enforced this regulation on all other Marines. But the acceptance of his request remained in question, because President Roosevelt, the "Big Boss," as Holcomb referred to him, could keep him on active duty as commandant indefinitely, if he chose to do so. Roosevelt did exercise this option, requiring Holcomb to remain commandant beyond August. And then the unexpected death of Charles Barrett on October 8 further delayed Holcomb's retirement until December.[89]

Meanwhile, Holcomb had long been grooming Vandegrift to lead the Marine Corps. As early as his inspection tour of Guadalcanal in October 1942, he had revealed to his former assistant and longtime confidant that he wanted him to succeed him. Careful planner that Holcomb was, he had doubtless looked to Vandegrift as the next commandant even before that. Vandergrift's superb leadership on Guadalcanal confirmed him as the best choice, in Holcomb's mind. Throughout 1943, Holcomb and Vandegrift consulted with each other regarding strategic plans in the Pacific, the expansion of the Corps' manpower, health conditions among Marines, the effectiveness of ongoing amphibious training, and the inner workings of Washington politics.[90]

Other Marines might have been named instead. Possible contenders included Major Generals Harry K. Pickett, Charles F. B. Price, Clayton B. Vogel, Roy S. Geiger, and Holland M. Smith. The first four had shortcomings of advanced age, poor performance, or insufficient command experience that weakened or disqualified them. Only Howlin' Mad Smith was a credible alternative because of his seniority, popularity, impeccable record, and intricate knowledge of amphibious operations. As Vandegrift's confidant Gerald C. Thomas said, "Holland was the only one that might have had some bitterness, because he has been so active, and he was not friendly with Holcomb. I think probably Holcomb might have thought he wasn't temperamentally as well fitted as Vandegrift. A great guy, a wonderful officer and all, but General Holcomb just thought that Vandegrift was the man to relieve him."[91]

Although no documentary evidence can confirm this, Holcomb seemed to model his selection process on the one Commandant John H. Russell had used in tapping him back in 1936.[92] What Russell wrote concerning his rationale for choosing a successor could equally well be applied to Holcomb's thinking. Neither commandant made seniority the primary factor in recommending his successor. Instead, Holcomb's choice of Vandegrift seemed to follow Russell's edict that "Efficiency should be the governing factor in his appointment."[93]

Holcomb submitted his retirement request to Navy Secretary Franklin Knox on November 30, 1943. Knox accepted it, and Roosevelt approved it a fortnight later. Holcomb turned over the commandancy to Vandegrift on January 1, 1944.[94] Another piece of good news was announced when Knox told Holcomb: "You will be the first officer of the Corps to hold the rank of general. . . . I know of no other officer to whom that distinction more fittingly belongs. You take with you in your retirement the admiration, the affection and the best wishes of the entire Naval Service."[95] Congress quickly approved awarding that fourth star. This honor stood as yet more proof of Holcomb's influence and importance to the Marine Corps and the nation's war effort.

Praise for Holcomb came from many quarters, including a 1944 report by COMINCH-CNO King. The admiral credited the commandant with expanding the Corps' two short-handed divisions, seven ill-equipped defense battalions, and twelve sub-par aviation squadrons into an effective wartime combat force of four divisions, nineteen defense battalions, and 85 aviation squadrons. Holcomb did much more, however, than increase the number of units and add thousands of new Marines to the Corps. King recognized Holcomb's other contributions when he unequivocally concluded that under Holcomb, "the Marine Corps successfully met the greatest test in its history by forging a huge mass of untrained officers and men into efficient tactical units especially organized, equipped, and trained for the complicated amphibious operations which have characterized the war in the Pacific."[96]

The transition from Holcomb to Vandegrift went smoothly, and the new commandant inherited a strong, yet flexible organization.[97] On New Year's Day of 1944, when Holcomb left his office in the Navy Annex for the last time, he made these parting remarks to his successor: "Vandegrift, when I go out this door I am placing twenty years on your shoulders and taking them off mine. You won't realize it at first but you will finally learn what I mean. . . . You have a good many friends in the Corps. I only hope that when you turn your job over to a successor you have the same number. The Commandant does not make many new friends if he does his job well."[98] Vandegrift went on to lead the Marines to victory in the Second World War. He then protected the Corps from extinction during the unification crisis in the postwar years. He definitely deserved much credit for his successes in both these tasks.

The eighteen months from July 1942 to Commandant Holcomb's retirement in December 1943 had marked a critical period for the Corps in the Second World War. The service firmly established itself as an essential part of the American military, a culmination of more than four decades of preparation for the right mission. All the while, Holcomb had demonstrated extraordinary skills as strategist, publicist, manager, and leader in meeting Corps' operational, manpower, and materiel needs. Nevertheless, because of the prejudices held by him and many other Marines, Holcomb failed to make the most effective use of African Americans and women to fill key combat and support roles in the Corps.

CHAPTER 7

FROM MARINE CORPS TO
DIPLOMATIC CORPS
TO RETIREMENT

D uring the first four months of 1944, General Holcomb advised the Navy Department regarding military organization and toured the country, making public appearances and inspecting Marine bases. In January he attended an Army-Navy war conference that brought together many of the high-ranking American leaders. Holcomb enjoyed a hero's welcome wherever he went. He had earned these accolades after having served seven years and one month as commandant during the Great Depression and Second World War. When Holcomb finished these activities, he hoped to move permanently back to Rose Croft with Beatrice.[1]

But his desire for the tranquil life of a gentleman farmer did not come to fruition in 1944. Having failed in his attempt to place Holcomb on the JCS, President Roosevelt decided on another course for his longtime friend to help in the nation's ongoing war effort. At the suggestion of Under Secretary of State Edward R. Stettinius Jr., the president appointed Holcomb as the new U.S. minister to the Union of South Africa. To observers, this appeared to be a waste of the retired com-

Holcomb wore his four stars at an Army-Navy war conference with Admiral William F. Halsey, January 8, 1944.

(Marine Corps University Archives, Holcomb Papers, Box 38)

General Thomas Holcomb with his wife, Beatrice, in early 1944.

(Marine Corps University Archives, Holcomb Papers, Box 39)

mandant's administrative skills, as well as of his amphibious-warfare knowledge. Stettinius disagreed with the naysayers, believing that the selection made sense on several levels. Holcomb's administrative expertise would be put to use maintaining a strong relationship with a valued ally. His combat experience would make him an ideal match for Jan Christian Smuts, the prime minister of South Africa and a combat veteran himself. Lastly, Holcomb's distinguished military career merited this appointment.[2]

That racial tension constituted a major political controversy in South Africa did not seem to concern Stettinius or Roosevelt. In 1944, race relations paled in comparison to diplomatic issues of paramount importance during the Second World War: the maintenance of the flow of raw materials from South Africa to the United States, and the negotiation of an equitable South African repayment for American Lend Lease support. Although no documentary evidence exists, it seems likely that Stettinius and Roosevelt believed Holcomb to be capable of dealing with racial tensions in South Africa because his attitudes and actions appeared to be similar to those of Prime Minister Smuts. But time would show that the two leaders did not, in fact, have the same beliefs about race.[3]

Roosevelt nominated Holcomb to the ministerial position on March 9, 1944, and the U.S. Senate unanimously confirmed him on March 20. One day later the retired commandant received his commission as U.S. Minister Plenipotentiary and Envoy Extraordinary to the Union of South Africa. Before Holcomb left the United States, the State Department briefed him regarding the political, economic, and social situations in that nation. In April, Secretary of State Cordell Hull gave Holcomb a formal letter with instructions to guide him in his ministerial activities. Hull confidently presumed that the new minister would reinforce the present "cordial relations" between the two countries.[4] As did all American ministers and ambassadors, Holcomb received more specific explanations of his duties: maintain close communications with the State Department regarding economic and political developments in South Africa, and interpret "faithfully the viewpoint of the American Government in any question at issue."[5]

Holcomb looked forward to his new assignment, not least because he could escape the harried existence and stultifying bureaucracy of the Navy Department in Washington. True, he would have to endure another bureaucracy in the State Department, but he hoped his ministerial duties would be less arduous than those of his last few long years as commandant. His friend and fellow Marine, Colonel James Roosevelt, predicted in March 1944 that Holcomb would find the job "profitable" and "enjoyable."[6] Just as important was relief for Beatrice and her recurring sinus problems. The climate in South Africa offered hope of reduced pain and less frequent headaches for her.[7]

On April 20, Holcomb departed from the United States. Joining him were several State Department officials as well as Beatrice and her nurse, a kind and caring woman identified as Mrs. Washington. The next six weeks took them on a circuitous route first to England, then Egypt, and finally South Africa. Holcomb made the most of each leg of the journey. During the last week of April while in London, he met with South Africa's Prime Minister Smuts, who was also there on state business. The First World War veteran and Boer War veteran took an immediate liking to one another. In fact, Holcomb admired Smuts for his active role in the creation of the United Nations.

While in London, Holcomb also spent an afternoon with the U.S. Army's General Dwight D. Eisenhower, the Supreme Allied Commander in Europe and the man responsible for Operation Overlord. Eisenhower asked for Holcomb's advice about amphibious assault doctrine and techniques to be used in the planned massive cross-channel invasion of Normandy, which would occur a few short weeks later. Lastly, Thomas and Beatrice Holcomb spent several delightful days with their son, Franklin, a major in the Marine Corps Reserve then stationed in Europe and serving with the Office of Strategic Services.[8]

From London the Holcombs flew to Cairo on May 3. There Thomas conferred with the Honorable Lincoln McVeagh, his predecessor as U.S. minister to South

Africa. They discussed the economic and diplomatic concerns that would confront the new American minister upon arrival. Beatrice fell ill in Egypt, and her recovery delayed their departure for three weeks. Holcomb finally arrived in the capital city of Pretoria, South Africa, on June 1, 1944. He presented to the South African government his letter of credence, which was promptly accepted.[9]

According to archivist and historian Gibson B. Smith, Holcomb took charge of the American legation and "immediately set out to run the legation as if it were a military post. He sized up his staff and the available resources to the job. His assessment resulted in a number of dispatches and telegrams to the State Department claiming that the legation at Pretoria was both understaffed and underpaid."[10] Insufficient resources plagued Holcomb's staff there, and Americans working in Capetown subsisted on still lower budgets and inadequate housing. South Africa's administrative capital was in Pretoria but its parliament met from January to June each year in Capetown, nearly 950 miles away by car. Holcomb wanted to establish an American chancery in the latter city to make interaction with the legislature easier during those months. But there was no reasonably priced housing and adequate transportation in Capetown.[11]

Having dealt with similar problems in the Marine Corps, Holcomb was no stranger to an under-strength and underfunded organization with a meager budget. He wrote to the State Department and requested a larger travel budget, better pay, and more clerks, attachés, and counselors. Those requests turned into demands when the State Department failed to respond in a timely or satisfactory manner. In November 1944, an aggravated Holcomb went so far as to tender his resignation over the dismal conditions at the legation. But President Roosevelt denied his resignation in January 1945. The ailing president would die in office four months later on April 12. Holcomb's reaction to hearing the sad news is not known, but the retired commandant certainly grieved the passing of his former commander in chief and friend. In the meantime, Minister Holcomb's urgent pleas produced some positive results: the State Department sent him the needed money and staff members. He even obtained a DC-3 aircraft to shuttle him from city to city—just over 800 miles by plane, in the case of the junket between Pretoria and Capetown.[12]

Regardless of the ebb and flow of his official duties, Holcomb enjoyed his time in South Africa, as his son recalled years later: "He liked the people," said Franklin. "He liked his staff. He loved the country. It was a tremendous slow down from the real pressures of being commandant. He had all the fun of decision-making. This was not a strange world to him. He had been living in China. He knew diplomacy, and he knew relations."[13]

Apart from interacting with the U.S. State Department, Holcomb found himself thrust into the middle of serious economic concerns affecting U.S.–South African diplomatic relations. Negotiations for a Lend Lease settlement stood as the major issue confronting the two nations in 1944.[14] Holcomb favored a strong American stance regarding the South African repayment of its war debt. As he wrote in February 1946 to the State Department: "Our government should adopt a just but firm attitude toward this Government which is obviously trying to evade its just debts."[15] The State Department concurred and instructed Holcomb to request $200 million for the direct and indirect Lend Lease aid from the United States.

That amount was actually much smaller than the State Department's internal estimates, totaling $800 million of aid. South African representatives countered with a paltry repayment figure between $40 and $60 million. From 1944 through 1946, Holcomb and the South Africans haggled endlessly over the exact sum. At last in 1946, negotiations resulted in the amount of $100 million, a settlement that the South Africans could easily afford.[16]

Holcomb deplanes while serving as U.S. minister to South Africa, c. 1944.

(Marine Corps University Archives, Holcomb Papers, Box 42)

Before the compromise regarding Lend Lease was finally struck, another matter arose that increasingly dwarfed the repayment negotiations in the postwar era. Beginning in early 1946, Holcomb devoted more and more of his time to reporting on South Africa's race relations. As minister, he routinely relayed to the State Department his observations about the government's treatment of blacks. At 8 million people, or nearly 75 percent of the population, blacks constituted an overwhelming majority. The South African government's oppressive racial policies shocked Holcomb, who increasingly viewed Prime Minister Smuts not as an admirably liberal leader but as an unrepentant white supremacist.[17] There was, of course, more than a little irony in Holcomb's impressions and observations: he had institutionalized segregation, as well as other policies in the Marine Corps that deprived African Americans of opportunities to serve in combat units or advance in rank. Minister Holcomb's official views on race relations thus gradually shifted away from what they had been when he was Commandant Holcomb.

Although Smuts and his United Party pursued racist programs, they did allow blacks to live and to work in urban areas, albeit with lower living standards and lower incomes than those of their white counterparts. In these ways, the United Party appeared to be less extreme on race relations than the more radical opposition Afrikaner Nationalist Party led by Daniel François Malan. The Afrikaner Nationalists favored a harsher policy of *Apartheid*, an Afrikaner word meaning "apart-ness." In reality, racism was an accepted and acceptable part of the cultural fabric of the country, as far as most white South Africans were concerned. Smuts had merely conceded that his nation's industry needed the cheap labor provided by blacks and that the white population could not or would not supply. Moreover, his United Party had long supported segregation of the races, incarceration of dissenters, disenfranchisement of blacks, and exploitation of non-European peoples.[18]

Holcomb witnessed one of the most blatant examples of abuse in the gold miners' strike of August 1946. The mine workers endured unhealthy conditions, paltry incomes unchanged in fifty years, and ever-rising costs of living. Months earlier Holcomb had warned the State Department that the situation was volatile and labor strife imminent. He also personally urged Smuts' government to grant more rights to the blacks' unions.[19] Holcomb warned the U.S. State Department that Smuts would handle a work stoppage by blacks "not through negotiation and reconciliation, but by repressive methods, since there is at present no Government machinery capable of dealing with the situation without force."[20]

Sadly, that prognostication proved true. Tens of thousands of black miners went on strike on August 12 in hopes of redressing their grievances without violence. The South African government, in collusion with the mine owners, reacted swiftly and violently. More than 1,500 armed police opened fire on thousands of striking miners, beat them with batons, and slashed them with bayonets. More than a dozen strikers died, and at least 1,200 sustained injuries in the melee that followed. The strike was crushed less than a week later on August 17, and some 60,000 battered and bloodied workers returned to the gold mines. Prime Minister Smuts justified these strike-breaking actions as a means to quell communist activism. Holcomb, for his part, seriously doubted the veracity of Smuts' claim.[21]

In November 1946, Holcomb described the white minority as having "been accustomed in the past to move 'in ways that are dark.'"[22] In this play on words, he explicitly referred to the way whites so easily accepted the racist practices of their government. He hoped that international ire would be awakened by exposure of those practices, and that resulting criticism might effect a "more sincere and enlightened attitude toward the non-European races in South Africa."[23] He was not merely parroting the State Department's line. Indeed, in another report submitted a month earlier in October, the minister had concurred with that department's own characterization of South Africa's racial policies as "narrow and backward."[24]

Beyond sending these stinging criticisms in his reports, Holcomb also consulted on the possible appointments from South Africa to serve the United Nations' newly forming Commission on Human Rights. In this role, he worked for and aligned himself with goals of the socially progressive Eleanor Roosevelt, widow of the late president and unquestioned champion of human, civil, and political rights. Unfortunately but not unsurprisingly, Holcomb believed that no black South African could legitimately serve on this commission, yet still be acceptable to Smuts and his party.[25] Moreover, Holcomb could suggest no white South African who could, as one UN document called for, "represent the principal races, religions, and linguistic groups" or "be familiar with the action conditions in different areas, including the 'backward' areas."[26] Once the UN Commission on Human Rights was established, Holcomb and his staff would report violations of principles of non-discrimination and social inequality to that body. They increasingly viewed the government of Smuts' United Party as an oppressive regime.[27]

Such stark realities of racism, albeit thinly veiled by South African government's public rhetoric, could not be ignored. The black majority enjoyed nothing even close to equitable political, economic, or civil rights relative to the white minority under Smuts' leadership, and Malan's Afrikaner Nationalist Party was even worse. Holcomb's own solution to the race problems entailed a compromise between "complete segregation" advocated by the Afrikaner Nationalists and "complete equality" desired by the black majority.[28] His hidebound racial beliefs had certainly moderated since 1942 and 1943, because of what he now observed in South Africa in 1946 and thereafter.[29]

In the spring of 1947, Holcomb helped craft the "State Department Policy and Information Statement on South Africa." This internally circulating document revealed the minister's view that the white minority would not relinquish their prerogative to solve "their racial problems in their own way without international interference."[30] External condemnation of their mistreatment of the black majority did not seem to affect Smuts and certainly did not influence Malan. Holcomb's 1947 Information Statement went so far as to predict that the South African solutions, whether under Smuts or Malan, would fail to solve the serious racial inequities and abuses. Indeed, he opined, the tensions and suffering would worsen over time. Thereafter, the U.S. State Department advocated cohabitation by whites and blacks in urban areas, as well as the improvement of economic, professional, and educational opportunities for blacks.

The 1947 Information Statement, according to historian Gibson Smith, "represented an enormous step forward in thinking on the race issue in South Africa much thanks to the careful and sensitive report by Holcomb and his staff." Smith's use of such terms indicates that Holcomb advocated a socially progressive solution to the racial problems in South Africa. Sadly, as Smith notes while pointing to acts of omission on the part of the United States, "it would take almost another twenty years for American policy-makers to openly argue the evils of Apartheid. By then the damage had been done."[31]

This observation is damning because it confirms American acquiescence to the post-1948 program of Apartheid in South Africa. Both the ruling United Party and the opposition Afrikaner Nationalist Party were absolutely committed to the preservation of white dominance. Any distinctions between the parties were those of degree, not kind.[32]

The Afrikaner Nationalist Party wanted complete subjugation of the black majority. White South Africans of both English and Afrikaner descent would remain in the cities, while blacks would be sent to farms, mines, or tribal reservations to work. Some Afrikaner Nationalists admired Adolf Hitler and Nazi Germany for their defense of racial purity and their fight against communism.[33] In a 1948 statement on policy, the Afrikaner Nationalist Party justified Apartheid on "Christian principles of justice and reasonableness," the goals of which were "the maintenance and the protection of the European population of the country as a pure white race."[34] Such rhetoric led both Holcomb and his staff to tag Malan's party as "centripetal in its outlook" and "anti-democratic in its tendencies" as early as October 1946.[35] Again, Holcomb's choice of unapologetic and unambiguous words shows that his views on race had moderated or even transformed.

Even in early 1948, Holcomb remained convinced that Smuts and his United Party would win the election later in the year. As he reported to the State Department, he fully expected the South African electorate to support Smuts and the status quo. He was certain that Malan and the Afrikaner Nationalist Party could never appeal to enough voters. And the differences between the two parties did frame the campaign. Perhaps surprisingly, the Afrikaner Nationalists succeeded in frightening enough of the white population into voting for them. Aside from playing on fears of race-mixing, they also aroused anxieties over possible communist ties. Despite Holcomb's forecast to the contrary, the Afrikaner Nationalist Party ousted the United Party in May 1948 and assumed control of the government for several decades.[36]

Under the new program of Apartheid, black South Africans found themselves living in horrific conditions in a system of political, economic, and social segregation from the white population. They were little better than human chattel. American diplomats may have complained about human rights violations such as those Holcomb brought up, but the new regime maintained control of South Africa by using Apartheid's ruthless means. The U.S. government could not condemn South Africa's maltreatment of blacks when Jim Crow laws and segregation still held sway in the United States. Pointing out racism in South Africa would only make a similar situation in the United States more noticeable and thus damage American credibility abroad.[37] Moreover, these reasons caused the United States to recognize and interact with the new South African government.

Supporting an Afrikaner Nationalist government—"centripetal in its outlook" and "anti-democratic in its tendencies," as Holcomb had written two years earlier—represented the moral cost of maintaining political stability in South Africa.[38] President Harry S. Truman's own progressive views on race did not extend to his foreign policies regarding that nation. Ultimately, South Africa's vast mineral resources and its strategic location at the southernmost tip of the continent made ensuring cooperative relations between the two nations an essential goal during the Cold War. Shamefully, the United States' national security and anticommunist ideology trumped human rights and racial equality as primary motivations for relations.[39]

One month before the election of May 1948, Thomas Holcomb stepped down as minister to South Africa, returned to the United States, and retired for a second and final time. He had performed his ministerial duties conscientiously for four years, but, as his son observed, Holcomb "was ready to quit South Africa. He wanted to come back to Rose Croft." After nearly five decades of military and public service, he and Beatrice finally took up permanent residence at their farm. They savored the peace and quiet on the Chesapeake Bay, while entertaining friends and family at lunches and dinners. Thomas gardened in a leisurely fashion, and Beatrice canned vegetables.[40] The subsequent eight years at Rose Croft were idyllic, except for Beatrice's chronic health problems.

In an interview in 2006, Suzanne Holcomb, widow of recently deceased Franklin, described her in-laws in retirement: Thomas "loved family. He loved to sail and to boat. He was happy at Rose Croft. He did a lot of small farming—that is their vegetable garden, the strawberry patch. He would take me out at dawn to eat the strawberries in the cool of the dawn. . . . Dinner was a feast because he grew so many things. They had their own cows. They would make their own ice cream." Suzanne and Franklin, both avid sailors, enjoyed visiting the farm by water. Suzanne remembered, "We would anchor at the dock. By the time we got in the dingy and rowed ashore, the general would have seen us. He would have come down to the dock. Then the three of us would sit at the end of the dock, nip up oysters, shuck them, and eat them. And, he would bring down a pitcher of martinis, so we would sit on the dock shucking oysters and drinking martinis." To his daughter-in-law, Thomas Holcomb always remained "The General."[41]

In 1956 Thomas and Beatrice moved to Chevy Chase, Maryland, where they stayed for the next six years and where Beatrice could more easily receive regular medical treatments. They lived on Oliver Street, and there the elderly Holcombs enjoyed time with family, especially Franklin and Suzanne's two young daughters, Clover and Sarah. Thomas took his granddaughters to steakhouses for dinners, to see parades at twilight at the Marine Barracks at "8th and I" in Washington, and to watch the Army-Navy football games in Annapolis. By all accounts, grandfather and granddaughters cherished these times together.[42]

Not all occasions on Oliver Street were so pleasant. Beatrice's physical condition, never strong, declined still further in those last years. She spent more and more time at nearby Bethesda Naval Hospital. Thomas kept track of her ups and downs in his diary in 1962. In May he wrote, "B continues to improve and talk of future plans," but later in July, he recorded how "B still in depressed condition," "was a bit confused," "unfriendly," and "quarrelsome." In a confession not of the usual matter-of-fact tone of these journal entries, Thomas confessed that he found her confusion "most discouraging."

But the devoted husband of forty-five years spent almost every day in the hospital room with his ailing wife. He frequently read to her. In early August Beatrice seemed to rebound. Thomas noted in his diary on August 6, "Nurse phoned me that B continues to improve. In particular, she is eating." This must have been cause for guarded optimism for Thomas, who had just turned eighty-three the day before. But after lingering for so many months, Beatrice Clover Holcomb soon passed away at age sixty-six on August 14, 1962. Thomas had left the hospital to return to his home for the evening. He wrote these words about that day: "Personally told of B's death at 2055. I went to hospital and finally saw her."[43]

Following his wife's funeral three days later, Thomas Holcomb moved into Washington proper. He experienced serious problems with his heart during the next year, 1963. His health had always been excellent, except for a bout with malaria decades earlier and minor complications from a wound suffered in the First World War. In fact, between 1933 and 1943, Holcomb spent only forty-one days "sick in quarters." When he retired in December 1943 at age sixty-four, his weight was just 24 pounds more than the 155 he weighed at commissioning in 1900, and his blood pressure read a respectable 130 over 64. But the intervening twenty years had taken their toll.

In early 1964 following his recovery, Holcomb moved back to his boyhood hometown of the Wilmington suburb of New Castle, Delaware. Ongoing difficulties with his calcific aortitis meant he traveled back and forth between Delaware and Bethesda Hospital for medical treatments every few weeks.[44] After returning from one of those hospital visits, Thomas Holcomb died of a heart attack in his home on May 24, 1965. He was eighty-five years old.[45]

The next day, Commandant Wallace M. Greene issued an official tribute: "Upon the death of General Thomas Holcomb we have not only lost an outstanding leader but also a beloved friend. The magnificent performance of the Marine Corps during World War II under the direction of General Holcomb is one of the highlights of the military history of this nation."[46] Services were held for him at the Fort Myer Chapel in Arlington, Virginia, on May 28. He was accorded full military honors and laid to rest next to Beatrice in Arlington National Cemetery, not far from the Navy Annex building where he had spent the momentous years of the Second

World War as commandant, in an office overlooking sobering rows of graves amid oaks, maples, and cedars.[47]

HOLCOMB'S LEGACIES AND ACHIEVEMENTS

During the eighty-five months between December 1, 1936, and December 31, 1943, Commandant Thomas Holcomb supervised the transformation of the U.S. Marine Corps from a marginal service to become the nation's premier amphibious assault force. He participated in all aspects of this process, including administrative oversight, resource allocation, strategic planning, and public relations. Without his efforts and without assistance from other officers and politicians, the U.S. Marine Corps could have gone the way of Britain's Royal Marines. They had confronted many of the same internal and external challenges as Holcomb and the American Marines had encountered in the 1930s and 1940s. But the Royal Marines never expanded beyond being a small, albeit highly specialized, force that could neither field full divisions nor conduct independent large-scale amphibious operations.[48]

Despite Holcomb's Herculean contributions to the U.S. Marine Corps and the American war effort, too few military historians have examined his achievements or acknowledged his legacies in any meaningful ways. My hope is that this book fills this void, as the first extensive study of his commandancy. The research presented here confirms that he played essential roles in mobilizing his service for the Second World War and directing the initial twenty-four months of that conflict. Holcomb modified accepted ideas, policies, and doctrines to fit new circumstances. His progressive management style made a virtue of such pragmatism.

But Holcomb was much more than adapter of what already existed in theory or practice. He frequently anticipated operational, technological, and administrative problems and initiated the necessary reforms ahead of time. Furthermore, his active roles in creating and applying amphibious assault and base defense doctrines in the Pacific helped carve a niche for the Marine Corps in the Navy's strategic plans. No other belligerent nation could boast having comparable forces in the Second World War, let alone since that conflict. Two examples best illustrate his innovative approach and capacity to effect needed reforms. Additionally, these instances can serve as lenses of organizational theory and leadership through which Holcomb's commandancy can be examined.

The first case occurred during his prewar years as commandant. As described earlier in this book, while observing a Japanese amphibious assault in China in 1937, Marine first lieutenant Victor H. Krulak photographed a landing craft with a special bow ramp that could be lowered so troops could run directly onto the beach. That photo and a small replica of the craft found their way to Holcomb's office at HQMC. Recognizing the design's potential led to the LCVP, so ubiquitous in amphibious assaults during the Second World War.[49] That a lowly lieutenant's proposal for an innovative design could reach the commandant's desk attested to an organizational culture in which communication lines functioned effectively, and where creative ideas became realities. Holcomb, as commandant, set the tone for this organizational culture.

Apart from such internal benefits of open communications, this process of identifying and procuring improvements in a weapon system established an equally, if not more beneficial, precedent for the Marine Corps. In his role as commandant, Holcomb helped set the stage for the Corps to be able to conduct independent research, development, testing, procurement, and employment of weapons, equipment, and other materiels in more recent years. His contribution cannot be overemphasized, because such practices helped make the service more autonomous over time within the U.S. military establishment. The Marine Corps remains part of the Navy Department, but it is hardly a minor or insignificant partner in national defense. Such a modern force-in-readiness as the Corps needs to exercise some independence if it is to be prepared to fight in any theater, environment, or operation.

The other illustration of Holcomb's reform-mindedness took place over several weeks in October and November 1942 in the South Pacific. He and Major General Alexander A. Vandegrift met with Navy commanders, ostensibly to determine the best course for future operations on Guadalcanal. Holcomb also wanted to reform the command structure for amphibious assaults. To this end, he drafted a policy change, as described earlier in detail. Holcomb wanted the naval officer to share operational control with the marine commander. In the planning stage, the two would exercise equal authority, but during the voyage and ship-to-shore stages, the naval commander would control all seaborne forces. After landing, as Marine units moved inland, the Marine commander would assume full control of his units on the ground. When Holcomb steered this vital reform in amphibious command relations to Washington and ultimate approval, he accomplished one of his most important contributions.[50]

Just as the bow ramp set a precedent for the Corps' independence in research and development, so did the new amphibious assault command relationships represent a landmark change. Bringing shore operations under the Marine Corps commander's control also foreshadowed the postwar development of the service's combined arms formation known as Marine Air-Ground Task Force. In a March 2009 report titled "Evolving the MAGTF for the 21st Century," the commanding general of the Marine Corps Command Development Command, Lieutenant General G. J. Flynn, praised the MAGTF concept as "designed to be deployed, employed, and sustained from the sea without reliance on host nation ports, airfields, or permissions." It remains, he said, "a fundamentally sound construct."[51]

This unique formation has various force sizes, such as the Marine Expeditionary Unit, the Marine Expeditionary Brigade, and the Marine Expeditionary Force. Each can be used in different capacities, according to operational requirements. All of the units integrate ground, aviation, and logistics elements under a single commander, yielding great flexibility, coordination, and self-sufficiency in operational capabilities. MAGTFs are thus able to conduct conventional, counterinsurgency, and humanitarian operations, or "hybrids" thereof.[52]

Although no documentation mentions Holcomb by name, the MAGTF's conceptual foundation was laid by Commandant Thomas Holcomb during his trip to Guadalcanal and his conference with Vice Admiral William Halsey at Noumea in October 1942. Holcomb's ghostwritten reform to *FTP 167* gave amphibious assault force commanders equality of command and autonomy of action in employing their ground and air assets once ashore. This has benefited every commander thereafter, from the Second World War to more recent conflicts. Holcomb thus deserves credit for presaging the modern concept of the MAGTF that allows Marine Corps units to be more effective forces-in-readiness.

Holcomb embraced many technological innovations and organizational reforms, but his openness to change did not extend to social issues. Most historians of the Marine Corps do not deal in detail with Holcomb's opposition to admitting to the service African Americans and women. If anything, they dismiss these failings as his being a product of his times. While true, this statement does not go far enough. One of the most striking examples of Holcomb's attitude regarding race relations occurred in January 1942, as detailed earlier. When members of the Navy's General Board questioned him about possible effects of admitting African Americans, the commandant cited efficiency. He appropriated the progressive principle of managerial efficiency to fit his own prejudices, as well as to justify fears that a racially integrated Corps would lose its combat effectiveness and elite status. However, when President Franklin Roosevelt, a man well known for his progressive social attitudes, mandated that the armed services admit minorities, Holcomb was bound to make inclusion as successful as he could.[53]

After retiring from the Corps, Holcomb's views on race relations moderated and transformed because of his tenure as U.S. minister to South Africa, from 1944 to 1948. Here he concluded that the government's racism was visible as well as ugly, and sharply criticized its oppression. Holcomb aligned himself with advocates of human rights in opposition to South Africa's racial policies.[54] Ultimately, while considering them fully and in depth, his beliefs on race and gender vis-à-vis Marine Corps service do not detract from the many significant achievements of his forty-eight years of public service.

Stepping back and looking at his career, a historical perspective shows that Commandant Thomas Holcomb performed instrumental roles in mobilizing the

Marines and preparing them to fight the Pacific War. His contributions cannot be denied and should not be ignored. The Corps' expansion from 18,000 Marines in 1936 to 385,000 in 1943 embodied just one telling measurement of his achievements. No better contemporary appraisal is available than the citation for the Distinguished Service Medal that President Franklin Delano Roosevelt presented to Holcomb on February 22, 1944. During the Second World War,

> General Holcomb was responsible for the development of an organization equal to extensive and pressing demands incident to the aggressive prosecution of the war. He has achieved brilliant success in the numerous phases of rapid expansion of the Corps to many times its normal size, at the same time, holding Marine Corps personnel to the traditional high level of combat readiness during a tremendously critical period. General Holcomb's forceful and inspiring leadership, his distinctive ability as an administrator and executive, and his tireless and unwavering devotion to duty have been major factors in the success of our offensive drive against the Japanese strongholds in the Pacific War Area and have contributed essentially to the high morale of the officers and men carrying the fight to the enemy.[55]

Setting aside official flourishes, this citation gets to the very essence of Thomas Holcomb's commandancy. It speaks to his rare combination of leadership talents and managerial skills combined with a strong intellect and calm temperament. Holcomb proved himself to be integral in making the Marine Corps into a truly modern force that is unique in the world's military history.

NOTES

ABBREVIATIONS

REPOSITORIES

Archives Branch, Alfred M. Gray Research Center, Marine Corps University, Quantico, Va.	MCUA
Dwight D. Eisenhower Library and Archives, Abilene, Kans.	DDEL
Marine Corps Oral History Collection	MCOHC
Minnesota Historical Society, Minneapolis, Minn.	MNHS
National Archives and Records Administration, College Park, Md.	NACP
National Archives and Records Administration, Washington, D.C.	NADC
Naval History and Heritage Command, Washington, D.C.	NHHC
Reference Branch, Marine Corps History Division, Marine Corps University, Quantico, Va.	HDRB
U.S. Army War College, U.S. Army Heritage and Education Center, Carlisle Barracks, Pa.	AHEC

ARCHIVAL COLLECTIONS

2nd Brigade Fleet Marine Force Geographic File	2ndBFMFGF
7th Defense Battalion Questionnaires	7thDBQ
Bureau of Medicine General Correspondence, 1941–1946	BMGC 1941–46
Commander in Chief U.S. Fleet, Plans Division Pacific Section, Records Regarding World War II Amphibious Operations, 1941–1946	COMINCH 1941–46
Committee to Defend America by Aiding the Allies	CDAAA
Division of Plans and Policies War Plans Section General Correspondence, 1926–1942	DPPWPSGC 1926–42
Division of Plans and Policies War Plans Section	DPPWPS 1915–45
General Board Subject File, 1900–1947	GBSF 1900–47
Headquarters Separate Correspondence, 1930–1971	HQSC 1930–71
History Amphibious File	HAF
Microfilm 971	M971

Microfilm 1421	M1421
Marine Corps Budget Estimates for FYs 1936–1943	MCBE FY 1936–43
Personnel Department General Correspondence, 1933–1938	PDGC 1933–38
Records Regarding World War II Organizations, Plans, and Military Operations, 1938–1945	WWIIOPMO 1938–45
Strategic Plans War Plans Division	StratPlnsWPD
Strategic Plans Division War Plans Division, 1912–1946	SPDWPD 1912–46
U.S. Marine Corps General Correspondence, 1939–1950	MCGC 1939–50
U.S. Navy and Related Operational, Tactical, and Industrial Publications, 1918–1970	USNROTIP 1918–70
War Plans and Related Materials, 1931–1944	WPRM 1931–44
World War II Collection	WWIIC
World War II–Solomons-Guadalcanal	WWIISG

JOURNALS

Army and Navy Journal	*A&NJ*
Journal of Military History	*JMH*
Marine Corps Gazette	*MCG*
Naval War College Review	*NWCR*

Introduction

1. For statements on originality and significance of a book-length study of Thomas
Holcomb's commandancy, see Allan R. Millett to David J. Ulbrich, 27 July 1994, in
Ulbrich's possession; Allan R. Millett, *In Many a Strife: General Gerald C. Thomas
and the U.S. Marine Corps, 1917–1956* (Annapolis: Naval Institute Press, 1993),
xviii; and Robert von Maier and Gregory J. W. Urwin, "Questions and Answers:
Allan R. Millett," *World War II Quarterly* 5 (Spring 2008): 55. For several histories
that only briefly refer to Holcomb yet provide context for his commandancy, see
Frank O. Hough, Verle D. Ludwig, and Henry I. Shaw Jr., *History of the U.S. Marines
in World War II*, vol. 1, *Pearl Harbor to Guadalcanal* (Washington, D.C.: Historical
Branch, HQMC, 1958), 44, 262, 341–42; Henry I. Shaw Jr., and Douglas T. Kane,
History of the U.S. Marines in World War II, vol. 2, *Isolation of Rabaul* (Washington,
D.C.: Historical Branch, HQMC, 1963), 35; Henry I. Shaw Jr., Bernard C. Nalty,
and Edwin T. Turnbladh, *History of the U.S. Marines in World War II*, vol. 3, *Central
Pacific Drive* (Washington, D.C.: Historical Branch, HQMC, 1966), 26, 585; Allan R.
Millett, *Semper Fidelis: The History of the United States Marine Corps*, rev. ed. (New
York: Macmillan, 1991), 335–37, 347, 359–60, 371–73, 390, 404; Robert Debs Heinl
Jr., *Soldiers of the Sea: The United States Marine Corps, 1775–1962* (1962; repr.,
Baltimore: Nautical and Aviation Publishing, 1991), 299–305, 312, 374–75, 388–89,
402–6; J. Robert Moskin, *The U.S. Marine Corps Story*, 3rd rev. ed. (New York:
McGraw-Hill, 1992), 255, 274, 306; Edwin H. Simmons, *The United States Marines:
A History*, 3rd ed. (Annapolis: Naval Institute Press, 1998), 120–22, 187–89; and
Edward S. Miller, *War Plan Orange: The U. S. Strategy to Defeat Japan, 1897–1945*
(Annapolis: Naval Institute Press, 1991), 181–83, 229, 277, 377–78, 329.

2. John W. Gordon, "General Thomas Holcomb and 'The Golden Age of Amphibious
Warfare,'" *Delaware History* 21 (September 1985): 269; and John W. Gordon,
"Thomas Holcomb, 1936–1943," in *Commandants of the Marine Corps*, ed. Allan R.
Millett and Jack Shulimson (Annapolis: Naval Institute Press, 2004), 253–81.

3. Gordon, "Holcomb and 'The Golden Age,'" 269.

4. Millett, *In Many a Strife*, 138, 150–52, 158, 202–5, 214, 228–30.

5. Alexander A. Vandegrift and Robert B. Asprey, *Once a Marine* (New York: Norton,
1964).

6. Although this article does not mention Holcomb by name, see Robin Higham and
Mark P. Parillo, "The Management Margin: Essential for Victory," *Aerospace Power
Journal* 16 (Spring 2002): 19–27.

7. Fred I. Greenstein, *The Presidential Difference: Leadership Style from FDR to
Clinton* (Princeton: Princeton University Press, 2000), 5–6, italics in original. For
a similar study, see Jameson W. Doig and Erwin C. Hargrove, eds., *Leadership and
Innovation: A Biographical Perspective on Entrepreneurs in Government* (Baltimore:
Johns Hopkins University Press, 1987).

8. Max Weber, "Bureaucracy," in *Max Weber: Essays in Sociology*, ed. H. Gerth and
C. W. Mills (Oxford: Oxford University Press, 1922); and Chester I. Barnard, *The
Functions of the Executive* (Cambridge, Mass.: Harvard University Press, 1938).

9. See Robert Wiebe, *The Search for Order, 1877–1920* (New York: Hill and Wang
Press, 1967); Ellis W. Hawley, *The Great War and the Search for a Modern Order:
A History of the American People and their Institutions, 1917–1933*, 2nd ed.

(New York: St. Martin's Press, 1992); and Henry Mintzberg, *The Structure of Organizations* (Englewood Cliffs, N.J.: Prentice-Hall Press, 1979).

10. Thomas Holcomb to Samuel W. Meek, 12 August 1943, Thomas Holcomb Papers (hereafter Holcomb Papers), Box 10, MCUA.

11. See Edward Mead Earle, ed., *Makers of Modern Strategy: Military Thought from Machiavelli to Hitler* (Princeton: Princeton University Press, 1943).

12. Russell F. Weigley, ed., *New Dimensions in Military History* (San Rafael, Calif.: Presidio, 1975); John Keegan, *The Face of Battle* (New York: Viking Press, 1976); John Whiteclay Chambers II, "The New Military History: Myth and Reality," *JMH* 55 (July 1991): 395–406; and John Shy, "The Cultural Approach to the History of War," *JMH* 57 (October 1993): 13–26.

13. Peter Karsten, ed., *The Military in America: From the Colonial Era to the Present*, rev. ed. (New York: Free Press, 1986), 1–3, 18.

14. Samuel P. Huntington, *The Soldier and the State: The Theory and Politics of Civil-Military Relations* (Cambridge, Mass.: Belknap Press of Harvard, 1957); Morris Janowitz, *The Professional Soldier: A Social and Political Portrait* (Glencoe, Ill.: Free Press, 1960); and Walter Millis, *Arms and Men: America's Military History and Military Policy from the Revolution to the Present* (New York: Capricorn Press, 1967).

15. See David M. Kennedy, *Freedom from Fear: The American People in Depression and War, 1929–1945* (New York: Oxford University Press, 1999); Akira Iriye, *Power and Culture: The Japanese-American War, 1941–1945* (Cambridge, Mass.: Harvard University Press, 1981); and Robert Dallek, *Franklin D. Roosevelt and American Foreign Policy, 1932–1945*, rev. ed. (New York: Oxford University Press, 1995).

16. In 1963, Thomas Holcomb donated seven boxes of his letters, memoranda, reports, speeches, and telegrams dating from 1936 through 1944 to the Marine Corps Historical Center, then at the Washington Navy Yard. The contents of these boxes were indexed and annotated in Gibson B. Smith, *Thomas Holcomb, 1879–1965: Register of his Personal Papers* (Washington, D.C.: History and Museums Division, HQMC, 1988). In 1999, Gibson Smith donated an additional two dozen boxes of primary sources he had amassed while preparing to write his own biography of Holcomb, which he never started. Most recently in 2006, Thomas Holcomb's heirs—his late daughter-in-law Suzanne Holcomb and his granddaughters Sarah Holcomb and Clover Holcomb Burgess—donated several more boxes of the commandant's documents and photographs. My book includes all three sets of documents and utilizes the more recent register of the Holcomb Papers completed in 2007. Much additional research in government archives went into this book. The MCUA holds the Alexander A. Vandegrift Personal Papers Collection (hereafter Vandegrift Papers) and dozens of oral history interviews with prominent Marines. Also of note are memoranda and reports culled from the Marine Corps General Correspondence, 1939–1950 Collection (MCGC 1939–50) found in Record Group 127 Records of the U.S. Marine Corps (hereafter RG 127) and housed at NACP. Two other collections in RG 127 provide significant yet previously classified documents: Division of Plans and Policies War Plans Section General Correspondence 1926–1942 (DPPWPSGC 1926–42); and Records Regarding World War II Organizations, Plans, and Military Operations 1938–1945 (WWIIOPMO 1938–45). Some boxes in these collections

surfaced when they were rearranged, cataloged, and moved from the National Records Center in Suitland, Maryland, to National Archives facilities in the 1990s.

Chapter 1

Holcomb's First Thirty-Six Years in the Marine Corps, 1900–1936

1. Holcomb to Daisy Holcomb Williamson, 11 September 1943, Holcomb Papers, Box 10, MCUA; Thomas Holcomb II, interview by Gibson B. Smith, 1978, transcript, p. 1, Holcomb Papers, Box 20, MCUA; and Franklin Holcomb, interview with G. Smith, c. 1978, audio recording, tape 2, sequence 4, Holcomb Papers, Box 24, MCUA (hereafter F. Holcomb, recording, tape 2, sequence 4).

2. "A General for the Marine Corps: The Career of Gen. Thomas Holcomb of Delaware, 1879–1945" (hereafter "Career of Thomas Holcomb"), by Gibson B. Smith, n.d., Holcomb Papers, Box 24, MCUA; Smith, *Register of Holcomb's Papers*, 220; Holcomb II, transcript, 1; F. Holcomb, recording, tape 3, sequence 4; and Suzanne Holcomb, Clover Holcomb Burgess, and Sarah Holcomb, interview with J. Michael Miller, James Ginther, and Alisa Whitley, 2006 (hereafter S. Holcomb et al.), video recording, Holcomb Papers, Box 24, MCUA.

3. F. Holcomb, recording, tape 3, sequence 4.

4. *Journal-Every Evening* (Wilmington, Del.), 11 December 1943; and Gordon, "Thomas Holcomb," 255.

5. *Journal-Every Evening* (Wilmington, Del.), 11 December 1943.

6. *Oxford English Dictionary*, 2nd ed., s.v. "gaff."

7. Thomas Holcomb Diary 11 December 1899 to 31 October 1901, 17 January 1899, 21 January 1899, 6 February 1900, 16 February 1900, 17 February 1900, and 24 February 1900, Holcomb Papers, Box 21, MCUA; F. Holcomb, recording, tape 3, sequence 4; and S. Holcomb et al., recording.

8. Holcomb Diary 1899–1901, 3 March, 7 March, 8 March, 9 March, 10 March, 12 March, 13 March, and 15 March 1900, Holcomb Papers, Box 21, MCUA; "Thomas Holcomb" Biographical File (hereafter Holcomb File), HDRB.

9. Holcomb Diary 1899–1901, 20 March 1900, Holcomb Papers, Box 21, MCUA.

10. Ibid., 21 March 1900, Holcomb Papers, Box 21, MCUA; Holcomb File, HDRB; and Gordon, "Thomas Holcomb," 256.

11. Holcomb File, HDRB; Leo J. Daugherty III, "Thomas Holcomb," in *American National Biography*, vol. 11, ed. John A. Garraty and Mark C. Carnes (New York: Oxford University Press, 1999), 30; "Military History of Thomas Holcomb," 13 September 1928 (hereafter Holcomb Military History) Holcomb Papers, Box 1, MCUA; Gordon, "Thomas Holcomb," 257; Millett, *Semper Fidelis*, 155–63, 213–6; George B. Clark, *Treading Softly: U.S. Marines in China, 1819–1949* (Westport, Conn.: Praeger Press, 2001), 86; and Heather Pace Marshall, "Crucible of Colonial Service: The Warrior Brotherhood and Mythos of the Modern Marine Corps, 1898–1934" (M.A. thesis, University of Hawaii, 2003), 72–79.

12. Chinese Secretary to Naval Attaché, 9 November 1913, Holcomb Papers, Box 3, MCUA.

13. Gordon, "Thomas Holcomb," 257; Kenneth W. Condit, John H. Johnstone, and Ella W. Nargele, *A Brief History of Headquarters Marine Corps*, rev. ed. (Washington, D.C.: History and Museums Division, HQMC, 1970), 7–9; Millett, *Semper Fidelis*, 136–37; Merrill L. Bartlett, *Lejeune: A Marine's Life, 1867–1942* (Columbia: University of South Carolina Press, 1991), 64; Holcomb Military History, Holcomb Papers, Box 1, MCUA; and F. Holcomb, recording, tape 1, sequence 2.

14. Robert E. Barde, *The History of Marine Corps Marksmanship* (Washington, D.C.: Marksmanship Branch, G-3 Division, 1961), 1–3, 8–17; Marine Corps Press Release, n.d. [c. November 1936], and Sam E. Conner, "Lt. Gen. Thomas Holcomb, Commander of All U.S. Marines As I Knew Him," *Lewiston Journal*, 22 August 1942, both in Holcomb File, HDRB; and Gordon, "Thomas Holcomb," 256.

15. Barde, *History of Marine Corps Marksmanship*, 13.

16. F. Holcomb, recording, tape 2, sequence 3.

17. Holcomb to Joseph Farnan, 19 April 1939, Holcomb Papers, Box 2, MCUA; Holcomb to E. C. Kalbfus, 12 February 1940, Holcomb Papers, Box 3, MCUA; and R. A. Madden to Holcomb, 4 May 1942, Holcomb Papers, Box 5, MCUA.

18. F. Holcomb, recording, tape 3, sequence 4; S. Holcomb et al., video recording; and Holcomb II, transcript, 6.

19. "Service Record of Thomas Holcomb" (hereafter Holcomb Service Record), Holcomb Papers, Box 31, MCUA; F. Holcomb, recording, tape 1, sequence 2; Condit et al., *Brief History of Headquarters Marine Corps*, 7; Jack Shulimson, "The First to Fight: Marine Corps Expansion, 1914–1918," *Prologue: The Journal of the National Archives* 8 (Spring 1976): 5–8; Edwin H. Simmons and Joseph H. Alexander, *Through the Wheat: The U.S. Marines in World War I* (Annapolis: Naval Institute Press, 2008), 5; Merrill L. Bartlett, "John A. Lejeune, 1920–1929," in *Commandants of the Marine Corps*, ed. Millett and Shulimson, 197–98, 212–13; Leo J. Daugherty III, "'To Fight Our Country's Battles': An Institutional History of the United States Marine Corps during the Interwar Era, 1919–1935," (Ph.D. diss., Ohio State University, 2001),78, 669.

20. Dirk A. Ballendorf and Merrill L. Bartlett, *Pete Ellis: An Amphibious Warfare Prophet, 1880–1993* (Annapolis: Naval Institute Press, 1997), 65–68.

21. Bartlett, *Lejeune*, 63–65.

22. Peter Karsten, "Armed Progressives: The Military Reorganizes for the American Century," in *Building the Organizational Society*, ed. Jerry Israel (New York: Free Press, 1972), 197–98.

23. Clayton Barrow Jr., "Looking for John A. Lejeune," *MCG* 74 (November 1990): 72.

24. Steven T. Ross, *American War Plans, 1890–1939* (Portland, Ore.: Frank Cass, 2002); 49, 80; Henry G. Gole, *The Road to Rainbow: Army Planning for Global War, 1934–1940* (Annapolis: Naval Institute Press, 2003), 11–15, 35; Miller, *War Plan Orange*; and Barrow, "Looking for John A. Lejeune," 73.

25. A. W. Hinds, "The Island of Guam as a Naval Base," *Proceedings of the United States Naval Institute* 41 (May 1915): 449–55; Robert William Neeser, *Our Navy in the Next War* (New York: Scribner, 1915), 163–65; George W. Baer, *One Hundred Years of Sea Power: The U.S. Navy, 1890–1990* (Stanford: Stanford University Press, 1994), 44, 51–53, 90–92, 119–28; Ross, *American War Plans, 1890–1939*, 7–9, 137, 167–74;

Gole, *Road to Rainbow*, 154–58; and David J. Ulbrich, "Clarifying the Origins and Strategic Mission of the U.S. Marine Corps Defense Battalion, 1898–1941," *War & Society* 17 (October 1999): 84–87.

26. Miller, *War Plan Orange*, 36, 77–82, 202–3, 226.

27. Daugherty, "'To Fight Our Country's Battles,'" 254–55, 331 note 5; Maier and Urwin, "Questions and Answers," 54–55; and Holland M. Smith, *The Development of Amphibious Tactics in the U.S. Navy* (Washington, D.C.: History and Museums Division, HQMC, 1992), 22.

28. John A. Lejeune, *The Reminiscences of a Marine* (1930; repr., Quantico, Va.: Marine Corps Association, 1990), 219–42; Bartlett, *Lejeune*, 63–65; Ballendorf and Bartlett, *Pete Ellis*, 66–67; Millett, *Semper Fidelis*, 174–75, 282–87; Condit et al., *Brief History of Headquarters Marine Corps*, 8–9; and "Historical Background" Subject File, HDRB.

29. Barrow, "Looking for John A. Lejeune," 72.

30. Edwin N. McClellan, *The United States Marine Corps in the World War* (Washington, D.C.: GPO, 1920), 14–27; Clyde H. Metcalf, *A History of the United States Marine Corps* (New York: G. P. Putnam and Sons, 1939), 455–56; Shulimson, "First to Fight," 5, 12–13, 16; and Daugherty, "'To Fight Our Country's Battles,'" 19–22.

31. John B. Wilson, *Maneuver and Firepower: The Evolution of Divisions and Separate Brigades* (Washington, D.C.: Center of Military History, 1998), 60–61; Millett, *Semper Fidelis*, 284–88; Lejeune, *Reminiscences*, 234–36; and Shulimson, "First to Fight," 9–12.

32. Kenneth J. Clifford, *Progress and Purpose: A Developmental History of the United States Marine Corps, 1900–1970* (Washington, D.C.: History and Museums Division, 1973), 23–24; Ballendorf and Bartlett, *Pete Ellis*, 77–78; Holcomb Service Record, Holcomb Papers, Box 31, MCUA; Millett, *Semper Fidelis*, 284, 654; McClellan, *Marine Corps in the World War*, 69–70; Gerald C. Thomas, interview with Gibson B. Smith, 1978, audio recording, 11591A, MCUA; and Peter Owen, *To the Limits of Endurance: A Battalion of Marines in the Great War* (College Station: Texas A&M University Press, 2007), 17–21, 33.

33. Holcomb Military History, Holcomb Papers, Box 1, MCUA.

34. Clifton B. Cates, oral history interview, cited in Owen, *To the Limits of Endurance*, 11.

35. Gordon, "Thomas Holcomb," 257; Daugherty, "Thomas Holcomb," 30; and F. Holcomb, recording, tape 1, sequence 2.

36. Holcomb II, transcript, 6.

37. Holcomb Service Record, Holcomb Papers, Box 31, MCUA; Holcomb Military History, Holcomb Papers, Box 1, MCUA; Lejeune, *Reminiscences*, 247; George B. Clark, *Devil Dogs: Fighting Marines of World War I* (Novato, Calif.: Presidio, 1999), 429–33; William K. Jones, *A Brief History of the 6th Marines* (Washington, D.C.: History and Museums Division, 1987), 3–5; and Second Division Association, *Commendations of Second Division, American Expeditionary Forces, 1917–1919* (Cologne, Germany: Second Division Association, 1919), 57.

38. Owen, *To the Limits of Endurance*, 38–42; McClellan, *Marine Corps in the World War*, 28; and Robert B. Asprey, *At Belleau Wood* (New York: G. P. Putnam's Sons, 1965), 32–38.

39. Thomas, recording with G. Smith, 11590A; James Roosevelt, interview with G. Smith, 1979, audio recording, 11586, MCUA; Vandegrift and Asprey, *Once a Marine*, 87; and Asprey, *At Belleau Wood*, 118.

40. Merwin H. Silverthorn, interview with G. Smith, 1979, audio recording, 11587A, MCUA; and Owen, *To Limits of Endurance*, 16, 76–77.

41. J. Roosevelt, recording, 11586.

42. Thomas, recording with G. Smith, 11590A; American Battle Monuments Commission (hereafter ABMC), *2nd Division Summary of Operations in the World War* (Washington, D.C.: GPO, 1944), 5–7; Shipley Thomas, *The History of the A.E.F.* (New York: George H. Dornan Company, 1920), 61–67; Jones, *Brief History of the 6th Marines*, 3; and Metcalf, *History of the Marine Corps*, 478.

43. Thomas, recording with G. Smith, 11590A.

44. James W. Thomason Jr., *The United States Army Second Division Northwest of Chateau Thierry in World War I*, ed. George B. Clark (Jefferson, N.C.: McFarland & Company, 2006), 38–40; ABMC, *2nd Division Summary*, 7–11; Clark, *Devil Dogs*, 80–81; Jones, *Brief History of the 6th Marines*, 5–6; Holcomb Service Record, Holcomb Papers, Box 31, MCUA; Holcomb Military History, Holcomb Papers, Box 1, MCUA; and Millett, *In Many a Strife*, 33–37.

45. Unreferenced quotation in Clark, *Devil Dogs*, 81. For other versions of this story, see Simmons and Alexander, *Through the Wheat*, 92; and Laurence Stallings, *The Doughboys: The Story of the A.E.F. 1917–1918* (New York: Harper & Row, 1963), 89.

46. Asprey, *At Belleau Wood*, 128–31; and Clark, *Devil Dogs*, 80–81.

47. George Barnett to Beatrice Holcomb, 2 July 1918, Holcomb Papers, Box 12, MCUA.

48. Dick Camp, *Devil Dogs at Belleau Wood: U.S. Marines in World War I* (Norwalk, Conn.: MBI Publishing, 2008), 82–89.

49. Holcomb to B. Holcomb, 6 June 1918, Holcomb Papers, Box 8, MCUA.

50. Thomason, *United States Army Second Division*, 105–8; Owen, *To the Limit of Endurance*, 73–83, 89–91; ABMC, *2nd Division Summary*, 11–17; Second Division Association, *Commendations of the Second Division*, 51–54; Asprey, *At Belleau Wood*, 190–200; Jones, *Brief History of the 6th Marines*, 9; Simmons and Alexander, *Through the Wheat*, 105–11; and Commanding General (hereafter CG), 7 June 1918, Diary of 4th Brigade, Marine Corps, American Expeditionary Force, 30 May–30 June 1918, *Records of the Second Division Operation Reports War Diaries Journal of Operations, 1918,* vol. 6 (Washington, D.C.: Second Division Historical Section, Army War College, 1929), n.p.

51. Holcomb to B. Holcomb, 8 June 1918, Holcomb Papers, Box 8, MCUA.

52. Ibid., 9 June 1918, Holcomb Papers, Box 8, MCUA.

53. Camp, *Devil Dogs at Belleau Wood*, 88.

54. Unreferenced quotation in McClellan, *Marine Corps in the World War*, 41. See also James G. Harbord, *Leaves from a War Diary* (New York: Dodd, Mead, & Company, 1925), 295.

55. *Croix de Guerre* citation, Holcomb Service Record, Holcomb Papers, Box 31, MCUA. See also General Order No. 40, 2nd Division, in Holcomb Service Record, Holcomb Papers, Box 31, MCUA.

56. Thomas, recording with G. Smith, 11590A. See also Silverthorn, recording with G. Smith, 11587A.

57. Thomas, recording with G. Smith, 11591A.

58. "Gas Warfare at Belleau Wood, June 1918," report by Rexmond C. Cochrane, U.S. Army Chemical Corps Historical Studies, 1957, 32–42, 63–75, loose copy held at MCUA; Owen, *To the Limits of Endurance*, 93–96; Heinl, *Soldiers of the Sea*, 200–202; and Simmons and Alexander, *Through the Wheat*, 111–16.

59. CG, 14 June 1918, Diary of the 4th Brigade, *Records of the Second Division*, n.p. See also Thomason, *United States Army Second Division*, 157.

60. Asprey, *At Belleau Wood*, 277–79; and Owen, *To the Limits of Endurance*, 96–99.

61. Jones, *Brief History of the 6th Marines*, 11–12; Heinl, *Soldiers of the Sea*, 203–4; and Colin Michael Colbourn, "Esprit de Marine Corps: The Making of the Modern Marine Corps through Public Relations, 1898–1929," (M.A. thesis, University of Southern Mississippi, 2009), 64–65.

62. Thomason, *United States Army Second Division*, 157, 216; Asprey, *At Belleau Wood*, 286; and Jones, *Brief History of the 6th Marines*, 11–12.

63. Douglas V. Johnson II and Rolfe Hillman Jr., *Soissons 1918* (College Station: Texas A&M University Press, 1999), 59–87, 103–5; Simmons and Alexander, *Through the Wheat*, 153–65; Thomas, *History of the A.E.F.*, 144–62; and Metcalf, *History of the Marine Corps*, 491–96.

64. Letter from Robert L. Denig, cited in *New York Times*, n.d., Holcomb File, HDRB.

65. Ibid.

66. Holcomb Service Record, Holcomb Papers, Box 31, MCUA. For similar praise for Holcomb's leadership at Soissons, see John A. Lejeune to Adjutant General of the Army, 31 March 1923, Holcomb Papers, Box 13, MCUA.

67. ABMC, *2nd Division Summary*, 31–32; Metcalf, *History of the Marine Corps*, 496–98; Jones, *Brief History of the 6th Marines*, 13–14; Clark, *Devil Dogs*, 26–52; Owen, *To the Limits of Endurance*, 117–30; and Johnson and Hillman, *Soissons*, 105–11.

68. Holcomb Service Record, Holcomb Papers, Box 31, MCUA; Lejeune, *Reminiscences*, 60–63, 470–72; Clifford, *Progress and Purpose*, 21–23; and Condit et al., *Brief History of Headquarters Marine Corps*, 10–13.

69. Owen, *To the Limits of Endurance*, 136–201; Simmons and Alexander, *Through the Wheat*, 177–241; George B. Clark, *Hiram Iddings Bears, U.S. Marine Corps: Biography of a World War I Hero* (Jefferson, N.C.: McFarland & Company, 2005), 236; ABMC, *2nd Division Summary*, 35–95; Second Division Association, *The Second Division American Expeditionary Force in France*, (New York: Hillman, 1937), 161–222; Holcomb Service Record, Holcomb Papers, Box 31, MCUA; and Holcomb Military History, Holcomb Papers, Box 1, MCUA.

70. Second Division Association, *Commendations of Second Division*, 18–53; Holcomb Service Record, Holcomb Papers, Box 31, MCUA; Holcomb Military History, Holcomb Papers, Box 1, MCUA; Silverthorn, recording with G. Smith, 11587A; and Second Division Association, *Second Division American Expeditionary Force*, 306–13.

71. Owen, *To the Limits of Endurance*, 204. See also Millett, *In Many a Strife*, 72–73.

72. Second Division Association, *Commendations of Second Division*, 54–55; "Origination and Meaning of the United States Marine Corps: 'Semper Fidelis,'" 4–5, n.d. [c. 1934], Ben H. Fuller Personal Papers Collection, Box 6, MCUA; Silverthorn, recording with G. Smith, 11587A; Owen, *To the Limits of Endurance*, 202–9; Millett, *Semper Fidelis*, 316–18; Gary L. Rutledge, "The Rhetoric of United States Marine Corps Enlisted Recruitment" (M.A. thesis, University of Kansas, 1974), 23–34; Marshall, "Crucible of Colonial Service," 94–102; Robert G. Lindsey, *This High Name: Public Relations and the U.S. Marine Corps* (Madison: University of Wisconsin Press, 1956), 67–73; Thomas, *History of the A.E.F.*, 83–84: and Colbourn, "Esprit de Marine Corps," 50–69.

73. Rutledge, "Rhetoric of Marine Corps," 23.

74. Robert L. Denig Sr., interviews by Benis M. Frank, Alvin M. Josephy Jr., and Robert L. Denig Jr., 1977–1979, transcript, 3–5, 26, MCUA; Fred Curtis Lash, "Media and the Marines: Marching, Music, and Movies" (M.A. thesis, American University, 1983), 6; and Colbourn, "Esprit de Marine Corps," 70–75.

75. Daugherty, "'To Fight Our Country's Battles,'" 77–78, 608.

76. Holcomb Service Record, Holcomb Papers, Box 31, MCUA; Metcalf, *History of the Marine Corps*, 520–22; McClellan, *Marine Corps in the World War*, 56–57, 80–81; Owen, *To the Limits of Endurance*, 202–3; Millett, *In Many a Strife*, 70–71; and Simmons and Alexander, *Through the Wheat*, 241–51.

77. Millett, *Semper Fidelis*, 319–20, 654.

78. McClellan, *Marine Corps in the World War*, 80–81; John A. Lejeune, "The United States Marine Corps: Present and Future," *Proceedings of the United States Naval Institute* 54 (October 1928): 861; and Holcomb Military History, Holcomb Papers, Box 1, MCUA.

79. Barrow, "Looking for John A. Lejeune," 74–75.

80. Merrill L. Bartlett, "John A. Lejeune, 1920–1929," in *Commandants of the Marine Corps*, ed. Millett and Shulimson, 197–98, 212–13; Lejeune, *Reminiscences*, 460–85; Metcalf, *History of the Marine Corps*, 546; Condit et al., *Brief History of Headquarters Marine Corps*, 12–15; Daugherty, "'To Fight Our Country's Battles,'" 122–31; and Millett, *Semper Fidelis*, 322–28.

81. Lejeune, "United States Marine Corps," 861.

82. Metcalf, *History of the Marine Corps*, 542–43.

83. Gerald C. Thomas to Alexander A. Vandegrift, 9 August 1945, HAF 204, MCUA; Lejeune, *Reminiscences*, 463; Metcalf, *History of the Marine Corps*, 545–46; Clifford, *Progress and Purpose*, 36–38; Daugherty, "'To Fight Our Country's Battles,'" 230 note 35, 331 note 5, 418–20, 440–51; and Donald F. Bittner, *Curriculum Evolution: Marine Corps Command and Staff College, 1920–1988* (Washington, D.C.: History and Museums Division, 1988), 1–15.

84. Diploma, U.S. Army Command and General Staff School, 19 June 1925, Class Standing, 19 June 1925, and Holcomb Service Record, all in Holcomb Military History, Holcomb Papers, Box 9, MCUA.

85. F. Holcomb, recording, tape 2 sequence 4.

86. Samuel B. Griffiths II, interview by B. Frank, 1970, transcript, 29, MCOHC, MCUA; Earl H. Ellis, *Advanced Base Operations in Micronesia* (Washington, D.C.: GPO,

1992), v–vi; Vandegrift and Asprey, *Once a Marine*, 61; Ballendorf and Bartlett, *Pete Ellis*, 123–41, 151–62; Hough et al., *Pearl Harbor to Guadalcanal*, 8–10; Moskin, *Marine Corps Story*, 459–61; Millett, *Semper Fidelis*, 325–26; Frank J. Infusino, "The U.S. Marines and War Planning, 1900–1941" (M.A. thesis, San Diego State Univeristy, 1974), 50–1, 78; and Simmons, *United States Marines*, 3rd ed., 125. For a dissenting view regarding the originality of Ellis' ideas relative to those of Robert H. Dunlap, see Leo J. Daugherty, III, *Pioneers of Amphibious Warfare, 1898–1945: Profiles of Fourteen American Military Strategists* (Jefferson, N.C.: McFarland & Company, 2009): 194–212.

87. Earl H. Ellis, *Navy Bases: Their Location, Resources, and Security* (Washington, D.C.: GPO, 1992), 3–6, 10–23, 30, 48.

88. Ellis, *Advanced Base Operations*, 39–50; and Daugherty, "'To Fight Our Country's Battles,'" 241–61.

89. Miller, *War Plan Orange*, 79; memo for General Board (hereafter GB), 11 February 1922, and GB to SecNav, 10 August 1932, both in GBSF 1900–47, GB 432, Box 163, RG 80, NADC; Thomas to Vandegrift, 9 August 1945, HAF 204, MCUA; and Daugherty, "'To Fight Our Country's Battles,'" 331 note 5.

90. Lejeune, "United States Marine Corps," 250; Millett, *Semper Fidelis*, 322–28; memo for the GB, 11 February 1922, GBSF 1900–47, GB 432, Box 163, RG 80, NADC; Russell N. Jordahl, interview by B. Frank, 1970, transcript, p. 13, MCUA; Director of the Marine Corps Institute to Commanding Officer of 19th Battalion, 17 December 1936, PDGC 1933–38, Box 4, RG 127, NADC; and Victor H. Krulak, *First to Fight: An Inside View of the U.S. Marine Corps* (Annapolis: Naval Institute Press, 1984), 142–43.

91. F. Holcomb, recording, tape 2, sequence 4.

92. Ibid.

93. Ibid., tape 3, sequence 5.

94. William E. Leuchtenberg, *Franklin D. Roosevelt and the New Deal, 1932–1940* (New York: Harper & Row, 1963), 1–3, 19–27; Dallek, *Roosevelt and American Foreign Policy*, 70, 86; Kennedy, *Freedom from Fear*, 36–69, 87–92, 390; and Heinl, *Soldiers of the Sea*, 668–69.

95. Michael A. Barnhart, *Japan Prepares for Total War: The Search for Economic Security* (Ithaca, N.Y.: Cornell University Press, 1987), 18–20, 116, 131; Yoshihisa Tak Matsusaka, *The Making of Japanese Manchuria, 1904–1932* (Cambridge, Mass.: Harvard University Asian Center, 2001), 312–411; Robert A. Divine, *The Illusion of Neutrality* (Chicago: University of Chicago Press, 1962), 23–30; and Fred Greene, "The Military View of American National Policy: 1904–1940," *American Historical Review* 66 (January 1961): 355–77.

96. Merrill L. Bartlett, "Wendell C. Neville," in *Commandants of the Marine Corps*, ed. Millett and Shulimson, 214–23; and Merrill L. Bartlett, "Ben Hebard Fuller and the Genesis of the United States Marine Corps, 1891–1934," *Journal of Military History* 69 (January 2005): 73–92.

97. W. C. Neville, "The Marine Corps," *Proceedings of the United States Naval Institute* 55 (October 1929): 863; and Daugherty, "'To Fight Our Country's Battles,'" 542–44.

98. John Hattendorf, B. Mitchell Simpson III, and John R, Wadliegh, *Sailors and Scholars: The Centennial History of the U.S. Naval War College* (Newport: Naval

War College Press, 1984), 140–46; and Certificate of Graduation, Naval War College, 27 May 1931, Holcomb Military History Holcomb Papers, Box 1, MCUA.

99. F. Holcomb, recording, tape 2, sequence 3.

100. "Report of Committee No. 6. Subject: Plans and Orders for the Seizure of Halifax," 29 March 1932, File Number 386-6, and "Analytical Studies, Synopsis of Report, Committee No. 5," 2 March 1932, File Number 388-5, both in AHEC; F. Holcomb, recording, tape 1, sequence 2; and Harry P. Ball, *Of Responsible Command: A History of the U.S. Army War College* (Carlisle Barracks, Penn.: Alumni Association of the Army War College), 212–25.

101. Holcomb, "The Marine Corps' Mission in National Defense, and Its Organization for a Major Emergency," 30 January 1932, pp. 1–4, File 387–30, AHEC.

102. Wilson, *Maneuver and Firepower*, 52–56, 86–95, 125–33.

103. Holcomb, "Discussion of the Marine Corps' Mission in National Defense, and Its Organization for a Major Emergency," 30 January 1932, p. 13, File 387–30, AHEC.

104. Holcomb, "The Marine Corps' Mission in National Defense," p. 3, File 387–30, AHEC.

105. Holcomb, "Discussion of the Marine Corps' Mission," p. 13, File 387–30, AHEC; Daugherty, "'To Fight Our Country's Battles,'" 440–51; Donald F. Bittner, "Taking the Right Fork in the Road: The Transition of the U.S. Marine Corps from an 'Expeditionary' to an 'Amphibious' Corps, 1918–1941," *Battle Near and Far: A Century of Overseas Deployment—The Chief of Army Military History Conference 2004*, ed. Peter Dennis and Jeffrey Grey (Canberra, Australia: Army History Unit, 2005), 116–40.

106. Miller, *War Plan Orange*, 36, 181, 183, 329, 377–78.

107. "Career of Thomas Holcomb," by G. Smith, Holcomb Papers, Box 29, MCUA; Gordon, "Thomas Holcomb," 260–61; and Holcomb Service Record, Holcomb Papers, Box 31, MCUA.

108. F. Holcomb, recording, tape 1, sequence 4.

109. Unsigned editorial, "Franklin Delano Roosevelt," *Marine Corps Gazette* 17 (February 1933): 5–6; Millett, *Semper Fidelis*, 335; Heinl, *Soldiers of the Sea*, 306; Leuchtenberg, *Roosevelt and the New Deal*, 214–15; Kennedy, *Freedom from Fear*, 398, 428; John C. Walter, "Congressman Carl Vinson and Franklin D. Roosevelt: Naval Preparedness and the Coming of World War II, 1939–1940," *Georgia Historical Quarterly* 64 (Fall 1980): 294, 298, 305; Julius Augustus Furer, *Administration of the Navy Department in World War II* (Washington, D.C.: GPO, 1959), 47–50; and Kenneth J. Hagan, *This People's Navy: The Making of American Seapower* (New York: Free Press, 1991), 281–87, 294.

110. Clifton B. Cates, interview by B. Frank, 1967, transcript, p. 97, MCOHC, MCUA; and Senator Phillip Lee Goldsborough to Estell Smith Kepler, 3 February 1933, Julian C. Smith Personal Papers Collection (hereafter J. Smith Papers), Box 28, MCUA.

111. "Maas Biography," and Ben H. Fuller to Melvin J. Maas, 12 January 1933, both in "Melvin J. Maas" Biographical File, HDRB; and Gladys Zehnpfennig, *Melvin J. Maas: Gallant Man of Action* (Minneapolis: T. S. Denison, 1967), 54–55, 65–70.

112. Leuchtenberg, *Roosevelt and the New Deal*, 218–21; Dallek, *Roosevelt and American Foreign Policy*, 102–4, 117–21, 137–47; and Kennedy, *Freedom from Fear*, 214–19, 350–58, 381–422.

113. Major General Commandant (hereafter MGC) to Louis McCarty Little, "Fleet Marine Force," 5 December 1933, PDGC 1933–38, Box 135, RG 127, NADC.

114. MGC to Chief of Naval Operations (hereafter CNO), "Expeditionary Force," 17 August 1933, File 1975-10, PDGC 1933–38, Box 135, RG 127, NADC; William J. Van Ryzin, interview by B. Frank and Graham A. Cosmas, 1975, transcript, pp. 74–76, MCUA; Millett, *Semper Fidelis*, 319, 330–37; Jeter A. Isely and Philip A. Crowl, *The U.S. Marines and Amphibious War: Its Theory, and Its Practice in the Pacific* (Princeton: Princeton University Press, 1951),74–75; Heinl, *Soldiers of the Sea*, 299–306; Thomas to Vandegrift, 9 August 1945, HAF 204, MCUA; and Daugherty, "'To Fight Our Country's Battles,'" 614–38.

115. Julian C. Smith to Little, 2 July 1936, Louis McCarty Little Personal Papers Collection (hereafter Little Papers) Folder 20, MCUA; Marine Corps Schools (hereafter MCS), *Tentative Manual for Landing Operations*, 1934, HAF 39, MCUA; MCS, *Tentative Manual for Defense of Advanced Bases*, 1936, HAF 906, MCUA; and Daughtery, *Pioneers of Amphibious Warfare*, 204–9.

116. Charles D. Melson, conversations with the author, July 2003.

117. MCS, *Tentative Manual for Landing Operations*, 1934, paragraphs 1.1, 1.2, 1.5, 1.8, 1.22, 3.120, MCUA; James C. Breckinridge to Russell, 6 November 1934, Holcomb Papers, Box 11, MCUA; Isely and Crowl, *U.S. Marines and Amphibious War*, 5, 36–44; Clifford, *Progress and Purpose*, 45–48, 58–59, 139–42; Hough et al., *Pearl Harbor to Guadalcanal*, 14–22; Millett, *Semper Fidelis*, 319, 331–37, 343; Millett, *In Many a Strife*, 111–16, 128–30; Ulbrich, "Clarifying the Origins," 88–90; Bittner, "Taking the Right Fork," 124–25; Gunther E. Rothenberg, "From Gallipoli to Guadalcanal," in *Assault from the Sea: Essays on the History of Amphibious Warfare*, ed. Merrill L. Bartlett (Annapolis: Naval Institute, 1983), 177–82; Timothy Moy, *War Machines: Transforming Technologies in the U.S. Military, 1920–1940* (College Station: Texas A&M University Press, 2001), 134–39, 147, 166–67; and Craig C. Felker, *Testing American Sea Power: U.S. Navy Strategic Exercises, 1923–1940* (College Station: Texas A&M University Press, 2007), 101–5.

118. F. Holcomb, recording, tape 1, sequence 1; MCS, *Tentative Manual for Defense of Advanced Bases*, 1936, War Plans and Related Material 1931–1944, Box 7, Entry 246, RG 127, NADC; Bittner, "Taking the Right Fork," 125–26; and David J. Ulbrich, "Document of Note: The Long-Lost *Tentative Manual for Defense of Advanced Bases* (1936)," *Journal of Military History* 71 (October 2007): 889–901.

119. MCS, *Tentative Manual for Defense of Advanced Bases*, preface.

120. MCS, Questionnaire, 11 April 1933, File "Military Correspondence, 1932–1937," Box 1, Vernon E. Megee Personal Papers Collection, DDEL; Clifford, *Progress and Purpose*, 45–48, 58–59, 139–42; Daugherty, "'To Fight Our Country's Battles,'" 222–23, 440–51; and Theodore L. Gatchel, *At the Water's Edge: Defending Against Modern Amphibious Assault* (Annapolis: Naval Institute Press, 1996), 1–24, 78–81.

121. Donald F. Bittner, "John H. Russell, 1934–1936," in *Commandants of the Marine Corps*, ed. Millett and Shulimson, 240–52.

122. John H. Russell, "Final Report of the Major General Commandant," *MCG* 20 (November 1936): 16.

123. Bittner, "John H. Russell," 246–47.

124. Russell, "Final Report," 16–21; and Bittner, "John H. Russell," 250.

125. Russell, "Final Report," 21.

126. John M. Arthur to Vandegrift, 21 August 1936, Vandegrift Papers, Box 1, MCUA. See also John Marston to Vandegrift, 3 November 1936, and Vandegrift to Marston, 4 December 1936, both in Vandegrift Papers, Box 1, MCUA; Oliver P. Smith, interview by B. Frank, 1969, transcription, p. 79, MCUA; Thomas, recording with G. Smith, 11590A; and Robert Hugh Williams, *The Old Corps: A Portrait of the U.S. Marine Corps between the Wars* (Annapolis: Naval Institute Press, 1982), 103–4.

127. "Service News and Gossip," *A&NJ*, 7 November 1936, p. 210, in Holcomb Papers, Box 25, MCUA; and Bittner, "John H. Russell," 251.

128. Lejeune to Cordell Hull, 11 May 1936, and Lejeune to Marvin MacIntyre, File 18E, original held at Franklin D. Roosevelt Library and Archives, Hyde Park New York (hereafter File 18E), and copy in Holcomb Papers, Box 11, MCUA.

129. Marston to Vandegrift, 3 November 1936, Vandegrift Papers, Box 1, MCUA; O. Smith, transcript, 79; and F. Holcomb, recording, tape 2, sequence 4.

130. F. Holcomb, recording, tape 1, sequence 2; Joseph A. Alexander, "Jacob Zeilin, 1864–1876," in *Commandants of the Marine Corps*, ed. Millett and Shulimson, 85–88, 96; Metcalf, *History of the Marine Corps*, 544; Simmons, *United States Marines*, 3rd ed., 120; Moskin, *U.S. Marine Corps Story*, 254; Gordon, "Thomas Holcomb," 261–62; Millett, *In Many a Strife*, 123; Millett, *Semper Fidelis*, 335–37; and Bittner, "John H. Russell," 251.

131. Franklin D. Roosevelt to SecNav, 12 November 1936, File 18E, in Holcomb Papers, Box 11, MCUA; Gordon, "Holcomb and 'The Golden Age,'" 260–61; and J. Roosevelt, recording, 11586, MCUA; "Army and Navy: Another Roosevelt," *Time*, 27 March 1933; and "Henry Roosevelt Dead in Capital," *New York Times*, 23 February 1936.

132. Keith B. Bickel, *Mars Learning: The Marine Corps Development of Small Wars Doctrine, 1915–1940* (Boulder: Westview Press, 2001), 205–8, 211–13; and Daugherty, *Pioneers of Amphibious Warfare*, 261–66.

133. Gordon, "Holcomb and 'The Golden Age,'" 260–61; Thomas, recording with G. Smith, 11590B; and J. Roosevelt, recording, 11586.

134. "Service News and Gossip," *A&NJ* of 14 November 1936, p. 230, in Holcomb Papers, Box 25, MCUA.

135. Greenstein, *Presidential Difference*, 5–6.

136. F. Holcomb, recording, tape 1, sequence 2.

137. Thomas, recordings with G. Smith, 11590A and 11591A; Vandegrift and Asprey, *Once a Marine*, 87, 89–90; Williams, *Old Corps*, 105; and Gordon, "Holcomb and 'The Golden Age,'" 269.

138. F. Holcomb, recording, tape 2, sequence 3.

139. *Advertiser* (Albion, N.Y.), 3 December 1936, Holcomb File, HDRB.

140. Robert H. Williams, interview with B. Frank, 1979, transcript, 65–66, MCUA; Vandegrift and Asprey, *Once a Marine,* 87; and Williams, *Old Corps,* 104–5.

141. William A. Worton, interview with B. Frank, 1967, transcript, pp. 327–28, MCUA.

142. F. Holcomb, recording, tape 2, sequence 3.

CHAPTER 2

Taking Charge of the Struggling Marine Corps, December 1936–August 1939

1. "General Holcomb Becomes Marine Corps Commandant," *A&NJ,* 5 December 1936, Holcomb Papers, Box 25, MCUA.

2. R. R. Wallace to Little, 14 November 1936, Little Papers, Folder 2, MCUA; Moskin, *U.S. Marine Corps Story,* 254; and *Advertiser,* 3 December 1936, Holcomb File, HDRB.

3. J. Smith to Holcomb, 25 February 1937, Holcomb Papers, Box 1, MCUA.

4. Smith, *Development of Amphibious Tactics,* 25–26; Isely and Crowl, *U.S. Marines and Amphibious War,* 46–51; and Millett, *Semper Fidelis,* 337–38.

5. Smith, *Development of Amphibious Tactics,* 26–27; Silverthorn, recording with G. Smith, 1158A, MCUA; Isely and Crowl, *U.S. Marines and Amphibious War,* 52–55; and Millett, *Semper Fidelis,* 38–39.

6. Clifford, *Progress and Purpose,* 48; Millett, *Semper Fidelis,* 339–40; and "A History of the U.S. Fleet Landing Exercises," report by B. W. Galley, 3 July 1939, HAF 73, MCUA.

7. Vandegrift and Asprey, *Once a Marine,* 88.

8. MGC to CNO, 18 February 1936, MCBE FY 1936–43, Entry 248, Box 1, RG 127, NADC; and General Statement of Thomas Holcomb to the Naval Subcommittee of the House Committee on Appropriations, 10 December 1936, Holcomb Papers, Box 27, MCUA; Melvin J. Maas, "Marine Corps Personnel Problem and the Only Solution," *MCG* (1936), pp. 7–8, in Melvin J. Maas Personal Papers Collection (hereafter Maas Papers), Box 8, MNHS.

9. Navy Department, *Naval Expenditures 1936* (Washington, D.C.: GPO, 1937), 1; Navy Department, *Naval Expenditures 1937* (Washington, D.C.: GPO, 1938), 1; *Annual Report of the Secretary of the Navy for FY 1937* (Washington, D.C.: GPO, 1937), 17–18; and Vandegrift and Asprey, *Once a Marine,* 89.

10. "Votes of Leading Isolationist Senators on Defense Measures, 1937–1941," unsigned report, n.d. [c. July 1941], Papers of the Committee to Defend America by Aiding the Allies (hereafter CDAAA), Box 2, MNHS; Kennedy, *Freedom from Fear,* 355–58; Leuchtenberg, *Roosevelt and the New Deal,* 194–95, 244, 256; and Divine, *Illusion of Neutrality,* 114–16.

11. Vandegrift and Asprey, *Once a Marine,* 90.

12. Ibid.

13. Vandegrift and Asprey, *Once a Marine,* 90. See also Silverthorn, recording with G. Smith, 11589A, MCUA; and Charles H. Lyman to Vandegrift, 22 July 1938, Vandegrift Papers, Box 2, MCUA.

14. Craig M. Cameron, *American Samurai: Myth, Imagination, and the Conduct of Battle in the First Marine Division, 1941–1951* (Cambridge: Cambridge University Press, 1994), 25.

15. Vandegrift and Asprey, *Once a Marine*, 90.

16. Roy Geiger to CNO, 10 December 1937, Holcomb Papers, Box 1, MCUA.

17. "The Contribution of the Marine Corps to National Defense," speech by Holcomb, 27 January 1927, Holcomb File, HDRB.

18. Ibid.

19. Lawrence H. Suid, *Guts and Glory: The Making of the American Military Image in Film*, rev. ed. (Lexington: University Press of Kentucky, 2002), 7, 53–56, 116–17; Lindsay, *This High Name*, 49; and Gordon, "Thomas Holcomb," 264.

20. Paul R. Watson to Holcomb, 15 January 1937, and Holcomb to Watson, 16 January 1937, both in Holcomb Papers, Box 1, MCUA.

21. Alexander Weir to Holcomb, 6 November 1937, and Holcomb to Weir, 10 November 1937, both in Holcomb Papers, Box 1, MCUA; and Lindsay, *This High Name*, 49.

22. Vandegrift and Asprey, *Once a Marine*, 90.

23. Western Recruiting Division (hereafter RD), "Publicity activities, etc., during the month of June 1937," n.d., RG 127, PDGC 1933–38, Box 70, RG 127, NADC.

24. Rutledge, "Rhetoric of the Marine Corps," 114. See also Cameron, *American Samurai*, 24–26, 38–40; and Peter G. Filene, *Him/Herself: Sex Roles in Modern America* (New York: Harcourt Brace Jovanovich, 1974), 153–66.

25. Christina S. Jarvis, *The Male Body at War: American Masculinity during World War II* (DeKalb: Northern Illinois University Press, 2004); 15–20; and Joan W. Scott, "Gender: A Useful Category of Analysis," *American Historical Review* 91 (December 1986): 1073–74.

26. John C. Beaumont, "Recruiting Situation," 16 April 1937, PDGC 1933–38, Box 70, RG 127, NADC.

27. "Statement of Recruiting, First Quarter Fiscal Year 1937," and "Statement of Recruiting, Second Quarter Fiscal 1937," both in PDGC 1933–38, Box 70, RG 127, NADC.

28. Beaumont, "Recruiting Situation," 16 April 1937, PDGC 1933–38, Box 70, RG 127, NADC.

29. "Statement of Recruiting, Second Quarter Fiscal Year 1937," PDGC 1933–38, Box 70, RG 127, NADC.

30. "Statement of Recruiting, First Quarter Fiscal Year 1937," PDGC 1933–38, Box 70, RG 127, NADC.

31. Commanding Officer of Recruit Depot to MGC, 12 June and 16 June 1937, both in PDGC 1933–38, Box 70, RG 127, NADC.

32. Malcolm Muir Jr., ed., *The Human Tradition in the World War II Era* (Wilmington, Del.: Scholarly Resources, 2001), xvi–xvii.

33. Beaumont, "Statement of Recruiting, Second Quarter Fiscal Year 1937," and "Recruiting Situation," 16 April 1937, both in PDGC 1933–38, Box 70, RG 127, NADC.

34. "Daily Report on Recruiting," 1 July 1937, and 30 December 1937, both in PDGC 1933–1938, Box 70, RG 127, NADC; H. Smith to Holcomb, 19 April 1937, Holcomb Papers, Box 1, MCUA; Silverthorn, recording with G. Smith, 11589A; and Vandegrift and Asprey, *Once a Marine*, 87–88.

35. F. Holcomb, recording, tape 1, sequence 1.

36. Ibid.

37. Joseph Fegan to Holcomb, 25 October 1938, Holcomb Papers, Box 2, MCUA; Edward L. Dreyer, *China at War, 1901–1945* (London: Longman, 1995), 200–216; and Mark R. Peattie, *Ishiwara Kanji and Japan's Confrontation with the West* (Princeton: Princeton University Press, 1975), 295–308.

38. Stephen R. MacKinnon, "The Sino-Japanese Conflict, 1931–1945," in *A Military History of China*, ed. David A. Graff and Robin Higham (Boulder: Westview Press, 2002), 213–15; Mark Eykholt et al., *The Nanjing Massacre in History and Historiography* (Berkeley: University of California Press, 2000); Saburo Hayashi with Alvin D. Coox, *Kōgun: The Japanese Army in the Pacific War* (1951; repr., Quantico, Va.: Marine Corps Association, 1959), 9; Dreyer, *China at War*, 219–20, 261–63; and Barnhart, *Japan Prepares for Total War*, 97–98.

39. Charles F. B. Price to Holcomb, 18 January 1938, MGC to CNO, 18 February 1938, both in Holcomb Papers, Box 1; Fegan to Holcomb, 25 October 1938, Holcomb Papers, Box 2, MCUA; Maxwell D. Taylor, "Strategical and Tactical Doctrines, Tactical Technique in China Operations," 3 August 1938, 2ndBFMFGF, Entry 238A, Box 13, RG 127, NADC; and Kenneth W. Condit and Edwin T. Turnbladh, *Hold High the Torch: A History of the 4th Marines* (Washington, D.C.: Historical Branch, HQMC, 1960), 167–74.

40. Price to Holcomb, 18 January 1938, Holcomb Papers, Box 1, MCUA. See also Harry E. Yarnell to Holcomb, 1 February 1938, Holcomb Papers, Box 1, MCUA; John W. Dower, *War Without Mercy: Race and Power in the Pacific War* (New York: Pantheon Books, 1986), 9–13, 20–21, 98–99; and Michael H. Hunt, *Ideology and U.S. Foreign Policy* (New Haven, Conn.: Yale University Press, 1987), 69–77, 140–45.

41. J. M. McHugh to Holcomb, 12 April 1938, Holcomb Papers, Box 1, MCUA; Condit and Turnbladh, *Hold High the Torch*, 184–85; Millett, *Semper Fidelis*, 234; Moskin, *U.S. Marine Corps Story*, 216–17; and Phyllis A. Zimmerman, "Military Missionary: The Riddle Wrapped in a Mystery inside an Enigma That Was Evans F. Carlson," in *New Interpretations in Naval History*, ed. Randy Carol Belano and Craig L. Symonds (Annapolis: Naval Institute Press, 2001), 252–58.

42. Holcomb to Fegan, 26 August 1938, Holcomb Papers, Box 1, MCUA; D. C. McDougal to Holcomb, 26 December 1937, Beaumont to Holcomb, 11 January 1938, and Yarnell to Holcomb, 1 February 1938, all in Holcomb Papers, Box 1, MCUA; Hayashi with Coox, *Kōgun*, 14–16; Iriye, *Power and Culture*, 1–25; Barnhart, *Japan Prepares for Total War*, 19–21, 142–43; Condit and Turnbladh, *Hold High the Torch*, 176–83; and Millett, *Semper Fidelis*, 232–34.

43. Iriye, *Power and Culture*, 1.

44. G-2 War Department General Staff, "Japan Combat Estimate," 31 March 1939, Record Group 38 Records of the Office of the CNO (RG 38), SPDWPD 1912–46, Series III, Misc. Subject File, Box 61, NACP; William L. Langer and S. Everett

Gleason, *The Undeclared War, 1940–1941* (New York: Harper & Brothers, 1953), 7–20; Dreyer, *China at War*, 207–10, 260–64; and Condit and Turnbladh, *Hold High the Torch*, 177–84.

45. Richard Overy, "Strategic Intelligence and the Outbreak of World War II," *War in History* 5 (November 1998): 451–79.

46. Frank Freidel, *Launching the New Deal* (Boston: Little, Brown, 1973), 377, cited in Kennedy, *Freedom from Fear*, 158. See also Robert A. Divine, *Reluctant Belligerent: American Entry into World War II*, 2nd ed. (New York: John Wiley & Sons, 1979), 47–48.

47. Ronald H. Spector, *Eagle Against the Sun: The American War Against Japan* (New York: Free Press, 1985), 59; D. Clayton James, "American and Japanese Strategies in the Pacific War," in *Makers of Modern Strategy from Machiavelli to the Nuclear Age*, ed. Peter Paret (Princeton: Princeton University Press, 1986), 710, 717; Ross, *American War Plans, 1890–1939*, 177–83; and Calvin L. Christman, "Franklin D. Roosevelt and the Craft of Strategic Assessment," in *Calculations: Net Assessment and the Coming of World War II*, ed. Williamson Murray and Allan R. Millett (New York: Free Press, 1992), 238–42.

48. "Joint Army and Navy Basic War Plan—Orange (1938)," Joint Board No. 325 (hereafter JB 325), Serial 618, p. 1, M1421, Reel 10, NACP.

49. Commander in Chief, Pacific Fleet (hereafter CINCPAC) to CNO, 27 July 1937, MCBE FY 1936–43, Box 1, Entry 248, RG 127, NADC; Thomas to Vandegrift, 9 August 1945, HAF 204, MCUA; Kinoaki Matsuo, *How Japan Plans to Win*, trans. Kilsoo K. Haan (1940; repr., Boston: Little, Brown, 1942), 182–99, 281–87; Ulbrich, "Clarifying the Origins," 93–96; David C. Evans and Mark R. Peattie, *Kaigun: Strategy, Tactics, and Technology in the Imperial Japanese Navy, 1887–1941* (Annapolis: Naval Institute Press, 1997), 464–67, 471–73; and James, "American and Japanese Strategies," 705–7.

50. Thomas to Vandegrift, 9 August 1945, HAF 204, MCUA; Vandegrift and Asprey, *Once a Marine*, 93, 118; Smith and Finch, *Coral and Brass*, 60–62; and Allan R. Millett, "Assault from the Sea: The Development of Amphibious Warfare between the Wars—The British, American, and Japanese Experiences," in *Military Innovation in the Interwar Period*, ed. Williamson Murray and Allan R. Millett (Cambridge: Cambridge University Press, 1996), 76–77.

51. "Report of the Board to Investigate and Report upon the Need, for Purposes of National Defense, for the Establishment of Additional Submarine, Destroyers, Mine, and Naval Air Bases on the Coasts of the United States, Its Territories and Possessions," 1 December 1938, pp. 1–6, 62–70, 87–89, SPDWPD 1912–46, Series III, Misc. Subject File, Box 50, RG 38, NACP; CNO to MGC, 21 September 1938, WWIIOPMO 1938–45, Box 3, RG 127, NACP; Miller, *War Plan Orange*, 241–43, 250–53; Gregory J. W. Urwin, *Facing Fearful Odds: The Siege of Wake Island* (Lincoln: University of Nebraska Press, 1997), 48–52; and Ulbrich, "Clarifying the Origins," 90–91.

52. MGC to CNO, 29 May 1937, MCBE FY 1936–43, Box 1, Entry 248, RG 127, NADC; Director of Operations and Training (hereafter O&T) to MGC, 21 September 1938, MGC to CNO, 21 September 1938, and CNO to MGC, 27 September 1938, all in WWIIOPMO 1938–45, Box 3, RG 127, NACP.

53. Smith, *Development of Amphibious Tactics*, 27–28; Isely and Crowl, *U.S. Marines and Amphibious War*, 56–57; and Millett, *Semper Fidelis*, 339–40.

54. McDougal to Holcomb, 5 March 1938, Holcomb Papers, Box 1, MCUA.

55. McDougal to Holcomb, 19 February 1938, and Malin Craig to CNO, 29 June 1938, both in Holcomb Papers, Box 1, MCUA; and Smith, *Development of Amphibious Tactics*, 28.

56. G. W. R. to John Kaluf, 10 March 1939, HAF 204, MCUA; Vandegrift and Asprey, *Once a Marine*, 93; Krulak, *First to Fight*, 88–92; Hough et al., *Pearl Harbor to Guadalcanal*, 23–25; Clifford, *Progress and Purpose*, 50–51; Moy, *War Machines*, 117–18, 150–57; and Jerry E. Strahan, *Andrew Jackson Higgins and the Boats That Won World War II* (Baton Rouge: Louisiana State University Press, 1994), 24–39.

57. Clifford, *Progress and Purpose*, 54–55.

58. Unreferenced quotation in Austin R. Brunelli, interview by Norman J. Anderson, 1984, transcript, p. 25, MCUA.

59. Gordon, "Thomas Holcomb," 262–63; Krulak, *First to Fight*, 100–102; Clifford, *Progress and Purpose*, 55–56; Hough et al., *Pearl Harbor to Guadalcanal*, 32–24; and Kenneth W. Estes, *Marines under Armor: The Marine Corps and the Armored Fighting Vehicle, 1916–2000* (Annapolis: Naval Institute Press, 2000), 32–33.

60. "Emergency Recruiting Plan," 1 January 1938, PDGC 1933–38, Box 256, RG 127, NADC; and Millett, *Semper Fidelis*, 654.

61. "Emergency Recruiting Plan," report by J. Smith, 14 June 1938, PDGC 1933–38, Box 256, RG 127, NADC.

62. "Daily Report on Recruiting," 30 December 1937, 1 July 1938, and 30 December 1938, all in PDGC 1933–38, Box 70, RG 127, NADC.

63. "Emergency Recruiting Plan [Statistical Report]," 1 January 1938, and "Emergency Recruiting Plan," reports by J. Smith, 14 June 1938, both in PDGC 1933–38, Box 256, RG 127, NADC.

64. Navy Department, *United States Marine Corps*, vol. 46a, *United States Naval Administration in World War II* (Washington, D.C.: Department of the Navy, [c. 1946]), 15.

65. "Emergency Recruiting Plan," report by J. Smith, 14 June 1938, PDGC 1933–38, Box 256, RG 127, NADC. See also Donald T. Winder to Holcomb, 29 March 1938, Holcomb Papers, Box 1, MCUA.

66. Rutledge, "Rhetoric of the Marine Corps," 111–18, 128; "Cost of Recruiting Literature Printed and Distributed by the M.C. Publicity Bureau to the Recruiting Service for the Month of September 1938," n.d., PDGC 1933–38, Box 4, RG 127, NADC; and "Daily Report of Recruiting," 30 December 1937, 1 July 1938, and 30 December 1938, all in PDGC 1933–38, Box 70, RG 127, NADC.

67. MGC to Officer in Charge of Central RD, 8 March 1938, PDGC 1933–38, Box 3, RG 127, NADC.

68. Ibid.; Officer in Charge to Holcomb, 18 March 1938; and Holcomb to Edgar Hornby, 22 March 1938, both in PDGC 1933–38, Box 3, RG 127, NADC.

69. Lyman to Holcomb, 8 December 1937, Holcomb Papers, Box 1, MCUA; MGC to CNO, 17 March 1938, and MGC to Quartermaster of the Marine Corps, 4 June 1938,

both in PDGC 1933–38, Box 3, RG 127, NADC; Officer in Charge of the Publicity Bureau to Director of Personnel–Recruiting, 16 September 1938, and Director of the Marine Corps Institute to Commanding Officer of 19th Battalion, 17 December 1936, both in PDGC 1933–38, Box 4, RG 127, NADC.

70. Holcomb to Lyman, 21 October 1938, Holcomb Papers, Box 2, MCUA.

71. General Statement of Thomas Holcomb to the Naval Subcommittee of the House Committee on Appropriations, 5 December 1937, Holcomb Papers, Box 1, MCUA.

72. Susan Landrum, "Carl Vinson: A Study in Military Preparedness" (M.A. thesis, Emory University, 1966), 53–57, 89; Calvin William Enders, "The Vinson Navy" (Ph.D. diss., Michigan State University, 1970), 106–22; John C. Walter, "Congressman Carl Vinson and Franklin D. Roosevelt: Naval Preparedness and the Coming of World War II, 1939–1940," *Georgia Historical Quarterly* 64 (Fall 1980): 294–305; James F. Cook, *Carl Vinson: Patriarch of the Armed Forces* (Macon, Ga.: Mercer University Press, 2004), 124–38; Zehnpfennig, *Melvin J. Maas*, 72–76; Dorothy G. Wayman, *David I. Walsh: Citizen Patriot* (Milwaukee, Wisc.: Bruce Publishing, 1952), 255–61; and James W. Hilty, "Voting Alignments in the United States Senate, 1933–1944," (Ph.D. diss., University of Missouri, 1973), 193–94, 232–37.

73. F. Holcomb, recording, tape 1, sequence 1.

74. James E. Van Zandt to Maas, 28 April 1938, and Maas, telegram to *Schlosser Literary Digest*, 22 December 1937, both in Maas Papers, Box 2, MNHS.

75. Maas, telegram to *Schlosser Literary Digest*, 22 December 1937, Maas Papers, Box 2, MNHS.

76. Maas, radio broadcast for NBC Red Network, 25 February 1938, Maas Papers, Box 6, MNHS.

77. Unsigned editorial, "Vinson Bill," *MCG* 22 (March 1938): 34–37.

78. House Committee on Naval Affairs, *Hearings on H.R. 9997* (hereafter *Hearings on H.R. 9997*), 75th Congress, 2nd and 3rd sessions, 7 April 1938, 3129–32; and unsigned editorial, "Status of Various Grades in Marine Corps," *MCG* 22 (March 1938): 28–29.

79. *Hearings on H.R. 9997*, 3129–32.

80. Ibid., 3134.

81. Ibid., 3134–37.

82. Ibid., 3137–38.

83. Holcomb to Gilder Jackson, 7 April 1938, Holcomb Papers, Box 1, MCUA.

84. Lejeune to Holcomb, 20 April 1938, Holcomb to Little, 25 April 1938, and Holcomb to Beaumont, 27 April 1938, all in Holcomb Papers, Box 1, MCUA; and unsigned editorial, "Legislation," *MCG* 22 (June 1938): 29.

85. Holcomb to Little, 6 June 1938, Holcomb Papers, Box 1, MCUA.

86. Holcomb to Little, 15 June 1938, and memorandum on "More important features of H.R. 9997, as affecting the Marine Corps," 22 June 1938, both in Holcomb Papers, Box 1, MCUA.

87. Holcomb to McDougal, 15 June 1938, Holcomb Papers, Box 1, MCUA.

88. Vandegrift and Asprey, *Once a Marine*, 88–90.

89. Lyman to Vandegrift, 22 July 1938, Vandegrift Papers, Box 2, MCUA.

90. Franklin D. Roosevelt, Address to Congress, 4 January 1939, *Peace and War: United States Foreign Policy, 1931–1941* (Washington, D.C.: GPO, 1943), 447–51; and F. Roosevelt, Message to Congress, 12 January 1939, *Peace and War*, 451–454.

91. Kennedy, *Freedom from Fear*, 394–413, 420; Dallek, *Roosevelt and American Foreign Policy*, 171–80; Divine, *Reluctant Belligerent*, 23–30, 40–52; and Hilty, "Voting Alignments," 192–94, 203–5.

92. General Statement of Thomas Holcomb to the Naval Subcommittee of the House Committee on Appropriations, 3 January 1939, pp. 1, 4–5, Holcomb Papers, Box 2, MCUA.

93. Ibid., 4.

94. Ibid., 5–7.

95. Ibid., 8.

96. Director of O&T to MGC, 19 January 1939, MCBE FY 1936–1943, Box 1, Entry 248, RG 127, NADC.

97. Fegan to Holcomb, 16 March 1939, Holcomb to David I. Walsh, 13 February 1939, Holcomb to Walter E. Noa, 8 March 1939, Holcomb to Arthur, 22 March 1939, Holcomb to A. S. Carpender, 27 March 1939, Holcomb to Walsh, 26 April 1939, Walsh to Holcomb 27 April 1939, all in Holcomb Papers, Box 2, MCUA; Vandegrift to Holcomb, 12 May 1939, Vandegrift Papers, Box 1, MCUA; Silverthorn, recording, with G. Smith 11589A, MCUA; unsigned editorial, "Legislation," *MCG* 23 (June 1939): 5; Dorothy G. Waymen, *David I. Walsh: Citizen Patriot* (Milwaukee, Wisc.: Bruce Publishing, 1952), 255–62; and Zehnpfennig, *Melvin J. Maas*, 73–76.

98. Rutledge, "Rhetoric of the United States Marine Corps," 114; Filene, *Him/Herself*, 153–66; Cameron, *American Samurai*, 24–30, 38, 79–81; and Jarvis, *Male Body at War*, 15–20.

99. "Daily Report on Recruiting," 3 January 1939, MCGC 1939–50, Box 617, RG 127, NACP; "Daily Report on Recruiting," 1 July 1939, MCGC 1939–50, Box 616, RG 127, NACP; and MGC to Officer in Charge of RD, 15 August 1939, MCGC 1939–50, Box 98, RG 127, NACP; F. J. Hall to Holcomb, 8 August 1940, and Holcomb to Hall, 12 August 1940, both in Holcomb Papers, Box 3, MCUA.

100. Charlotte Keyser, interview by G. Smith, 1978, audio recording, 11655, MCUA; and Holcomb to Roosevelt, 1 February 1939 and 3 February 1939, and Holcomb to Fred T. Bishop, 14 February 1939, all in Holcomb Papers, Box 2, MCUA.

101. Little to Holcomb, 1 February 1939, Holcomb Papers, Box 2, MCUA.

102. F. Holcomb, recording, tape 1, sequence 1; and Robert E. Mattingly, *Herringbone Cloak—GI Dagger: Marines of the OSS* (Washington, D.C.: History and Museums Division, HQMC, 1989), 28–30, 39.

103. Alexander Kiralfy, "Japanese Naval Strategy," in *Makers of Modern Strategy*, ed. Earle, 457–61, 480–84; George C. Dyer, ed., *On the Treadmill to Pearl Harbor: The Memoirs of Admiral James O. Richardson* (Washington, D.C.: Naval History Division, 1973), 272–77; B. Mitchell Simpson III, *Admiral Harold R. Stark: Architect of Victory, 1939–1945* (Columbia: University of South Carolina Press, 1989),

13–14; Miller, *War Plan Orange*, 215–17, 226–29; James, "American and Japanese Strategies," 708–9; Brian M. Linn, *Guardians of Empire: The U. S. Army and the Pacific, 1902–1940* (Chapel Hill: University of North Carolina Press, 1997), 180–82; Baer, *One Hundred Years of Sea Power*, 148–49; and Ross, *American War Plans, 1890–1939*, 182–83.

104. "Joint Army and Navy Basic War Plans, Rainbow Nos. 1, 2, 3, 4 and 5," 9 April 1940, JB 325, Serial 642, M1421, Reel 11, NACP; George Carroll Dyer, *Amphibians Came to Conquer: The Story of Richmond Kelly Turner* (Washington, D.C.: Department of the Navy, 1973), 162–65; Dyer, *On the Treadmill to Pearl Harbor*, 282–306; John Major, "Navy Plans for War, 1937–1941," in *In Peace and War: Interpretations of American Naval History, 1775–1984*, ed. Kenneth J. Hagan, 2nd ed. (Westport, Conn.: Greenwood Press, 1984), 246–47; Miller, *War Plan Orange*, 1, 83–4, 214–16, 324; Gole, *Road to Rainbow*, 177–21: James, "American and Japanese Strategies," 709–11; Baer, *One Hundred Years of Sea Power*, 146–47; Simpson, *Admiral Harold R. Stark*, 13–14; and Ross, *American War Plans, 1890–1939*, 164–78.

105. Linn, *Guardians of Empire*, 177–80, 244–46; Gole, *Road to Rainbow*, 108–9; and "Industrial Mobilization Plan," n.d. [c. 1939], Henry S. Aurand Personal Papers Collection, Box 58, DDEL.

106. Memorandum from the CNO, "Report of the Hepburn Board–Defense Facilities," 16 February 1939, and CNO to Department Chiefs, 16 February 1939, DPPWPSGC 1926–42, Box 4, RG 127, NACP. See also MGC to CNO, 11 May 1936, HAF 38, MCUA; unsigned editorial, "The Idea of the Fleet Marine Force," *MCG* 23 (June 1939): 61; Miller, *War Plan Orange*, 227; and Ulbrich, "Clarifying the Origins," 93.

107. Vandegrift and Asprey, *Once a Marine*, 92.

108. Millett, *Semper Fidelis*, 339; Smith, *Development of Amphibious Tactics*, 28; William Upshur to Holcomb, 22 January 1939, 29 January 1939, 20 February 1939, 26 February 1939, H. Smith to Holcomb, 30 January 1939 and 25 February 1939, and McDougal to Holcomb, 8 February 1939, 1 March 1939, all in Holcomb Papers, Box 2, MCUA.

109. Upshur to Holcomb, 22 January 1939, Holcomb Papers, Box 2, MCUA.

110. Upshur to Holcomb, 22 January 1939, H. Smith to Holcomb, 25 February 1939, Upshur to Holcomb, 8 February 1939, and Schedule for Demonstration, 1 March 1939, all in Holcomb Papers, Box 2, MCUA; "A History of the U.S. Fleet Landing Exercises," HAF 73, MCUA; Smith, *Development of Amphibious Tactics*, 28; Millett, *Semper Fidelis*, 339–40; and Hough et al., *Pearl Harbor to Guadalcanal*, 14–22.

111. Upshur to Holcomb, 26 February 1939, Holcomb Papers, Box 2, MCUA.

112. Victor H. Krulak, interview by B. Frank, 1970, transcript, pp. 68–69, MCUA; Upshur to Holcomb, 20 February 1939, Holcomb Papers Box 2, MCUA; George Rappleyea to John Kaluf, 10 March 1939, and unsigned memorandum, 20 March 1939, both in HAF 204, MCUA; Holland M. Smith and Percy Finch, *Coral and Brass* (New York: Scribners, 1948), 65–66; Strahan, *Andrew Jackson Higgins*, 38–40; Millett, *Semper Fidelis*, 339–40; Moy, *War Machines*, 156–58; and Norman V. Cooper, *A Fighting General: The Biography of General Holland "Howlin' Mad" Smith* (Quantico, Va.: Marine Corps Association, 1987), 64–67.

113. Krulak, *First to Fight*, 92–94; Moy, *War Machines*, 158–59; Clifford, *Progress and Purpose*, 55; Millett, *Semper Fidelis*, 340; Isely and Crowl, *U.S. Marines and*

Amphibious War, 57; and William F. Royall, "Landing Operations and Equipment," August 1939, HAF 5, MCUA.

114. Millett, *In Many a Strife*, 131.

115. Cook, *Carl Vinson*, 138–39; and Ulbrich, "Clarifying the Origins," 90–92.

116. Hepburn Board Report, pp. 1–6, 62–70, 87–89, SPDWPD 1912–46, Series III, Miscellaneous Subject File, Box 50, RG 38, NACP; Holcomb to Harry K. Pickett, 12 December 1938, WWIIOPMO 1938–45, Box 1, RG 127, NACP; CNO to MGC, 16 February 1939, Holcomb Papers, Box 3, MCUA; and Furer, *Administration of the Navy Department*, 550.

117. JCF to Holcomb, 11 February 1939, and CNO to MGC, 16 February 1939, both in Holcomb Papers, Box 2, MCUA; George F. Eliot, *Defending America* (New York: Foreign Policy Association, 1939), 161–76; Charles D. Melson, *Condition Red: Marine Defense Battalions in World War II* (Washington, D.C.: History and Museums Division, HQMC, 1996), 1–2; Urwin, *Facing Fearful Odds,* 190–91; William W. Buchanan, interview by Frank, 1969, transcript, pp.12–14, MCUA; Hough et al., *Pearl Harbor to Guadalcanal*, 59–62; Millett, *In Many a Strife*, 130–32; and Ulbrich, "Clarifying the Origins," 86–87, 93.

118. Holcomb to CG of Fleet Marine Force (hereafter FMF), 28 March 1939, DPPWPSGC 1926–42, Box 4, RG 127, NACP.

119. Robert D. Heinl, "Defense Battalions," 15 August 1939, and unsigned memorandum, "Material Requirements for Four Defense Battalions," 15 August 1939, both in DPPWPSGC 1926–42, Box 4, RG 127, NACP; memorandum for MGC, 22 December 1939, DPPGC 1921–43, Box 34, RG 127, NACP; Holcomb to John Greenslade, 31 January 1941, GBSF 1900–47, GB 432, Box 163, RG 80, NACP; Isley and Crowl, *U.S. Marines and Amphibious War,* 74–75; Melson, *Condition Red*, 4–5; and Ulbrich, "Clarifying the Origins," 91–92.

120. John H. Craige, *What the Citizen Should Know about the Marines* (New York: Norton, 1941), 187, cited in Urwin, *Facing Fearful Odds,* 193. See also memorandum for MGC, 22 December 1939, DPPGC 1921–43, Box 34, RG 127, NACP; and Annual Report of the MGC to the SecNav for FY 1940, 27 August 1940, pp. 24, 38–40, MCUA.

121. The quotations appear in three sources: Urwin, *Facing Fearful Odds,*192; Heinl, *Soldiers of the Sea*, 306; and Vandegrift and Asprey, *Once a Marine*, 91–92. For other evidence that Holcomb recognized the importance of advanced base defense, see Holcomb to McDougal, 25 May 1937, Holcomb Papers, Box 1, MCUA.

122. Heinl, *Soldiers of the Sea*, 306–7; Urwin, *Facing Fearful Odds,* 192; Cameron, *American Samurai*, 36–37; and Ulbrich, "Clarifying the Origins," 93.

123. Navy Department, *United States Marine Corps*, vol. 46a, 126–78; Furer, *Administration of the Navy Department*, 553–55; and Condit et al., *Brief History of Headquarters Marine Corps*, 17; Silverthorn, recording with G. Smith, 11588B; and Pedro del Valle, *Semper Fidelis: An Autobiography* (Hawthorne: Christian Book Club of America, 1976), 110–11.

124. Navy Department, *United States Marine Corps,* vol. 46a, 5, 126–78; Furer, *Administration of the Navy Department*, 553–55; excerpt from *United States Marine Corps*, "Installations and Logistics" Subject File, HDRB; and Millett, *In Many a Strife*, 136.

125. Ernest J. King, *The U.S. Navy at War, 1941–1945: Official Reports to the Secretary of the Navy* (Washington, D.C.: Department of the Navy, 1946), 37; Baer, *One Hundred Years of Sea Power*, 152–53; and Smith and Finch, *Coral and Brass*, 64–65.

126. Chairman of the GB, memorandum for the SecNav, "Are We Ready," 31 August 1939, File 325, GB Records, cited in Millett, *Semper Fidelis*, 342–43.

127. Holcomb to Stark, 16 March 1939, Holcomb Papers, Box 2, MCUA.

128. Holcomb to John W. Thomason, 23 March 1939, Holcomb Papers, Box 2, MCUA; Thomas Holcomb, summary notes from interview by Robert D. Heinl, 1949, p. 1, Marine Corps Oral History Collection (hereafter MCOHC), Box 75, MCUA; Harold R. Stark, summary notes from interview by Robert D. Heinl, 1949, p. 2, MCOHC, Box 142, MCUA; Silverthorn, recording with G. Smith, 11588A; and Stark to Holcomb, 7 August 1939, DPPWPSGC 1926–42, Box 4, RG 127, NACP.

CHAPTER 3

Holcomb and the Marine Corps Transition from Peace toward War, 1939–1941

1. F. Roosevelt, "The Five Hundred and Seventy-Seventh Press Conference (Excerpts)," 8 September 1939, in *The Public Papers and Addresses of Franklin D. Roosevelt, 1939*, vol. 8, *War and Neutrality* (New York: Macmillan, 1941), 483–84. See also James W. Hammond Jr., *The Treaty Navy: The Story of the U.S. Naval Service Between the World Wars* (Victoria, B.C.: Wesley Press, 2001), 191–92.

2. Dyer, *On the Treadmill to Pearl Harbor*, 154–57; Furer, *Administration of the Navy Department*, 42, 560; unsigned report, "Votes of Leading Isolationist Senators on Defense Measures, 1937–1941," July 1941, CDAAA, Box 2, MNHS; Hilty, "Voting Alignments," 207, 230–37, 308–9; Dallek, *Roosevelt and American Foreign Policy*, 196–200, 202–5; Kennedy, *Freedom from Fear*, 432–35, Wayman, *David I. Walsh*, 266–68; Zehnpfennig, *Melvin J. Maas*, 74–75; and Cook, *Carl Vinson*, 140–44.

3. James, "American and Japanese Strategies," 705–6, 710–11; Millett, *Semper Fidelis*, 344–45; Christman, "Roosevelt and the Craft of Strategic Assessment," 243–45; and Linn, *Guardians of Empire*, 180–82.

4. Millett, *Semper Fidelis*, 344–45; Gordon, "Thomas Holcomb," 264–65; Smith and Finch, *Coral and Brass*, 64–65; Holcomb to J. Roosevelt, 22 March 1939, and Holcomb to Thomason, 23 March 1939, both in Holcomb Papers, Box 2, MCUA; Rutledge, "Rhetoric of the Marine Corps," 129; "Golden Gate International Exposition Key Plan of the Grounds," c. 1939, A. J. Hepburn to CNO, 16 November 1939, and pamphlet on "The United States Marine Corps Exhibit," 1939, all in MCGC 1939–50, Box 97, RG 127, NACP.

5. Rutledge, "Rhetoric of United States Marine Corps," 114, 119–29; Jarvis, *Male Body at War*, 123, 138; Leila Montague Barnett, *What the Mothers of Marines Should Know* (New York: U.S. Marine Corps Publicity Bureau [c. 1940]), n.p., Holcomb Papers, Box 3, MCUA; Franklin Knox to Arthur Capper, 1 August 1940, and W. R Sexton to Morton Deyo, 17 September 1940, both in Morris J. MacGregor and Bernard C. Nalty, eds., *Blacks in the United States Armed Forces*, vol. 6, *Blacks in World War II Naval Establishment* (Wilmington, Del.: Scholarly Resources, 1977), 3–7; and Bernard C. Nalty, *Strength for the Fight: A History of Black Americans in the Military* (New York: Free Press, 1986), 126–42.

6. "Daily Report of Recruiting," 1 July 1939 and 1 January 1940, both in MCGC 1939–50, Box 616, RG 127, NACP.

7. MGC, memorandum on Emergency Recruiting Activities, 14 November 1939, HQSC 1930–71, Box 1, RG 127, NACP.

8. "Daily Report of Recruiting," 1 January 1940, MCGC 1939–50, Box 616, RG 127, NACP; Officer in Charge at Salt Lake City, Utah, to Officer in Charge of Western RD, 12 October 1939, and HQMC to Department of the Pacific, 17 October 1939, both in MCGC 1939–50, Box 620, RG 127, NACP.

9. "Daily Report of Recruiting," 1 January 1940 and 1 July 1940, both in MCGC 1939–50, Box 616, RG 127, NACP.

10. Holcomb to Jackson, 21 October 1939, Holcomb Papers, Box 3, MCUA.

11. Officer in Charge of the Central RD to MGC, 6 September 1939, and H. P. McGinley to Francis T. Maloney, both in HQSC 1930–1971, Box 1, RG 127, NACP; and Medical Examiner to Recruiting Officer, 27 August 1940, MCGC 1939–50, Box 624, RG 127, NACP.

12. MGC, Circular Letter 311, 8 September 1939, MCGC, Box 294, RG 127, NACP; and Chief of the Bureau of Medicine and Surgery to MGC, 12 September 1939, HQSC 1930–71, Box 1, RG 127, NACP.

13. Holcomb to all Commanding Officers and Recruiting Officers, 13 September 1939, HQSC 1930–71, Box 1, RG 127, NACP.

14. Vandegrift to Maloney, 21 August 1940, HQSC 1930–71, Box 1, RG 127, NACP; Elmore A. Champie, *A Brief History of the Marine Corps Base and Recruitment Depot, San Diego*, rev. ed. (Washington, D.C.: Historical Branch, HQMC, 1960), 14–16; Champie, *A Brief History of the Marine Corps Base and Recruitment Depot, Parris Island, South Carolina*, rev. ed. (Washington, D.C.: Historical Branch, HQMC, 1960), 8–9; Victor H. Krulak, "This Precious Few . . . The Evolution of Marine Recruit Training," *MCG* 66 (April 1982): 46–55; and Cameron, *American Samurai*, 50–51, 59–60.

15. General Statement of Thomas Holcomb to the Naval Subcommittee of the House Committee on Appropriations, 3 November 1939, and MGC's Statement for Supplemental Estimates for FY 1941, 18 December 1939, both in Holcomb Papers, Box 33, MCUA.

16. Kennedy, *Freedom from Fear*, 458–60; Kenneth S. Davis, *FDR: The War President, 1940–1943* (New York: Random House, 2000), 12–14; Divine, *Reluctant Belligerent*, 135–37; and V. R. Cardozier, *The Mobilization of the United States in World War II: How the Government, Military, and Industry Prepared for War* (Jefferson, N.C.: McFarland & Company, 1995), 72–80, 84–89.

17. Navy Department, *Naval Expenditures, 1940* (Washington, D.C.: GPO, 1941), 1; and Statement of Brigadier General Seth Williams, Budget Officer, Marine Corps, 27 May 1940, House Subcommittee on Naval Affairs of the Committee on Appropriations, *Supplemental Hearings on the Navy Department Bill for 1941*, 76th Congress, 3rd session, 1940, 184–86, Holcomb Papers, Box 33, MCUA; and Annual Report of the MGC to the SecNav for FY 1940, 27 August 1940, pp. 4–5, MCUA.

18. MGC to CNO, 30 October 1939, Vogel to Holcomb, 5 December 1939, Upshur to Holcomb, 7 December 1939, MGC to CNO, 8 December 1939, all in Clayton B.

Vogel Personal Papers Collection (Vogel Papers), File 66, MCUA; MGC to Officer
in Charge of Eastern RD, 15 May 1940, MCGC, Box 614, RG 127, NACP; MGC to
all Commanding Officers of Ships' Detachments, 7 August 1940, HQSC 1930–71,
Box 1, RG 127, NACP; Eliot to Holcomb, 17 August 1940, Holcomb Papers, Box 3,
MCUA; Adjutant and Inspector (hereafter A&I) to Marine Corps Budget Officer, 8
July 1940, Budget Officer of Navy Department to HQMC, 11 July 1940, memorandum from MGC, 19 October 1939, Lists of Witnesses to Appear before the Bureau of
the Budget, 25 October 1940, and E. G. Allen, memo for HQMC, 9 January 1941, all
in Holcomb Papers, Box 31, MCUA.

19. Statement of Thomas Holcomb, 13 September 1940, House Committee on Naval
Affairs, *Hearings on Sundry Legislation Affecting the Naval Establishment 1941*,
4108–4109, Holcomb Papers, Box 33, MCUA.

20. Ibid., 4112.

21. Holcomb to Maas, 27 December 1940, Holcomb Papers, Box 3, MCUA.

22. Furer, *Administration of the Navy Department*, 42; Langer and Gleason, *Undeclared
War*, 2, 16–17, 24–26; Cardozier, *Mobilization of the United States*, 11–12; and
Kennedy, *Freedom from Fear*, 421, 427–34, 462–64, 476.

23. Langer and Gleason, *Undeclared War*, 199–212; Dallek, *Roosevelt and American
Foreign Policy*, 248–53; Kennedy, *Freedom from Fear*, 454–75; Davis, *FDR*,
16–33, 54–57; Divine, *Reluctant Belligerent*, 105–7; and Ulbrich, "Clarifying the
Origins," 94.

24. Holcomb to Stark, 24 November 1940, Holcomb Papers, Box 3, MCUA.

25. Thomas, recording with G. Smith, 11590A; Silverthorn, recording with G. Smith,
11589B; and Holcomb to Stark, 24 November 1940, Box 3, Holcomb Papers, MCUA.

26. Thomas Holcomb–Report on Fitness of Officer of the United States Marine Corps
(hereafter Holcomb Fit Rep), 29 August 1939–30 September 1939, Holcomb Papers,
Box 13, MCUA.

27. Holcomb Fit Rep, 1 October 1939–24 June 1940, Holcomb Papers, Box 13, MCUA.

28. Holcomb Fit Rep, 25 June 1940–30 September 1940, Holcomb Papers, Box 13,
MCUA.

29. Knox, memo for the President, 18 November 1940, Holcomb Papers, Box 13,
MCUA.

30. Holcomb Fit Rep, 29 August 1939–30 September 1939, 1 October 1939–24 June
1940, and 25 June 1940–30 September 1940, all in Holcomb Papers, Box 13,
MCUA; and Greenstein, *Presidential Difference*, 5–6, italics in original.

31. Unsigned editorial, "National Defense," *Time*, 11 November 1940, 21–24.

32. Naval Aide to the Secretary to the President of the United States, 26 November 1940,
Holcomb Papers, Box 13, MCUA.

33. Gilder Jackson to Holcomb, 15 November 1940, Holcomb Papers, Box 3, MCUA.
See also Mabel and John H. Russell, telegram to Holcomb, 29 November 1940,
Robert L. Ghormley to Holcomb, 30 November 1940, Cogswell to Holcomb,
30 November 1940, Henry Williams to Holcomb, 30 November 1940, Mass to
Holcomb, 3 December 1940, and Walter A. Shanley to Holcomb, 14 December 1940,
all in Holcomb Papers, Box 3, MCUA.

34. Holcomb to Lejeune, 27 December 1940, Holcomb Papers, Box 3, MCUA.

35. Holcomb to E. C. Kalbfus, 12 February 1940, Holcomb Papers, Box 3, MCUA; Mass to Holcomb, 3 December 1940, Holcomb Papers, Box 3, MCUA; and F. Holcomb, recording, tape 1, sequences 1–2.

36. Iriye, *Power and Culture*, 19–25; Christman, "Roosevelt and the Craft of Strategic Assessment," 243–46; James, "American and Japanese Strategies," 709–710; Evans and Peattie, *Kaigun*, 464–67; Spector, *Eagle Against the Sun*, 63–65; and Thomas C. Hone, "The Evolution of the U.S. Fleet, 1933–1941: How the President Mattered," in *FDR and the U.S. Navy*, ed. Edward J. Marolda (New York: St. Martin's Press, 1998), 92–96.

37. "Joint Army and Navy Basic War Plans, Rainbow Nos. 1, 2, 3, 4, and 5," 9 April 1940, JB 325, Serial 642, M1421, Reel 11, NACP; R. S. Crenshaw, "War Plans," lecture at the Naval War College, 10 May 1940, SPDWPD 1912–46, Series I, Lectures and Speeches, Box 3, RG 38, NACP; Stetson Conn, "Changing Concepts of National Defense in the United States, 1937–1947," *Military Affairs* 28 (Spring 1964), 1–4; and Miller, *War Plan Orange*, 260–61, 270.

38. Holcomb to Eliot, 24 July 1940, Holcomb Papers, Box 3, MCUA; MGC to CNO, 30 October 1939, Vogel to Holcomb, 5 December 1939, Upshur to Holcomb, 7 December 1939, and MGC to CNO, 8 December 1939, all in Vogel Papers, File 66, MCUA; memorandum for the MGC, 16 June 1940, DPPGC 1921–43, Box 34, RG 127, NACP; Millett, *Semper Fidelis*, 345; Miller, *War Plan Orange*, 277–78; and Ulbrich, "Clarifying the Origins," 93–94.

39. Memorandum for the MGC, 16 June 1940, DPPGC 1921–43, Box 34, RG 127, NACP; Annual Report of the MGC to the SecNav for FY 1940, 15 August 1939, pp. 2–3, MCUA; James H. Strother to Director of Plans and Policies, 3 July 1940, MCBE FY 1936–43, Entry 248, Box 1, RG 127, NADC; Gordon, "Thomas Holcomb," 265; Baer, *One Hundred Year of Sea Power*, 149, 153; and Miller, *War Plan Orange*, 277–78.

40. Smith and Finch, *Coral and Brass*, 58, 66–71; Dyer, *Amphibians Came to Conquer*, 206–8; Robert D. Heinl Jr., "The U.S. Marine Corps: Author of Modern Amphibious Warfare," in *Assault from the Sea: Essays on the History of Amphibious Warfare*, ed. Merrill L. Bartlett, 189; Millett, "Assault from the Sea," 76–77; and Cooper, *Fighting General*, 60–62.

41. Smith, *Development of Amphibious Tactics*, 29.

42. Ibid., 29–30; Isely and Crowl, *U.S. Marines and Amphibious War*, 57–58; Millett, *In Many a Strife*, 132–33; and Upshur to Holcomb, 21 January 1940, Holcomb Papers, Box 3, MCUA.

43. Annual Report of the MGC to the SecNav for FY 1940, 15 August 1939, pp. 61–63, MCUA; Strother to Director of Plans and Policies, 3 July 1940, MCBE FY 1936–43, Entry 248, Box 1, RG 127, NADC; Smith and Finch, *Coral and Brass*, 67, 97; Krulak, *First to Fight*, 101–4; Silverthorn, recording with G. Smith, 11588B, MCUA; Smith, *Development of Amphibious Tactics*, 32–34; Strahan, *Andrew Jackson Higgins*, 42–50; Moy, *War Machines*, 157–60; and Millett, "Assault from the Sea," 76–77.

44. Harry K. Pickett and Alfred Pefley, "The Defense of Wake Island," 14 October 1939, Division Plans and Policies General Correspondence 1921–43, Box 33, RG 127,

NACP; Holcomb to Eliot, 24 July 1940, Holcomb Papers, Box 3, MCUA; SecNav to Bureaus and Offices of the Navy Department, 15 April 1940, Holcomb Papers, Box 20, MCUA; J. B. Earle to CNO, 8 September 1939, Stark to the SecWar, 24 October 1939, Director of P&P to MGC, 12 October 1939, and H. B. Sayler to Holcomb, 3 October 1940, all in DPPWPSGC 1926–42, Box 4, RG 127, NACP; Holcomb to Robert L. Denig, 5 November 1939, Holcomb Papers, Box 3, MCUA; Hough et al., *Pearl Harbor to Guadalcanal*, 64–69; Melson, *Condition Red*, 4–6, 29–31; and Ulbrich, "Clarifying the Origins," 93–94.

45. Stark, memorandum for SecNav, p. 4, 12 November 1940 (hereafter Stark Memorandum), in Stark, summary notes, Box 142, MCOHC, MCUA. Various drafts of the Stark Memorandum can be found in Steven D. Ross, ed., *American War Plans, 1919–1941*, vol. 3, *Plans to Meet the Axis Threat* (New York: Garland, 1992), 225–30.

46. Gordon W. Prange with Donald Goldstein and Katherine Dillon, *At Dawn We Slept: The Untold Story of Pearl Harbor* (New York: McGraw-Hill, 1981), 38–40; Simpson, *Admiral Harold R. Stark*, 62–71; and Mark M. Lowenthal, "The Stark Memorandum and the American National Security Process, 1940," in *Changing Interpretations and New Sources in Naval History*, ed. Robert W. Love (New York: Garland, 1980), 353–55.

47. Stark Memorandum, 2–3, 21–24; Dyer, *Amphibians Came to Conquer*, 158–59; Lowenthal, "Stark Memorandum," 355–56; Miller, *War Plan Orange*, 267–70; and Baer, *One Hundred Years of Sea Power*, 152–55.

48. Stark Memorandum, 18–19, 24–26; and Marshall to Stark, 29 November 1940 and 2 December 1940, in *The Papers of George Catlett Marshall*, vol. 2, *"We Cannot Delay,"* ed. Larry I. Bland and Sharon R. Stevens (Baltimore: Johns Hopkins University Press, 1986), 360–63.

49. Louis Morton, "Germany First: The Basic Concept of Allied Strategy in World War II," in *Command Decisions*, ed. Kent R. Greenfield (New York: Harcourt, Brace, 1959), 26, quoted in Baer, *One Years of Sea Power*, 154. See also Gole, *Road to Rainbow*, 102–3, 108–10, 121; Linn, *Guardians of Empire*, 177–83; Lowenthal, "Stark Memorandum," 358–59; Simpson, *Admiral Harold R. Stark*, 70–75; and Jonathan G. Utley, "Franklin Roosevelt and Naval Strategy, 1933–1941," in *FDR and the U.S. Navy*, ed. Edward J. Marolda, 57–59.

50. Stark Memorandum, 14–15, 23–26; Baer, *One Hundred Years of Sea Power*, 154–57; and Ulbrich, "Clarifying the Origins," 94.

51. Marshall to Stark, 29 November 1940 and 2 December 1940, both in *Papers of George Catlett Marshall*, vol. 2, 360–63; Joint Board Meeting Minutes, 11 December 1940, JB 301, M1421, Reel 1, NACP; James, "American and Japanese Strategies," 711; Gole, *Road to Rainbow*, 102–3, 108–10, 121; Linn, *Guardians of Empire*, 177–83; Baer, *One Hundred Years of Sea Power*, 156–57; Simpson, *Admiral Harold R. Stark*, 70–76; Hone, "Evolution of the U.S. Fleet," 91–92; and Dyer, *Amphibians Came to Conquer*, 158–59.

52. Simpson, *Admiral Harold R. Stark*, 76; and Kennedy, *Freedom from Fear*, 481–82.

53. Omar T. Pfeiffer, interview by Lloyd E. Tatem, 1968, transcript, pp. 132–41, 152–53, 158, MCUA.

54. Pfeiffer, transcript, 158; Simpson, *Admiral Harold R. Stark*, 76; and Kennedy, *Freedom from Fear*, 481–82.

55. Pfeiffer, transcript, 159.

56. Ibid., 163.

57. "United States–British Staff Conversations Report," 27 March 1941, pp. 5–6, SPDWPD 1912–46, Series IX, Part III, Box 147G, RG 38, NACP; Pfeiffer, transcript, 236–37; Miller, *War Plan Orange*, 271; Spector, *Eagle Against the Sun*, 66–67; Christman, "Roosevelt and the Craft of Strategic Assessment," 248–49; and Baer, *One Hundred Years of Sea Power*, 156–57.

58. "Navy Basic War Plan–Rainbow No. 5," May 1941, pp. 14, 27, StratPlnsWPD, WPL Series, Box 34, RG 38, NACP; Joint Board Meeting Minutes, 14 May 1941, JB 301, M1421, Reel 1, NACP; memorandum from CNO, 31 May 1941, Office of Naval Intelligence, Box 7, RG 38, NACP; Grace P. Hayes, *The History of the Joint Chiefs of Staff in World War II: The War Against Japan* (Annapolis: Naval Institute Press, 1982), 9–10; Miller, *War Plan Orange*, 271–72; Baer, *One Hundred Years of Sea Power*, 156–58, 171; and Hone, "Evolution of the U.S. Fleet," 91–94.

59. "U.S. Pacific Fleet Operating Plan–Rainbow 5," July 1941, p. 30, USNROTIP 1918–70, Box 84, RG 38, NACP.

60. Urwin, *Facing Fearful Odds*, 113–16; Miller, *War Plan Orange*, 284; Husband E. Kimmel to Stark copied to Holcomb, 28 February 1941, WWIIOPMO 1938–45, Box 1, RG 127, NACP; "Marine Corps Plan C-5, Part II, Rainbow No. 5," July 1941, pp. 2–4, 9, 26, WPRM 1931–44, Box 6, Entry 246, RG 127, NADC; "United States–British Staff Conversations Report, Annex III," 27 March 1941, *Hearings before the Joint Committee on the Investigation of the Pearl Harbor Attack, Joint Committee Exhibits Part 15*, 79th Congress, 1st session (hereafter *Pearl Harbor Hearings Pt 15*), 1511–15; and "U.S. Pacific Fleet Operating Plan–Rainbow 5," July 1941, pp. 19–31, USNROTIP 1918–70, Box 84, RG 38, NACP.

61. Kimmel to Hart, 12 November 1940, *Pearl Harbor Hearings Pt 15*, 2448–51; A. G. Kirk to Stark, 20 February 1941, General Correspondence of the CNO and SecNav 1940–1947, Box 54, RG 80, NACP; Miller, *War Plan Orange*, 272–74; Urwin, *Facing Fearful Odds,* 107–10; and Hone, "Evolution of U.S. Fleet," 99.

62. Urwin, *Facing Fearful Odds*, 114.

63. Holcomb to Kimmel, 15 February 1941, Holcomb Papers, Box 3, MCUA. See also Holcomb to Kimmel, 15 January 1941, and Kimmel to Holcomb, 27 January 1941, both in Holcomb Papers, Box 3, MCUA.

64. Harry I. Shaw Jr., *Opening Moves: The Marines Gear Up for War* (Washington, D.C.: History and Museums Division, HQMC, 1991), 12–13.

65. Pfeiffer, transcript, 165–66. See also Miller, *War Plan Orange*, 274–75.

66. Kimmel to Stark, 26 July 1941, *Pearl Harbor Hearings Pt 15*, 2240; "Marine Corps Plan, C-2, Rainbow No. 5," June 1941, pp. 4–7, WPRM 1931–44, Box 8, Entry 246, RG 127, NADC; "Marine Corps Plan C-5, Part II, Rainbow No. 5," July 1941, pp. 2–4, 9, 26, WPRM 1931–144, Box 6, Entry 246, RG 127, NADC; and Samuel Eliot Morison, *Rising Sun in the Pacific, 1931–April 1942,* vol. 3*, History of the United States Naval Operations in World War II* (Boston: Little, Brown, 1948), 51–52.

67. Donald F. Bittner, *The Lion and the White Falcon: Britain and Iceland in the World War II Era* (Hamden: Archon Books, 1983), 1–4, 125–29; Dallek, *Roosevelt and American Foreign Policy*, 276–77; Hough et al., *Pearl Harbor to Guadalcanal*, 35–36; and James A. Donovan, *Outpost in the North Atlantic: Marines in the Defense of Iceland* (Washington, D.C.: History and Museums Division, HQMC, 1992), 1–4.

68. Stark to Marston, 16 June 1941, SPDWPD 1912–46, Series III, Misc. Subject File, Box 50, RG 38, NACP; Marshall to Stark, 29 August 1941, *Papers of George Catlett Marshall*, vol. 2, 587; Marston to Vandegrift, 3 October 1941, and Vandegrift to Marston, 14 October 1941, both in Vandegrift Papers, Box 9, MCUA; Donovan, *Outpost in the North Atlantic*, 7–21; Hough et al., *Pearl Harbor to Guadalcanal*, 42–44; and Bittner, *Lion and the White Falcon*, 129–39.

69. Marston to Vandegrift, 24 September 1941, Vandegrift Papers, Box 9, MCUA.

70. Donovan, *Outpost in the North Atlantic*, 30–32; and Bittner, *Lion and the White Falcon*, 139–43.

71. Chief of the Bureau of Ships to CNO, 5 June 1941, Holcomb Papers, Box 20, MCUA. See also Kimmel to Chester W. Nimitz, 16 February 1941, *Pearl Harbor Hearings Pt 15*, 2461–62; memorandum for MGC, 16 September 1941, DPPWPS 1915–45, Box 15, RG 127, NACP; Pickett to Vandegrift, 12 August 1941, Vandegrift Papers, Box 1, MCUA; Christman, "Roosevelt and the Craft of Strategic Assessment," 243; and Ulbrich, "Clarifying the Origins," 95–99.

72. Kimmel to Stark, 12 September 1941, *Pearl Harbor Hearings Pt 15*, 2248–49; Hayes, *History of the JCS*, 22–23; Morison, *Rising Sun in the Pacific*, 58–64; Hiroyuki Agawa, *The Reluctant Admiral: Yamamoto and the Imperial Navy*, trans. John Bester (1969; repr., Tokyo: Kodansha International, 1979), 208–12, 226–28; Baer, *One Hundred Years of Sea Power*, 164–69; and Dallek, *Roosevelt and American Foreign Policy*, 274–75.

73. CNO to Director of Ship Movements Division copied to MGC, 17 January 1941, and Kimmel to Stark, 26 July 1941, both in WWIIOPMO 1938–45, Box 1, RG 127, NACP; SecNav, 3 February 1941, Senate Subcommittee on the Naval Affairs of the Committee on Appropriations, *Hearings on the Navy Department Appropriations Bill for 1942*, 77th Congress, 1st session (hereafter *Navy Appropriations FY 1942 Hearings*), 1–3, copy in Holcomb Papers, Box 33, MCUA; memorandum from the CNO, 3 April 1941, *Pearl Harbor Hearings Pt 15*, 2462–63; Kimmel to Stark, 26 July 1941, *Pearl Harbor Hearings Pt 15*, 2239–42; Vandegrift and Asprey, *Once a Marine*, 96; and Thomas C. Hart, "War on the Horizon," in *The Pacific War Remembered: An Oral History Collection*, ed. James T. Mason Jr. (Annapolis: Naval Institute Press, 1986), 18–22.

74. Statements of Maj. Gen. Thomas Holcomb and others, 13 February 1941, *Navy Appropriations FY 1942 Hearings*, 611–12, copy in Holcomb Papers, Box 33, MCUA.

75. Ibid., 616.

76. Millett, *In Many a Strife*, 150–51.

77. Statements of Maj. Gen. Thomas Holcomb and others, 13 February 1941, *Navy Appropriations FY 1942 Hearings*, 615–20, 644–45.

78. Holcomb to Carl Vinson, 9 January 1941, Holcomb Papers, Box 3, MCUA.

79. Shaw, *Opening Moves*, 6. See also Gordon, "Thomas Holcomb," 253–55, 267.

80. Holcomb to William D. Leahy, 22 August 1941, Holcomb Papers, Box 4, MCUA.

81. Holcomb to Vinson, 9 January 1941, and Holcomb to McDougal, 30 January 1941, both in Holcomb Papers, Box 3; Holcomb to Ernest J. King, 10 March 1941, Holcomb Papers, Box 4, MCUA; Shaw, *Opening Moves*, 9–10; and Hough et al., *Pearl Harbor to Guadalcanal*, 51–52.

82. Landrum, "Carl Vinson," 77; Cook, *Carl Vinson*, 173; "Bases-Outlying," n.d., GBSF 1900–47, GB 425, Box 135, RG 80, NACP; CNO to Director of Ship Movement Division, 17 January 1941, Kimmel to Stark, 11 February 1941, and Stark to Kimmel, 26 February 1941, all in WWIIOPMO 1938–45, Box 1, RG 127, NACP; and Hough et al., *Pearl Harbor to Guadalcanal*, 95.

83. R. E. Ingersoll to Holcomb, 10 January 1941, DPPWPSGC 1926–42, Box 4, RG 127, NACP; MGC to CNO, 28 April 1941, Holcomb Papers, Box 20, MCUA; and Millett, *Semper Fidelis*, 347.

84. CNO to MGC, 29 April 1941, DPPWPSGC 1926–42, Box 4, RG 127, NACP. See also "Bases-Outlying," n.d., GBSF 1900–47, GB 425, Box 135, RG 80, NACP; Ulbrich, "Clarifying the Origins," 95–97; Melson, *Condition Red*, 4–6; Kimmel to Stark, 26 August 1941, *Pearl Harbor Hearings Pt 15*, 2247; and memorandum for MGC, 16 September 1941, DPPWPS 1915–45, Box 15, RG 127, NACP.

85. Wayne S. Cole, *America First: The Battle Against Intervention, 1940–1941* (Madison: University of Wisconsin Press, 1953), 44–46, 157–65; Manfred Jonas, *Isolationism in America, 1935–1941* (Ithaca, N.Y.: Cornell University Press, 1966), 244–45, 260; Claude Pepper, speech on George Washington's Birthday in Topeka, Kansas, 22 February 1941, CDAAA, Box 2, MNHS; Cook, *Carl Vinson*, 174–75; Dallek, *Roosevelt and American Foreign Policy*, 255–60; and Kennedy, *Freedom from Fear*, 470–76, 484–85, 505.

86. Officer in Charge of Eastern RD to A&I, 25 March 1941, MCGC 1939–50, Box 614, RG 127, NACP.

87. "Daily Report of Recruiting," 28 June 1940, 30 December 1940, 2 January 1941, 1 March 1941, 1 April 1941, all in MCGC 1939–50, Box 616, RG 127, NACP.

88. Cole, *America First*, 100–103; Dallek, *Roosevelt and American Foreign Policy*, 262–70; and Kennedy, *Freedom from Fear*, 482–85.

89. 1 July 1941, all in MCGC 1939–50, Box 616, RG 127, NACP; and Rutledge, "Rhetoric of the Marine Corps," 131.

90. Holcomb to J. G. Harbord, 17 June 1941, Holcomb Papers, Box 4, MCUA.

91. "Daily Report of Recruiting," 30 December 1940, 1 July 1941, and 9 December 1941, all in MCGC 1939–50, Box 616, RG 127, NACP.

92. Officer in Charge of Eastern RD to A&I, 25 March 1941, MCGC 1939–50, Box 614, RG 127, NACP. For corroborating assessments, see Officer in Charge of Central RD to A&I, 29 October 1941, MCGC 1939–50, Box 614, RG 127, NACP; and Price to Vandegrift, 8 May 1941, Vandegrift Papers, Box 1, MCUA.

93. Officer in Charge of Eastern RD to A&I, 25 March 1941, MCGC 1939–50, Box 614, RG 127, NACP.

94. Ibid.

95. Ibid.

96. Holcomb to King, 10 March 1941, Holcomb to Harbord, 17 June 1941, Holcomb to Walsh, 21 July 1941, and Holcomb to Marston, 12 August 1941, all in Holcomb Papers, Box 4, MCUA; Lindsay, *This High Name*, 50; Rutledge, "Rhetoric of the Marine Corps," 129–31; Cameron, *American Samurai*, 26; and "Daily Report of Recruiting," 30 December 1940, 1 July 1941, and 9 December 1941, all in MCGC 1939–50, Box 616, RG 127, NACP.

97. Denig, transcript, 5, 26.

98. Condit et al., *Brief History of Headquarters Marine Corps*, 15.

99. Greenstein, *Presidential Difference*, 5.

100. Navy Department, *United States Marine Corps*, vol. 46a, 11b; Lindsay, *This High Name*, 50–51; Rutledge, "Rhetoric of the Marine Corps," 131–33; Condit et al., *Brief History of Headquarters Marine Corps*, 15; and Lash, "Media and the Marines," 31–32.

101. Denig, transcript, 3–4.

102. Ibid.

103. "The Marines in Print," lecture by Robert L. Denig, 28–31 July 1941, transcript, pp. 17–24, "Public Relations–Navy" Subject File, HDRB. See also Holcomb to King, 10 March 1941, Holcomb Papers, Box 4, MCUA; excerpts of correspondence, 15–21 April 1941, Vandegrift Papers, Box 1, MCUA; and Lash, "Media and the Marines," 6.

104. Rutledge, "Rhetoric of the Marine Corps," 129, 141–42; Jarvis, *Male Body at War*, 39–40; A&I to Officer in Charge of Recruiting District of Detroit, Michigan, 8 April 1941, MCGC 1939–1950, Box 97, RG 127, NACP; and Officer in Charge of Recruiting District of Detroit, Michigan, to A&I, 31 March 1941, MCGC 1939–1950, Box 97, RG 127, NACP.

105. "The Marines in Print," lecture by Denig, pp. 17–24, "Public Relations–Navy" Subject File, HDRB.

106. H. H. Allen to W. E. Burke, 23 July 1941, and M. C. Gregory to Denig, 31 July 1941, both in MCGC 1939–50, Box 617, RG 127, NACP. See also Clay Barrow, "Marine Mystique," *Naval History* 3 (Fall 1989): 37–42; Dennis Showalter, "The Evolution of the U.S. Marine Corps into a Military Elite in the Twentieth Century," *MCG* 63 (November 1979), 44, 50–51; John W. Gordon, "The U.S. Marine Corps and an Experiment in Military Elitism," in *Changing Interpretations and New Sources in Naval History*, ed. Robert William Love (New York: Garland, 1980), 362–73; Cameron, *American Samurai*, 24–29, 38; and Lindsay, *This High Name*, 26–28, 90.

107. Holcomb to King, 10 March 1941, and Holcomb to A. E. Eggleston, 26 September 1941, both in Holcomb Papers, Box 4, MCUA; Roland L. MacDonald to Holcomb, 10 July 1941, MCGC 1938–50, Box 198, RG 127, NACP; and Holcomb, radio broadcast, 22 November 1941, Holcomb Papers, Box 27, MCUA.

108. Craige, *What the Citizen Should Know*, 187, quoted in Urwin, *Facing Fearful Odds*, 193.

109. William W. Rogers, interview by Tatem, 1969, transcript, 56, MCUA.

110. 7thDBQ, WWIIC, Box 1, MCUA.

111. Lash, "Media and the Marines," 36–37.

112. Daniel Pope, *The Making of Modern Advertising* (New York: Basic Books, 1983), 193. See also 193 note 18, which contains references to Daniel Boostin, *The Image* (New York: Harper & Row, 1964), 211–28; and Daniel Boorstin, "Advertising and American Civilization," in *Advertising and American Society*, ed. Yale Brozen, (New York: New York University Press, 1974), 11–23.

113. Ingersoll to Holcomb, 10 January 1941, DPPWPSGC 1926–42, Box 4, RG 127, NACP.

114. "Plan for Expansion of the U.S. Marine Corps," 6 May 1941, GBSF 1900–47, GB 425, Box 135, RG 80, NACP; Robert A. McGill, "Island Defense," *MCG* 25 (March 1941): 16–18; and R. D. Heinl Jr., "On the Mobility of Base Defense Artillery," *MCG* 25 (September 1941): 23–25, 42–43.

115. "Training of Units of the FMF," unsigned report, n.d. [c. February 1941], GBSF 1900–1947, GB 425, Box 135, RG 80, NACP; Vandegrift to Price, 11 March 1941, Vandegrift Papers, Box 1, MCUA; Leo D. Hermle, interview by Tatem, 1968, transcript, p. 59, MCUA; Millett, *Semper Fidelis*, 348–49; and Holcomb to Marston, 22 November 1941, Holcomb Papers, Box 4, MCUA.

116. Wilson, *Maneuver and Firepower*, 143–47; Gordon L. Rottman, *U.S. Marine Corps World War II Order of Battle: Ground and Air Units in the Pacific War, 1939–1945* (Westport, Conn.: Greenwood, 2002), 113–17; Isely and Crowl, *U.S. Marines and Amphibious War*, 60; and Gordon, "Thomas Holcomb," 265–66.

117. "Marine Corps' Mission," p. 2, File 387–30, AHEC.

118. Smith, *Development of Amphibious Tactics*, 34; Smith and Finch, *Coral and Brass*, 73–76; and Isely and Crowl, *U.S. Marines and Amphibious War*, 59–60.

119. Smith and Finch, *Coral and Brass*, 74–79; Cooper, *Fighting General*, 71–73; Millett, *Semper Fidelis*, 349; Gordon, "Thomas Holcomb," 265–66; Smith, *Development of Amphibious Tactics*, 34–35; and Isely and Crowl, *U.S. Marines and Amphibious War*, 59–62.

120. King to Holcomb, 11 February 1941, Holcomb Papers, Box 4, MCUA; and MGC to CNO, 15 February 1941, MCGC, Box 189, RG 127, NACP.

121. Smith and Finch, *Coral and Brass*, 75–77; Thomas B. Buell, *Master of Sea Power: A Biography of Fleet Admiral Ernest J. King* (Boston: Little, Brown, 1980), 121–22; and Cooper, *Fighting General*, 71–72.

122. Millett, *In Many a Strife*, 151.

123. Smith and Finch, *Coral and Brass*, 78–80; Cooper, *Fighting General*, 73; Buell, *Master of Sea Power*, 122; Gordon, "Thomas Holcomb," 265; Frederick Roy, interview by B. Frank, 1976, transcript, pp. 30–31, MCUA; and Thomas, recording with G. Smith, 11591A.

124. Holcomb to McDougal, 30 January 1941, Holcomb Papers, Box 4, MCUA.

125. Holcomb to J. Smith, 24 February 1941, and "Report of Board to Submit Plans for Establishment of Division Training Center, New River, North Carolina," 10 April 1941, both in J. Smith Papers, Box 11, MCUA; and Millett, *Semper Fidelis*, 348.

126. Seth Williams to William P. T. Hill, 12 March 1941, and Hill to Williams, 15 May 1941, William P. T. Hill Personal Papers Collection (hereafter Hill Papers), Box 4, MCUA; J. Smith to Chief of the Bureau of Docks and Yards, 20 March 1941, and "Report of Board to Submit Plans for Establishment of Division Training Center,

New River, North Carolina," 10 April 1941, both in J. Smith Papers, Box 11, MCUA; Vandegrift to Holcomb, 19 May 1941, and Vandegrift to F. E. Beatty, 15 July 1941, both in Vandegrift Papers, Box 2, MCUA; Hough et al., *Pearl Harbor to Guadalcanal*, 51–52; and Millett, *Semper Fidelis*, 350.

127. Isely and Crowl, *U.S. Marines and Amphibious War*, 63.

128. H. Smith to CNO via MGC, 10 September 1941, H. Smith to King, 14 November 1941, and Deputy Chief of Staff of the U.S. Army to CNO, 10 October 1941, all in Holcomb Papers, Box 27, MCUA; Smith, *Development of Amphibious Tactics*, 36–38; and Isely and Crowl, *U.S. Marines and Amphibious War*, 64–65.

129. Russell F. Weigley, *The American Way of War: A History of United States Military Strategy and Policy* (1973; repr., Bloomington: Indiana University Press, 1977), 264.

130. Krulak, *First to Fight*, 90.

131. Andrew Jackson Higgins to Stark, 26 May 1941, and Holcomb to Stark, 6 June 1941, both in SPDWPD 1912–46, Series III, Miscellaneous Subject File, Box 50, RG 38, NACP; Higgins to Holcomb, 1 August 1941, Holcomb Papers, Box 4, MCUA; Smith and Finch, *Coral and Brass*, 71–72; Strahan, *Andrew Jackson Higgins*, 57–58, 89; Krulak, *First to Fight*, 90–96; Isely and Crowl, *U.S. Marines and Amphibious War*, 60–65; Hough et al., *Pearl Harbor to Guadalcanal*, 28; John W. Mountcastle, "From Bayou to Beachhead: The Marines and Mr. Higgins," *Military Review* (March 1980): 25–26; Millett, *Semper Fidelis*, 340; Millett, "Assault from the Sea," 84; and Moy, *War Machines*, 160–62.

132. H. Smith to CNO via MGC, 10 September 1941, Holcomb Papers, Box 20, MCUA.

133. Holcomb to Stark, 31 July 1941, Holcomb Paper, Box 4, MCRUA.

134. Strahan, *Andrew Jackson Higgins*, 86–114.

135. "Minutes of Meeting of the Marine Corps Equipment Board," 24 April 1941, Hill Papers, Box 4, MCUA; "Report No. 2–41, Department Continuing Board for Development of Landing Boats," 10 June 1941, Holcomb Papers, Box 20, MCUA; Holcomb to Stark, 6 June 1941, SPDWPD 1912–46, Series III, Miscellaneous Subject File, Box 50, RG 38, NACP; H. Smith to CNO via MGC, 10 September 1941, and H. Smith to King, 14 November 1941, Holcomb Papers, Box 20, MCUA; Strahan, *Andrew Jackson Higgins*, 56–65; Mountcastle, "From Bayou to Beachhead," 27; Moy, *War Machines*, 167–68; and Millett, *Semper Fidelis*, 340–41

136. Millett, "Assault from the Sea," 94.

137. Shaw, *Opening Moves*, 11; and Joseph H. Alexander, *The Battle History of the U.S. Marines: A Fellowship of Valor* (New York: HarperPerennial, 1999), 125, 264.

138. Chandler B. Gardner, "The Johnson Semi-Automatic Rifle," *MCG* 23 (March 1939): 8–13; Melvin M. Johnson Jr., "The M1 Rifle," *MCG* 25 (March 1941): 42; and unsigned article, "Marine Corps Rifle Tests," *MCG* 25 (June 1941): 14–16, 54–57.

139. Holcomb to Elliot, 27 December 1940, Holcomb Papers, Box 3, MCUA.

140. Knox to John J. Cochran, 20 August 1940, Holcomb to D. J. Callaghan, 5 September 1940, Callaghan to F. Roosevelt, 5 September 1940, all in File 18E, Holcomb Papers, Box 11, MCUA; Johnson, "M1 Rifle," 42; unsigned editorial, "National Defense," *Time* 36 (March 3, 1941): 20; MGC to all Commanding Officers, 23 April 1941, HQSC 1930–71, Box 1, RG 127, NACP; Gordon, "Thomas Holcomb," 279; and

Bernard C. Nalty, *Cape Gloucester: The Green Inferno* (Washington, D.C.: History and Museums Division, HQMC, 1994), 32.

141. Holcomb Fit Rep, 1 April 1941–30 September 1941, Holcomb Papers, Box 13, MCUA.

142. Shaw, *Opening Moves*, 22, 24; MGC to Commanding Officers, 18 July 1941, MCGC, Box 294, RG 127, NAC; Holcomb to Callaghan, 5 September 1944, File 18E, Holcomb Papers, Box 11, MCUA; Mountcastle, "From Bayou to Beachhead," 27–28; Dyer, *Amphibians Came to Conquer*, 208–10; and Strahan, *Andrew Jackson Higgins*, 65–94. For examples of Marines with good morale prior to the Japanese attack on Pearl Harbor, see 7thDBQ, WWIIC, Box 1, MCUA.

143. Holcomb to Leahy, 22 August 1941, Holcomb Papers, Box 4, MCUA. For Holcomb's sense of duty, see Holcomb to John A. Lejeune, 27 December 1940, Holcomb Papers, Box 3, MCUA.

144. Holcomb to Breckinridge, 25 July 1941, Holcomb Papers, Box 4, MCUA.

145. F. Holcomb, recording, tape 1, sequence 2; Holcomb to Walsh, 21 July 1941, Holcomb to Upshur, 4 August 1941, and Holcomb to Harold F. Wirgman, 23 September 1941, all in Holcomb Papers, Box 4, MCUA; Holcomb to Joseph Farnan, 19 April 1939, Holcomb Papers, Box 2, MCUA; and Holcomb to E. C. Kalbfus, 12 February 1940, Holcomb Papers, Box 3.

146. Vandegrift to McDougal, 16 August 1941, Vandegrift Papers, Box 1, MCUA.

147. F. Roosevelt, Press Conference, 28 November 1941, in *The Public Papers and Addresses of Franklin D. Roosevelt, 1941*, vol. 10, *The Call to Battle Stations* (New York: Harper & Row, 1950), 499–502; Hart, "War on the Horizon," 18–22; Dallek, *Roosevelt and American Foreign Policy*, 274–99; Spector, *Eagle Against the Sun*, 68; and Saburō Ienaga, *The Pacific War, 1931–1945: A Critical Perspective on Japan's Role in World War II*, trans. Frank Baldwin (1968; repr., New York: Pantheon Books, 1978), 132–33.

148. "Combined Fleet Top Secret Order 1," issued by Isoroku Yamamoto, 5 November 1941, Office of Naval Intelligence, Box 26, RG 38, NACP; Agawa, *Reluctant Admiral*, 32–38; and Evans and Peattie, *Kaigun*, 455, 477–80.

149. Akira Iriye, ed., *Pearl Harbor and the Coming of the Pacific War: A Brief History with Documents and Essays* (Boston: Bedford/St. Martin's Press, 1999), 74–95.

150. Stark and Marshall to FDR, 27 November 1941, SPDWPD 1912–46, Series III, Miscellaneous Subject File, Box 47, RG 38, NACP; "Fortnightly Summary of Current National Situation," report by T. S Wilkinson, 1 December 1941, Office of Naval Intelligence, Box 26, RG 38, NACP; "Narrative of Events, Asiatic Fleet, Leading Up to War and from 8 December 1941 to 15 February 1942," report by Thomas C. Hart, pp. 34–35, *Annual Reports of Fleets and Task Forces of the U.S. Navy*, M971, Reel 14, NACP; Agawa, *Reluctant Admiral*, 236–37, 242–54; Langer and Gleason, *Undeclared War*, 479–80; 871–930; Morrison, *Rising Sun in the Pacific*, 73–81; Kennedy, *Freedom from Fear*, 513–17; Simpson, *Admiral Harold R. Stark*, 107–12; and Hough et al., *Pearl Harbor to Guadalcanal*, 60.

151. Hart, "Narrative of Events, Asiatic Fleet," pp. 28–29, 32–33, *Annual Reports of Fleets and Task Forces of the U.S. Navy*, M971, Reel 14, NACP; J. Michael Miller, *From Shanghai to Corregidor: The Marines in Defense of the Philippines*

(Washington, D.C.: History and Museums Division, HQMC, 1997), 1–4; W. W. Rogers to Holcomb, 28 November 1941, WWIIOPMO 1938–45, Box 4, RG 127, NACP; and Shaw, *Opening Moves*, 13–21.

152. Francis B. Loomis Jr., interview by B. Frank, 1970, transcript, pp. 98–102, MCUA; Stark to Kimmel, 17 October 1941, DPPWPSGC 1926–42, Box 4, RG 127, NACP; Kimmel to Stark, 2 December 1941, *Pearl Harbor Hearings Pt 15*, 2481–84; and Urwin, *Facing Fearful Odds*, 105–12, 209, 217.

153. Holcomb to Stark, 5 September 1941, DPPWPSGC 1926–42, Box 4, RG 127, NACP; Kimmel to Stark, 28 November 1941, *Pearl Harbor Hearings Pt 15*, 2481; Kimmel to Stark, 2 December 1941, *Pearl Harbor Hearings Pt 15*, 2253–55; James P. S. Devereux, interview by B. Frank, 1970, transcript, pp. 93–94, 104–5, MCUA; Pfeiffer, transcript, 179; and Urwin, *Facing Fearful Odds*, 183–93, 203–19.

154. Joint Board, Meeting Minutes, 3 November 1941, JB 301, MF 1421, Reel 1, NACP; "Joint Army and Navy Basic War Plan–Rainbow No. 5," 19 November 1941, SPDWPD 1912–46, Series IX, Part II, Box 147J, RG 38, NACP; Marshall to L. T. Gerow, 27 November 1941, SPDWPD 1912–46, Series III, Miscellaneous Subject File, Box 47, RG 38, NACP; Baer, *One Hundred Years of Sea Power*, 169–77; Christman, "Roosevelt and the Craft of Strategic Assessment," 231–35, 250–52; Alvin D. Coox, "Japanese Net Assessment in the Era before Pearl Harbor," in *Calculations*, ed. Murray and Millett, 298; Ienaga, *Pacific War*, 138–41; Morison, *Rising Sun in the Pacific*, 63–64; and Spector, *Eagle Against the Sun*, 78–84.

155. Rogers, transcript, 56.

156. Holcomb to Marshall, 7 August 1942, Box 9, MCUA.

157. Holcomb to Marston, 22 November 1941, Holcomb Papers, Box 4, MCUA; and Holcomb to Marshall, 7 August 1942, Box 9, MCUA.

158. Prange et al., *At Dawn We Slept*, 468–75; Jon Bridgeman, "Saturday, December 6, 1941," in *Pearl Harbor Revisited*, ed. Robert W. Love Jr. (New York: St. Martin's Press, 1995), 160–65; Simpson, *Harold R. Stark*, 112; Divine, *Reluctant Belligerent*, 160–62; and Davis, *FDR*, 336–38.

Chapter 4

Marine Mobilization in the First Seven Months of War, December 1941–June 1942

1. *Pearl Harbor Hearings Pt 26*, 135; Morison, *Rising Sun*, 94–126; and Prange et al., *At Dawn We Slept*, 503–40.

2. *Pearl Harbor Hearings Pt 14*, 1411; Davis, *FDR*, 338–41, 347; and Simpson, *Admiral Harold R. Stark*, 112–15.

3. Rogers, transcript, 56; Brunelli, transcript, 15–16, 19–21; James P. Berkeley, interview by B. Frank, 1969, transcript, pp. 189–90, MCUA; and Smith and Finch, *Coral and Brass*, 86–87.

4. Unreferenced recollection by Harry Sanders, quoted in Buell, *Master of Seapower*, 138.

5. Brunelli, transcript, 15.

6. Rogers, transcript, 56.

7. Brunelli, transcript, 15–17; and Rogers, transcript, 56–57.

8. *Pearl Harbor Hearings Pt 19*, 3503–4; Urwin, *Facing Fearful Odds*, 225–59; Hough et al., *Pearl Harbor to Guadalcanal*, 75–80, 160–62; Millett, *Semper Fidelis*, 354–55; Morison, *Rising Sun*, 160–77; Pfeiffer, transcript, 174–77; and Kimmel to Stark, 12 December 1941, *Pearl Harbor Hearings Pt 15*, 2257–58.

9. Roosevelt, speech, 8 December 1941, *Public Papers of FDR in 1941*, 514–16.

10. Holcomb to Knox, 11 December 1941, Holcomb Papers, Box 4, MCUA.

11. Millett, *Semper Fidelis*, 354–55; Robert J. Cressman, *"A Magnificent Fight": The Battle for Wake Island* (Annapolis: Naval Institute Press, 1995), 111–29; Urwin, *Facing Fearful Odds*, 115–20, 309–42; and Hough et al., *Pearl Harbor to Guadalcanal*, 150.

12. Excerpts, Roosevelt's Press Conference, 12 December 1941, *Public Papers of FDR in 1941*, 445–46.

13. Urwin, *Facing Fearful Odds*, 7–11; George H. Roeder Jr., *The Censored War: American Visual Experience during World War Two* (New Haven, Conn.: Yale University Press, 1993), 4–5, 63–65; and Cameron, *American Samurai*, 58, 88, 96–98.

14. Hough, *Pearl Harbor to Guadalcanal*, 132–50; Urwin, *Facing Fearful Odds*, 408–26; and Cressman, *"Magnificent Fight,"* 138–69.

15. Urwin, *Facing Fearful Odds*, 447–524; Cressman, *"Magnificent Fight,"* 186–247; Berkeley, transcript, 190–91; and Holcomb, summary notes, MCOHC, Box 75, MCUA.

16. Pfeiffer, transcript, 178–79.

17. Urwin, *Facing Fearful Odds*, 524–38, 553; and Millett, *Semper Fidelis*, 355–56.

18. *New York Times,* 29 December 1941, cited in Gregory J. W. Urwin, "The Defenders of Wake Island and Their Two Wars, 1941–1945," in *The Pacific War Revisited*, ed. Gunter Bischoff and Robert L. Dupont (Baton Rouge: Louisiana State University Press, 1996), 114.

19. Holcomb to Knox, 11 December 1941, Holcomb to Nimitz, 12 December 1941, Geiger to Holcomb, 20 December 1941, Barrett to Holcomb, 21 December 1941, Holcomb to King, 22 December 1941, Geiger to Holcomb, 22 December 1941, Holcomb to Geiger, 29 December 1941, and Holcomb to Price, 4 February 1942, all in Holcomb Papers, Box 4, MCUA.

20. Greenstein, *Presidential Difference*, 6.

21. Holcomb to Marshall Andrews, 27 December 1941, Holcomb Papers, Box 4, MCUA. For an example of encouragement that buoyed Holcomb's own morale, see Henry H. Arnold to Holcomb, 7 January 1942, Holcomb Papers, Box 4, MCUA.

22. Vandegrift and Asprey, *Once a Marine*, 98.

23. "Narrative of Events, Asiatic Fleet," pp. 38–42, *Annual Reports of Fleets and Task Forces of the U.S. Navy*, M971, Reel 14, NACP.

24. Joint Board, Meeting Minutes, 8 December 1941, JB 301, M1421, Reel 1, NACP.

25. Stark to Kimmel, 12 December 1941, *Pearl Harbor Hearings Pt 15*, 2257–58; Joint Board Meeting Minutes, 9, 10, 13, 17, and 21 December 1941, JB 301, M1421, Reel

1, NACP; Memo from CNO, 11 December 1941, SPDWPD 1912–46, Series IX, Part III, Box 147J, RG 38, NACP; Geiger to Holcomb, 20 December 1941, Holcomb Papers, Box 4, MCUA; Hayes, *History of the JCS*, 27–29; Simpson, *Admiral Harold R. Stark*, 115–18; Buell, *Master of Sea Power*, 137–38; and Baer, *One Hundred Years of Sea Power*, 184–210.

26. Holcomb to Barron, 26 December 1941, and Henrik Shipstead to Walsh, 21 January 1942, Holcomb Papers, Box 4, MCUA; and Gordon, "Thomas Holcomb," 270.

27. Ernest J. King and Walter M. Whitehall, *Fleet Admiral King: A Naval Record* (New York: Norton, 1953), 349–59; Morison, *Rising Sun*, 255–57; Simpson, *Admiral Harold R. Stark*, 118, 127–35; Buell, *Master of Sea Power*, 138–39, 160–62; and Jeffrey G. Barlow, "Roosevelt and King: The War in the Atlantic and European Theaters," in *FDR and the U.S. Navy*, ed. Marolda, 177–78.

28. Holcomb to Stark, 2 April 1942, Holcomb Papers, Box 5, MCUA; and Brunelli, transcript, 27.

29. Roy, transcript, 30–31.

30. Thomas, transcript, 525–26, 548–56; Worton, transcript, 102, 327–28; Merwin H. Silverthorn, interview with B. Frank, 1969, transcript, 244; Roy, transcript, 24–25; Stark, summary notes, p. 2, MCOHC, Box 142, MCUA; Vandegrift and Asprey, *Once a Marine*, 87–90; and Gordon, "Thomas Holcomb," 278–81.

31. Kennedy, *Freedom from Fear*, 544. See also Weigley, *American Way of War*, 274; Millett, *In Many a Strife*, 151; Eric Larrabee, *Commander in Chief: Franklin Delano Roosevelt, His Lieutenants, and Their War* (New York: Harper & Row, 1987), 153–58; and Barlow, "Roosevelt and King," 177–78.

32. Thomas, transcript, 550.

33. Brunelli, transcript, 21.

34. "Policy for Conduct of Operations in the Pacific–Annex J," n.d. [c. April 1942], p. 2, StratPlnsWPD, WPL Series, Box 35, RG 38, NACP; King and Whitehall, *Fleet Admiral King*, 360–64; Simpson, *Admiral Harold R. Stark*, 119–23; Davis, *FDR*, 365, 379–86; Hayes, *History of the JCS*, 38–42; and Gordon, "Thomas Holcomb," 269–70.

35. Vandegrift and Asprey, *Once a Marine*, 105.

36. O. Smith to Silverthorn, 4 January 1942, O. Smith Papers, Box 17, MCUA; Louis Morton, *Strategy and Command: The First Two Years* (Washington, D.C.: Office of the Chief of Military History, 1962), 199–206; Hayes, *History of the JCS*, 51–60; Hough et. al., *Pearl Harbor to Guadalcanal*, 84–85; and Millett, *Semper Fidelis*, 356–57.

37. "Combined Fleet Top Secret Order 1," issued by Isoroku Yamamoto, 5 November 1941, Office of Naval Intelligence, Box 26, RG 38, NACP; "Estimate of the World Situation, 10 January 1942–15 May 1945," pp. 1–3, 8–10, 23–26, SPDWPD 1912–46, Series III, Miscellaneous Subject File, Box 46, RG 38, NACP; "Narrative of Events, Asiatic Fleet," pp. 36–39, *Annual Reports of Fleets and Task Forces of the U.S. Navy*, M971, Reel 14, NACP; Morton, *Strategy and Command*, 201–12, 290–92; Hough et al., *Pearl Harbor to Guadalcanal*, 235–37; Millett, *Semper Fidelis*, 357–59; and Buell, *Master of Sea Power*, 156–57.

38. King to Marshall, 2 March 1942, quoted in Hayes, *History of the JCS*, 138.

39. Report by Navy War Plans Division, 16 April 1942, cited in Hayes, *History of the JCS*, 139, and in Dyer, *Amphibians Came to Conquer*, 252–53; "Policy for Conduct of Operations in the Pacific–Annex J," n.d. [c. April 1942], pp. 3–8, StratPlnsWPD, WPL Series, Box 35, RG 38 NACP; King, memorandum for the President, 5 March 1942, appended in Buell, *Master of Sea Power*, 503–5; Ghormley to Turner, 24 April 1942, FSDCD, Box 5, RG 38, NACP; Thomas to Vandegrift, 9 August 1945, HAF 204, MCUA; Samuel Eliot Morison, *Coral Sea, Midway, and Submarine Actions, May 1942–August 1942*, vol. 4, *History of the United States Naval Operations in World War II* (Boston: Little, Brown, 1949), 248; Isely and Crowl, *U.S. Marines and Amphibious War*, 73–85; Vandegrift and Asprey, *Once a Marine*, 107–9; Miller, *War Plan Orange*, 331–39; Smith, *Development of Amphibious Tactics*, 39–40; Millett, *In Many a Strife*, 158–62; and Millett, *Semper Fidelis*, 357–59, 362–64.

40. Morton, *Strategy and Command*, 242–63; King and Whitehall, *Fleet Admiral King*, 386–87; and Morison, *Coral Sea*, 249–53.

41. Spector, *Eagle Against the Sun*, 152–78; and Baer, *One Hundred Years of Sea Power*, 216–21.

42. Ienaga, *Pacific War*, 132–33.

43. Vandegrift and Asprey, *Once a Marine*, 107–9; King, *U.S. Navy at War*, 37–49; Miller, *War Plan Orange*, 334–36; Weigley, *American Way of War*, 270–74; and Isely and Crowl, *U.S. Marines and Amphibious War*, 87–95.

44. King to Nimitz, n.d. [c. April 1942], pp. 1–2, StratPlnsWPD, WPL Series, Box 35, RG 38, NACP; Miller, *War Plan Orange*, 333–35; Hayes, *History of the JCS*, 105–7, 117–18; Morton, *Strategy and Command*, 299–302; Buell, *Master of Sea Power*, 171–72, 197–200; Gordon, "Thomas Holcomb," 268–70; Vandegrift and Asprey, *Once a Marine*, 105–9; and John Kennedy Ohl, *Supplying the Troops: General Somervell and American Logistics in WWII* (DeKalb: Northern Illinois University Press, 1994), 181–200.

45. Clark M. Eichelberger to Chapter Representatives of the CDAAA, 8 December 1941, press release by Citizens for Victory, n.d. [c. early 1942], and Willem Luyten to Hendrik Shipstead, 14 December 1941, all in CDAAA, Box 2, MNHS; Dallek, *Franklin D. Roosevelt*, 311–19; Cole, *America First*, 185–97; and Jonas, *Isolationism in America*, 271–73.

46. Cited in Cole, *America First*, 199.

47. Holcomb to Price, 17 January 1942, Holcomb Papers, Box 4, MCUA.

48. Holcomb to Lejeune, 11 December 1941, and Holcomb to Nimitz, 12 December 1941, both in Holcomb Papers, Box 4, MCUA; Statements by Maj. Gen. Thomas Holcomb and others, United States Marine Corps, 15 January 1942, Senate Naval Affairs Subcommittee of the Committee on Appropriations, *Supplemental Navy Department Appropriation for 1942*, 77th Congress, 2nd session, 178–89; Statements by Lt. General T. Holcomb and others, 28 May 1942, House Committee on Appropriations, *Seventh Supplemental National Defense Appropriation Bill for 1942* (hereafter *Seventh Supplemental Bill for 1942*), 77th Congress, 2nd session, 51–64; and Statements by Lt. Gen. Thomas Holcomb and Maj. Gen. Seth Williams, 5 June 1942, Senate Naval Affairs Subcommittee of the Committee of Appropriations,

Seventh Supplemental Bill for 1942, 77th Congress, 2nd session, 21–22, Holcomb Papers, Box 33, MCUA.

49. Statements by Lt. General T. Holcomb and others, 28 May 1942, *Seventh Supplemental Bill for 1942*, 52.

50. Navy Department, *Naval Expenditures, 1942* (Washington, D.C.: GPO, 1943), 1; Navy Department, *Naval Expenditures, 1943* (Washington, D.C.: GPO, 1944), 1; and House Committee on Appropriations, 23 January 1942, *Report on the Fourth Supplemental National Defense Appropriation Bill for 1942*, 77th Congress, 2nd session, 16, 24; and Statement of Frank Knox, House Committee on Appropriations, 29 January 1942, *Navy Department Appropriation Bill for 1943*, 77th Congress, 2nd session, 1–8, Holcomb Papers, Box 33, MCUA.

51. George W. Killen Questionnaire, 7thDBQ, WWIIC, Box 1, MCUA.

52. Stewart Robertson, telegram to HQMC, 7 January 1942, and HQMC to Robertson, 8 January 1942, both in Holcomb Papers, Box 4, MCUA.

53. Denig, transcript, 8; Denig to Holcomb, 26 February 1942, and Turnage to Holcomb, 27 March 1942, both in MCGC 1939–50, Box 613, RG 127, NACP; Lindsay, *This High Name*, 51–55, 62; and Lash, "Media and the Marines," 32, 73.

54. Commandant of the Marine Corps (hereafter CMC) to SecNav, 10 March 1942, MCGC 1939–50, Box 99, RG 127, NACP.

55. R. M. Montague to Holcomb, 28 February 1942, James to Montague, 4 March 1942, Holcomb to Crawford, 10 March 1942, and Rappleyea to Higgins, 11 December 1941, all in Holcomb Papers, Box 4, MCUA; George T. Van der Hoef to H. Schlye, 13 March 1942, MCGC 1939–50, Box 99, RG 127, NACP; Officer in Charge of Central RD to Denig, 19 March 1942, and Officer in Charge of Central RD to Holcomb, both in MCGC 1939–50, Box 197, RG 127, NACP; Lindsay, *This High Name*, 53–54; and Lash, "Media and the Marines," 7–10, 32, 54–59.

56. Denig to Holcomb, 20 May 1942, MCGC 1939–50, Box 197, RG 127, NACP.

57. Roger Whitman to Denig, 5 March 1942, MCGC 1939–50, Box 99, RG 127, NACP.

58. Rutledge, "Rhetoric of Marine Corps," 114, 129; Lash, "Media and the Marines," 24, 30–31, 99; Millett, *Semper Fidelis*, 360–61; Cameron, *American Samurai*, 24–25, 48–50, 62–81; Showalter, "Evolution of U.S. Marine Corps," 51; and Lemuel C. Shepherd Jr., interview by B. Frank, 1967, transcript, pp. 264–66, MCOHC, MCUA.

59. Cameron, *American Samurai*, 30.

60. Lindsay, *This High Name*, 53–55; Jarvis, *Male Body at War*, 48–55; and Cameron, *American Samurai*, 30, 48.

61. See Rutledge, "Rhetoric of Marine Corps," 131–32, 139, 143–46.

62. Roeder, *Censored War*, 2.

63. Memo from Lyman Munson with enclosure on propaganda by Eric Knight, 26 May 1942, in *Film and Propaganda in America: A Documentary History*, vol. 2, pt. 2, ed. David Culbert (New York: Greenwood Press, 1990), 106–7; Cedric Larson, "The Domestic Motion Picture Work of the Office of War Information," *Hollywood Quarterly* 3 (Summer 1948): 434–43; Roeder, *Censored War*, 9–12, 19–22, 55, 83–89, 125; Urwin, *Facing Fearful Odds*, 5, 11–12; and Suid, *Guts and Glory*, 65–66, 71–76, 90–91.

64. 7thDBQ, WWIIC, Box 1, MCUA; Wilbur D. Jones Jr., *Gyrene: The World War II United States Marine* (Shippensburg, Pa.: White Mane Books, 1998), 15–19; and E. Anthony Rotundo, *American Manhood: Transformations in Masculinity from the Revolution to the Modern Era* (New York: Basic Books, 1993), 232–34.

65. Cameron, *American Samurai*, 48.

66. "Daily Report of Recruiting," 24 November 1941, 9 December 1941, 17 December 1941, 24 December 1941, and 1 January 1942, all in MCGC 1939–50, Box 616, RG 127, NACP; and Millett, *In Many a Strife*, 155.

67. Holcomb to Francis Sullivan, 7 January 1942, Holcomb Papers, Box 4, MCUA; and Millett, *Semper Fidelis*, 359–60.

68. C. H. Wheeler, memorandum for Recruiting Section, 10 December 1941, MCGC 1939–50, Box 619, RG 127, NACP.

69. Holcomb, Letter of Instruction No. 61, 28 December 1941, and Letter of Instruction No. 71, 20 January 1942, both in MCGC 1939–50, Box 297, RG 127, NACP; Navy Department, *United States Marine Corps*, 12; Holcomb to Knox, 11 December, and Holcomb to Nimitz, 12 December 1941, both in Box 4, Holcomb Papers, MCUA; and "Daily Report of Recruiting," 31 January 1942, MCGC 1939–50, Box 616, RG 127, NACP.

70. Muir, *Human Tradition*, xvi–xvii; Jarvis, *Male Body at War*, 55–64; and Cameron, *American Samurai*, 52, 58.

71. Omar Lee Clark to Holcomb, 27 February 1942, and Burke to Clark, 2 March 1942, both in MCGC 1939–50, Box 624, RG 127, NACP; and "Report for Physical Examination," 19 March 1942, 4 April 1942, and 20 April 1942, all in MCGC 1939–50, Box 906, RG 127, NACP.

72. "Report for Physical Examination," 19 March 1942, 4 April 1942, and 20 April 1942, all in MCGC 1939–50, Box 906, RG 127, NACP. See also Lewis H. Loeser, "The Sexual Psychopath in the Military Service," *American Journal of Psychiatry* 102 (July 1945): 92–101, reprinted in *Gay Warriors: A Documentary History from the Ancient World to the Present*, ed. B. R. Burg (New York: New York University Press, 2002), 239, 242–43.

73. Forrest M. Harrison to Winfred Overholzer, 5 August 1942, and John C. Whitehorn and Overholzer to Harrison, 3 November 1942, both in BMGC 1941–46, Box 165, Entry 15B, Record Group 52, Records of the Bureau of Medicine of the U.S. Navy (RG 52), NACP; Forrest M. Harrison, "Psychiatry in the Navy," *War Medicine* 3 (February 1943): 114–26, 137; Allan Bérubé, *Coming Out under Fire: The History of Gay Men and Women in World War II* (New York: Free Press, 1990), 149–54; and Beth Bailey, *Sex in the Heartland* (Cambridge, Mass.: Harvard University Press, 1999), 56–61.

74. Gordon, "Thomas Holcomb," 274; Janowitz, *Professional Soldier*, 100; Jarvis, *Male Body at War*, 123, 140–41; Richard M. Dalfiume, *Desegregation of the Armed Forces: Fighting on Two Fronts, 1939–1953* (Columbia: University of Missouri Press, 1969), 26, 53–55; Beth Bailey and David Farber, "The 'Double-V' Campaign in World War II in Hawaii: African Americans, Racial Ideology, and Federal Power," *Journal of Social History* 26 (December 1993): 817–43; and Jack D. Forbes, "'Indian' and 'Black' As Radically Different Types of Categories," in *The Social*

Construction of Race and Ethnicity in the United States, ed. Joan Ferrante and Prince Brown Jr. (New York: Longman, 1998), 120–22.

75. Roeder, *Censored War*, 44.

76. Morris J. McGregor Jr., *Integration of the Armed Forces, 1940–1965* (Washington, D.C.: Center of Military History, 1981), 64–65; Dalfiume, *Desegregation of the Armed Forces*, 54–55; Nalty, *Strength for the Fight*, 184–87; Bernard C. Nalty, *The Right to Fight: African-American Marines in World War II* (Washington, D.C.: Marine Corps Historical Center, 1995), 1–2; Millett, *Semper Fidelis*, 374–75; Cardozier, *Mobilization of the United States*, 162–63; and Kennedy, *Freedom from Fear*, 711–13, 765–70.

77. Louis C. Padillo Jr. to F. Roosevelt, 11 December 1941, MCGC 1939–50, Box 619, RG 127, NACP.

78. Burke to Padillo, 29 December 1941, MCGC 1939–50, Box 619, RG 127, NACP. See also Jarvis, *Male Body at War*, 131, 135–36.

79. Jarvis, *Male Body at War*, 125–27; Cameron, *American Samurai*, 34; and Paul A. Kramer, "Race-Making and Colonial Violence in the U.S. Empire: The Philippine-American War As Race War," *Diplomatic History* 30 (April 2006): 169–210.

80. Holcomb, testimony in hearings of the General Board of the Navy, 23 January 1942, Subject: "Enlistment of Men of Colored Race (201)," Navy Operational Archives, cited in Henry I. Shaw Jr. and Ralph W. Donnelly, *Blacks in the Marine Corps* (Washington, D.C.: History and Museums Division, HQMC, 1975), 1.

81. Ibid.

82. See also McGregor, *Integration of the Armed Forces*, 100–101.

83. W. R. Poage to Knox, 10 December 1941, in McGregor and Nalty, *Blacks in the United States Armed Forces*, 12; Knox to Gifford Pinchot, 19 January 1942, in McGregor and Nalty, *Blacks in the United States Armed Forces*, 13–14; Knox to William H. Smathers, 6 February 1942, in MacGregor and Nalty, *Blacks in the United States Armed Forces*, 17; McGregor, *Integration of the Armed Forces*, 62–67; Nalty, *Strength for the Fight*, 185–87; Dalfiume, *Desegregation of the Armed Forces*, 37–38, 53–55; and Steven J. Ramold, *Slaves, Soldiers, Citizens: African Americans in the Union Navy* (DeKalb: Northern Illinois University Press, 2002), 182–86.

84. Chairman of the General Board to SecNav, 3 February 1942, File 18E, Holcomb Papers, Box 11, MCUA.

85. General Board Study of Men of the Colored Race in Other Than Messman Branch, 20 March 1942, p. 9, File 18E, Holcomb Papers, Box 11, MCUA. For commentary on Holcomb's own perspective, see Gordon, "Thomas Holcomb," 275.

86. Roosevelt to Knox, 9 February 1942, File 18E, Holcomb Papers, Box 11, MCUA. See also Knox to W. R. Sexton, 14 February 1942, and Roosevelt to Knox, 31 March 1942, both in MacGregor and Nalty, *Blacks in the United States Armed Forces*, 65, 102.

87. Nalty, *Strength for the Fight*, 186–87.

88. Chairman of the General Board to SecNav, 20 March 1942, Knox to Roosevelt, 27 March 1942, and Roosevelt to Knox, 31 March 1942, all in File 18E, Holcomb Papers, Box 11, MCUA; memorandum from Holcomb, 25 May 1942, in McGregor

and Nalty, *Blacks in the United States Armed Forces*, 416; Gordon, "Thomas Holcomb," 273–75; Shaw and Donnelly, *Blacks in the Marine Corps*, 1–3; Millett, *Semper Fidelis*, 374–75; Nalty, *Right to Fight*, 1–3; McGregor, *Integration of the Armed Forces*, 65–67, 99–103; and Nalty, *Strength for the Fight*, 187–90, 199–200.

89. Thomas, recording with G. Smith, 11591A. In an interview for the Marine Corps Historical Center ten years earlier in 1968, Gerald Thomas attributed to Holcomb the common racial slur for the word "black" when he related the same episode of Holcomb's interaction with King (Thomas, transcript with B. Frank, 550). This disparity in usage presents a historical conundrum. Without Holcomb, King, and Gerald Thomas still alive, there can be no certain clarification of the disparities between usages and memories in the 1968 and 1978 interviews with Thomas.

90. Nimitz to Holcomb, 13 April 1942, Holcomb Papers, Box 5, MCUA; and Millett, *Semper Fidelis*, 375.

91. Chairman of the General Board to SecNav, 3 February 1942, File 18E, Holcomb Papers, Box 11, MCUA; McGregor, *Integration of the Armed Forces*, 3–16; Millett, *In Many a Strife*, 236; Cameron, *American Samurai*, 237; Gordon, "Thomas Holcomb," 274; and Kennedy, *Freedom from Fear*, 713, 773–74.

92. Marshall, "Crucible of Colonial Service," 34–51, 114–20, 165. See also Routledge M. Dennis, "Social Darwinism, Scientific Racism, and the Metaphysics of Race," *Journal of Negro Education* 64 (Summer 1995): 243–46; Gordon, "Thomas Holcomb," 274; Janowitz, *Professional Soldier*, 100; Cameron, *American Samurai*, 34; Kristin L. Hoganson, *Fighting for American Manhood: How Gender Politics Provoked the Spanish-American and Philippine-American Wars* (New Haven, Conn.: Yale University Press, 1998), 12–13, 131–50; and Kramer, "Race-Making and Colonial Violence," 169–210.

93. Jarvis, *The Male Body at War*, 125–27, 139–41; Cameron, *American Samurai*, 34; Hoganson, *Fighting for American Manhood*, 7, 12–13, 131–50; and Forbes, "'Indian' and 'Black,'" 120–24.

94. Vogel to Holcomb, 6 March 1942, MCGC 1939–50, Box 613, RG 127, NACP.

95. Turnage to Holcomb, 20 March 1942, and Holcomb to Vogel, 2 April 1942, both in MCGC 1939–50, Box 613, RG 127, NACP; and Berkeley, transcript, 183–86.

96. Millett, *Semper Fidelis*, 374–75; Jeanne Holm, *Women in the Military: An Unfinished Revolution*, rev. ed. (Novato, Calif.: Presidio, 1993), 21–25; and Janann Sherman, "Margaret Chase Smith: Wartime Congresswomen," in *The Human Tradition in the World War II Era*, ed. Malcolm Muir Jr. (Wilmington, Del.: Scholarly Resources, 2001), 129–30.

97. Holcomb, summary notes, p. 5, Box 75, MCUA; DeWitt Peck, interview by B. Frank, 1967, transcript, p. 43, MCUA; Price to Holcomb, 29 February 1942, Holcomb Papers, Box 4, MCUA; "Mission of the Marine Corps," n.d. [c. spring 1942], O. Smith Papers, Box 17, MCUA; Harry W. Edwards, *A Different War: Marines in Europe and North Africa*, (Washington, D.C.: Marine Corps Historical Center, 1994), 1–3; and Donovan, *Outpost in the North Atlantic*, 30–32.

98. Price to Holcomb, 24 March 1942, Holcomb Papers, Box 4, MCUA.

99. Nimitz to King, 1 January 1942, WWIIOPMO 1938–45, Box 1, RG 127, NACP; Pfeiffer to Vandegrift, 21 March 1942, WWIIOPMO 1938–45, Box 5, RG 127,

NACP; "First Marine Amphibious Corps–Enclosure A," 9 April 1942, FSDCD, Box 5, RG 28, NACP; Pfeiffer to Holcomb, 21 March 1942, WWIIOPMO 1938–45, Box 5, RG 127, NACP; "A Study in Logistics of the Guadalcanal Campaign," report by Thomas P. Bartleson Jr., pp. 1–3, n.d. (hereafter "Study in Logistics"), WWIISG, Box 3, MCUA; King, *U.S. Navy at War*, 34–36; and Millett, *In Many a Strife*, 357–59.

100. Nimitz to Holcomb, 2 June 1942, WWIIOPMO 1938–45, Box 5, RG 127, NACP. See also Bagley to Holcomb via Nimitz, 2 June 1942, and Nimitz, telegram to Holcomb, 6 June 1942, both in WWIIOPMO 1938–45, Box 5, RG 127, NACP.

101. Emile P. Moses to Holcomb, 6 May 1942, and Holcomb to Moses, 8 May 1942, both in Holcomb Papers, Box 5, MCUA; and Millett, *Semper Fidelis*, 359.

102. Cameron, *American Samurai*, 56.

103. Price to Holcomb, 26 February 1942, Holcomb Papers, Box 4, MCUA; Cameron, *American Samurai*, 56–60; Champie, *Brief History of Recruitment Depot, San Diego*, 16–17; and Champie, *Brief History of Recruitment Depot, Parris Island*, 9–11.

104. Jones, *Gyrene*, 55–65.

105. Barrett to Holcomb, 27 January 1942, Holcomb Papers, Box 4, MCUA.

106. Shepherd, transcript, 264–66; Millett, *Semper Fidelis*, 360–61; and 7thDBQ, WWIIC, Box 1, MCUA.

107. "Study in Logistics," p. 9, WWIISG, Box 3, MCUA; Price to Holcomb, 29 February 1942, Holcomb Papers, Box 4, MCUA; Pfeiffer to Vandegrift, 21 March 1942, WWIIOPMO 1938–45, Box 5, RG 127, NACP; Holcomb to Henry K. Hewitt, 14 July 1942, Holcomb Papers, Box 5, MCUA; and Millett, *Semper Fidelis*, 359, 362.

108. Holcomb to Price, 17 January 1942, Holcomb Papers, Box 4, MCUA.

109. Vandegrift and Asprey, *Once a Marine*, 99.

110. Melson, *Condition Red*, 6–29; Ulbrich, "Clarifying the Origins," 83–85, 98–99; and Millett, *Semper Fidelis*, 346–47.

111. Pfeiffer, transcript, 194–95; Thomas, transcript, 537–40; memorandum from H. Smith, 2 June 1942, Records Regarding World War II Plans, Policies, Aviation, and Amphibious Operations 1942–1972, Box 1, RG 127, NACP; Gordon, "U.S. Marine Corps and an Experiment in Military Elitism," 362–65; Gordon, "Thomas Holcomb," 268–69; and Jon T. Hoffman, *From Makin to Bougainville: Marine Raiders in the Pacific* (Washington, D.C.: Marine Corps Historical Center, 1995), 1–4.

112. J. Roosevelt, audio recording, 11586; Pfeiffer, transcript, 193–94; Thomas, transcript, 537; Showalter, "Evolution of U.S. Marine Corps," 44, 50–51; and Gordon, "U.S. Marine Corps and an Experiment in Military Elitism," 362–63, 366–70.

113. Holcomb, summary notes, p. 4, MCOHC, Box 75, MCUA.

114. Ibid. See also Gordon, "Thomas Holcomb," 368–69; and Hoffman, *From Makin to Bougainville*, 3–4.

115. Millett, *In Many a Strife*, 156; Hoffman, *From Makin to Bougainville*, 4–5; and Millett, *Semper Fidelis*, 346.

116. Vandegrift and Asprey, *Once a Marine*, 99.

117. Zimmerman, "Military Missionary," 258–59; Hoffman, *From Makin to Bougainville*, 5; Pfeiffer, transcript, 198–99; Worton, transcript, 153–56; and Krulak, transcript, 69–71.

118. Holcomb, summary notes, p. 4, MCOHC, Box 75, MCUA.

119. Worton, transcript, 106–107.

120. Vandegrift and Asprey, *Once a Marine*, 98; Smith, *Development of Amphibious Tactics*, 37–38; Cooper, *Fighting General*, 88–90; Joel Thacker, "First Marine Division," 3, HAF 186, MCRUA; Merrill B. Twining, *No Bended Knee: The Battle for Guadalcanal, the Memoir of Gen. Merrill B. Twining, USMC (Ret.)*, ed. Neil Carey (Novato, Calif.: Presidio, 1996), 9–10; and Merle T. Cole, *Cradle of Invasion: A History of the U.S. Naval Amphibious Training Base, Solomons, Maryland, 1942– 1945* (Solomons, Md.: Calvert Marine Museum, 1984), 2–6.

121. Price to Holcomb, 24 March 1942, Holcomb Papers, Box 4, MCUA. See also Twining, *No Bended Knee*, 9; and David S. Barry, memorandum for A&I, 11 March 1942, Holcomb Papers, Box 4, MCUA.

122. William White and Ben Wofford, *The Marine: A Guadalcanal Survivor's Final Battle* (Annapolis: Naval Institute Press, 2002), 14. For reflections about another inspection tour by Holcomb, see George B. Bell Questionnaire, 7thDBQ, WWIIC, Box 1, MCUA.

123. Holcomb to Price, 4 February 1942; Holcomb to J. L. McCrea, 23 March 1942, and Price to Holcomb, 24 March 1942, all in Holcomb Papers, Box 4, MCUA.

124. Cooper, *Fighting General*, 90; and Millett, *In Many a Strife*, 156–57.

125. Thacker, "First Marine Division," 2, HAF 186, MCUA; and Pfeiffer, transcript, 184–85.

126. Vandegrift and Asprey, *Once a Marine*, 99–100.

127. Vandegrift and Asprey, *Once a Marine*, 100; Twining, *No Bended Knee*, 13–16; and Millett, *In Many a Strife*, 158–62.

128. Vandegrift and Asprey, *Once a Marine*, 100.

129. Noble to Holcomb, 14 June 1942, WWIIOPMO 1938–45, Box 4, RG 127, NACP; "Study in Logistics," 10, 16–18, WWIISG, Box 3, MCUA; Vandegrift and Asprey, *Once a Marine*, 100–103; Twining, *No Bended Knee*, 23–27; Millett, *In Many a Strife*, 164; Thacker, *First Marine Division*, 3–4; and Eric Hammel, *Guadalcanal: Starvation Island* (New York: Crown Publishers, 1987), 28–31.

130. Memorandum for King, 17 September 1942, SPDWPD 1912–46, Series III, Misc. Subject File, Box 48, RG 38, NACP.

131. Vandegrift and Asprey, *Once a Marine*, 104.

132. Twining, *No Bended Knee*, 28–29; Theodore L. Gatchel, "Marines in Support of a Naval Campaign: Guadalcanal As a Prototype," *MCG* 70 (January 1986): 40–43; Thacker, "First Marine Division," 3–4, HAF 186, MCUA; Buell, *Master of Sea Power*, 198–200; Millett, *In Many a Strife*, 163–65; "Study in Logistics," 19, 39, WWIISG, Box 3, MCUA; and Millett, *Semper Fidelis*, 363–64.

133. Holcomb Fit Rep, 1 October 1941–31 March 1942, Holcomb Papers, Box 13, MCUA.

Chapter 5

Guadalcanal: The First Big Test for Holcomb and the Marine Corps,
July 1942–February 1943

1. King to Ghormley, 5 June 1942, Records Regarding Plans, Policies, Aviation, and
   Amphibious Operations 1942–1972, Box 1, RG 127, NACP; King, telegram to
   Ghormley, MacArthur, and Marshall, 2 July 1942, SPDWPD 1912–46, Series III,
   Misc. Subject File, Box 48, RG 38, NACP; "Estimate of the Situation (Tulagi-
   Guadalcanal Area)," report by Frank B. Goettge, 11 July 1942, WWIISG, Box 7,
   MCUA; "Estimate of the Situation," report by Maas, 15 July 1942, Box 7, Maas
   Papers, MNHS; Alexander A. Vandegrift, "Operation Order No 7–42," 20 July
   1942, appended in Hough et al., *Pearl Harbor*, 396–98; Dyer, *Amphibians Came
   to Conquer*, 271–90; Morton, *Strategy and Command*, 299–311, 318–19; Weigley,
   American Way of War, 270–74; Miller, *War Plan Orange*, 334–36; and Spector, *Eagle
   Against the Sun*, 184–87.

2. Vandegrift and Asprey, *Once a Marine*, 114–15; Vandegrift to Holcomb, 8 July 1942,
   Holcomb Papers, Box 21, MCUA; and "The Marine Corps' Mission," File 387–30,
   AHEC.

3. "Division Commander's Final Report on Guadalcanal—Phase I," report by
   Vandegrift, May 1943 (hereafter "Guadalcanal Final Report"), pp. 1–6 and Annex
   L, WWIISG, Box 11, MCUA; Vandegrift and Asprey, *Once a Marine*, 100; Thacker,
   "First Marine Division," HAF 186, MCUA; John Miller, *Guadalcanal: The First
   Offensive* (Washington, D.C.: Office of the Chief of Military History, Department of
   the Army, 1949), 41–50, 58; Thomas, transcript, 276–78; Thomas M. Kane, *Military
   Logistics and Strategic Performance* (London: Frank Cass, 2001), 51–53; Richard
   M. Leighton and Robert W. Coakley, *Global Logistics and Strategy, 1940–1943*
   (Washington, D.C.: Office of the Chief of Military History, Department of the Army,
   1960), 722–25, 736–37; and "Study in Logistics," 21–23, WWIISG, Box 3, MCUA.

4. Hough et al., *Pearl Harbor*, 244–46; Thomas, recording with G. Smith, 11591A; and
   Twining, *No Bended Knee*, 33.

5. Vandegrift and Asprey, *Once a Marine*, 115.

6. For examples of reports, see references cited in Isely and Crowl, *U.S. Marines and
   Amphibious War*, 103–18.

7. Vandegrift and Asprey, *Once a Marine*, 107–9.

8. Robert L. Ghormley, "The Tide Turns," n.d., 59 (emphasis in original), World War II
   Command File, Forces–South Pacific Naval Forces History, Box 288, NHHC.

9. Nimitz to Ghormley, n.d. [c. June or July 1942], Box 6, Richmond Kelly Turner
   Personal Papers Collection (hereafter Turner Papers), NHHC; Ghormley, "Tide
   Turns," 40–52; Richard B. Frank, *Guadalcanal* (New York: Random House, 1990),
   52–57; John B. Lundstrom, *Black Shoe Carrier Admiral: Frank Jack Fletcher at
   Coral Sea, Midway, and Guadalcanal* (Annapolis: Naval Institute Press, 2006), 318–
   23; James Joseph Henry IV, "A Historical Review of the Development of Doctrine
   for Command Relationships in Amphibious Warfare" (M.S. thesis, U.S. Army
   Command and General Staff College, 2000), 54–55; Morison, *Coral Sea*, 268–75;
   Dyer, *Amphibians Came to Conquer*, 285–94; King, *U.S. Navy at War*, 34; Holcomb,
   summary notes, p. 3, MCOHC, Box 75, MCUA; and Thomas, transcript, 259–61.

10. United States Navy, *FTP 167(Fleet Training Publication 167), Landing Operations Doctrine, 1938*, paragraph 201, HAF 638, MCUA; memo for Colonel Handy, 17 March 1942, F. P. Thomas, memo for Turner, 18 March 1942, Dewitt Peck, memo for Turner, 18 March 1942, and memo by A. H. Noble, 24 July 1942, all in COMCINCH 1941–46, Box 2, RG 38, NACP; and 22 May 1942, Turner to King, 13 May 1942, and Nimitz to King, both in Turner Papers, Box 6, NHHC, and Tentative [draft] Memo by Turner, n.d. [c. July 1942], Turner Papers, Box 9, NHHC.

11. Vandegrift to Holcomb, 11 August 1942, Holcomb Papers, Box 21, MCUA.

12. Dyer, *Amphibians Came to Conquer*, 290–94; Morison, *Coral Sea*, 268–75; Harry I. Shaw Jr., *First Offensive: The Marine Campaign for Guadalcanal* (Washington, D.C.: Marine Corps Historical Center, 1992), 2–4; Larrabee, *Commander in Chief*, 264; and W. H. P. Blandy, "Command Relations in Amphibious Warfare," U.S. Naval Institute *Proceedings* 77 (June 1951): 573–74.

13. Ghormley, "Tide Turns," 50–51. See also Chester W. Nimitz to Ghormley, n.d. [c. June or July 1942], Box 6, Turner Papers, NHHC.

14. Thomas, transcript, 259–61; Alfred G. Ward, interview by John T. Mason Jr., 1970, transcript, p. 46, NHHC; Hason T. Baldwin, interview with Mason, 1975, transcript, p. 345, NHHC; King and Whitehall, *Fleet Admiral King*, 388–89, 428–30; King, *U.S. Navy at War*, 34; Dyer, *Amphibians Came to Conquer*, 285–88; Millett, *Semper Fidelis*, 364; Morton, *Strategy and Command*, 306–7; Samuel B. Griffith II, *The Battle for Guadalcanal* (Philadelphia: Lippincott, 1963), 28–32, 35; Holcomb, summary notes, p. 3, MCOHC, Box 75, MCUA; and McDill to King, 24 September 1945, StratPlns SPDWPD 1912–46, Series III, Misc. Subject File, Box 48, RG 38, NACP.

15. Hammel, *Guadalcanal*, 38–39; Frank, *Guadalcanal*, 54–55; "Study in Logistics," 28–30, WWIISG, Box 3, MCUA; R. R. Keene, "Preparing for Guadalcanal," *Leatherneck* 55 (June 1972), 37; Dyer, *Amphibians Came to Conquer*, 299–302; Vandegrift and Asprey, *Once a Marine*, 120; Millett, *In Many a Strife*, 369–71; Twining, *No Bended Knee*, 44–46; Lundstrom, *Black Shoe Carrier Admiral*, 313, 320–23, 329–42; and Larrabee, *Commander in Chief*, 264–65.

16. Vandegrift and Asprey, *Once a Marine*, 120.

17. Greenstein, *Presidential Difference*, 6.

18. Keene, "Preparing for Guadalcanal," 35.

19. Dyer, *Amphibians Came to Conquer*, 307–9; Isely and Crowl, *U.S. Marines and Amphibious War*, 115–17; and William H. Bartsch, "Operation Dovetail: Bungled Guadalcanal Rehearsal, July 1942," *Journal of Military History* 66 (April 2002): 443–76.

20. Griffith, *Battle for Guadalcanal*, 36; Millett, *In Many a Strife*, 171–72; and White and Wofford, *Marine*, 37.

21. Williams, transcript, 65–66; and Holcomb to Vandegrift, 14 August 1942, Vandegrift Papers, Box 2, MCUA.

22. Berkeley, transcript, 191–92.

23. Ibid.

24. Marshall to Holcomb, 4 August 1942, Holcomb Papers, Box 5, MCUA.

25. Holcomb to Marshall, 7 August 1942, Holcomb Papers, Box 5, MCUA. For similarly toned letters, see Holcomb to Nimitz, 1 August 1942, Holcomb Papers, Box 5, MCUA; and Holcomb to Vandegrift, 15 September 1942, Vandegrift Papers, Box 2, MCUA.

26. Vandegrift to Holcomb, 11 August 1942, Holcomb Papers, Box 21, MCUA; "Guadalcanal Final Report—Phase II," 1–8, WWIISG, Box 11, MCUA; Isely and Crowl, *U.S. Marines and Amphibious War*, 122–25; Hough et al., *Pearl Harbor to Guadalcanal*, 253–67; Frank, *Guadalcanal*, 59–79; Millett, *In Many a Strife*, 174–86; Dana T. Hughes, *The Old Breed: A Combat Marine's Odyssey through the Pacific, 1941–1945* (Denver: Outskirts, 2008), 226–27; Stanley Coleman Jersey, *Hell's Island: The Untold Story of Guadalcanal* (College Station: Texas A&M University Press, 2008), 113–22, 123–63; and James F. Christ, *The Battalion of the Damned: The 1st Marine Paratroopers at Gavutu and Bloody Ridge, 1942* (Annapolis: Naval Institute Press, 2007), 46–159.

27. CG of 1st Marine Division to Headquarters Marine Corps, n.d. [c. August 1942], cited in Isely and Crowl, *U.S. Marines and Amphibious War*, 121.

28. "Guadalcanal Final Report—Phase II," 8–10, WWIISG, Box 11, MCUA; Thomas, transcript, 289–90; Griffith, *Battle for Guadalcanal*, 40–41; Isely and Crowl, *U.S. Marines and Amphibious War*, 118–22; Hough et al., *Pearl Harbor to Guadalcanal*, 254–58; and Miller, *Guadalcanal*, 67–71, 75–78.

29. Unreferenced quotation cited in Herbert C. Merillat, *Guadalcanal Remembered* (New York: Dodd, Mead, 1982), 55.

30. Thomas G. Miller Jr., *The Cactus Air Force* (New York: Harper & Row, 1969), 7–9; Jersey, *Hell's Island*, 189; and Lundstrom, *Black Shoe Carrier Admiral*, 362–76.

31. Vandegrift and Asprey, *Once a Marine*, 127. For the full seven-page original report, see Vandegrift to Holcomb, 14 August 1942, Holcomb Papers, Box 21, MCUA.

32. "Guadalcanal Final Report—Phase II," 11–12, WWIISG, Box 11, MCUA; Cates, transcript, 132–33; Jersey, *Hell's Island*, 113; and Frank, *Guadalcanal*, 79–82.

33. Miller to Isely, 28 February 1949, "Amphibious Doctrine" Subject File, HDRB; Dyer, *Amphibians Came to Conquer*, 290–95, Vandegrift and Asprey, *Once a Marine*, 128–29; Frank, *Guadalcanal* , 94–95; and Samuel Eliot Morison, *History of the United States Naval Operations in World War II*, vol. 5, *The Struggle for Guadalcanal, August 1942–February 1943* (Boston: Little, Brown, 1949), 29–30.

34. Unreferenced quotation in Larrabee, *Commander in Chief*, 274.

35. Lundstrom, *Black Shoe Carrier Admiral*, 357–82; and "South Pacific Campaign," report by Halsey, 3 September 1944, n.p. [3], Folder: South Pacific Campaign (hereafter Halsey Report), Commander, South Pacific Area and South Pacific Forces (hereafter COMSOPAC), NHHC. For more on commentary on Lundstrom's defense of Fletcher, see also David J. Ulbrich, "Thomas Holcomb, Alexander A. Vandegrift, and Reforms in Amphibious Command Relations on Guadalcanal in 1942," *War & Society* 28 (May 2009): 122–23, 127–28.

36. Agawa, *Reluctant Admiral*, 323–24; Paul S. Dull, *A Battle History of the Imperial Japanese Navy: 1941–1945* (Annapolis: Naval Institute Press, 1978), 190–203; Morison, *Struggle for Guadalcanal*, 17–21, 35–55; and Frank, *Guadalcanal*, 99–122.

37. Vandegrift to Holcomb, 14 August 1942, Holcomb Papers, Box 21, MCUA; and Hough et al., *Pearl Harbor to Guadalcanal*, 260–61.

38. Twining, *No Bended Knee*, 73.

39. Buell, *Master of Sea Power*, 203–8; Davis, *FDR*, 583–85, 654–55; and Griffith, *Battle for Guadalcanal*, 72, 77.

40. Unsigned article, *Gazette* (Worcester, Mass.), 14 August 1942, Holcomb File, HDRB. See also Gordon, "Thomas Holcomb," 270; Walter Sykes Sr. to Holcomb, 17 August 1942, Holcomb Papers, Box 5, MCUA; and Holcomb to Linscott, 18 August 1942, Vandegrift Papers, Box 2, MCUA.

41. Holcomb to Vandegrift, 14 August 1942, Vandegrift Papers, Box 2, MCUA.

42. Vandegrift to Holcomb, 11 August 1942 and 14 August 1942, Holcomb Papers, Box 21, MCUA; Vandegrift and Asprey, *Once a Marine*, 17–19, 131–33; Baldwin, transcript, 348–49; Griffith, *Battle for Guadalcanal*, 66–70; Twining, *No Bended Knee*, 73–78; Larrabee, *Commander in Chief*, 279–80; "Guadalcanal Final Report—Phase III," 1–3, WWIISG, Box 11, MCUA.

43. Merillat, *Guadalcanal Remembered*, 73. See also Twining, *No Bended Knee*, 73–83; and Miller, *Guadalcanal*, 93–97.

44. Vandegrift and Asprey, *Once a Marine*, 134.

45. Vandegrift to Holcomb, 11 August 1942 and 14 August 1942, both in Holcomb Papers, Box 21, MCUA; Twining, *No Bended Knee*, 79, 86–87; Millett, *In Many a Strife*, 184; and Vandegrift and Asprey, *Once a Marine*, 149.

46. Vandegrift to Holcomb, 22 August 1942, Holcomb Papers, Box 21, MCUA.

47. Ibid., 31 August 1942, Holcomb Papers, Box 21, MCUA; and "Guadalcanal Final Report—Phase III," 12–13, WWIISG, Box 11, MCUA; Vandegrift and Asprey, *Once a Marine*, 149; Millett, *Semper Fidelis*, 368–69; "Air Power Is Key to Victory in Pacific, Says General in Marines," article by Josiah P. Rowe Jr., Louis E. Wood Papers, Box 6, MCUA; Miller, *Cactus Air Force*; Robert Sherrod, *History of the Marine Corps Aviation in World War II* (Washington, D.C.: Combined Forces Press, 1952), 78–87; and Peter Mersky, *U.S. Marine Corps Aviation, 1912 to the Present*, 3rd ed. (Baltimore: Nautical and Aviation Press, 1997), 40–52.

48. "Guadalcanal Final Report—Phase IV," 1–4, WWIISG, Box 11, MCUA; "Estimate of the Enemy Situation," report by Buckley, 25 August 1942, WWIISG, Box 7, MCUA; Thomas, recording with G. Smith, 11591A; Griffith, *Battle for Guadalcanal*, 78–88; Vandegrift and Asprey, *Once a Marine*, 133–43; and Hough et al., *Pearl Harbor to Guadalcanal*, 274–93.

49. Vandegrift to Holcomb, 22 August 1942, Holcomb Papers, Box 21, MCUA. For an excerpted version, see Vandegrift and Asprey, *Once a Marine*, 143.

50. See an April 1942 article in the *Infantry Journal* reprinted as Paul W. Thompson, "The Japanese Army: Tailor-Made for the Far East," *MCG* 26 (June 1942): 12–17.

51. Vandegrift to Holcomb, 22 August 1942, cited in Griffith, *Battle for Guadalcanal*, 87. See also Vandegrift and Asprey, *Once a Marine*, 141–42.

52. Vandegrift's quotation in *MCG* (1943), cited in Cameron, *American Samurai*, 105.

53. Ronald H. Spector, "The Pacific War and the Fourth Dimension of Strategy," in *The Pacific War Revisited*, ed. Günter Bischof and Robert L. Dupont (Baton Rouge: Louisiana State University Press, 1997), 41–56; Dower, *War Without Mercy*, 11, 98–99, 116–17, 187–90; Cameron, *American Samurai*, 101–5; and Peter Schrijvers, *The GI War Against Japan: American Soldiers in Asia and the Pacific during World War II* (New York: New York University Press, 2002),178–83.

54. Turner to Vandegrift, 28 September 1942, Vandegrift Papers, Box 9, MCUA; "Guadalcanal Final Report—Phase IV," 8–13, WWIISG, Box 11, MCUA; Vandegrift and Asprey, *Once a Marine*, 154–58; Twining, *No Bended Knee*, 98–102; Hough et al., *Pearl Harbor to Guadalcanal*, 294–309; Frank, *Guadalcanal*, 218–46; Christ, *Battalion of the Damned*, 202–90; William H. Bartsch, "Crucial Battle Ignored," *MCG* 81 (September 1997): 82–89; and Jersey, *Hell's Island*, 219–44.

55. Vandegrift to Holcomb, 15 September 1942, Holcomb Papers, Box 21, MCUA.

56. Holcomb to Lindscott, 12 September 1942, Vandegrift Papers, Box 2, MCUA. .

57. Holcomb, summary notes, p. 3, MCOHC, Box 75, MCUA; Vandegrift to Turner, 24 September 1942, Vandegrift Papers, Box 2, MCUA; Turner to Vandegrift, 23 August 1942, and Turner to Vandegrift, 16 November 1942, both in Tuner Papers, Box 1, NHHC; Dyer, *Amphibians Came to Conquer*, 404, 408–24; Robert B. Carney, "Logistical Planning for War," *NWCR* 1 (October 1948): 3–16; Millett, *In Many a Strife*, 196–97; and Lundstrom, *Black Shoe Carrier Admiral*, 404.

58. Ghormley, "Tide Turns," 58–60, 104–17, 126–30, 134–38, 140–43; Baldwin, transcript, 345, 365; Thomas, transcript, 369–71, 381–82; Pfeiffer, transcript, 210–12; Griffith, *Battle for Guadalcanal*, 127, 162–64; Hough et al., *Pearl Harbor to Guadalcanal*, 302, 310–11; Isely and Crowl, *U.S. Marines and Amphibious War*, 156–58; Millett, *In Many a Strife*, 191; Lundstrom, *Black Shoe Carrier Admiral*, 405, 424–25, 460–64, 468; Buell, *Master of Sea Power*, 208–9; Morison, *Struggle for Guadalcanal*, 178–79; and Merrill B. Twining, "Head for the Hills," *MCG* 71 (August 1987): 48–50.

59. Twining, *No Bended Knee*, 96–97; Pfeiffer, transcript, 201–6, 158; Griffith, *Battle for Guadalcanal*, 113–15, 140–41; Vandegrift and Asprey, *Once a Marine*, 152–55, 173; Millett, *In Many a Strife*, 191, 200; Dyer, *Amphibians Came to Conquer*, 419–21; Dull, *Battle History*, 244–58; Worrall Reed Carter, *Beans, Bullets, and Black Oil: The Story of Fleet Logistics Afloat in the Pacific during World War II* (Washington, D.C.: Department of the Navy, 1953), 42–47; and Spector, *Eagle Against the Sun*, 199–201, 210–13.

60. Baldwin, transcript, 356–57; Davis, *FDR*, 643; Dyer, *Amphibians Came to Conquer*, 412–14; Hayes, *History of the JCS*, 188–91; and Kevin Smith, *Conflict over Convoys: Anglo-American Logistics Diplomacy in the Second World War* (Cambridge: Cambridge University Press, 1996), 83–84.

61. W. D. Puleston to Holcomb, 31 August 1942, Holcomb Papers, Box 5, MCUA.

62. Holcomb to Puleston, 1 September 1942, Holcomb Papers, Box 5, MCUA.

63. Vandegrift to Holcomb, 15 September 1942, Holcomb Papers, Box 21, MCUA; "Estimate of the Situation—Own Force," unsigned report, 10 October 1942, WWIISG, Box 7, MCUA; "Medical Experiences and Problems in the Guadalcanal Campaign—Phase V," unsigned report, n.d., WWIISG, Box 7, MCUA; Hughes, *Old*

Breed, 259–60; Schrijvers, *GI War Against Japan*, 130–34; and Frank, *Guadalcanal*, 256–91.

64. Halsey Report, n.p., COMSOPAC, NHHC; Pfeiffer, transcript, 210–12; Baldwin, transcript, 354, 364–66; Griffith, *Battle for Guadalcanal*, 127, 162–64; William F. Halsey and J. Bryan III, *Admiral Halsey's Story* (New York: Whittlesey House, 1947), 108–13; Hughes, *Old Breed*, 258–62; Miller, *Guadalcanal*, 170–72; Thomas, transcript, 397–98; Twining, *No Bended Knee*, 125–26; Morison, *Struggle for Guadalcanal*, 178–87; Buell, *Master of Sea Power*, 208–9; Vandegrift and Asprey, *Once a Marine*, 181–82; Merillat, *Guadalcanal Remembered*, 191–92; and Ghormley, "Tide Turns," 138–39.

65. Vandegrift and Asprey, *Once a Marine*, 181–82.

66. Twining, *No Bended Knee*, 125: and Merillat, *Guadalcanal Remembered*, 191–92.

67. Griffith, *Battle for Guadalcanal*, 162–64; Larrabee, *Commander in Chief*, 294–96; Millett, *In Many a Strife*, 202–3; and "News and Comment," *Army-Navy Register*, 14 November 1942.

68. Holcomb to Vandegrift, 15 September 1942, Vandegrift Papers, Box 2, MCUA.

69. Ibid., 29 September 1942, Vandegrift Papers, Box 2, MCUA.

70. Vandegrift to Holcomb, 11 August 1942, Holcomb Papers, Box 21, MCUA; Holcomb, summary notes, p. 3, MCOHC, Box 75, MCUA. See also Vandegrift and Asprey, *Once a Marine*, 169–72; Pfeiffer, transcript, 202–4; Isely and Crowl, *U.S. Marines and Amphibious War*, 154–56; Henry, "Historical Review of Command Relationships," 58–59; Hoffman, *From Makin to Bougainville*, 6–9, 24–25; Gordon, "Thomas Holcomb," 253–81; and Millett, *Semper Fidelis*, 370–71.

71. Nimitz to Holcomb, 24 September, and Nimitz to Turner, 23 October 1942, both in Turner Papers, Box 6, NHHC; Austin R. Brunelli, interview by Norman J. Anderson, 1984, transcript, 26–27, MCUA; Holcomb, summary notes, p. 3, MCOHC, Box 75, MCUA; Pfeiffer, transcript, 213; Gordon, "Thomas Holcomb," 271–72; and Jon T. Hoffman, "Alexander A. Vandegrift," in *Commandants of the Marine Corps*, ed. Millett and Shulimson, 289–90.

72. Brunelli, transcript, 26–36, and appendices A1–A3.

73. Pfeiffer, transcript, 213; Brunelli, transcript, 27; and Hoffman, "Alexander A. Vandegrift," 289–90.

74. Brunelli, transcript, 27.

75. Ibid., 27–28.

76. Ibid., 29–30.

77. "News and Comment," *Army-Navy Register*, 14 November 1942; Twining, *No Bended Knee*, 130; Frank, *Guadalcanal*, 344–45; Millett, *In Many a Strife*, 202; Frank, *Guadalcanal*, 344; and Hammel, *Guadalcanal*, 335.

78. Thomas, transcript, 429.

79. Brunelli, transcript, 30; and Merillat, *Guadalcanal Remembered*, 186–87.

80. Vandegrift and Asprey, *Once a Marine*, 182.

81. Holcomb to B. Holcomb, 23 October 1942, Holcomb Papers, Box 5, MCUA.

82. Ibid.

83. Thomas, recording with G. Smith, 11591A. See also Silverthorn, recording with G. Smith, 11589A.

84. Greenstein, *Presidential Difference*, 6.

85. Vandegrift and Asprey, *Once a Marine*, 183. See also Thomas, transcript, 429; Hammel, *Guadalcanal*, 335; and Millett, *In Many a Strife*, 203.

86. Roy, transcript, 29; Thomas, transcript, 523, 547–48; and Hoffman, "Alexander A. Vandegrift," 290–91.

87. Holcomb to Vandegrift, 29 September 1942, Vandegrift Papers, Box 2, MCUA.

88. Silverthorn, recording with G. Smith, 11589A; Williams, transcript, 270–71; Thomas, transcript, 609–10; Dyer, *Amphibians Came to Conquer*, 599–601; Hoffman, "Alexander A. Vandegrift," 290–91; and Millett, *Semper Fidelis*, 372–73, 392–93.

89. Brunelli, transcript, 31; Vandegrift and Asprey, *Once a Marine*, 183–84; and Hammel, *Guadalcanal*, 335–37.

90. Hammel, *Guadalcanal*, 336; and Frank, *Guadalcanal*, 351.

91. Vandegrift and Asprey, *Once a Marine*, 184.

92. Ibid.

93. Vandegrift and Asprey, *Once a Marine*, 183; Hoffman, "Alexander A. Vandegrift," 289–90; and Millett, *Semper Fidelis*, 370–71.

94. Brunelli, transcript, 32–34; Millett, *Semper Fidelis*, 371; Hoffman, "Alexander A. Vandegrift," 290; and John Creswell, *Generals and Admirals: The Story of Amphibious Command* (London: Longmans, Green and Company, 1952), 174–75.

95. Unreferenced quotation by Holcomb, cited in Brunelli, transcript, 34. See also King, *U.S. Navy at War*, 36–37; and Vandegrift and Asprey, *Once a Marine*, 185.

96. Pfeiffer, transcript, 213; Millett, *Semper Fidelis*, 371; and Hoffman, "Alexander A. Vandegrift," 290.

97. Brunelli, transcript, 34. See also Hammel, *Guadalcanal*, 336.

98. Pfeiffer, transcript, 213; and Brunelli, transcript, 34.

99. Brunelli, transcript, 34; and Hammel, *Guadalcanal*, 337.

100. COMSOPAC, Dispatch 321216 to CINCPAC, 3 November 1942, COMINCH 1941–46, Box 2, RG 38, NACP.

101. CINCPAC, Dispatch 030201 to Commander in Chief, U.S. Fleet (hereafter COMINCH), 3 November 1942, COMINCH 1941–46, Box 2, RG 38, NACP.

102. Brunelli, transcript, 35.

103. Pfeiffer, transcript, 213; Vandegrift and Asprey, *Once a Marine*, 185; Millett, *Semper Fidelis*, 371; and Hammel, *Guadalcanal*, 337.

104. *FTP 143a (Fleet Tactical Publication 143a), War Instructions, United States Navy, 1944* (Washington, D.C.: GPO, 1944), http://www.history.navy.mil/library/online/warinst-14.htm; Blandy, "Command Relations in Amphibious Warfare," 573–79; and Henry, "Historical Review of Command Relationships," 65–68, 83–84.

105. *FTP 143a (1944)*, paragraphs 1400–1418.

106. Ibid., paragraph 1400.

107. *FTP 143a (1944)*, paragraphs 1407, 1409, 1418. See also Creswell, *Generals and Admirals*, 175; and U.S. Army's 1944 version of *FM 31-5 Landing Operations on Hostile Shores* (Washington, D.C.: GPO, 1944), 9–11.

108. Vandegrift, memo for King, 25 May 1944, and R. S. Edwards to Marshall, 1 June 1943, both in COMINCH 1941–46, Box 2, NACP; "General Instructions for Amphibious Phase of Galvanic Operation," report by Turner, 24 October 1943, Turner Papers, Box 16, NHHC; Nimitz, report to King, "Operations in the Pacific Ocean Area," Annex E and Annex E: Plate I, 28 February 1944, World War II Command File, Box 236, NHHC; Halsey Report, n.p. (10–12), COMSOPAC, NHHC; David C. Fuquea, "Bougainville: The Amphibious Assault Enters Maturity," *NWCR* 50 (Winter 1997): 104–11; Blandy, "Command Relations in Amphibious Warfare," 576–79; and Henry, "Historical Review of Command Relationships," 60–69.

109. "News and Comment," *Army-Navy Register*, 14 November 1942.

110. Ibid.

111. "Inspection of Marine Corps Activities in the Pacific," report by Rogers, 14 November 1942, WWIIOPMO 1938–45, Box 4, RG 127, NACP; Hough et. al, *Pearl Harbor to Guadalcanal*, 342–43; and Gordon, "Thomas Holcomb," 270–71.

112. Holcomb to George H. Hartlein, 10 November 1942, Holcomb Papers, Box 5, MCUA. See also Harry A. Schmidt to Robert A. Taft, 7 November 1942, Holcomb Papers, Box 5, MCUA.

113. Halsey and Bryan, *Admiral Halsey's Story*, 116–19; Brunelli, transcript, 32–34; Twining, *No Bended Knee*, 138; Merillat, *Guadalcanal Remembered*, 211–13; Griffith, *Battle for Guadalcanal*, 163–64; Vandegrift and Asprey, *Once a Marine*, 184–91; Miller, *Guadalcanal*, 170–83; Hough et al., *Pearl Harbor to Guadalcanal*, 341–43; and Frank, *Guadalcanal*, 351.

114. "[Japanese] Order of Battle, Guadalcanal, Solomons," report by W. D. Long, n.d. [c. October 1942], WWIISG, Box 3, MCUA; "Guadalcanal Final Report—Phase V," report by Vandegrift, 24 May 1943, pp. 1–35, WWIISG, Box 11, MCUA; Frank, *Guadalcanal*, 346–89; Jersey, *Hell's Island*, 264–93; Spector, *Eagle Against the Sun*, 210–13; Kane, *Military Logistics*, 55–56; Dull, *Battle History*, 244–58; Hayashi with Coox, *Kōgun*, 60–66; Iriye, *Power and Culture*, 96–97; Ienaga, *Pacific War*, 144–47; Evans and Peattie, *Kaigun*, 494–501, 509; and Mark P. Parillo, *The Japanese Merchant Marine in World War II* (Annapolis: Naval Institute Press, 1993), 174–76, 211.

115. Vandegrift to Holcomb, 6 December 1942, Holcomb Papers, Box 21, MCUA.

116. "Guadalcanal Final Report—Phase V," 24 May 1943, WWIISG, Box 11, MCUA; Ienaga, *Pacific War,* 101, 143–44, 147; Pfeiffer, transcript, 223–24; Alexander A. Vandegrift, "Amphibious Miracle of Our Time," *MCG* 28 (October 1944): 3–9; Dull, *Battle History*, 269; Frank, *Guadalcanal*, 598–616; and Jersey, *Hell's Island*, 402–4.

117. "Gen. Holcomb States U.S. at Turning Point," *The Chevron* (Marine Base, San Diego), 20 December 1942, Holcomb File, HDRB.

Chapter 6
Preparing the Corps for a New Commandant, July 1942–December 1943

1. Keller E. Rockey to Holcomb, 12 August 1942, Holcomb Papers, Box 10, MCUA; Holcomb to Nimitz, 15 December 1942, and "Proposed Deployment of Marine Corps and Fleet Marine Force Aviation in 1943," report by Silverthorn, 7 March 1943, both in Commander in Chief U.S. Navy War Plans Division, Box 2, RG 38, NACP; Vandegrift to Holcomb, 14 October 1943, Holcomb to Nimitz, 13 August 1943, and Pfeiffer to Charles M. Cook, 13 August 1943, all in Vandegrift Papers, Box 9, MCUA; Pfeiffer, transcript, 241–43; and Vandegrift and Asprey, *Once a Marine*, 238–39.

2. Smith and Finch, *Coral and Brass*, 102–9; Holcomb to Vogel, 19 September 1942, Holcomb Papers, Box 5, MCUA; Cooper, *Fighting General*, 91–97; Rottman, *Marine Corps Order of Battle*, 85–95, 103–4; and Millett, *Semper Fidelis*, 372–77.

3. Vandegrift and Asprey, *Once a Marine*, 218–20; Holcomb to Vogel, 19 September 1942, Holcomb Papers, Box 5, MCUA; Rottman, *Marine Corps Order of Battle*, 66–67, 92–95, 103–11; Cooper, *Fighting General*, 94–95; Millett, *In Many a Strife*, 215–26; and Millett, *Semper Fidelis*, 372–77.

4. Harold O. Deakin, interview by B. Frank, 1968, transcript, pp. 20–21, MCUA; Condit et al., *Brief History of Headquarters Marine Corps*, 14, 18–21; Rottman, *Marine Corps Order of Battle*, 12, 20–21, 42–44; Furer, *Administration of the Navy Department*, 551–53, 586–87; and Millett, *Semper Fidelis*, 376.

5. Bernard C. Nalty, *Inspection in the U.S. Marine Corps, 1775–1957: Historical Background* (Washington, D.C.: Historical Branch, HQMC, 1960), 41–42; Furer, *Administration of the Navy Department*, 554–56; Condit et al., *Brief History of Headquarters Marine Corps*, 14–15, 20–21; and Hoffman, "Alexander A. Vandegrift," 293.

6. Greenstein, *Presidential Difference*, 5; Weber, "Bureaucracy"; and Barnard, *Functions of the Executive*.

7. Statement by Lt. Gen. Thomas Holcomb, 8 May 1943, House Committee on Naval Affairs, *Hearings on H.R. 2583*, 78th Congress, 1st session, 825–26, Holcomb Papers, Box 33, MCUA; Condit et al., *Brief History of Headquarters Marine Corps*, 20–22; Navy Department, *United States Marine Corps*, 54–55; Nalty, *Inspection in the U.S. Marine Corps*, 42–43; Rottman, *Marine Corps Order of Battle*, 43; and Rockey to Holcomb, 12 August 1942, Holcomb Papers, Box 10, MCUA.

8. Vandegrift and Asprey, *Once a Marine*, 87; Thomas, transcript, 525–26, 614; Berkeley, transcript, 192; Letter of Instruction No 421, 14 May 1943, in McGregor and Nalty, *Blacks in the United States Armed Forces*, 431–32; and Holcomb, Letter of Instruction No. 275, 9 December 1942, MCGC 1939–50, Box 296, RG 127, NACP. Box 296, in MCGC 1939–50, contains several dozen wartime Letters of Instruction issued by Holcomb.

9. Berkeley, transcript, 193. For a similar affirmation of Holcomb's system, see Deakin, transcript, 21–22.

10. Holcomb to Meek, 12 August 1943, Holcomb Papers, Box 6, MCUA.

11. Speech by Holcomb, quoted in John G. Norris, "Holcomb, Retiring Leader," unreferenced newspaper clipping, n.d., Holcomb File, HDRB.

12. Quoted in Lindsay, *This High Name*, 54.

13. Quoted in Millett, *Semper Fidelis*, 390–91.

14. "On Broadway," *Detroit Evening News*, 13 December 1942, Holcomb Papers, Box 6, MCUA; Lindsay, *This High Name*, 53–54; Lash, "Media and the Marines," 9–10, 31–32, 47; George Landy to Garrett Graham, 15 July 1943, Woods Papers, Box 6, MCUA; Jason A. Joy to Holcomb, 6 August 1942, and Thomas H. Beck to Holcomb, 12 November 1942, both in Holcomb Papers, Box 5, MCUA.

15. William L. Chenery, 16 December 1943, Holcomb Papers, Box 6, MCUA.

16. Millett, *Semper Fidelis*, 390–91; Lash, "Media and the Marines," 31–32; and Lindsay, *This High Name*, 55.

17. Denig, transcript, 23–24.

18. Denig, transcript, 28–30, 37–38, 58; J. Smith to Jeter A. Isely, 7 April 1950, "Amphibious Doctrine" Subject File, HDRB; "Public Relations Report on Solomons Operation," report by John W. Thomason III, 12 September 1942, WWIISG, Box 1, MCUA; memorandum for all Combat Correspondents, 4 November 1942, Combat Correspondents July 1942–August 1944 Subject File, HDRB; Heinl, *Soldiers of the Sea*, 507; Roeder, *Censored War*, 58; Lash, "Media and the Marines," 74, 99; and Jarvis, *Male Body at War*, 94–95.

19. Lash, "Media and the Marines," 32–33; Lindsay, *This High Name*, 55–56; and Cameron, *American Samurai*, 100–101.

20. Millett, *Semper Fidelis*, 391.

21. Jeanne R. Schomburg to Holcomb, 31 December 1942, Holcomb Papers, Box 6, MCUA.

22. Cameron, *American Samurai*, 100–106, 125–26; Millett, *Semper Fidelis*, 391; Roeder, *Censored War*, 1–2, 11, 25, 34–35; and Lila Armstrong to Vandegrift, Vandegrift Papers, Box 2, MCUA.

23. John G. Norris, "Tough, Quiet: That's the Officer Code of the Marine Corps under Holcomb, Retiring Leader," *Washington Post*, 5 December 1943, Holcomb File, HDRB.

24. Statement by Lt. Gen. Thomas Holcomb on FY 1944 to the Naval Subcommittee of the House Committee on Appropriations, n.d. [c. January–February 1943], Holcomb Papers, Box 33, MCUA; Statements by SecNav and others, 8 February 1943, House Subcommittee of the Committee on Appropriations, *Supplemental Navy Department Appropriation for 1943*, 78th Congress, 1st session, 22–23; SecNav to Speaker of the House of Representative regarding H.R. 2583, 1 May 1943, House Committee on Naval Affairs, 78th Congress, 1st session, 725–27, Holcomb Papers, Box 33, MCUA; Deakin, transcript, 23; Landrum, "Carl Vinson," 100–101; Zehnpfennig, *Melvin J. Maas*, 115; Wayman, *David I. Walsh*, 307–20; Millett, *In Many a Strife*, 229; and Hilty, "Voting Alignments," 310–12.

25. Holcomb to Nimitz, 3 February 1943, Holcomb Papers, Box 6, MCUA.

26. Navy Department, *United States Marine Corps*, 12–13; Millett, *Semper Fidelis*, 360; and Jones, *Gyrene*, 12–18.

27. Officer in Charge of Southern RD to Burke, 18 January 1943, MCGC 1939–50, Box 615, NACP; Navy Department, *United States Marine Corps*, 14–17; Cameron,

American Samurai, 56–62; Millett, *Semper Fidelis*, 373–74; Jarvis, *Male Body at War*, 57–69; and Paul V. McNutt to SecNav, 23 April 1943, MCGC 1939–50, Box 904, NACP.

28. Bureau of Naval Personnel, memorandum to all Appointment Unit Officers and Section Heads, 10 November 1942, MCGC 1939–50, Box 619, NACP.

29. Webb C. Hayes to Chief of Naval Personnel, 11 May 1943, and Charles R. Rowan, Camp Lejeune General Order Number 61–Venereal Disease Control, 28 June 1943, both in MCGC 1939–50, Box 917, NACP; memorandum for Army Assistant Chief of Staff G-1, 21 May 1945, and Wethered Woodworth to Schmidt, 8 June 1943, both in MCGC 1939–50, Box 904, NACP; MCGC 1939–50, Box 917, NACP; and Wayne McMillen to the Surgeon General of the U.S. Navy, 26 March 1942, and L. Sheldon Jr. to McMillen, 1 June 1942, both in BMGC 1941–46, Box 165, Entry 15B, RG 52, NACP.

30. Hayes to Chief of Naval Personnel, 11 May 1943, MCGC 1939–50, Box 917, NACP; Cardozier, *Mobilization of the United States*, 298–302; and Jarvis, *Male Body at War*, 78–84.

31. Holcomb to the Chief of the Bureau of Naval Personnel, 9 June 1943, MCGC 1939–50, Box 904, NACP.

32. Ibid.

33. Ibid.

34. Holcomb to all Officers in Charge of all Induction and Recruitment Districts, 12 June 1943, MCGC 1939–50, Box 904, NACP.

35. Navy Department, *United States Marine Corps*, 14–16; Furer, *Administration of the Navy Department*, 566–67; Holcomb to SecNav, 2 February 1943, Woodworth to Schmidt, 8 June 1943, memorandum for Army Assistant Chief of Staff G-1, 21 May 1943, and Hayes to Chief of Naval Personnel, 11 May 1943, all in MCGC 1939–50, Box 904, NACP.

36. Burke to Officer in Charge of the Eastern RD, 23 February 1943, MCGC 1939–50, Box 613, NACP; Cameron, *American Samurai*, 61; Navy Department, *United States Marine Corps*, 15; Furer, *Administration of the Navy Department*, 566–67; Millett, *Semper Fidelis*, 372–74; and Cardozier, *Mobilization of the United States*, 198.

37. Burke to Officer in Charge of the Eastern RD, 23 February 1943, MCGC 1939–50, Box 613, NACP; Holcomb to all Officers in Charge of all Induction and Recruitment Districts, 12 June 1943, MCGC 1939–50, Box 904, NACP; Cameron, *American Samurai*, 61; Furer, *Administration of the Navy Department*, 566–68; Millett, *Semper Fidelis*, 374; and Millett, *In Many a Strife*, 234.

38. Ferguson Questionnaire, 7thDBQ, WWIIC, Box 1, MCUA.

39. Mary V. Stremlow, *Free a Marine to Fight: Women Marines in World War II* (Washington, D.C.: Marine Corps Historical Center, 1994), 1–2; Holm, *Women in the Military*, 21–25; Millett, *Semper Fidelis*, 374–75; and Cardozier, *Mobilization of the United States*, 166–80.

40. Zehnpfennig, *Melvin J. Maas*, 114–15.

41. Sherman, "Margaret Chase Smith," 130; and Millett, *Semper Fidelis*, 374–75.

42. Holcomb and R. T. McIntire to all Commanding Officers, Marine Corps, and all Navy Hospitals, 14 May 1943, MCGC 1939–50, Box 619, NACP; Stremlow, *Free a Marine to Fight*, 1–2; and Gordon, "Thomas Holcomb, 273–74.

43. CMC to SecNav via Judge Advocate General of the Navy (hereafter JAG) and CNO-COMINCH, 12 October 1942, File 18E, Holcomb Papers, Box 11, MCUA.

44. JAG to SecNav via CNO-COMINCH, 26 October 1942, and CNO-COMINCH to SecNav (with initialed approval by F. Roosevelt on 7 November 1942), 30 October 1942, File 18E, Holcomb Papers, Box 11, MCUA; and Pat Meid, *Marine Corps Women's Reserve in World War II* (Washington, D.C.: Historical Branch, HQMC, 1964), 4–5.

45. Holcomb interview, *Life*, 27 March 1944, cited in Stremlow, *Free a Marine to Fight*, 2. See also Holcomb to Bertha McCaulley Foster, 16 April 1943, Holcomb Papers, Box 6, MCUA.

46. Millett, *Semper Fidelis*, 374–75.

47. Edna Hill Schultz, "'Free a Marine to Fight,'" *Naval History* (February 2003): 46; "Women Marines: News Clippings—WWII" Subject File, HDRB; and Office of War Information *Women in the War . . . for the Final Push to Victory* (Washington, D.C: GPO, 1944), 1–2, 9.

48. "Marine Corps Women's Reserve Information Concerning the Aptitude Test," n.d. [c. 1944], Folder 1, Gladys O'Laughlin Papers, World War II Participants and Contemporaries, DDEL.

49. Holcomb to Price, 27 May 1943, Holcomb Papers, Box 6, MCUA. See also Meid, *Marine Corps Women's Reserve*, 8–9.

50. Office of War Information, *Women in the War*, 3–5; Bérubé, *Coming Out under Fire*, 28–33, 42–43, 142, 147, 258–59; and Leisa D. Meyer, *Creating G. I. Jane: Sexuality and Power in the Women's Army Corps in World War II* (New York: Columbia University Press, 1996), 33–51, 107–20, 148–79.

51. Medical Offices in Command at Parris Island to Senior Medical Officer of MCWR Schools at Camp Lejeune, 4 October 1943, and George Donabedian to Commandant of MCWR Schools, 18 October 1943, both in MCGC 1939–50, Box 594, NACP; "Class VI (b) Rejects February–December 1943," report by Marine Corps Procurement District, 6 December 1943, MCGC 1939–50, Box 619, NACP.

52. Holcomb, Letter of Instruction No. 382, 27 March 1942, Holcomb, Letter of Instruction No. 426, 18 May 1943, Director of Marine Corps Reserve to Officer in Charge of Marine Corps Officer Procurement in Seattle, Washington, 4 April 1943, and Ruth Cheney Streeter to all Officers in the WMCR, 17 July 1943, all in MCGC 1939–50, Box 594, NACP; MCWR, "1st Anniversary—February 13, 1944, 'Thumbnail' History," n.d. [c. February 1944], "Women Marines: News Clippings—WWII," HDRB; "Research Material USMCWR—New River," unsigned report, n.d. [c. 1944], "Women Marines: Specialist Training," HDRB; Stremlow, *Free a Marine to Fight*, 9–14; Meid, *Marine Corps Women's Reserve*, 12–21, 26–52; Millett, *Semper Fidelis*, 374–75; and Cardozier, *Mobilization of the United States*, 175–76.

53. Gordon, "Thomas Holcomb," 274; and Janowitz, *Professional Soldier*, 100.

54. CMC, 20 March 1943, in McGregor and Nalty, *Blacks in the United States Armed Forces*, 423–25; Price to Rockey, 24 April 1943, cited in MacGregor, *Integration of*

*the Armed Forces,*110–11; "The Negro Marine, 1942–1946," report by T. N. Greene, n.d., "Black Marines in World War II" Subject File, HDRB; Gordon, "Thomas Holcomb," 274–75; Millett, *Semper Fidelis,* 375–76; and Millett, *In Many a Strife,* 236.

55. Walter Pritchard, "Paving the Way: First Black Marines Recall Battle Against Racism," *Marine Corps Scholarship Foundation, Inc., Newsletter,* n.d., "Black Marines History" Subject File, HDRB; Nalty, *Strength for the Fight,* 198–99; McGregor, *Integration of the Armed Forces,* 103–7; Gordon, "Thomas Holcomb," 374–75; Roeder, *Censored War,* 44–46; Shaw and Donnelly, *Blacks in the Marine Corps,* 2–8, 15–46; Edwin H. Simmons, "Montford Point Marines," *Fortitudine* (Summer 1991): 3–7; John W. Davis, "The Negro in the United States Navy, Marine Corps, and Coast Guard," *Journal of Negro Education* 12 (Summer 1943): 347–48; Philip McGuire, "Desegregation of the Armed Forces: Black Leadership, Protest and World War II," *Journal of Negro History* 68 (Spring 1983): 152–55; Nalty, *Right to Fight,* 3–8, 28; Nalty, *Strength for the Fight,* 199–202; and Melson, *Condition Red,* 21–24, 52.

56. Memorandum for the Director of Plans and Policies, 26 December 1942, in McGregor and Nalty, *Blacks in the United States Armed Forces,* 421–22.

57. Ibid.

58. Holcomb to Distribution List, 20 March 1943, in McGregor and Nalty, *Blacks in the United States Armed Forces,* 423–26; and Holcomb, Letter of Instruction No. 421, 14 May 1943, in McGregor and Nalty, *Blacks in the United States Armed Forces,* 431–33.

59. Holcomb to SecNav, 2 February 1943, Burke to Officer in Charge of the Eastern RD, 23 February 1943, Fred H. Bock, memorandum for R. A. Robinson, 21 May 1943, Holcomb to Officer in Charge Western Procurement Division, 31 December 1943, Woodworth to the Officers in Charge of all RD, 2 February 1943, and Ray A. Robinson, memorandum for the Division of Recruiting, 6 January 1942, all in MCGC 1939–50, Box 613, NACP; McGregor, *Integration of the Armed Forces,*103–12; Shaw and Donnelly, *Blacks in the Marine Corps,* 15–44; and Kennedy, *Freedom from Fear,* 769–76, 817, 857–58.

60. Samuel A. Wood Jr. to Holcomb, 14 August 1943, Holcomb Papers, Box 6, MCUA.

61. Holcomb to Price, 27 May 1943, Holcomb Papers, Box 6, MCUA.

62. Jarvis, *Male Body at War,* 74–78, 84–85; and Cameron, *American Samurai,* 79–80.

63. Cardozier, *Mobilization of the United States,* 79.

64. John E. Sholley to F. Roosevelt, 16 October 1942, MCGC 1939–50, Box 619, NACP.

65. Burke to Sholley, 24 October 1942, MCGC 1939–50, Box 619, NACP.

66. "Report for Physical Examination," MCGC 1939–50, Box 906, RG 127, NACP; and Loeser, "Sexual Psychopath," 239.

67. Bérubé, *Coming Out under Fire,* 14–17; Howard N. Montgomery to Holcomb, 18 November 1943, and Murray Banks to Surgeon General of the U.S. Navy, June 1944, both in BMGC 1941–46, Box 165, Entry 15B, RG 52, NACP; Loeser, "Sexual Psychopath," 242–43; and Jarvis, *Male Body at War,* 74–78, 84–85.

68. CG of I Marine Amphibious Corps, 1 March 1943, forwarding SecNav to all Ships and Stations, 1 January 1943, Fleet Marine Force Pacific General Correspondence

(hereafter FMFPacGC) 1944–1945, Box 43, RG 127, NACP; Estelle Friedman, "'Uncontrolled Desires': The Response to the Sexual Psychopath, 1920–1960," *Journal of American History* 74 (June 1987): 84–97; Bérubé, *Coming Out under Fire*, 154–69; Jarvis, *Male Body at War*, 73–75; Bailey, *Sex in the Heartland*, 54–61; David J. Ulbrich, "Managing Marine Mobilization: Thomas Holcomb and the U.S. Marine Corps, 1936–1943" (Ph.D. diss., Temple University, 2007), 388–91; Holcomb to Bureau of Medicine and Surgery, and 10 November 1943, and Montgomery to Holcomb, 18 November 1943, both in BMGC 1941–46, Box 165, Entry 15B, RG 52, NACP; and District Medical Officer to District Medical Officers of 11th, 12th, and 13th Naval Districts, 22 December 1943, MCGC 1939–50, Box 917, NACP.

69. Bailey, *Sex in the Heartland*, 54–55.

70. Friedman, "'Uncontrolled Desires,'" 100, 103–4; Bailey, *Sex in the Heartland*, 51–54; Chief of Neuropsychiatric Service to Chief of Bureau of Naval Personnel, 13 April 1944, BMGC 1941–46, Box 165, Entry 15B, RG 52, NACP; and Vandegrift to all Commanding Officers, 31 October 1944, FMFPacGC 1944–45, Box 43, NACP.

71. Holcomb to Virginia and Charles Willard, 11 January 1943, Holcomb Papers, Box 6, MCUA.

72. Baer, *One Hundred Years of Sea Power*, 225–26, 239.

73. Hayes, *History of the JCS*, 251–71, 278–81; James, "American and Japanese Strategies," 713–30; King, *U.S. Navy at War*, 39, 63–70; King and Whitehall, *Fleet Admiral King*, 414–27; Buell, *Master of Sea Power*, 247–49; Samuel Eliot Morison, *History of the United States Naval Operations in World War II*, vol. 7, *Aleutians, Gilberts and Marshalls, June 1942–April 1944* (Boston: Little, Brown, 1951), 102–8; and Morton, *Strategy and Command*, 376–86.

74. King, *Fleet Admiral King*, 428–44; Marshall to King, 29 July 1943, in *The Papers of George Catlett Marshall*, vol. 4, *"Aggressive and Determined Leadership,"* ed. Larry I. Bland and Sharon R. Stevens (Baltimore: Johns Hopkins University Press, 1996), 73–74; Vandegrift and Asprey, *Once a Marine*, 214–21; Vandegrift to H. Smith, 22 October 1943, Vandegrift Papers, Box 9, MCUA; Hayes, *History of the JCS*, 386–409; and Millett, *Semper Fidelis*, 372, 377–80.

75. Millett, *Semper Fidelis*, 377–80; Charles D. Melson, *Up the Slot: Marines in the Central Solomons* (Washington, D.C.: History and Museums Division, HQMC, 1993), 1–35; and Shaw and Kane, *Isolation of Rabaul*, 55–118.

76. Vandegrift and Asprey, *Once a Marine*, 226–29; Hoffman, "Alexander A. Vandegrift," 292–93; and Millett, *Semper Fidelis*, 373.

77. Vandegrift and Asprey, *Once a Marine*, 230. For the entire report, see Vandegrift to Holcomb, 4 November 1943, Vandegrift Papers, Box 9, MCUA.

78. Fuquea, "Bougainville," 104–21; Harry A. Gailey, *Bougainville, 1943–1945: The Forgotten Campaign* (Lexington: University Press of Kentucky, 1991), 93–212; John C. Chapin Jr., *Top of the Ladder: Marine Operations in the Northern Solomons* (Washington, D.C.: History and Museums Division, HQMC, 1993), 1–31; Pfeiffer, transcript, 242–45; Millett, *Semper Fidelis*, 381–87; Hoffman, "Alexander A. Vandegrift," 294; Melson, *Up the Slot*, 36; and Shaw and Kane, *Isolation of Rabaul*, 161–63.

79. "Estimate of the Situation—Gilberts, 5 October 1943, and Supplementary Estimate of the Situation, 25 October 1943," report by Merritt A. Edson, World War II–Gilberts-Tarawa Collection, Box 2, MCUA; Pfeiffer, transcript, 245–46; Isely and Crowl, *U.S. Marines and Amphibious War*, 205–17; Joseph H. Alexander, *Utmost Savagery: The Three Days of Tarawa* (Annapolis: Naval Institute Press, 1995), xvii, 13–22; Smith and Finch, *Coral and Brass*, 109–21; Millett, *Semper Fidelis*, 387–90, 393–95; Shaw et al., *Central Pacific Drive*, 3–13, 35–53; Baer, *One Hundred Years of Sea Power*, 237–43; and Theodore L Gatchel, *At the Water's Edge: Defending Against Modern Amphibious Assault* (Annapolis: Naval Institute Press, 1996), 119–24.

80. Turner to King, 4 December 1942, World War II–Gilberts-Tarawa Collection, Box 4, MCUA; Shaw et al., *Central Pacific Drive*, 55–79; Alexander, *Utmost Savagery*, 79–84, 106–59; Isely and Crowl, *The U.S. Marines and Amphibious War*, 235–46; Rottman, *Marine Corps Order of Battle*, 310–15; and Gatchel, *At the Water's Edge*, 125–28.

81. Quoted in Joseph H. Alexander, *Across the Reef: The Marine Assault on Tarawa* (Washington, D.C.: Marine Corps Historical Center, 1993), 26.

82. Shaw et al., *Central Pacific Drive*, 79–85; Alexander, *Utmost Savagery*, 170–93; and Gatchel, *At the Water's Edge*, 128–29.

83. David Shoup, radio message to J. Smith, service number 198, 2nd Marine Division D-3 Journal, cited in Shaw et al., *Central Pacific Drive*, 79.

84. Holcomb to J. Smith, 25 November 1943, Holcomb Papers, Box 7, MCUA.

85. Alexander, *Across the Reef*, 46–50; Isely and Crowl, *U.S. Marines and Amphibious War*, 251; Millett, *In Many a Strife*, 226; and Vandegrift and Asprey, *Once a Marine*, 232–36.

86. Holcomb to Vandegrift, 14 July 1943, Vandegrift Papers, Box 9, MCUA; Russell to Holcomb, 18 July 1943, Holcomb Papers, Box 6, MCUA; Millett, *Semper Fidelis*, 390; Heinl, *Soldiers of the Sea*, 387–88; and Millett, *In Many a Strife*, 227–29.

87. Holcomb to Meek, 5 April 1943, Holcomb to L. B. Browne, 21 June 1943, Holcomb to H. Smith, 34 June 1943, and Holcomb to Laura Clover, 26 July 1943, all in Holcomb Papers, Box 6, MCUA.

88. Holcomb to Forrestal, 28 June 1943, Holcomb Papers, Box 6, MCUA.

89. Holcomb to Clifton B. Cates, 13 August 1943, and Holcomb to R. P. Williams, 20 September 1943, both in Holcomb Papers, Box 6, MCUA; Holcomb to Vandegrift, 14 July 1943, Vandegrift Papers, Box 9, MCUA; and Thomas, transcript, 497–99.

90. Merwin H. Silverthorn, interview by B. Frank, 1969, transcript, 244; Vandegrift and Asprey, *Once a Marine*, 218; Hoffman, "Alexander A. Vandegrift," 294–95; Holcomb to Vandegrift, 6 April 1943, Vandegrift to Holcomb, 14 April 1943, Holcomb to Vandegrift, 14 July 1943, and Holcomb to Vandegrift, 23 November 1943, all in Vandegrift Papers, Box 9, MCUA; and Holcomb to Vandegrift, 19 November 1943, Holcomb Papers, Box 7, MCUA.

91. Thomas, transcript, 609.

92. Memorandum for the Naval Aide to the President, 16 September 1943, File 18E, Holcomb Papers, Box 11, MCUA; Thomas, transcript, 608–10; Roy, transcript, 28–30; Williams, transcript, 270–71; and Gordon, "Thomas Holcomb," 276–77.

93. Russell, "Final Report," 17.

94. Holcomb to Knox, 30 November 1943, Holcomb Papers, Box 7, MCUA; Knox to F. Roosevelt, 30 November 1943, File 18E, Holcomb Papers, Box 1, MCUA; Knox to Holcomb, 1 December 1943, and Holcomb to Knox, 2 December 1943, both in Holcomb Papers, Box 7, MCUA.

95. Press release, 31 December 1943, Holcomb File, HDRB.

96. King, *U.S. Navy at War*, 25.

97. Vandegrift and Asprey, *Once a Marine*, 232–43; Hoffman, "Alexander A. Vandegrift," 295–304; and Millett, *In Many a Strife*, 223–27.

98. Vandegrift and Asprey, *Once a Marine*, 237.

CHAPTER 7

From Marine Corps to Diplomatic Corps to Retirement

1. Gibson B. Smith, "The Flying Diplomat: General Thomas Holcomb in South Africa," *Shipmate* 41 (November 1978): 26; Gordon, "Thomas Holcomb," 277; "Gen. Holcomb, USMC," 14 July 1964, Holcomb File, HDRB; "Joint Civic, Service, and Veteran Dinner honoring General Holcomb, DuPont Hotel, Wilmington, Delaware, February 17, 1944," Holcomb File, HDRB; and Paul R. Rinard to Holcomb 14 February 1944, Holcomb Papers, Box 7, MCUA.

2. Thomas, recording with G. Smith, 11591A; Eliot to Holcomb, 21 March 1944, Holcomb Papers, Box 7, MCUA; "General Thomas Holcomb and American Relations with South Africa," unpublished draft article by Gibson B. Smith, n.d. [c. 1980], pp. 2–3, Holcomb Papers, Box 31, MCUA (hereafter "Holcomb and American Relations with South Africa"); and Thomas Borstelmann, *Apartheid's Reluctant Uncle: The United States and Southern Africa in the Early Cold War* (New York: Oxford University Press, 1993), 50–52.

3. "Holcomb and American Relations with South Africa," 1, 3–4, 10, Holcomb Papers, Box 32, MCUA; Borstelmann, *Apartheid's Reluctant Uncle*, 89–91; and T. R. H. Davenport and Christopher Saunders, *South Africa: A Modern History*, 5th ed. (New York: St. Martin's Press, 2000), 344–79.

4. Cordell Hull to Holcomb, 14 April 1944, quoted in "Holcomb and American Relations with South Africa," 3.

5. The exact explanations to Holcomb in 1944 are not available, but for a similar list, see G. Rowland Shaw to Julia St. John, 28 August 1941, quoted in "Holcomb and American Relations with South Africa," 3.

6. J. Roosevelt to Holcomb, 29 March 1944, and Vandegrift to Holcomb, n.d., Holcomb Papers, Box 7, MCUA; and Smith, "Flying Diplomat," 27.

7. F. Holcomb, recording, sequence 1, tape 4.

8. Holcomb II, transcript, 6; "Holcomb and American Relations with South Africa," 3; Smith, "Flying Diplomat," 27; and Gordon, "Thomas Holcomb," 275.

9. "Holcomb and American Relations with South Africa," 5; Smith, "Flying Diplomat," 27–28; and "Presentation of Credentials by General Thomas Holcomb, American Minister to South Africa," 14 June 1944, Holcomb Papers, Box 13, MCUA.

10. "Holcomb and American Relations with South Africa," 3; and Smith, "Flying Diplomat," 27.

11. Smith, "Flying Diplomat," 27.

12. "South Africa—Chronology," Holcomb Papers, Box 31, MCUA; "Holcomb and American Relations with South Africa," 4–5; and Smith, "Flying Diplomat," 27.

13. F. Holcomb, recording, sequence 1, side 4.

14. "Holcomb and American Relations with South Africa," 10–12; and Smith, "Flying Diplomat," 29.

15. Holcomb to the Secretary of State (hereafter SecState), 23 February 1946, quoted in Borstelmann, *Apartheid's Reluctant Uncle*, 79.

16. "Holcomb and American Relations with South Africa," 10–17; and Borstelmann, *Apartheid's Reluctant Uncle*, 79–80.

17. "Holcomb and American Relations with South Africa," 17; and Borstelmann, *Apartheid's Reluctant Uncle*, 87–89.

18. Davenport and Saunders, *South Africa*, 270–73, 306–11, 324–55; "Holcomb and American Relations with South Africa," 23–26; Borstelmann, *Apartheid's Reluctant Uncle*, 87–88, 199–201; and Anthony W. Marx, "Race-Making and the Nation-State," *World Politics* 48 (January 1996): 180–82, 188–91, 196–98.

19. For examples, see Holcomb to SecState, 22 March 1946, and Holcomb to SecState, 15 April 1946, both quoted in Borstelmann, *Apartheid's Reluctant Uncle*, 71.

20. Holcomb to SecState, 21 May 1946, quoted in Borstelmann, *Apartheid's Reluctant Uncle*, 70–71.

21. Dan O'Meara, "The 1946 African Mine Workers' Strike and the Political Economy of South Africa," *Journal of Commonwealth and Comparative Politics* 13 (July 1975): 147–58; Davenport and Saunders, *South Africa*, 356–60; and Borstelmann, *Apartheid's Reluctant Uncle*, 71–72.

22. Holcomb to SecState, 22 November 1946, Holcomb Papers, Box 17, MCUA.

23. Ibid.

24. Comments on "Current U.S. Policy toward the Union of South Africa," enclosed in Holcomb to SecState, 8 October 1946, Holcomb Papers, Box 17, MCUA.

25. Holcomb to SecState, 19 February 1947, and memo for Undersecretary of State, 11 June 1947, both in Holcomb Papers, Box 14, MCUA.

26. Memo on the United States Position on Size and Composition of the Commission on Human Rights, 1 April 1946, Holcomb Papers, Box 14, MCUA.

27. Memo for Robert A. Lovett, 1 July 1947, and American Consulate General in South Africa to SecState, 26 September 1947, both in Holcomb Papers, Box 14, MCUA.

28. Holcomb to SecState, 27 January 1948, quoted in Borstelmann, *Apartheid's Reluctant Uncle*, 89.

29. Borstelmann, *Apartheid's Reluctant Uncle*, 35–37, 89; George M. Frederickson, *White Supremacy: A Comparative Study in American and South African History* (New York: Oxford University Press, 1981), 221–83; and Marx, "Race-Making and the Nation-State," 180–208.

30. Comments on "Policy and Information Statement on South Africa," enclosed in Dale Maher to SecState, 19 June 1947, quoted in "Holcomb and American Relations with South Africa," 27.

31. "Holcomb and American Relations with South Africa," 28.

32. Marx, "Race-Making and the Nation-State," 189–94; Borstelmann, *Apartheid's Reluctant Uncle*, 35–36; and "Holcomb and American Relations with South Africa," 24.

33. Davenport and Saunders, *South Africa*, 335–36, 342–49; and Borstelmann, *Apartheid's Reluctant Uncle*, 33–37, 68, 88–90.

34. "Statement on the Nationalist Party's 'Apartheid' Policy, 29 March 1949, quoted in Borstelmann, *Apartheid's Reluctant Uncle*, 87. See also Deborah Posel, "The Meaning of Apartheid before 1948: Conflicting Interests and Forces with the Afrikaner Nationalist Alliance," *Journal of Southern African Studies* 14 (October 1987): 125–26.

35. Comments on "Current U.S. Policy toward the Union of South Africa," enclosed in Holcomb to SecState, 8 October 1946, Holcomb Papers, Box 17, MCUA.

36. Davenport and Saunders, *South Africa*, 369–74, Borstelmann, *Apartheid's Reluctant Uncle*, 71–74, 86–87; and Smith, "Flying Diplomat," 28–29.

37. Robert K. Carr to Marshall, 5 June 1947, and Memo for SecState, 15 July 1947, both in Holcomb Papers, Box17, MCUA; Borstelmann, *Apartheid's Reluctant Uncle*, 83–84, 117–23, 199–201; "Holcomb and American Relations with South Africa," 23; and Frederickson, *White Supremacy*, 239–82.

38. Comments on "Current U.S. Policy toward the Union of South Africa," enclosed in Holcomb to SecState, 8 October 1946, Holcomb Papers, Box 17, MCUA.

39. Thomas J. Noer, "Truman, Eisenhower, and South Africa: The 'Middle Road' and Apartheid," *Journal of Ethnic Studies* 11 (Spring 1983): 75–104; Davenport and Saunders, *South Africa*, 378–92, 520–21; Hunt, *Ideology*, 165, 177; Borstelmann, *Apartheid's Reluctant Uncle*, 83–89, 199–202; Thomas Borstelmann, *The Cold War and the Color Line: American Race Relations in the Global Arena* (Cambridge, Mass.: Harvard University Press, 2001), 48–53, 72–78; and H. W. Brands, *The Devil We Knew: Americans and the Cold War* (New York: Oxford University Press, 1993), 3–4, 132–33, 145.

40. Holcomb II, transcript, 6; and F. Holcomb, recording, tape 2, sequence 3.

41. S. Holcomb et al., recording.

42. "Gen. Holcomb, USMC," HDRB; and S. Holcomb et al., recording.

43. Holcomb Diary 1962–1963, 16 May 1962, 22 May 1962, 8 July 1962, 9 July 1962, 14 July 1962, 15 July 1962, 23 July 1962, 28 July 1962, 6 August 1962, 9 August 1962, and 14 August 1962, Holcomb Papers, Box 23, MCUA. See also "Wife of Former Commandant Dies," *Washington Post*, 15 August 1962.

44. Gordon, "Thomas Holcomb," 278.

45. Thomas Holcomb obituary, *Evening Star* (Washington, D.C.), 25 May 1965.

46. Commandant of the Marine Corps, Telegram to all Marines, 25 May 1965, Holcomb File, HDRB.

47. Gordon, "Thomas Holcomb," 278.

48. Creswell, *Generals and Admirals*, 146–49; Kenneth J. Clifford, *Amphibious Warfare Development in Britain and America from 1920 to 1940* (Laurens, N.Y.: Edgewood, 1983), 50–56; and, most significantly, Donald F. Bittner, "Britannia's Sheathed Sword: The Royal Marines and Amphibious Warfare in the Interwar Years— A Passive Response," *JMH* 55 (July 1991): 345–64.

49. See section on "Holcomb's Impact on Amphibious Preparations and Innovations" in Chapter 3.

50. See section on "Holcomb's Ground-Breaking Tour of Guadalcanal" in Chapter 5.

51. U.S. Marine Corps Combat Development Command, "Evolving the MAGTF for the 21st Century," 20 March 2009, "Marine Air Ground Task Force" Subject File, HDRB.

52. Ibid. See also Millett, *Semper Fidelis*, 547–48, 636–52; Michael R. Kennedy, "MAGTF Area of Operation: Turf War or Doctrinal Necessity," *Joint Force Quarterly* 32 (Autumn 2002): 93–97; and Fleet Marine Force Reference Publication 2-12, *Marine Air-Ground, Task Force: A Global Capability* (1991), 2–3, 14–23.

53. See section on "Racial Restriction in the Marine Corps" in Chapter 4; and "Holcomb's Exclusionary Personnel Policies" in Chapter 6.

54. Holcomb to SecState, 21 May 1946, quoted in Borstelmann, *Apartheid's Reluctant Uncle*, 70–71.

55. F. Roosevelt, Distinguished Service Medal Citation, 22 February 1944, Holcomb File, HDRB. For similar pronouncements, see also Furer, *Administration of the Navy Department*, 594–95; and F. Holcomb, recording, tape 1, sequence 2.

BIBLIOGRAPHY

MANUSCRIPTS

ARMY HERITAGE AND EDUCATION CENTER, CARLISLE BARRACKS, PENNSYLVANIA
Army War College Files

DWIGHT D. EISENHOWER LIBRARY AND ARCHIVES, ABILENE, KANSAS
Henry S. Aurand Personal Papers Collection
Vernon E. Megee Personal Papers Collection
World War II Participants and Contemporaries Collection
 – Gladys O'Laughlin Papers

MARINE CORPS UNIVERSITY, HISTORY DIVISION, QUANTICO, VIRGINIA
Reference Branch, Biographical Files
 – Thomas Holcomb
 – Melvin J. Maas
Reference Branch, Subject Files
 – Amphibious Doctrine
 – Black Marines in History
 – Black Marines in World War II
 – Combat Correspondents, July 1942–August 1944
 – Headquarters Marine Corps: Historical Background
 – Installations and Logistics
 – Marine Air Ground Task Force
 – Public Relations—Navy
 – Women Marines: News Clippings—World War II

MARINE CORPS UNIVERSITY, ARCHIVES BRANCH, GRAY RESEARCH CENTER,
QUANTICO, VIRGINIA
Annual Reports of the Major General Commandant of the United States Marine
Corps to the Secretary of the Navy, 1935–1945
History Amphibious File
Marine Corps Administrative History
Oral History Collection
 – Thomas Holcomb Interview Summary Notes
 – Harold R. Stark Interview Summary Notes
Oral History Interview Transcriptions
 – Thomas E. Bourke
 – Austin R. Brunelli
 – Pedro del Valle

– Harold O. Deakin
– Robert L. Denig Sr.
– James P. S. Devereux
– Leo D. Hermle
– Thomas Holcomb II
– Victor H. Krulak
– Francis B. Loomis Jr.
– Omar T. Pfeiffer
– William Riley
– William W. Rogers
– James Roosevelt
– Frederick Roy
– Lemuel C. Shepherd Jr.
– Merwin H. Silverthorn
– Julian C. Smith
– Samuel G. Taxis
– Gerald C. Thomas
– William J. Van Ryzin
– Robert Hugh Williams
– William A. Worton

Oral History Interview Audio or Video Recordings
– Franklin Holcomb
– Suzanne Holcomb, Clover Holcomb Burgess, and Sarah Holcomb
– Charlotte Keyser
– James Roosevelt
– Merwin H. Silverthorn
– Gerald C. Thomas

Personal Papers Collections
– Ben H. Fuller Papers
– William P. T. Hill Papers
– Thomas Holcomb Papers
– John A. Lejeune Papers
– Louis M. Little Papers
– John H. Russell Papers
– Holland M. Smith Papers
– Julian C. Smith Papers
– Oliver P. Smith Papers
– Alexander A. Vandegrift Papers
– Clayton B. Vogel Papers
– Louis E. Woods Papers

World War II Collection
– 7th Defense Battalion Questionnaire
– Gilberts—Tarawa
– Solomons—Guadalcanal

MINNESOTA HISTORY SOCIETY, MINNEAPOLIS, MINNESOTA
Papers of the Committee to Defend America by Aiding the Allies
Melvin J. Maas Personal Papers Collection

NATIONAL ARCHIVES AND RECORDS ADMINISTRATION, COLLEGE PARK, MARYLAND

Microfilm Collection
- Annual Reports of Fleets and Task Forces of the U.S. Navy Joint Board Records

Record Group 38, Records of the Office of the Chief of Naval Operations
- Commander in Chief U.S. Fleet, Plans Division Pacific Section, Records Regarding World War II Amphibious Operations, 1941–1946
- Formerly Security Declassified Correspondence of the Director
- Office of Naval Intelligence
- Strategic Plans Division War Plans Division, 1912–1946
- Strategic Plans War Plans Division
- U.S. Navy and Related Operational, Tactical, and Industrial Publications, 1918–1970

Record Group 52, Records of the Bureau of Medicine of the United States Navy
- Bureau of Medicine General Correspondence, 1941–1946

Record Group 80, General Records of the United States Navy
- General Board Subject File, 1900–1947
- General Correspondence of Chief of Naval Operations and the Secretary of the Navy, 1900–1947
- Records of the Logistics Plans Division, Office of the Chief of Naval Operations, 1941–1946
- Strategic and Operational Planning Documents, 1939–1950

Record Group 127, Records of the United States Marine Corps
- Adjutant and Inspector's Office General Correspondence, 1798–1949
- Division of Plans and Policies General Correspondence, 1921–1943
- Division of Plans and Policies War Plans Section General Correspondence, 1926–1942
- Division of Plans and Policies War Plans Section, 1915–1946
- Fleet Marine Force General Correspondence, 1944–1945
- Headquarters Separate Correspondence, 1930–1971
- Records Regarding Plans, Policies, Aviation, and Amphibious Operations, 1942–1972
- Records Regarding World War II Organizations, Plans, and Military Operations, 1938–1945
- U.S. Marine Corps General Correspondence, 1939–1950
- War Plans and Related Material, 1931–1944

NATIONAL ARCHIVES AND RECORDS ADMINISTRATION, WASHINGTON, D.C.

Record Group 127, Records of the United States Marine Corps
- 2nd Brigade Fleet Marine Force, Geographic File, Entry 238A
- Marine Corps Budget Estimates for Fiscal Years 1936–1943, Entry 248
- Personnel Department General Correspondence, 1933–1938
- U.S. Marine Corps General Correspondence, 1933–1938
- War Plans and Related Materials, 1931–1944, Entry 246

NAVAL HISTORY AND HERITAGE COMMAND, WASHINGTON, D.C.

Papers of Commander, South Pacific Area and South Pacific Forces
Richmond K. Turner Personal Papers Collection

Oral History Interview Transcripts
- Hanson W. Baldwin
- Alfred G. Ward

World War II Command File—Forces–South Pacific Naval Forces History
- Robert L. Ghormley, "The Tide Turns" (unpublished memoir)

CONGRESSIONAL DOCUMENTS

U.S. Congress. House. Committee on Appropriations. *Navy Department Appropriation Bill for 1943*, 77th Congress, 2nd session, 29 January 1942.

_____. Committee on Appropriations. *Report on the Fourth Supplemental National Defense Appropriation Bill for 1942*, 77th Congress, 2nd session, 23 January 1942.

_____. Committee on Appropriations. *Seventh Supplemental National Defense Appropriation Bill for 1942*, 77th Congress, 2nd session, 28 May 1942.

_____. Committee on Appropriations. Subcommittee on Naval Affairs. *Hearings on the Navy Department Bill for 1941*, 76th Congress, 3rd session, 4 January 1940 and 9 January 1940.

_____. Committee on Appropriations. Subcommittee on Naval Affairs. *Supplemental Hearings on the Navy Department Bill for 1941*, 69th Congress, 3rd session, 27 May 1940.

_____. Committee on Appropriations. Subcommittee on Naval Affairs. *Supplemental Navy Department Appropriation for 1943*, 78th Congress, 1st session, 8 February 1943.

_____. Committee on Naval Affairs. *Hearings on H.R. 2583*, 78th Congress, 1st session, 8 May 1943.

_____. Committee on Naval Affairs. *Hearings on H.R. 9997*, 75th Congress, 2nd session, 7 April 1938.

_____. Committee on Naval Affairs. Secretary of the Navy, letter to the Speaker of the House of Representatives. 78th Congress, 1st session, 1 May 1942.

_____. Committee on Naval Affairs. *Sundry Legislation Affecting the Naval Establishment in 1941*, 77th Congress, 1st session, 6 March 1941.

U.S. Congress. Joint Committee. *Hearings before the Joint Committee on the Investigation of the Pearl Harbor Attack, Joint Committee Exhibits Parts 14, 15, 19, and 26*, 79th Congress, 1st session, 1946.

U.S. Congress. Senate. Committee on Appropriations. Subcommittee on Naval Affairs. *Hearings on the Navy Department Appropriations Bill for 1942*, 77th Congress, 1st session, 3 February 1941.

_____. Committee on Appropriations. Subcommittee on Naval Affairs. *Seventh Supplemental National Defense Appropriation Bill for 1942*, 77th Congress, 2nd session, 5 June 1942.

_____. Committee on Appropriations. Subcommittee on Naval Affairs. *Supplemental Navy Department Appropriation for 1942*, 77th Congress, 2nd session, 15 January 1942.

PUBLISHED PRIMARY SOURCES AND MEMOIRS

Barnett, Leila Montague. *What the Mothers of Marines Should Know*. New York: Marine Corps Publicity Bureau, n.d.

Bland, Larry I., and Sharon R. Stevens, eds. *The Papers of George Catlett Marshall*. 5 vols. Baltimore: Johns Hopkins University Press, 1981–2003.

Burg, B. R., ed. *Gay Warriors: A Documentary History from the Ancient World to the Present*. New York: New York University Press, 2002.

Craige, John H. *What the Citizen Should Know about the Marines*. New York: Norton, 1941.

Culbert, David, ed. *Film and Propaganda in America: A Documentary History*. Volume 2, Part 2. New York: Greenwood Press, 1990.

Davis, John W. "The Negro in the United States Navy, Marine Corps, and Coast Guard." *Journal of Negro Education* 12 (Summer 1943): 345–49.

Dyer, George C., ed. *On the Treadmill to Pearl Harbor: The Memoirs of Admiral James O. Richardson*. Washington, D.C.: Naval History Division, 1973.

Eisenhower, Dwight D. "The Leavenworth Course." *Infantry Journal* 35 (June 1927): 589–600.

Eliot, George F. *Defending America*. New York: Foreign Policy Association, 1939.

Ellis, Earl H. *Advanced Base Operations in Micronesia*. Reprint, Washington, D.C.: GPO, 1992.

_____. *Navy Bases: Their Location, Resources, and Security*. Reprint, Washington, D.C.: GPO, 1992.

Gardner, Chandler B. "The Johnson Semi-Automatic Rifle." *MCG* 23 (March 1939): 8–13.

Greene, Wallace M., Jr. "Selection and Training of Recruits." *MCG* 20 (November 1936): 10–14.

Griffith, Samuel B., II. *The Battle for Guadalcanal*. Philadelphia: Lippincott, 1963.

Halsey, William F, and J. Bryan III. *Admiral Halsey's Story*. New York: Whittlesey House, 1947.

Harbord, James G. *Leaves from a War Diary*. New York: Dodd, Mead, & Company, 1925.

Harrison, Forrest M. "Psychiatry in the Navy." *War Medicine* 3 (February 1943): 114–37.

Heinl, R. D., Jr. "The Future of the Defense Battalion." *MCG* 26 (September 1942): 14–15, 60–61.

_____. "On the Mobility of Base Defense Artillery." *MCG* 25 (September 1941): 23–25, 42–43.

Hinds, A. W. "The Island of Guam as a Naval Base." *Proceedings of the United States Naval Institute* 41 (May 1915): 449–55.

Holcomb, Thomas. "The Marines' Task." *Leatherneck* 27 (January 1944): 70.

Hughes, Dana T. *The Old Breed: A Combat Marine's Odyssey through the Pacific, 1941–1945*. Denver: Outskirts, 2008.

"The Idea of the Fleet Marine Force." *MCG* 23 (June 1939): 61.

Iriye, Akira, ed., *Pearl Harbor and the Coming of the Pacific War: A Brief History with Documents and Essays*. Boston: Bedford/St. Martin's Press, 1999.

Johnson, Melvin M., Jr. "The M1 Rifle." *MCG* 25 (March 1941): 42.

Ketcham, Charles E. "Legislation." *MCG* 24 (June 1940): 10.

King, Ernest J. *U.S. Navy at War 1941–1945: Official Reports to the Secretary of the Navy*. Washington, D.C.: Department of the Navy, 1946.

King, Ernest J., and Walter M. Whitehall. *Fleet Admiral King: A Naval Record*. New York: Norton, 1953.

Krulak, Victor H. *First to Fight: An Inside View of the U.S. Marine Corps*. Annapolis: Naval Institute Press, 1984.

_____. "This Precious Few . . . The Evolution of Marine Recruit Training." *MCG* 66 (April 1982): 46–55.

"Legislation." *MCG* 23 (June 1939): 5.

Lejeune, John A. *Reminiscences of a Marine*. 1930. Reprint, Quantico, Va.: Marine Corps Association, 1990.

_____. "The United States Marine Corps: Present and Future." *Proceedings of the United States Naval Institute* 54 (October 1928): 859–61.

Maas, Melvin J. "Marine Corps Personnel Problem and the Only Solution," *MCG* (1936): 7–8.

MacGregor, Morris J., and Bernard C. Nalty, eds. *Blacks in the United States Armed Forces*. Vol. 6, *Blacks in World War II Naval Establishment*. Wilmington, Del.: Scholarly Resources, 1977.

"Marine Corps Rifle Tests." *MCG* 25 (June 1941): 14–16, 54–57.

Martin, C. "The Selection and Defense of Naval Bases." *Journal of the United States Artillery* 25 (January–February 1911): 1–6.

Mason, James T., Jr., ed. *The Pacific War Remembered: An Oral History Collection*. Annapolis: Naval Institute Press, 1986.

Matsuo, Kinoaki. *How Japan Plans to Win*, trans. Kilsoo K. Haan. 1940. Reprint, Boston: Little, Brown, 1942.

McGill, Robert A. "Island Defense." *MCG* 25 (March 1941): 16–18.

Merillat, Herbert C. *Guadalcanal Remembered*. New York: Dodd, Mead, 1982.

"National Defense." *Time*, 3 March 1941, 20.

"National Defense." *Time*, 11 November 1940, 21–24.

Navy Department. *Naval Expenditures 1936–1943*. Washington, D.C.: GPO, 1937–1944.

Neeser, Robert William. *Our Navy in the Next War*. New York: Scribner, 1915.

Neville, W. C. "The Marine Corps." *Proceedings of the United States Naval Institute* 55 (October 1929): 863–86.

Office of War Information. *Women in the War . . . for the Final Push for Victory*. Washington, D.C.: GPO, 1944.

Peace and War: United States Foreign Policy, 1931–1941. Washington, D.C.: GPO, 1943.

The Public Papers and Addresses of Franklin D. Roosevelt, 1941. Vol. 11, *Humanity on the Defensive*. New York: Harper & Row, 1950.

The Public Papers and Addresses of Franklin D. Roosevelt, 1939. Vol. 8, *War and Neutrality*. New York: Macmillan, 1941.

Records of the Second Division Operation Reports War Diaries Journal of Operations, 1918. Vol. 6. Washington, D.C.: Second Division Historical Section, Army War College, 1929.

"The Rifleman's New Weapon." *Infantry Journal* 45 (September–October 1938): 393–97.

Ross, Steven D., ed. *American War Plans, 1919–1941*. Vol. 3, *Plans to Meet the Axis Threat*. New York: Garland, 1992.

Russell, John H. "Final Report of the Major General Commandant." *MCG* 20 (November 1936): 16–21.

Second Division Association. *Commendations of Second Division, American Expeditionary Forces, 1917–1919*. Cologne, Germany: Second Division Association, 1919.

Secretary of the Navy. *Annual Reports of the Secretary of the Navy for the Fiscal Years 1933–1942*. Washington, D.C.: GPO, 1933–1942.

Schultz, Edna Hill. "'Free a Marine to Fight.'" *Naval History* (February 2003): 46–49.

Sledge, E. B. *With the Old Breed at Peleliu and Okinawa*. Novato, Calif.: Presidio, 1981.

Smith, Holland M. *Development of Amphibious Tactics in the U.S. Navy*. Washington, D.C.: History and Museums Division, HQMC, 1992.

Smith, Holland M., and Percy Finch. *Coral and Brass*. New York: Scribners,1948.

Sprout, Harold, and Margaret Sprout. *Toward a New Order of Sea Power: American Naval Policy, 1918–1922*. 1940. Reprint, New York: Greenwood Press, 1969.

"Status of Various Grades in Marine Corps." *MCG* 22 (March 1938): 28–29.

Stevens, Michael E. *Women Remember the War, 1941–1945*. Madison: State Historical Society of Wisconsin, 1993.

Thomason, James W., Jr. *The United States Army Second Division Northwest of Chateau Thierry in World War I*, ed. George B. Clark. Jefferson, N.C.: McFarland & Company, 2006.

Thompson, Paul W. "The Japanese Army: Tailor-Made for the Far East." *MCG* 26 (June 1942): 12–17.

Thorpe, George C. *Pure Logistics: The Science of War Preparation*. 1917. Reprint, Washington, D.C.: National Defense University Press, 1986.

Tregaskis, Richard. *Guadalcanal Diary*. New York: Random House, 1943.

Twining, Merrill B. *No Bended Knee: The Battle for Guadalcanal, the Memoir of Gen. Merrill B. Twining, USMC (Ret)*, ed. Neil Carey. Novato, Calif.: Presidio, 1996.

_____. "Head for the Hills," *MCG* 71 (August 1987): 48–50.

U.S. Army. *FM 31-5 Landing Operations on Hostile Shores*. Washington, D.C.: GPO, 1944.

U.S. Marine Corps. Fleet Marine Force Reference Publication 2-12, *Marine Air-Ground. Task Force: A Global Capability* (1991).

U.S. Navy. *FTP 143a (Fleet Tactical Publication 143a), War Instructions, United States Navy, 1944* (Washington, D.C.: GPO, 1944), accessed at http://www.history.navy. mil/library/online/warinst–14.htm.

Vandegrift, Alexander A. "Amphibious Miracle of Our Time." *MCG* 28 (October 1944): 3–9.

_____, and Robert B. Asprey. *Once a Marine*. New York: Norton, 1964.

"Vinson Bill." *MCG* 22 (March 1938): 34–37.

War Department. *Report of the Secretary of War to the President 1939*. Washington, D.C.: GPO, 1939.

White, William, and Ben Wofford. *The Marine: A Guadalcanal Survivor's Final Battle*. Annapolis: Naval Institute Press, 2002.

Williams, Robert Hugh. *The Old Corps: A Portrait of the U.S. Marine Corps Between the Wars*. Annapolis: Naval Institute Press, 1982.

Wood, Robert E. *Our Foreign Policy*. Chicago: America First Committee, n.d.

NEWSPAPERS

Advertiser (Albion, New York), 3 December 1936
Army and Navy Journal, 7 November 1936, 14 November 1936, and 2 December 1936
Army-Navy Register, 14 November 1942
Chevron (Marine Corps Base, San Diego), 20 December 1942
Chicago Daily Tribune, 4 December 1941
Detroit Evening News, 13 December 1942
Evening Star (Washington, D.C.), 25 May 1965
Gazette (Worcester, Massachusetts), 14 August 1942
Journal-Every Evening (Wilmington, Del.), 11 December 1943
Lewiston Journal, 22 August 1942
New York Times, 27 and 29 December 1941, 18 October 1942, and 1 January 1944
Plane Talk (USS *Saratoga*), 28 December 1941
Washington Post, 27 December 1941, 15 August 1942, 3 December 1942, and
    15 August 1962

BOOKS

Agawa, Hiroyuki. *The Reluctant Admiral: Yamamoto and the Imperial Navy*. Trans. by
    John Bester. 1969. Reprint, Tokyo: Kodansha International, 1979.
Alexander, Joseph H. *The Battle History of the U.S. Marines: A Fellowship of Valor*. New
    York: HarperPerennial, 1999.
_____. *Utmost Savagery: The Three Days of Tarawa*. Annapolis: Naval Institute Press,
    1995.
_____. *Across the Reef: The Marine Assault on Tarawa*. Washington, D.C.: Marine Corps
    Historical Center, 1993.
American Battle Monuments Commission. *2d Division Summary of Operations in the
    World War*. Washington. D.C.: GPO, 1944.
Asprey, Robert B. *At Belleau Wood*. New York: G. P. Putnam's Sons, 1965.
Baer, George W. *One Hundred Years of Sea Power: The U.S. Navy, 1890–1990*. Stanford,
    Calif.: Stanford University Press, 1994.
Bailey, Beth. *Sex in the Heartland*. Cambridge, Mass.: Harvard University Press, 1999.
Ballantine, Duncan S. *U.S. Naval Logistics in the Second World War*. Princeton: Princeton
    University Press, 1947.
Ballendorf, Dirk A., and Merrill L. Barrlett. *Pete Ellis: An Amphibious Warfare Prophet,
    1880–1993*. Annapolis: Naval Institute Press, 1997.
Barde, Robert B. *The History of Marine Corps Marksmanship*. Washington, D.C.:
    Marksmanship Branch, G-3 Division, 1961.
Barnard, Chester I. *The Functions of the Executive*. Cambridge, Mass.: Harvard
    University Press, 1938.
Barnhart, Michael A. *Japan Prepares for Total War: The Search for Economic Security*.
    Ithaca, N.Y.: Cornell University Press, 1987.
Bartlett, Merrill L. *Lejeune: A Marine's Life, 1867–1942*. Columbia: University of South
    Carolina Press, 1991.

_____, ed. *Assault from the Sea: Essays on the History of Amphibious Warfare*. Annapolis: Naval Institute Press, 1983.

Belano, Randy Carol, and Craig L. Symonds, eds. *New Interpretations in Naval History*. Annapolis: Naval Institute Press, 2001.

Bérubé, Allan. *Coming Out under Fire: The History of Gay Men and Women in World War II*. New York: Free Press, 1990.

Bickel, Keith B. *Mars Learning: The Marine Corps Development of Small Wars Doctrine, 1915–1940*. Boulder: Westview Press, 2001.

Bischoff, Gunter, and Robert L. Dupont, eds. *The Pacific War Revisited*. Baton Rouge: Louisiana State University Press, 1996.

Bittner, Donald F. *Curriculum Evolution: Marine Corps Command and Staff College, 1920–1988*. Washington, D.C.: History and Museums Division, HQMC, 1988.

_____. *The Lion and the White Falcon: Britain and Iceland in the World War II Era*. Hamden: Archon Books, 1983.

Borstelmann, Thomas. *The Cold War and the Color Line: American Race Relations in the Global Arena*. Cambridge, Mass.: Harvard University Press, 2001.

_____. *Apartheid's Reluctant Uncle: The United States and Southern Africa in the Early Cold War*. New York: Oxford University Press, 1993.

Brands, H. W. *The Devil We Knew: Americans and the Cold War*. New York: Oxford University Press, 1993.

Brozen, Yale, ed. *Advertising and American Society*. New York: New York University Press, 1974.

Buell, Thomas B. *Master of Sea Power: A Biography of Fleet Admiral Ernest J. King*. Boston: Little, Brown, 1980.

Cameron, Craig M. *American Samurai: Myth, Imagination, and the Conduct of Battle in the First Marine Division, 1941–1951*. Cambridge: Cambridge University Press, 1994.

Camp, Dick. *Devil Dogs at Belleau Wood: U.S. Marines in World War I*. Norwalk, Conn.: MBI Publishing, 2008.

Cardozier, V. R. *The Mobilization of the United States in World War II: How the Government, Military, and Industry Prepared for War*. Jefferson, N.C.: McFarland & Company, 1995.

Carter, Worrall Reed. *Beans, Bullets, and Black Oil: The Story of Fleet Logistics Afloat in the Pacific during World War II*. Washington, D.C.: Department of the Navy, 1953.

Champie, Elmore A. *A Brief History of the Marine Corps Base and Recruitment Depot, Parris Island, South Carolina*. Rev. ed. Washington, D.C.: Historical Branch, HQMC, 1960.

_____. *A Brief History of the Marine Corps Base and Recruitment Depot, San Diego*. Rev. ed. Washington, D.C.: Historical Branch, HQMC, 1960.

Chandler, Alfred D. *The Visible Hand: The Managerial Revolution in American Business*. Cambridge, Mass.: Belknap Press of Harvard, 1977.

Chapin, John C., Jr., *Top of the Ladder: Marine Operations in the Northern Solomons*. Washington, D.C.: History and Museums Division, HQMC, 1993.

Christ, James F. *The Battalion of the Damned: The 1st Marine Paratroopers at Gavutu and Bloody Ridge, 1942*. Annapolis: Naval Institute Press, 2007.

Clark, George B. *Hiram Iddings Bearss, U.S. Marine Corps: Biography of a World War I Hero*. Jefferson, N.C.: McFarland & Company, 2005.

_____. *Treading Softly: U.S. Marines in China, 1819–1949*. Westport, Conn.: Praeger, 2001.

_____. *Devil Dogs: Fighting Marines of World War I*. Novato, Calif.: Presidio, 1999.

Clifford, Kenneth J. *Amphibious Warfare Development in Britain and America from 1920–1940*. Laurens, N.Y.: Edgewood, 1983.

_____. *Progress and Purpose: A Developmental History of the United States Marine Corps 1900–1970*. Washington, D.C.: History and Museums Division, HQMC, 1973.

Cole, Merle T. *Cradle of Invasion: A History of the U.S. Naval Amphibious Training Base, Solomons, Maryland, 1942–1945*. Solomons, Md.: Calvert Marine Museum, 1984.

Cole, Wayne S. *Roosevelt and the Isolationists, 1932–1945*. Lincoln: University of Nebraska Press, 1983.

_____. *America First: The Battle against Intervention, 1940–1941*. Madison: University of Wisconsin Press, 1953.

Condit, Kenneth W., John H. Johnstone, and Ella W. Nargele. *A Brief History of Headquarters Marine Corps Staff Organization*. Rev. ed. Washington, D.C.: History and Museums Division, HQMC, 1970.

Condit, Kenneth W., and Edwin T. Turnbladh. *Hold High the Torch: A History of the 4th Marines*. Washington, D.C.: Historical Branch, HQMC, 1960.

Cook, James F. *Carl Vinson: Patriarch of the Armed Forces*. Macon, Ga.: Mercer University Press, 2004.

Cooper, Norman V. *A Fighting General: The Biography of General Holland "Howlin' Mad" Smith*. Quantico, Va.: Marine Corps Association, 1987.

Cowley, Robert, ed. *No End Save Victory: Perspectives on World War II*. New York: G. P. Putnam's Sons, 2001.

Cressman, Robert J. *"A Magnificent Fight": The Battle for Wake Island*. Annapolis: Naval Institute Press, 1995.

Creswell, John. *Generals and Admirals: The Story of Amphibious Command*. London: Longmans, Green and Company, 1952.

Dalfiume, Richard. *Desegregation of the U.S. Armed Forces: Fighting on Two Fronts, 1939–1953*. Columbia: University of Missouri Press, 1969.

Dallek, Robert. *Franklin D. Roosevelt and American Foreign Policy, 1932–1945*. Rev. ed. New York: Oxford University Press, 1995.

Daugherty, Leo J., III. *Pioneers of Amphibious Warfare, 1898–1945: Profiles of Fourteen American Military Strategists*. Jefferson, N.C.: McFarland & Company, 2009.

Davenport, T. R. H., and Christopher Saunders. *South Africa: A Modern History*. 5th ed. New York: St. Martin's Press, 2000.

Davis, Kenneth S. *FDR: The War President, 1940–1943*. New York: Random House, 2000.

Dennis, Peter, and Jeffrey Grey, eds. *Battle Near and Far: A Century of Overseas Deployment—The Chief of Army Military History Conference 2004*. Canberra, Australia: Army History Unit, 2005.

Divine, Robert A. *The Reluctant Belligerent: American Entry into World War II*. 2nd ed. New York: John Wiley & Sons, 1979.

_____. *The Illusion of Neutrality*. Chicago: University of Chicago Press, 1962.

Doig, Jameson W., and Erwin C. Hargrove, eds. *Leadership and Innovation: A Biographical Perspective on Entrepreneurs in Government*. Baltimore: Johns Hopkins University Press, 1987.

Donovan, James A. *Outpost in the North Atlantic: Marines in the Defense of Iceland*. Washington, D.C.: History and Museums Division, HQMC, 1992.

Dower, John W. *War Without Mercy: Race and Power in the Pacific War*. New York: Pantheon Books, 1986.

Dreyer, Edward L. *China at War, 1901–1945*. London: Longman, 1995.

Dull, Paul S. *A Battle History of the Imperial Japanese Navy: 1941–1945*. Annapolis: Naval Institute Press, 1978.

Dyer, George Carroll. *The Amphibians Came to Conquer: The Story of Admiral Kelly Turner*. 2 vols. Washington, D.C.: GPO, 1971.

Earl, Edward Meade, ed. *Makers of Modern Strategy: Military Thought from Machiavelli to Hitler*. Princeton: Princeton University Press, 1943.

Edwards, Harry W. *A Different War: Marines in Europe and North Africa*. Washington, D.C.: Marine Corps Historical Center, 1994.

Elshtain, Jean Bethke. *Women and War*. New York: Basic Books, 1987.

Estes, Kenneth W. *Marines under Armor: The Marine Corps and the Armored Fighting Vehicle, 1916–2000*. Annapolis: Naval Institute Press, 2000.

Evans, David C., and Mark R. Peattie. *Kaigun: Strategy, Tactics, and Technology in the Imperial Japanese Navy, 1887–1941*. Annapolis: Naval Institute Press, 1997.

Eykholt, Mark, et al. *The Nanjing Massacre in History and Historiography*. Berkeley: University of California Press, 2000.

Ferrante, Joan, and Prince Brown Jr., eds. *The Social Construction of Race and Ethnicity in the United States*. New York: Longman, 1998.

Filene, Peter G. *Him/Herself: Sex Roles in Modern America*. New York: Harcourt Brace Jovanovich, 1974.

Frank, Richard B. *Guadalcanal*. New York: Random House, 1990.

Frederickson, George M. *White Supremacy: A Comparative Study in American and South African History*. New York: Oxford University Press, 1981.

Fuller, Stephen M., and Graham A. Cosmas. *Marines in the Dominican Republic, 1916–1924*. Washington, D.C.: History and Museums Division, HQMC, 1974.

Furer, Julius Augustus. *Administration of the Navy Department in World War II*. Washington, D.C.: GPO, 1959.

Gailey, Harry A. *Bougainville, 1943–1945: The Forgotten Campaign*. Lexington: University Press of Kentucky, 1991.

Garraty, John A., and Mark C. Carnes, eds. *American National Biography*. 24 vols. Oxford: Oxford University Press, 1999.

Gatchel, Theodore L. *At the Water's Edge: Defending Against Modern Amphibious Assault*. Annapolis: Naval Institute Press, 1996.

Gerth, H. H., and C. W. Mills, eds. *Max Weber: Essays in Sociology*. Oxford: Oxford University Press, 1922.

Gole, Henry G. *The Road to Rainbow: Army Planning for Global War, 1934–1940*. Annapolis: Naval Institute Press, 2003.

Graff, David A., and Robin Higham, eds. *A Military History of China*. Boulder: Westview, 2002.

Greenstein, Fred I. *The Presidential Difference: Leadership Style from FDR to Clinton.* Princeton: Princeton University Press, 2000.

Gulick, Luther, and Lindall Urwick, eds. *Papers on the Science of Administration.* New York: Institute for Public Administration, 1937.

Hagan, Kenneth J. *This People's Navy: The Making of American Seapower.* New York: Free Press, 1991.

_____, ed. *In Peace and War: Interpretations of American Naval History, 1775–1984.* 2nd ed. Westport, Conn.: Greenwood, 1984.

Hagan, Kenneth J., and William R. Roberts, eds. *Against All Enemies: Interpretations of American Military History from Colonial Times to the Present.* Westport, Conn.: Greenwood, 1986.

Hammel, Eric. *Guadalcanal: Starvation Island.* New York: Crown Publishers, 1987.

Hammond, James W., Jr. *The Treaty Navy: The Story of the U.S. Naval Service Between the World Wars.* Victoria, B.C.: Wesley Press, 2001.

Hattendorf, John, B. Mitchell Simpson III, and John R, Wadliegh. *Sailors and Scholars: The Centennial History of the U.S. Naval War College.* Newport: Naval War College Press, 1984.

Hawley, Ellis W. *The Great War and the Search for a Modern Order: A History of the American People and Their Institutions, 1917–1933.* 2nd ed. New York: St. Martin's Press, 1992.

Hayashi, Saburo, with Alvin D. Coox. *Kōgun: The Japanese Army in the Pacific War.* 1951. Reprint, Quantico, Va.: Marine Corps Association, 1959.

Hayes, Grace P. *The History of the Joint Chiefs of Staff in World War II: The War against Japan.* Annapolis: Naval Institute Press, 1982.

Heinl, Robert Debs, Jr. *Soldiers of the Sea: The United States Marine Corps, 1775–1962.* 1962. Reprint, Baltimore: Nautical and Aviation Publishing, 1991.

Hewes, James E., Jr. *From Root to McNamara: Army Organization and Administration, 1900–1963.* Washington, D.C.: Center of Military History, 1975.

Hoffman, Jon T. *Chesty: The Story of Lieutenant General Lewis B. Puller, USMC.* New York: Random House, 2001.

_____. *From Makin to Bougainville: Marine Raiders in the Pacific.* Washington, D.C.: Marine Corps Historical Center, 1995.

Hoganson, Kristin L. *Fighting for American Manhood: How Gender Politics Provoked the Spanish-American and Philippine-American Wars.* New Haven, Conn.: Yale University Press, 1998.

Holm, Jeanne. *Women in the Military: An Unfinished Revolution.* Rev. ed. Novato, Calif.: Presidio, 1993.

Hough, Frank O., Verle D. Ludwig, and Henry I. Shaw Jr. *History of the U.S. Marines in World War II.* Vol. 1, *Pearl Harbor to Guadalcanal.* Washington, D.C.: Historical Branch, HQMC, 1958.

Hoyt, Edwin P. *Japan's War: The Pacific Conflict, 1853–1952.* 1986. Reprint, New York: Da Capo Press, 1989.

Hunt, Michael H. *Ideology and U.S. Foreign Policy.* New Haven, Conn.: Yale University Press, 1987.

Huntington, Samuel P. *The Soldier and the State: The Theory and Politics of Civil-Military Relations*. Cambridge, Mass.: Belknap Press of Harvard, 1957.

Ienaga, Saburō. *The Pacific War, 1931–1945: A Critical Perspective on Japan's Role in World War II*. Trans. by Frank Baldwin. 1968. Reprint, New York: Pantheon Books, 1978.

Iriye, Akira. *The Origins of the Second World War in Asia and the Pacific*. London: Longman, 1987.

_____. *Power and Culture: The Japanese-American War, 1941–1945*. Cambridge, Mass.: Harvard University Press, 1981.

Isely, Jeter A., and Philip A. Crowl. *The U.S. Marines and Amphibious War: Its Theory, and Its Practice in the Pacific*. Princeton: Princeton University Press, 1951.

Israel, Jerry D., ed. *Building the Organizational Society: Essays on Associational Activities in Modern America*. New York: Free Press, 1972.

Janowitz, Morris. *The Professional Soldier: A Social and Political Portrait*. Glencoe, Ill.: Free Press, 1960.

Jarvis, Christina S. *The Male Body at War: American Masculinity during World War II*. DeKalb: Northern Illinois University Press, 2004.

Jersey, Stanley Coleman. *Hell's Island: The Untold Story of Guadalcanal*. College Station: Texas A&M University Press, 2008.

Johnson, Douglas V., II, and Rolfe Hillman Jr. *Soissons 1918*. College Station: Texas A&M University Press, 1999.

Jonas, Manfred. *Isolationism in American, 1935–1941*. Ithaca, N.Y.: Cornell University Press, 1966.

Jones, Archer. *Elements of Strategy: An Historical Approach*. Westport, Conn.: Praeger, 1996.

Jones, Wilbur D., Jr. *Gyrene: The World War II United States Marine*. Shippensburg, Pa.: White Mane Books, 1998.

Jones, William K. *A Brief History of the 6th Marines*. Washington, D.C.: History and Museums Division, HQMC, 1987.

Kane, Thomas M. *Military Logistics and Strategic Performance*. Portland, Ore.: Frank Cass, 2001.

Karsten, Peter, ed. *The Military in America: From the Colonial Era to the Present*. Rev. ed. New York: Free Press, 1986.

Kennedy, David M. *Freedom from Fear: The American People in Depression and War, 1929–1945*. New York: Oxford University Press, 1999.

Kimmel, Michael. *Manhood in America: A Cultural History*. New York: Free Press, 1996.

LaFrance, Edward. *Men, Media, and Masculinity*. 2nd ed. Dubuque, Iowa: Kendall/Hunt Publishing Company, 1995.

Langer, William L., and S. Everett Gleason. *The Undeclared War, 1940–1941*. New York: Harper & Brothers, 1953.

Larrabee, Eric. *Commander in Chief: Franklin Delano Roosevelt, His Lieutenants, and Their War*. New York: Harper & Row, 1987.

Leighton, Richard M., and Robert W. Coakley. *Global Strategy and Logistics, 1940–1943*. Washington, D.C.: Office of the Chief of Military History, Department of the Army, 1960.

Leuchtenberg, William E. *Franklin D. Roosevelt and the New Deal, 1932–1940.* New York: Harper & Row, 1963.

Lindsey, Robert. *This High Name: Public Relations and the U.S. Marine Corps.* Madison: University of Wisconsin Press, 1956.

Linn, Brian M. *Guardians of Empire: The U. S. Army and the Pacific, 1902–1940.* Chapel Hill: University of North Carolina Press, 1997.

Love, Robert William, Jr., ed. *Pearl Harbor Revisited.* New York: St. Martin's Press, 1995.

_____. *Changing Interpretations and New Sources in Naval History.* New York: Garland, 1980.

Lundstrom, John B. *Black Shoe Carrier Admiral: Frank Jack Fletcher at Coral Sea, Midway, and Guadalcanal.* Annapolis: Naval Institute Press, 2006.

MacGregor, Morris J. *Integration of the Armed Forces, 1940–1965.* Washington, D.C.: Center of Military History, 1981.

Marchand, Roland. *Advertising the American Dream: Making Way for Modernity, 1920–1940.* Berkeley: University of California Press, 1985.

Marolda, Edward J., ed. *Theodore Roosevelt, the U.S. Navy, and the Spanish-American War.* New York: Palgrave, 2001.

_____. *FDR and the U.S. Navy.* New York: St. Martin's Press, 1998.

Mattingly, Robert E. *Herringbone Cloak—GI Dagger: Marines of the OSS.* Washington, D.C.: History and Museums Division, HQMC, 1989.

McClellan, Edwin N. *The United States Marine Corps in the World War.* Washington, D.C.: GPO, 1920.

Meid, Pat. *Marine Corps Women's Reserve in World War II.* Washington, D.C.: Historical Branch, HQMC, 1964.

Melson, Charles D. *Condition Red: Marine Defense Battalions in World War II.* Washington, D.C.: Marine Corps Historical Center, 1996.

_____. *Up the Slot: Marines in the Central Solomons.* Washington, D.C.: Marine Corps Historical Center, 1993.

Mersky, Peter. *U.S. Marine Corps Aviation, 1912 to the Present.* 3rd ed. Baltimore: Nautical and Aviation Publishing, 1997.

Metcalf, Clyde H. *A History of the United States Marine Corps.* New York: G. P. Putnam and Sons, 1939.

Meyer, Leisa D. *Creating G.I. Jane: Sexuality and Power in the Women's Army Corps in World War II.* New York: Columbia University Press, 1996.

Miller, Edward S. *War Plan Orange: The U.S. Strategy to Defeat Japan, 1897–1945.* Annapolis: Naval Institute Press, 1991.

Miller, J. Michael. *From Shanghai to Corregidor: The Marines in Defense of the Philippines.* Washington, D.C.: History and Museums Division, HQMC, 1997.

Miller, John. *Guadalcanal: The First Offensive.* Washington, D.C.: Office of the Chief of Military History, Department of the Army, 1949.

Millett, Allan R. *In Many a Strife: General Gerald C. Thomas and the U.S. Marine Corps, 1917–1956.* Annapolis: Naval Institute Press, 1993.

_____. *Semper Fidelis: The History of the United States Marine Corps.* Rev. ed. New York: Macmillan, 1991.

Millett, Allan R., and Peter Maslowski. *For the Common Defense: A Military History of the United States of America.* Rev. ed. New York: Free Press, 1994.

Millett, Allan R., and Jack Shulimson, eds. *Commandants of the Marine Corps.* Annapolis: Naval Institute Press, 2004.

Mintzberg, Henry. *The Structure of Organizations.* Englewood Cliffs, N.J.: Prentice-Hall Press, 1979.

Morison, Samuel Eliot. *History of the United States Naval Operations in World War II.* 15 Vols. Boston: Little, Brown, 1947–1962.

Morton, Louis. *Strategy and Command: The First Two Years.* Washington, D.C.: Office of the Chief of Military History, 1962.

Moskin, J. Robert. *The U.S. Marine Corps Story.* 3rd rev. ed. New York: McGraw-Hill, 1992.

Moy, Timothy. *War Machines: Transforming Technologies in the U.S. Military, 1920–1940.* College Station, Tex.: Texas A&M University Press, 2001.

Muir, Malcolm, Jr., ed. *The Human Tradition in the World War II Era.* Wilmington, Del.: Scholarly Resources, 2001.

Murray, Williamson, and Allan R. Millett, eds. In *Military Innovations in the Interwar Period.* Cambridge: Cambridge University Press, 1996.

_____. *Calculations: Net Assessment and the Coming of World War II.* New York: Free Press, 1992.

Nalty, Bernard C. *The Right to Fight: African-American Marines in World War II.* Washington, D.C.: Marine Corps Historical Center, 1995.

_____. *Cape Gloucester: The Green Inferno.* Washington, D.C.: History and Museums Division, HQMC, 1994.

_____. *Strength for the Fight: A History of Black Americans in the Military.* New York: Free Press, 1986.

_____. *Inspection in the U.S. Marine Corps, 1775–1957: Historical Background.* Washington, D.C.: Historical Branch, HQMC, 1960.

Navy Department. *United States Marine Corps.* Volume 46a, *United States Naval Administration in World War II.* Washington, D.C.: Office of Naval History [c. 1946].

Ohl, John Kennedy. *Supplying the Troops: General Somervell and American Logistics in WWII.* DeKalb, Ill.: Northern Illinois University Press, 1994.

Owen, Peter. *To the Limits of Endurance: A Battalion of Marines in the Great War.* College Station, Tex.: Texas A&M University Press, 2007.

Paret, Peter, ed. *Makers of Modern Strategy from Machiavelli to the Nuclear Age.* Princeton: Princeton University Press, 1986.

Parillo, Mark P. *The Japanese Merchant Marine in World War II.* Annapolis: Naval Institute Press, 1993.

Peattie, Mark R. *Ishiwara Kanji and Japan's Confrontation with the West.* Princeton: Princeton University Press, 1975.

Pope, Daniel. *The Making of Modern Advertising.* New York: Basic Books, 1983.

Prange, Gordon W., with Donald Goldstein and Katherine Dillon. *At Dawn We Slept: The Untold Story of Pearl Harbor.* New York: McGraw-Hill, 1981.

Ramold, Steven J. *Slaves, Sailors, Citizens: African Americans in the Union Navy.* DeKalb: Northern Illinois University Press, 2002.

Reserve Officers of Public Affairs Unit. *The Marine Corps Reserve: A History.* Washington, D.C.: History and Museums Division, HQMC, 1966.

Roeder, George H., Jr. *The Censored War: American Visual Experience during World War Two*. New Haven, Conn.: Yale University Press, 1993.

Ross, Steven T. *American War Plans, 1890–1939*. Portland, Ore.: Frank Cass, 2002.

Rottman, Gordon L. *U.S. Marine Corps World War II Order of Battle: Ground and Air Units in the Pacific War, 1939–1945*. Westport, Conn.: Greenwood, 2002.

Rotundo, E. Anthony. *American Manhood: Transformations in Masculinity from the Revolution to the Modern Era*. New York: Basic Books, 1993.

Schmidt, Hans. *Maverick Marine: General Smedley D. Butler and the Contradictions of American Military History*. Lexington: University Press of Kentucky, 1987.

Schrijvers, Peter. *The GI War Against Japan: American Soldiers in Asia and the Pacific during World War II*. New York: New York University Press, 2002.

Second Division Association. *The Second Division American Expeditionary Force in France, 1917–1919*. New York: Hillman, 1937.

Shafritz, Jay M., and J. Steven Ott, eds. *Classics of Organization Theory*. 4th ed. Belmont, Calif.: Wadsworth, 1996.

Shaw, Harry I., Jr. *First Offensive: The Marine Campaign for Guadalcanal*. Washington, D.C.: Marine Corps Historical Center, 1992.

_____. *Opening Moves: The Marine Gear Up for War*. Washington, D.C.: Marine Corps Historical Center, 1991.

Shaw, Henry I., Jr., and Ralph W. Donnelly. *Blacks in the Marine Corps*. Washington, D.C.: History and Museums Division, HQMC, 1975.

Shaw, Henry I., Jr., and Douglas T. Kane. *History of the U.S. Marines in World War II*. Vol. 2, *Isolation of Rabaul*. Washington, D.C.: Historical Branch, HQMC, 1963.

Shaw, Henry I., Jr., Bernard C. Nalty, and Edwin T. Turnbladh. *History of the U.S. Marines in World War II*. Vol. 3, *Central Pacific Drive*. Washington, D.C.: Historical Branch, HQMC, 1966.

Sherrod, Robert. *History of Marine Corps Aviation in World War II*. Washington, D.C.: Combined Forces Press, 1952.

Sherry, Michael S. *In the Shadow of War: The United States since the 1930s*. New Haven, Conn.: Yale University Press, 1995.

Shulimson, Jack. *The Marine Corps' Search for a Mission, 1880–1898*. Lawrence: University Press of Kansas, 1993.

Simmons, Edwin H. *The United States Marines: A History*. 3rd ed. Annapolis: Naval Institute Press, 1998.

_____. *The United States Marines, 1775–1975*. New York: Viking Press, 1976.

Simmons, Edwin H., and Joseph H. Alexander. *Through the Wheat: The U.S. Marines in World War I*. Annapolis: Naval Institute Press, 2008.

Simpson, B. Mitchell, III. *Admiral Harold R. Stark: Architect of Victory, 1939–1945*. Columbia: University of South Carolina Press, 1989.

Smith, Daniel E., and Joseph E. Siracusa. *The Testing of America: 1914–1945*. Saint Louis: Forum Press, 1979.

Smith, Gibson B. *Thomas Holcomb, 1879–1965: Register of His Personal Papers*. Washington, D.C.: History and Museums Division, HQMC, 1988.

Smith, Kevin. *Conflict over Convoys: Anglo-American Logistics Diplomacy in the Second World War*. Cambridge: Cambridge University Press, 1996.

Spector, Ronald H. *Eagle Against the Sun: The American War Against Japan.* New York: Free Press, 1985.

Stallings, Laurence. *The Doughboys: The Story of the A.E.F., 1917–1918.* New York: Harper & Row, 1963.

Strahan, Jerry E. *Andrew Jackson Higgins and the Boats That Won World War II.* Baton Rouge: Louisiana State University Press, 1994.

Stremlow, Mary V. *Free a Marine to Fight: Women Marines in World War II.* Washington, D.C.: Marine Corps Historical Center, 1994.

Suid, Lawrence H. *Guts and Glory: The Making of the American Military Image in Film.* Rev. ed. Lexington: University Press of Kentucky, 2002.

Thomas, Shipley. *The History of the A.E.F.* New York: George H. Dornan, 1920.

Updegraph, Charles L., Jr. *U.S. Marine Corps Special Units of World War II.* Washington, D.C.: History and Museums Division, HQMC, 1977.

Urwin, Gregory J. W. *Facing Fearful Odds: The Siege of Wake Island.* Lincoln: University of Nebraska Press, 1997.

Utley, Jonathan G. *Going to War with Japan, 1937–1941.* Knoxville: University of Tennessee Press, 1985.

Wayman, Dorothy G. *David I. Walsh: Citizen Patriot.* Milwaukee, Wisc.: Bruce Publishing, 1952.

Weigley, Russell F. *The American Way of War: A History of United States Military Strategy and Policy.* 1973. Reprint, Bloomington: Indiana University Press, 1977.

_____, ed. *New Dimensions in Military History.* San Rafael, Calif.: Presidio, 1975.

Whisenhunt, Donald G., ed. *The Human Tradition in America between the Wars, 1920–1945.* Wilmington, Del.: Scholarly Resources, 2002.

White, David H., and John W. Gordon, ed. *Proceedings of the Citadel Conference on War and Diplomacy.* Charleston, S.C.: Citadel Press, 1977.

Wiebe, Robert. *The Search for Order, 1877–1920.* New York: Hill and Wang, 1967.

Wilson, John B. *Maneuver and Firepower: The Evolution of Divisions and Separate Brigades.* Washington, D.C.: Center for Military History, 1998.

Winkler, Allan M. *The Politics of Propaganda: The Office of War Information, 1942–1945.* New Haven, Conn.: Yale University Press, 1978.

Yamamoto, Masahiro. *Nanjing: Anatomy of an Atrocity.* Westport, Conn.: Praeger, 2000.

Young, Louise. *Japan's Total Empire: Manchuria and the Culture of Wartime Imperialism.* Berkeley: University of California Press, 1998.

Zehnpfennig, Gladys. *Melvin J. Maas: Gallant Man of Action.* Minneapolis: T. S. Denison, 1967.

Zimmerman, John. *The Guadalcanal Campaign.* Washington, D.C.: Historical Section, HQMC, 1949.

ARTICLES

Bailey, Beth, and David Farber. "The 'Double-V' Campaign in World War II Hawaii: African Americans, Racial Ideology, and Federal Power." *Journal of Social History* 26 (June 1993): 817–43.

Barrow, Clayton, Jr. "Looking for John A. Lejeune." *MCG* 74 (November 1990): 72.

_____. "Marine Mystique." *Naval History* 3 (Fall 1989): 37–42.

Bartlett, Merrill L. "Ben Hebard Fuller and the Genesis of the United States Marine Corps, 1891–1934." *JMH* 69 (January 2005): 73–92.

Bartsch, William H. "Operation DOVETAIL: Bungled Guadalcanal Rehearsal, July 1942," *JMH* 66 (April 2002): 443–76.

_____. "Crucial Battle Ignored." *MCG* 81 (September 1997): 82–89.

Bittner, Donald F. "Britannia's Sheathed Sword: The Royal Marines and Amphibious Warfare in the Interwar Years—A Passive Response." *JMH* 55 (July 1991): 345–64.

Blandy, W. H. P. "Command Relations in Amphibious Warfare." U.S. Naval Institute *Proceedings* 77 (June 1951): 569–81.

Carney, Robert B. "Logistical Planning for War." *NWCR* 1 (October 1948): 3–16.

Chambers, John Whiteclay, II. "The New Military History: Myth and Reality." *JMH* 55 (July 1991): 395–406.

Conn, Stetson. "Changing Concepts of National Defense in the United States, 1937–1947." *Military Affairs* 28 (Spring 1964): 1–7.

Dennis, Routledge M. "Social Darwinism, Scientific Racism, and the Metaphysics of Race." *Journal of Negro Education* 64 (Summer 1995): 243–52.

Freedman, Estelle B. "'Uncontrolled Desires': The Response to the Sexual Psychopath, 1920–1960." *Journal of American History* 74 (June 1987): 83–106.

Fuquea, David C. "Bougainville: The Amphibious Assault Enters Maturity." *NWCR* 50 (Winter 1997): 104–21.

Gatchel, Theodore L. "Marines in Support of a Naval Campaign: Guadalcanal As a Prototype." *MCG* 70 (January 1986): 40–42.

Gordon, John W. "General Thomas Holcomb and 'The Golden Age of Amphibious Warfare.'" *Delaware History* 21 (September 1985): 256–70.

Greene, Fred. "The Military View of American National Policy: 1904–1940." *American Historical Review* 66 (January 1961): 354–77.

Higham, Robin, and Mark P. Parillo. "The Management Margin: Essential for Victory." *Aerospace Power Journal* 16 (Spring 2002): 19–27.

Keene, R. R. "Preparing for Guadalcanal." *Leatherneck* 55 (July 1972): 31–37.

Kramer, Paul A. "Race-Making and Colonial Violence in the U.S. Empire: The Philippine-American War As Race War." *Diplomatic History* 30 (April 2006): 169–210.

Larson, Cedric. "The Domestic Motion Picture Work of the Office of War Information." *Hollywood Quarterly* 3 (Summer 1948): 434–43.

Maier, Robert von, and Gregory J. W. Urwin. "Questions and Answers: Allan R. Millett." *World War II Quarterly* 5 (Spring 2008): 50–59.

Marx, Anthony W. "Race-Making and the Nation-State." *World Politics* 48 (January 1996): 190–208.

McGuire, Phillip. "Desegregation of the Armed Forces: Black Leadership, Protest, and World War II." *Journal of Negro History* 68 (Spring 1983): 147–58.

Mountcastle, John W. "From Bayou to Beachhead: The Marine and Mr. Higgins." *Military Review* 60 (March 1980): 20–29.

Noer, Thomas J. "Truman, Eisenhower, and South Africa: The 'Middle Road' and Apartheid." *Journal of Ethnic Studies* 11 (Spring 1983): 85–99.

O'Connor, Raymond G. "Naval Strategy in the Twentieth Century." *NWCR* 21 (February 1961): 4–12.

O'Meara, Dan. "The 1946 African Miner Workers' Strike and the Political Economy of South Africa." *Journal of Commonwealth and Comparative Politics* 13 (July 1975): 147–58.

Overy, Richard. "Strategic Intelligence and the Outbreak of World War II." *War in History* 5 (November 1998): 451–79.

Posel, Deborah. "The Meaning of Apartheid before 1948: Conflicting Interests and Forces with the Afrikaner Nationalist Alliance." *Journal of Southern African Studies* 14 (October 1987): 123–39.

Scott, Joan W. "Gender: A Useful Category of Analysis." *American Historical Review* 91 (December 1986): 1053–75.

Showalter, Dennis. "The Evolution of the U.S. Marine Corps into a Military Elite in the Twentieth Century." *MCG* 63 (November 1979): 44–58.

Shulimson, Jack. "The First to Fight: Marine Corps Expansion, 1914–1918." *Prologue: The Journal of the National Archives* 8 (Spring 1976): 5–16.

Shy, John. "The Cultural Approach to the History of War." *JMH* 57 (October 1993): 13–26.

Simmons, Edwin H. "Montford Point Marines." *Fortitudine* (Summer 1991): 3–7.

Smith, Gibson B. "The Flying Diplomat: General Thomas Holcomb in South Africa." *Shipmate* 41 (November 1978): 26–29.

Ulbrich, David J. "Thomas Holcomb, Alexander A. Vandegrift, and Reforms in Amphibious Command Relations on Guadalcanal in 1942." *War & Society* 28 (May 2009): 113–47.

_____. "Document of Note: The Long-Lost *Tentative Manual for the Defense of Advanced Bases* (1936)." *JMH* 71 (July 2007): 899–901.

_____. "Clarifying the Origins and Strategic Mission of the U.S. Marine Corps Defense Battalion, 1898–1941." *War & Society* 17 (October 1999): 81–109.

Walter, John C. "Congressman Carl Vinson and Franklin D. Roosevelt: Naval Preparedness and the Coming of World War II, 1939–1940." *Georgia Historical Quarterly* 64 (Fall 1980): 294–305.

DISSERTATIONS AND THESES

Colbourn, Colin Michael. "Esprit de Marine Corps: The Making of the Modern Marine Corps through Public Relations, 1898–1929." M.A. thesis, University of Southern Mississippi, 2009.

Daugherty, Leo J., III. "'To Fight Our Country's Battles': An Institutional History of the United States Marine Corps during the Interwar Era, 1919–1935." Ph.D. diss., Ohio State University, 2001.

Enders, Calvin William. "The Vinson Navy." Ph.D. diss., Michigan State University, 1970.

Henry, James Joseph, IV. "A Historical Review of the Development of Doctrine for Command Relationships in Amphibious Warfare." M.S. thesis, U.S. Army Command and General Staff College, 2000.

Hilty, James W. "Voting Alignment in the United States Senate, 1933–1944." Ph.D. diss., University of Missouri, 1973.

Infusio, Frank J. "The U.S. Marines and War Planning, 1900–1941." M.A. thesis, San Diego State University, 1974.

Landrum, Susan. "Carl Vinson: A Study in Military Preparedness." M.A. thesis, Emory University, 1966.

Lash, Fred Curtis. "Media and the Marines: Marching, Music, and Movies." M.A. thesis, American University, 1983.

Marshall, Heather Pace. "Crucible of Colonial Service: The Warrior Brotherhood and the Mythos of the Modern Marine Corps, 1898–1934." M.A. thesis, University of Hawaii, 2003.

Rutledge, Gary L. "The Rhetoric of United States Marine Corps Enlisted Recruitment." M.A. thesis, University of Kansas, 1974.

Ulbrich, David J. "Managing Marine Mobilization: Thomas Holcomb and the U.S. Marine Corps, 1936–1943." Ph.D. diss., Temple University, 2007.

INDEX

▼

About the Author

DAVID J. ULBRICH is a historian at the U.S. Army Engineer School and senior instructor in Norwich University's Masters in Military History program. He received the 2003–2004 General Lemuel Shepherd Dissertation Fellowship from the Marine Corps Heritage Foundation. He earned his doctorate in history at Temple University.